MICROSOFT® OFFICE

Outlook 2003

Introductory Concepts and Techniques

Gary B. Shelly
Thomas J. Cashman
Jeffrey J. Webb

COURSE TECHNOLOGY
25 THOMSON PLACE
BOSTON MA 02210

Australia • Canada • Denmark • Japan • Mexico • New Zealand • Philippines • Puerto Rico • Singapore
South Africa • Spain • United Kingdom • United States

THOMSON
COURSE TECHNOLOGY

Microsoft Office Outlook 2003 Introductory Concepts and Techniques

Gary B. Shelly
Thomas J. Cashman
Jeffrey J. Webb

Executive Editor:
Cheryl Costantini

Senior Acquisitions Editor:
Dana Merk

Senior Product Manager:
Alexandra Arnold

Associate Product Manager:
Reed Cotter

Editorial Assistant:
Selena Coppock

Print Buyer:
Laura Burns

Signing Representative:
Cheryl Costantini

Series Consulting Editor:
Jim Quasney

Director of Production:
Becky Herrington

Production Editor:
Becky Herrington

Production Assistant:
Jennifer Quiambao

Development Editor:
Ginny Harvey

Copy Editor:
Ginny Harvey

Proofreaders:
Nancy Lamm
Lori Silfen

Interior Designer:
Becky Herrington

Cover Designer:
Richard Herrera

Illustrator:
Richard Herrera

Compositors:
Jeanne Black
Andrew Bartel

Indexer:
Cristina Haley

Printer:
Banta Menasha

Printed in the United States of America

4 5 6 7 8 9 10
BM 08 07 06 05

For more information, contact
Course Technology
25 Thomson Place
Boston, Massachusetts 02210

Or find us on the World Wide Web at:
www.course.com

ISBN 0-619-25537-4

MICROSOFT® OFFICE

Outlook® 2003

Introductory Concepts and Techniques

Contents

Appendix A

Microsoft Outlook Help System

Appendix B

Speech and Handwriting Recognition

Appendix C

Publishing Office Web Pages to a Web Server

Appendix D

Changing Screen Resolution and Resetting the Outlook Toolbars and Menus

Appendix E

Microsoft Office Specialist Certification

Preface

The Shelly Cashman Series® offers the finest textbooks in computer education. We are proud of the fact that our series of Microsoft Office 4.3, Microsoft Office 95, Microsoft Office 97, Microsoft Office 2000, and Microsoft Office XP textbooks have been the most widely used books in education. With each new edition of our Office books, we have made significant improvements based on the software and comments made by the instructors and students. The *Microsoft Office 2003* books continue with the innovation, quality, and reliability that you have come to expect from the Shelly Cashman Series.

In this *Microsoft Office Outlook 2003* book, you will find an educationally sound, highly visual, and easy-to-follow pedagogy that combines a vastly improved step-by-step approach with corresponding screens. All projects and exercises in this book are designed to take full advantage of the Outlook 2003 enhancements. The project material is developed to ensure that students will see the importance of learning Outlook for future coursework. The popular Other Ways and More About features offer in-depth knowledge of Outlook 2003. The new Q&A feature offers students a way to solidify important personal information management concepts. The Learn It Online page presents a wealth of additional exercises to ensure your students have all the reinforcement they need.

Objectives of This Textbook

Microsoft Office Outlook 2003: Introductory Concepts and Techniques is intended for a course that covers a brief introduction to Outlook 2003. No experience with a computer is assumed, and no mathematics beyond the high school freshman level is required. The objectives of this book are:

- To teach the fundamentals of Outlook 2003
- To expose students to practical examples of the computer as a useful tool
- To acquaint students with personal information management (PIM)
- To develop an exercise-oriented approach that allows learning by doing
- To introduce students to new input technologies
- To encourage independent study and help those who are working alone

Approved by Microsoft as Courseware for Microsoft Office Specialist Certification

Microsoft Office Outlook 2003: Introductory Concepts and Techniques has been approved by Microsoft as courseware for Microsoft Office Specialist certification. After completing the projects and exercises in this book, students will be prepared to take the specialist-level examination for Microsoft Office Outlook 2003.

By passing the certification exam for a Microsoft software application, students demonstrate their proficiency in that application to employers. This exam is offered at participating centers, corporations, and employment agencies. See Appendix E for additional information about obtaining Microsoft Office Specialist certification and for a table that includes the Microsoft Office Outlook 2003 skill sets and corresponding page numbers where a skill is discussed in the book, or visit the Web site microsoft.com/officespecialist.

The Shelly Cashman Series Microsoft Office Specialist Center (Figure 1 on the next page) has links to valuable information on the certification program. The Web page (scsite.com/winoff2003/cert) includes links to general information on certification, choosing an application for certification, preparing for the certification exam, and taking and passing the certification exams.

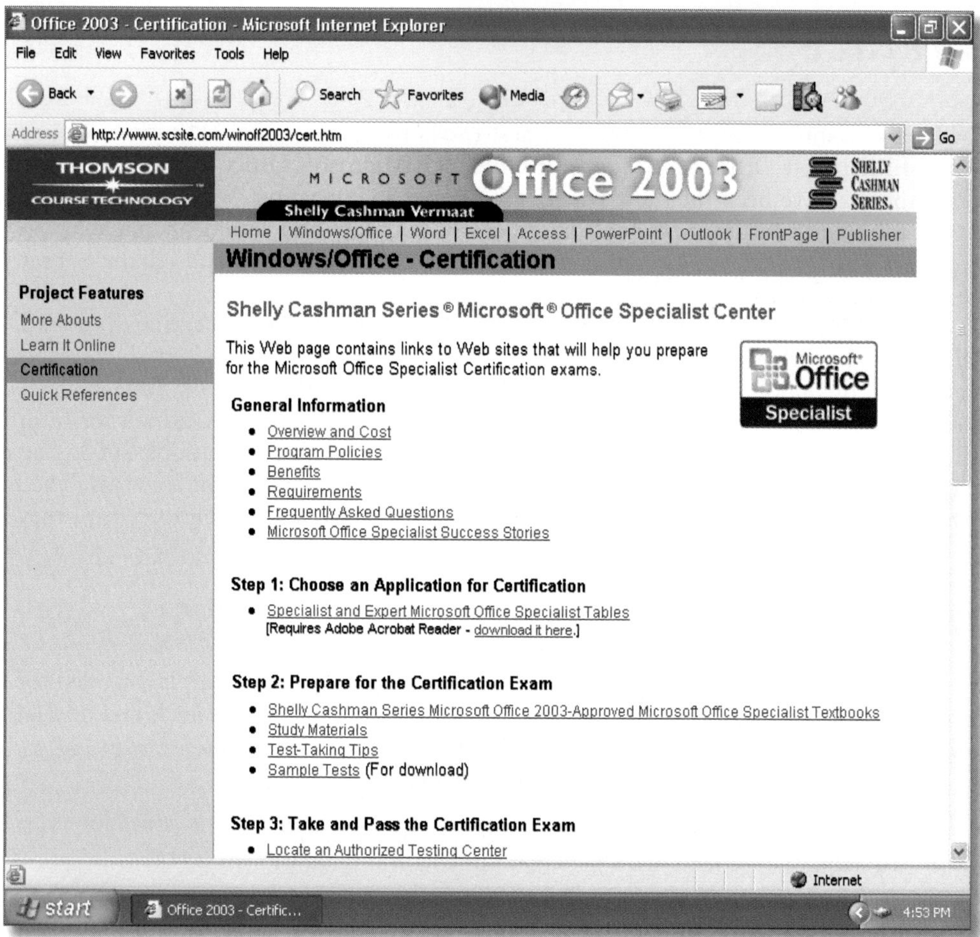

FIGURE 1

The Shelly Cashman Approach

Features of this Shelly Cashman Series *Microsoft Office Outlook 2003* book include:

- Project Orientation: Each project in the book presents a practical problem and complete solution in an easy-to-understand approach.
- Step-by-Step, Screen-by-Screen Instructions: Each of the tasks required to complete a project is identified throughout the project. Full-color screens accompany the steps.
- Thoroughly Tested Projects: Unparalleled quality is ensured because every screen in the book is produced by the author only after performing a step, and then each project must pass Course Technology's award-winning Quality Assurance program.
- Other Ways Boxes and Quick Reference Summary: The Other Ways boxes displayed at the end of most of the step-by-step sequences specify the other ways to do the task completed in the steps. Thus, the steps and the Other Ways box make a comprehensive reference unit.
- More About and Q&A Features: These marginal annotations provide background information, tips, and answers to common questions that complement the topics covered, adding depth and perspective to the learning process.
- Integration of the World Wide Web: The World Wide Web is integrated into the Outlook 2003 learning experience by (1) More About annotations that send students to Web sites for up-to-date information and alternative approaches to tasks; (2) a Microsoft Office Specialist Certification Web page so students can prepare for the certification examinations; (3) an Outlook 2003 Quick Reference Summary Web page that summarizes the ways to complete tasks (mouse, menu, shortcut menu, and keyboard); and (4) the Learn It Online page at the end of each project, which has project reinforcement exercises, learning games, and other types of student activities.

Organization of This Textbook

Microsoft Office Outlook 2003: Introductory Concepts and Techniques provides basic instruction on how to use Outlook 2003. The material is divided into two projects, five appendices, and a Quick Reference Summary.

Project 1 – E-Mail and Contact Management with Outlook In this project, students learn to read and send e-mail messages, and work with contacts. Topics include reading, replying to, forwarding, and deleting e-mail messages; composing, formatting, inserting a file attachment; sending new e-mail messages; flagging, sorting, and configuring e-mail options; generating and maintaining a contacts list; and creating a personal folder for contacts.

Project 2 – Schedule Management and Instant Messaging Using Outlook In this project, students discover the benefits of personal information management systems by using Outlook to create a schedule of classes, meetings, and extracurricular activities. Students learn how to enter both one-time and recurring appointments and events, send out meeting requests, assign tasks, and use Windows Messenger with Outlook. Topics include starting and quitting the Calendar folder; generating and managing daily, weekly, and monthly schedules; printing and saving a calendar; creating, importing, and exporting personal subfolders; creating and assigning tasks; accepting a task assignment; printing tasks; inviting attendees to a meeting; accepting a meeting request; enabling instant messaging; sending an instant message; and sending a file with instant messaging.

Appendices The book includes five appendices. Appendix A presents an introduction to the Microsoft Outlook Help system. Appendix B describes how to use Outlook's speech and handwriting recognition capabilities. Appendix C explains how to publish Web pages to a Web server. Appendix D shows how to change the screen resolution and reset the menus and toolbars. Appendix E introduces students to Microsoft Office Specialist certification.

Quick Reference Summary In Outlook 2003, you can accomplish a task in a number of ways, such as using the mouse, menu, shortcut menu, and keyboard. The Quick Reference Summary at the back of the book provides a quick reference to each task presented.

End-of-Project Student Activities

A notable strength of this Shelly Cashman Series *Microsoft Outlook 2003* book is the extensive student activities at the end of each project. Well-structured student activities can make the difference between students merely participating in a class and students retaining the information they learn. The activities in this Shelly Cashman Series Microsoft Outlook 2003 book include the following.

- What You Should Know A listing of the tasks completed within a project together with the pages on which the step-by-step, screen-by-screen explanations appear.
- Learn It Online Every project features a Learn It Online page that comprises twelve exercises. These exercises include True/False, Multiple Choice, Short Answer, Flash Cards, Practice Test, Learning Games, Tips and Tricks, Newsgroup Usage, Expanding Your Horizons, Search Sleuth, Office Online Training, and Office Marketplace.
- Apply Your Knowledge This exercise usually requires students to open and manipulate a file on the Data Disk that parallels the activities learned in the project. To obtain a copy of the Data Disk, follow the instructions on the inside back cover of this textbook.
- In the Lab Three in-depth assignments per project require students to utilize the project concepts and techniques to solve problems on a computer.
- Cases and Places Five unique real-world case-study situations, including one small-group activity.

Instructor Resources CD-ROM

The Shelly Cashman Series is dedicated to providing you with all of the tools you need to make your class a success. Information on all supplementary materials is available through your Course Technology representative or by calling one of the following telephone numbers: Colleges and Universities, 1-800-648-7450; High Schools, 1-800-824-5179; Private Career Colleges, 1-800-347-7707; Canada, 1-800-268-2222; Corporations with IT Training Centers, 1-800-648-7450; and Government Agencies, Health-Care Organizations, and Correctional Facilities, 1-800-477-3692.

The Instructor Resources for this textbook include both teaching and testing aids. The contents of each item on the Instructor Resources CD-ROM (ISBN 0-619-20048-0) are described below.

INSTRUCTOR'S MANUAL The Instructor's Manual is made up of Microsoft Word files, which include detailed lesson plans with page number references, lecture notes, teaching tips, classroom activities, discussion topics, projects to assign, and transparency references. The transparencies are available through the Figure Files described below.

LECTURE SUCCESS SYSTEM The Lecture Success System consists of intermediate files that correspond to certain figures in the book, allowing you to step through the creation of an application in a project during a lecture without entering large amounts of data.

SYLLABUS Sample syllabi, which can be customized easily to a course, are included. The syllabi cover policies, class and lab assignments and exams, and procedural information.

FIGURE FILES Illustrations for every figure in the textbook are available in electronic form. Use this ancillary to present a slide show in lecture or to print transparencies for use in lecture with an overhead projector. If you have a personal computer and LCD device, this ancillary can be an effective tool for presenting lectures.

POWERPOINT PRESENTATIONS PowerPoint Presentations is a multimedia lecture presentation system that provides slides for each project. Presentations are based on project objectives. Use this presentation system to present well-organized lectures that are both interesting and knowledge based. PowerPoint Presentations provides consistent coverage at schools that use multiple lecturers.

SOLUTIONS TO EXERCISES Solutions are included for the end-of-project exercises, as well as the Project Reinforcement exercises.

RUBRICS AND ANNOTATED SOLUTION FILES The grading rubrics provide a customizable framework for assigning point values to the laboratory exercises. Annotated solution files that correspond to the grading rubrics make it easy for you to compare students' results with the correct solutions whether you receive their homework as hard copy or via e-mail.

TEST BANK & TEST ENGINE The ExamView test bank includes 110 questions for every project (25 multiple-choice, 50 true/false, and 35 completion) with page number references, and when appropriate, figure references. A version of the test bank you can print also is included. The test bank comes with a copy of the test engine, ExamView, the ultimate tool for your objective-based testing needs. ExamView is a state-of-the-art test builder that is easy to use. ExamView enables you to create paper-, LAN-, or Web-based tests from test banks designed specifically for your Course Technology textbook. Utilize the ultra-efficient QuickTest Wizard to create tests in less than five minutes by taking advantage of Course Technology's question banks, or customize your own exams from scratch.

DATA FILES FOR STUDENTS All the files that are required by students to complete the exercises are included. You can distribute the files on the Instructor Resources CD-ROM to your students over a network, or you can have them follow the instructions on the inside back cover of this book to obtain a copy of the Data Disk.

ADDITIONAL ACTIVITIES FOR STUDENTS These additional activities consist of Project Reinforcement Exercises, which are true/false, multiple choice, and short answer questions that help students gain confidence in the material learned.

Online Content

Course Technology offers textbook-based content for Blackboard, WebCT, and MyCourse 2.1.

BLACKBOARD AND WEBCT As the leading provider of IT content for the Blackboard and WebCT platforms, Course Technology delivers rich content that enhances your textbook to give your students a unique learning experience. Course Technology has partnered with WebCT and Blackboard to deliver our market-leading content through these state-of-the-art online learning platforms.

MYCOURSE 2.1 MyCourse 2.1 is Course Technology's powerful online course management and content delivery system. Completely maintained and hosted by Thomson, MyCourse 2.1 delivers an online learning environment that is completely secure and provides superior performance. MyCourse 2.1 allows nontechnical users to create, customize, and deliver World Wide Web-based courses; post content and assignments; manage student enrollment; administer exams; track results in the online gradebook; and more.

MICROSOFT

Office Outlook 2003

MICROSOFT OFFICE

OUTLOOK

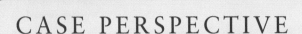

MICROSOFT
Office Outlook 2003

E-Mail and Contact Management with Outlook

PROJECT 1

CASE PERSPECTIVE

Maria Rosado is the captain of the Woodland Community College High Flyers championship women's basketball team. You attend several classes with Maria, and you always support her by attending the games. Maria's responsibilities as captain of the team include scheduling team meetings, notifying team members of schedule changes, and reporting team concerns and/or problems to the coach. She also likes to keep track of team and personal statistics, scores, standings, and home court winning streaks.

You work as a part-time Help desk specialist at the Woodland Community College computer lab, which has given you the opportunity to work with Outlook and become familiar with its information management and communications features. Maria has visited the Help desk and has watched you easily manage e-mail, contacts, and appointments. She knows that Outlook could help her, and she would like to use it to communicate with her teammates and coach and simplify team scheduling, but she needs some direction in getting started.

Maria has asked you to help her in familiarizing herself with Outlook's e-mail and contact management capabilities. She feels that becoming proficient with Outlook will make it easier to keep her teammates abreast of team meetings and schedule changes.

As you read through this project, you will learn how to use Outlook to open, read, create, send, and organize e-mail messages. You also will learn how to insert a file attachment to an e-mail message, and create and attach an electronic signature. In addition, you will learn how to create, organize, and print a contact list. Finally, you will learn how to create a distribution list and track activities of a contact.

MICROSOFT Office Outlook 2003

E-Mail and Contact Management with Outlook

PROJECT

Objectives

You will have mastered the material in this project when you can:

- Start Outlook
- Open, read, print, reply to, and delete electronic mail messages
- View a file attachment
- Create and insert an e-mail signature
- Compose, format, and send electronic mail messages
- Insert a file attachment in an e-mail message
- Flag and sort e-mail messages
- Set e-mail importance, sensitivity, and delivery options
- Create a personal folder
- Create and print a contact list
- Use the Find a Contact feature
- Organize the contact list
- Track activities of a contact
- Quit Outlook

What Is Microsoft Office Outlook 2003?

Microsoft Office Outlook 2003 is a powerful communications and scheduling program that helps you communicate with others (Figures 1-1a through 1-1d), keep track of your contacts, and organize your busy schedule. Outlook allows you to send and receive electronic mail and permits you to engage in real-time messaging with family, friends, or coworkers using instant messaging. Outlook also provides you with the means to organize your contacts. Users easily can track e-mail messages, meetings, and notes with a particular contact. Outlook's Calendar, Contacts, Tasks, and Notes components aid in this organization. Contact information readily is available from the Outlook Calendar, Mail, Contacts, and Task components by accessing the Find a Contact feature. Personal information management (PIM) programs such as Outlook provide a way for individuals and workgroups to organize, find, view, and share information easily.

This latest version of Outlook has many new features, including a completely new look. The new Reading Pane takes the place of the Preview pane and allows for viewing twice as much information. A Junk E-mail filter has been added to help prevent unwanted messages. Quick flags make it easy to categorize and find your messages. Search Folders make it easy to find specific messages. Another new feature in Outlook allows you to have a unique signature for each e-mail account.

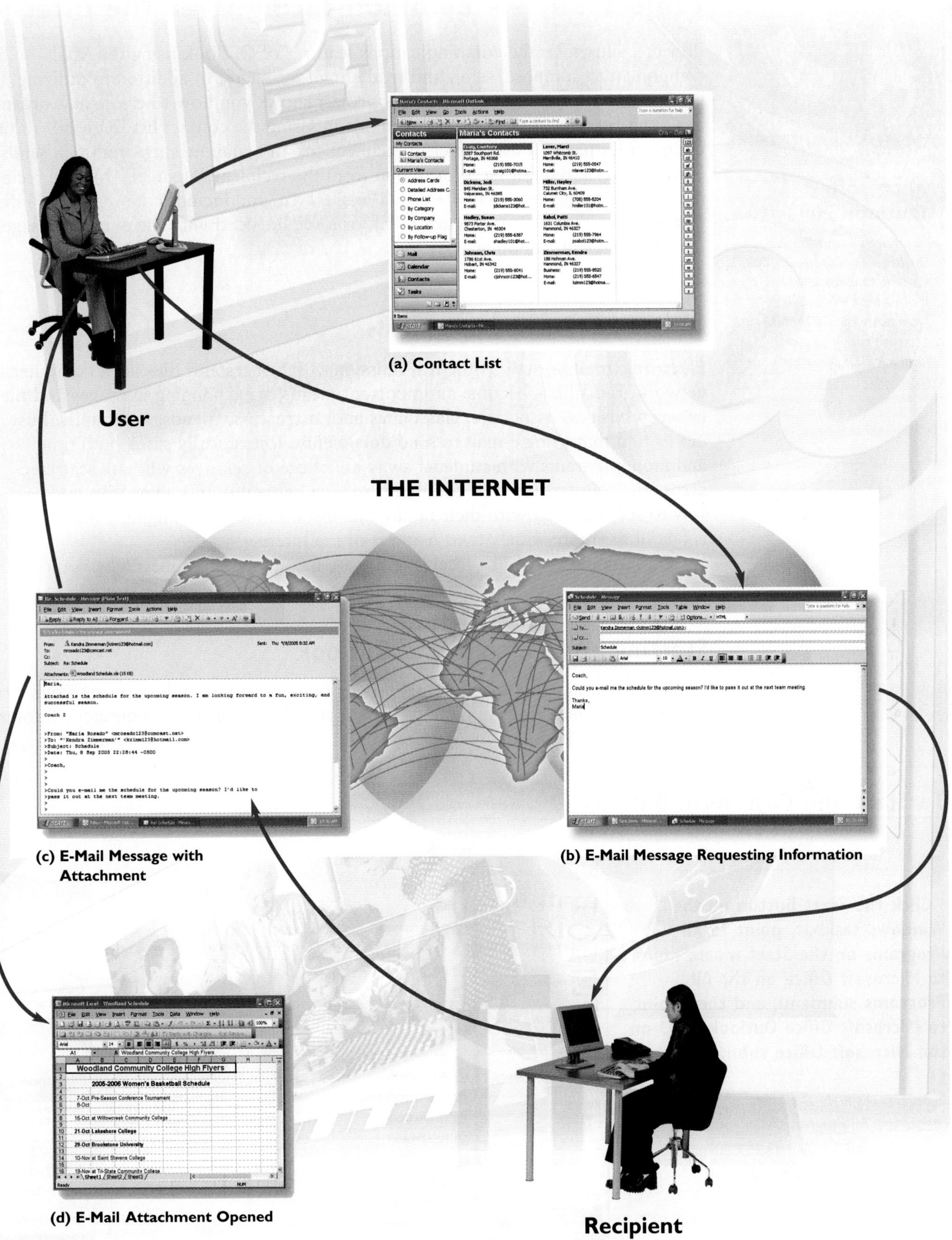

(a) Contact List

(b) E-Mail Message Requesting Information

(c) E-Mail Message with Attachment

(d) E-Mail Attachment Opened

FIGURE 1-1

Project One — Communicating Over the Internet

Project 1 illustrates the communications features of Outlook using the Mail component to compose, send, and read e-mail messages. In addition to utilizing Outlook's communications tools, this project shows you how to create and organize a contact list using the Contacts component. Using the contact list (Figure 1-1a on the previous page), a user selects a recipient for an e-mail message and then sends an e-mail message requesting information from the recipient (Figure 1-1b). The recipient replies by sending an e-mail message (Figure 1-1c) and includes the requested information as an attachment (Figure 1-1d), or a file included with the e-mail message, that the recipient can open.

> *More About*
>
> **Microsoft Outlook 2003**
>
> For more information about the features of Outlook 2003, visit the Outlook 2003 More About Web page (scsite.com/out2003/more) and then click Microsoft Outlook 2003 features.

Electronic Mail (E-Mail)

Electronic mail (**e-mail**) is the transmission of messages and files via a computer network. E-mail has become an important means of exchanging messages and files between business associates, classmates and instructors, friends, and family. Businesses find that using e-mail to send documents electronically saves both time and money. Parents with students away at college or relatives who are scattered across the country find that communicating via e-mail is an inexpensive and easy way to stay in touch with their family members. In fact, exchanging e-mail messages is one of the more widely used features of the Internet.

Outlook allows you to receive and store incoming e-mail messages, compose and send e-mail messages, and maintain a list of frequently used e-mail addresses.

Starting and Customizing Outlook

If you are stepping through this project on a computer and you want your screen to agree with the figures in this book, then you should set your computer's resolution to 800 × 600. The following steps start Outlook and customize its window.

To Start and Customize Outlook

1

• **Click the Start button on the Windows taskbar, point to All Programs on the Start menu, point to Microsoft Office on the All Programs submenu, and then point to Microsoft Office Outlook 2003 on the Microsoft Office submenu.**

Windows displays the Start menu, the All Programs submenu, and the Microsoft Office submenu (Figure 1-2).

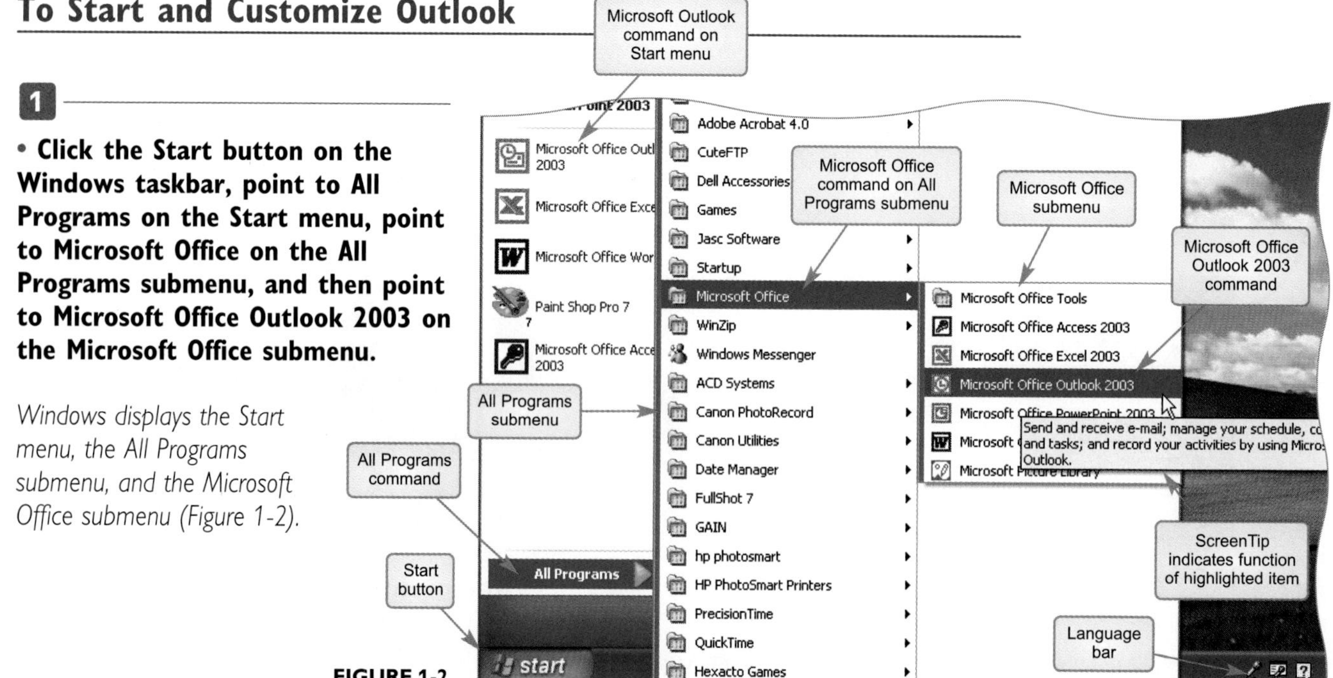

FIGURE 1-2

2

- **Click Microsoft Office Outlook 2003. If necessary, click the Mail button in the Navigation Pane and then click the Inbox folder in the All Mail Folders pane.**
- **If the Inbox – Microsoft Office Outlook window is not maximized, double-click its title bar to maximize it.**
- **Drag the right border of the Inbox message pane to the right so that the Inbox message pane and Reading Pane have the same width.**
- **If the Language bar shows, right-click it and then click Close the Language bar on the shortcut menu.**

Outlook starts and displays the Inbox – Microsoft Outlook window as shown in Figure 1-3.

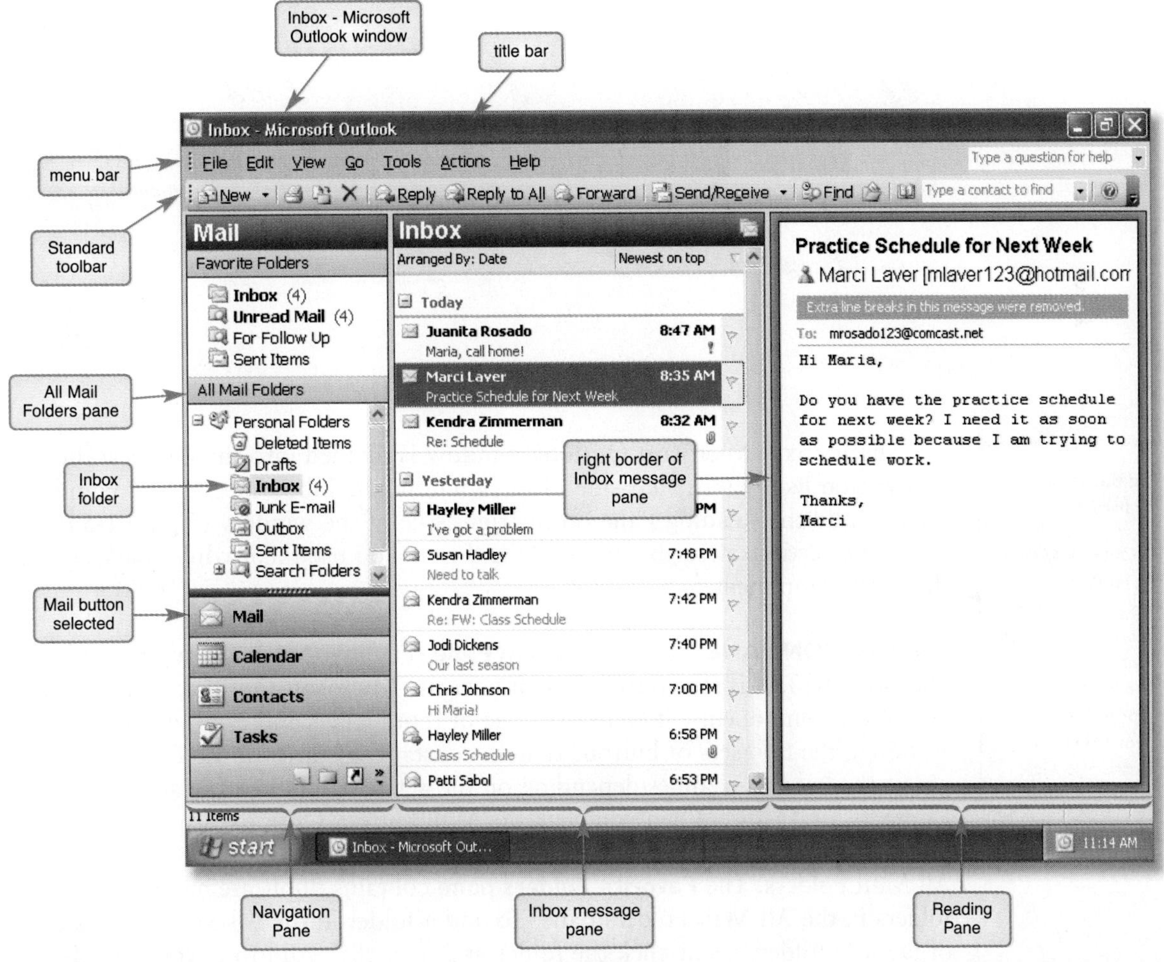

FIGURE 1-3

The screen shown in Figure 1-3 illustrates how the Outlook window looks the first time you start Outlook after setting up an e-mail account on most computers. If the Office Speech Recognition software is installed and active on your computer, then when you start Outlook, the Language bar may appear on the screen (Figure 1-2). The **Language bar** allows you to speak commands and dictate text. It usually is located on the right side of the Windows taskbar next to the notification area and changes to include the speech recognition functions available in Outlook. In this book, the Language bar is closed because it takes up computer resources

Other Ways

1. Double-click Microsoft Outlook icon on desktop
2. Click Start button on Windows taskbar, click Microsoft Outlook icon on Start menu

and with the Language bar active, the microphone can be turned on accidentally causing your computer to act in an unstable manner.

The Inbox - Microsoft Outlook Window

The Inbox - Microsoft Outlook window shown in Figure 1-3 on the previous page comprises a number of elements that you will use consistently as you work in the Outlook environment. Figure 1-4 illustrates the Standard toolbar, located below the title bar and the menu bar. The Standard toolbar contains buttons specific to Outlook. The button names indicate their functions. Each button can be clicked to perform a frequently used task, such as creating a new mail message, printing, or sending and receiving mail.

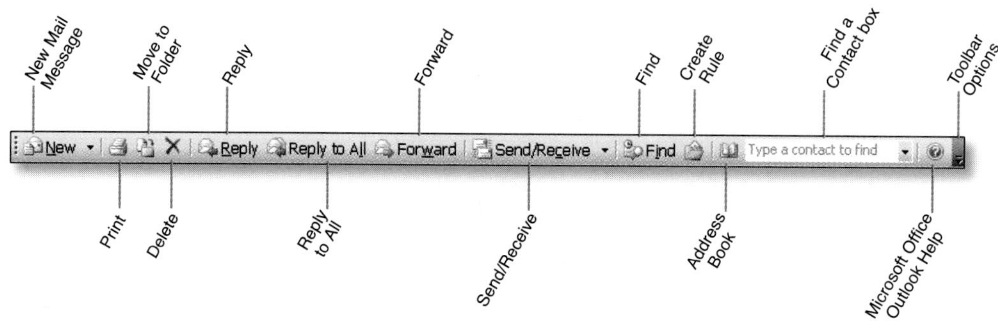

FIGURE 1-4

> **Q&A**
>
> **Q:** Can I find the Outlook folders on my hard disk?
>
> **A:** No. The Outlook folders in the Navigation Pane do not correspond to any folders on your hard disk. Outlook takes all your information and stores it in one large file based on the properties specified for your Personal Folders information service.

The Inbox – Microsoft Outlook window is divided into three panes: the Navigation Pane on the left side of the window, the Inbox message pane in the middle, and the Reading Pane on the right side of the window (Figure 1-5a). The following sections describe the panes and how you use them while working within the Mail component.

NAVIGATION PANE The **Navigation Pane** (Figure 1-5a) is a new feature in Outlook 2003. It is set up to help you navigate Microsoft Outlook while using any of the components. It comprises one or more panes and two sets of buttons. Although the two sets of buttons remain constant, the area of the Navigation Pane above the buttons changes depending on the active component (Mail, Calendar, Contacts, or Tasks). When you click the Mail button, Outlook displays Mail in the title bar of the Navigation Pane. This pane includes two panes: Favorite Folders and All Mail Folders. The **Favorite Folders pane** contains duplicate names of your favorite folders in the All Mail Folders pane. To add a folder in the All Mail Folders to the list of favorite folders, right-click the folder and then click Add to Favorite Folders.

Below the Favorite Folders pane, the **All Mail Folders** pane contains a set of folders associated with the communications tools of Outlook Mail (Deleted Items, Drafts, Inbox, Junk E-mail, Outbox, Sent Items, and Search Folders).

The **Deleted Items folder** holds messages that you have deleted. As a safety precaution, you can retrieve deleted messages from the Deleted Items folder if you later decide to keep them. Deleting messages from the Deleted Items folder removes the messages permanently. The **Drafts folder** retains copies of messages that you are not yet ready to send. The **Inbox folder** is the destination for incoming mail. The **Junk E-mail folder** is the destination folder for unwanted messages or messages of an unknown origin. You can customize the settings in Outlook to direct only messages that meet certain criteria to the Inbox folder. Messages not meeting those criteria are sent to the Junk E-mail folder. The **Outbox folder** temporarily holds messages you

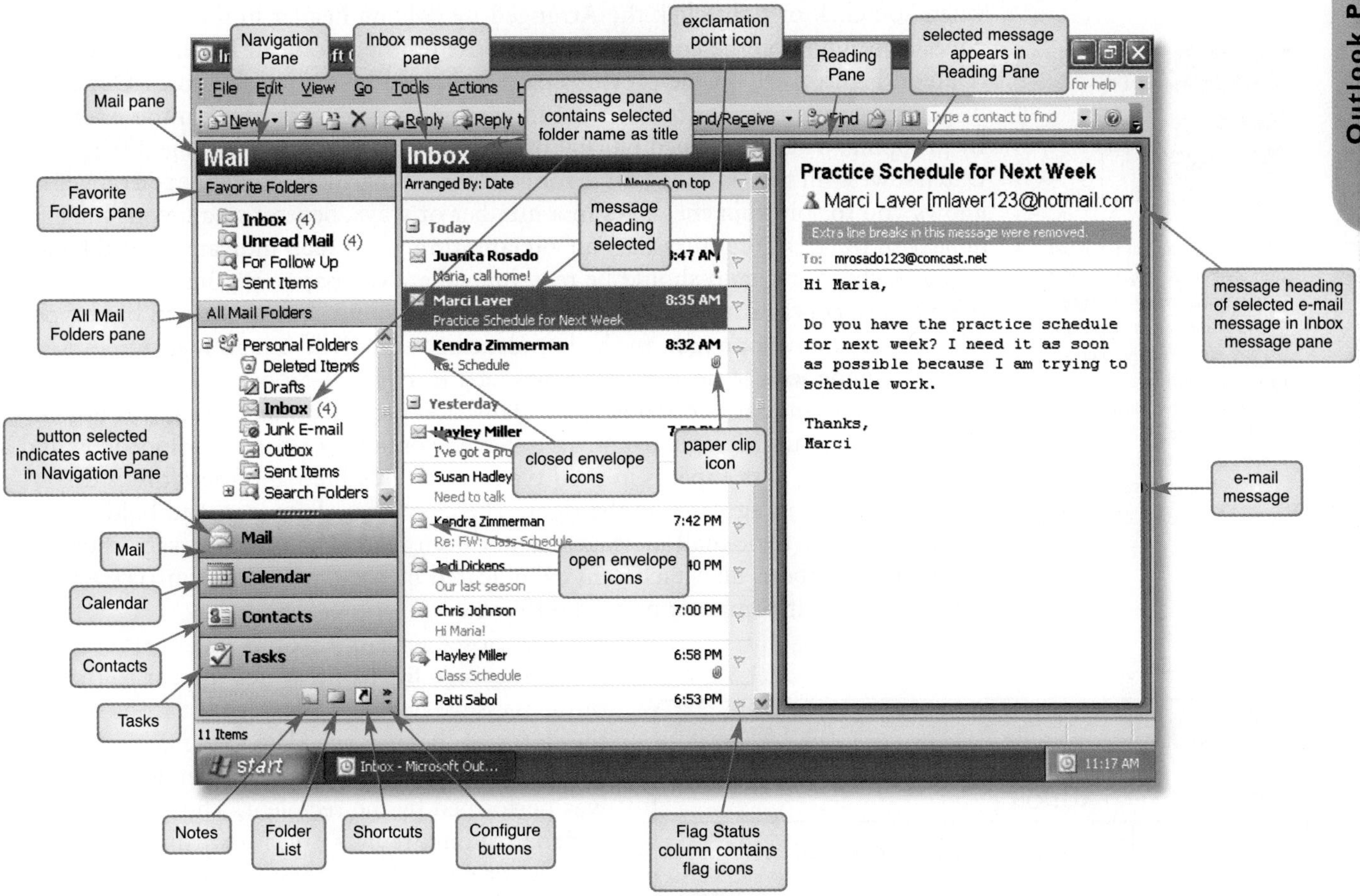

FIGURE 1-5a

send until Outlook delivers the messages. The **Sent Items folder** retains copies of messages that you have sent. The **Search Folders folder** is actually a group of folders that allows you to group your messages easily in one of three ways — messages for follow up, large messages, or unread messages.

Folders can contain e-mail messages, faxes, and files created in other Windows applications. Folders in bold type followed by a number in parentheses (**Inbox** (4)) indicate the number of messages in the folder that are unopened. Other folders may appear on your computer instead of or in addition to the folders shown in Figure 1-5a.

The two sets of buttons at the bottom of the Navigation Pane contain shortcuts to the major components of Outlook (Mail, Calendar, Contacts, Tasks, Notes, Folder List, Shortcuts, and Configure buttons).

MESSAGE PANE The Inbox **message pane** (shown in Figure 1-5a) lists the contents of the folder selected in the All Mail Folders pane. In Figure 1-5a, the Inbox folder is selected. Thus, the message pane lists the e-mails received. Figure 1-5b shows the Arranged By shortcut menu that appears

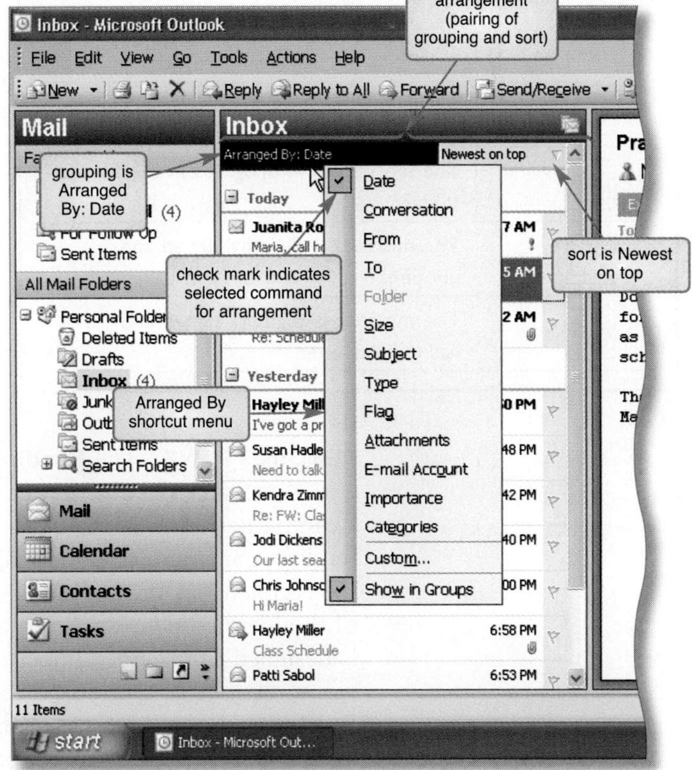

FIGURE 1-5b

when you click or right-click the Arranged By column header in the Inbox message pane. Depending on the command you choose on the Arranged By shortcut menu (Date in Figure 1-5b on the previous page indicated by the check mark), Outlook displays a column header to the right indicating the sort order within the Arranged By grouping. This predefined pairing of a grouping and a sort (Arranged By: Date/Newest on top) is called an **arrangement.** Using these predefined arrangements allows you to sort your messages in a number of ways. Several small icons may appear to the right of a message: an **exclamation point icon** indicates that the message is high priority and should be read immediately, a **paper clip icon** indicates that the message contains an attachment. A message heading that appears in bold type with a **closed envelope icon** to the left identifies an unread e-mail message. An **open envelope icon** indicates a read message. In Figure 1-5a on the previous page, the first e-mail message contains the exclamation point icon indicating it is urgent. The second e-mail message, from Marci Laver, contains a closed envelope icon and a message heading that appears in bold type. It is highlighted and therefore is displayed in the Reading Pane on the right. The closed envelope icon and bold message heading indicate the e-mail message has not been read. The third message shown in Figure 1-5a contains an attachment as indicated by the paper clip icon. The e-mail messages on your computer may be different.

More About

Reading E-Mail Messages

If Outlook is not the active window on your screen, it still provides a mail notification alert informing you when you receive a new message. Outlook displays a semitransparent ScreenTip momentarily by the Outlook icon in the notification area showing the sender's name, subject of the message, and the first few words of the message body.

The closed envelope icon is one of several icons, called **message list icons**, which appear to the left of the message heading. Message list icons indicate the status of the message. The icon may indicate an action that was performed by the sender or one that was performed by the recipient. The actions may include reading, replying to, forwarding, digitally signing, or encrypting a message. Table 1-1 contains a partial list of message list icons and the action performed on the mail message.

Table 1-1 Message List Icons and Actions

MESSAGE LIST ICON	ACTION
	The message has been opened.
	The message has not been opened.
	The message has been replied to.
	The message has been forwarded.
	The message is in progress in the Drafts folder.
	The message is digitally signed and unopened.
	The message is digitally signed and has been opened.

Flag icons are displayed when the Flag Status column is visible (Figure 1-5a). To the right of the message header, a **flag icon** indicates the status of the message. Outlook allows you to prioritize messages in a manner you choose using message flags. To set priorities, you right-click a flag icon and then choose colors and notes on the shortcut menu. To view the information about the message flag, point to the flag in the message heading and Outlook will display information about the message in a ScreenTip. Flagging and sorting e-mail messages using the Flag Status column are discussed later in this project.

READING PANE The **Reading Pane** (Figure 1-5a) contains the text of the selected e-mail message (Marci Laver). The **message header** appears at the top of the Reading Pane and contains the e-mail subject (Practice Schedule for Next Week), the sender's name and/or e-mail address (Marci Laver [mlaver123@hotmail.com]), and the recipient's e-mail address (mrosado123@comcast.net). Outlook displays the text of the highlighted e-mail message below the message header. The new Reading Pane is designed to provide almost twice as much information as the preview pane in previous versions of Outlook. In addition, using the View menu, you can display the Reading Pane to the right of the message pane (vertically), as shown in Figure 1-5a, or you can display it at the bottom of the message pane (horizontally) according to your personal preference.

Note: If you are stepping through this project on a computer and you want your screen to appear the same as the figures in the Mail Component section of this project, then you should ask your instructor to assist you (or see page OUT 61) to import Maria's Inbox from the Data Disk. Once you have imported Maria's Inbox, click the plus sign (+) next to the Inbox folder in the All Mail Folders list, and then select the Maria's Inbox folder. See the inside back cover of this book for instructions for downloading the Data Disk or see you instructor for information about accessing files for this book.

Opening and Reading E-Mail Messages

In Figure 1-5a on page OUT 9, the message headings for each message appear in the message pane. Double-clicking the closed envelope icon in any heading opens the e-mail message and displays the text of the message in a separate window. The following step shows how to open the e-mail message from Marci Laver.

To Open (Read) an E-Mail Message

1

• **Double-click the Marci Laver message heading in the Inbox Message pane (Figure 1-5a) and then maximize the Practice Schedule for Next Week window.**

Outlook displays the maximized Message window (Figure 1-6). The Message window contains a menu bar, Standard toolbar, identifying information about the e-mail message, and message pane. The subject of the e-mail message (Practice Schedule for Next Week) becomes the window title.

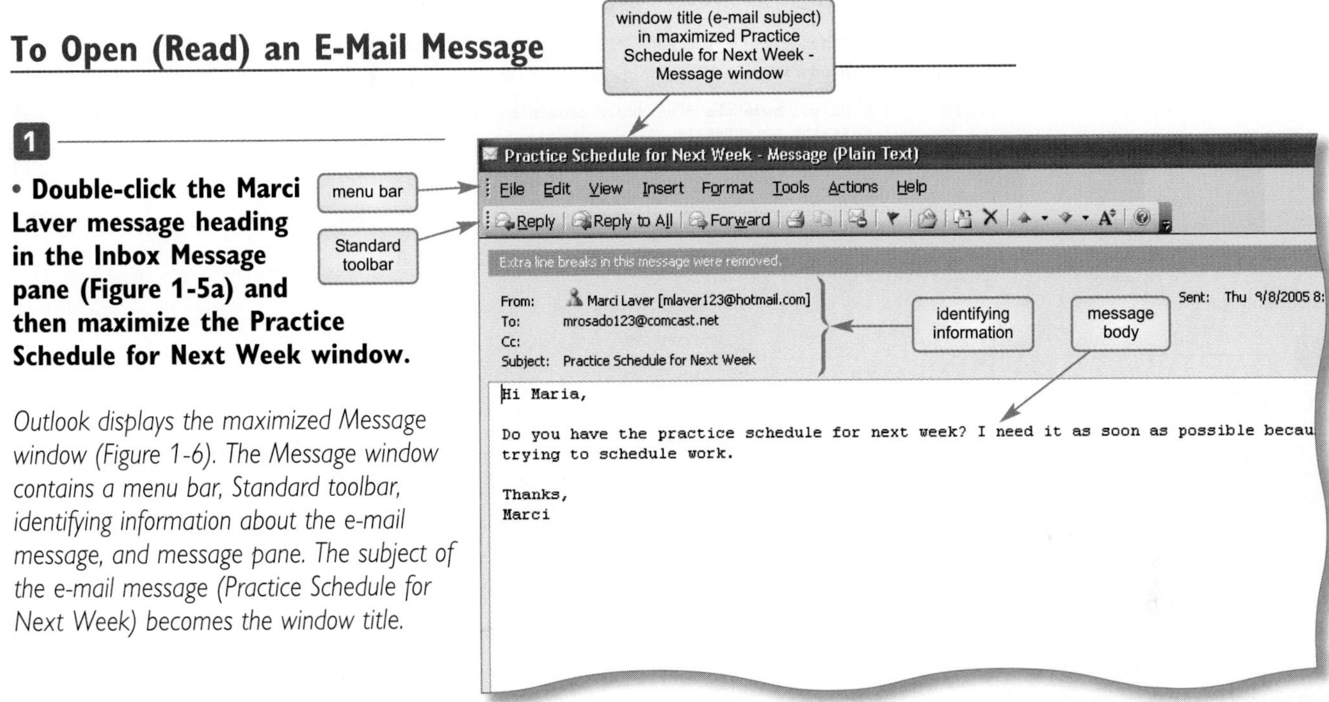

FIGURE 1-6

Other Ways

1. Right-click message heading, click Open on shortcut menu
2. Click message heading, on File menu point to Open, click Selected Items on Open submenu
3. Select message heading, press CRTL+O

When you double-click a message heading in the message pane, Outlook displays the message in a separate window, changes the closed envelope icon to an opened envelope icon, and no longer displays the message heading in bold type.

Figure 1-7 illustrates the Standard toolbar in the Message window. The Standard toolbar is located below the title bar and menu bar. The buttons on the Standard toolbar allow you to select easily from a list of the most common responses to an e-mail.

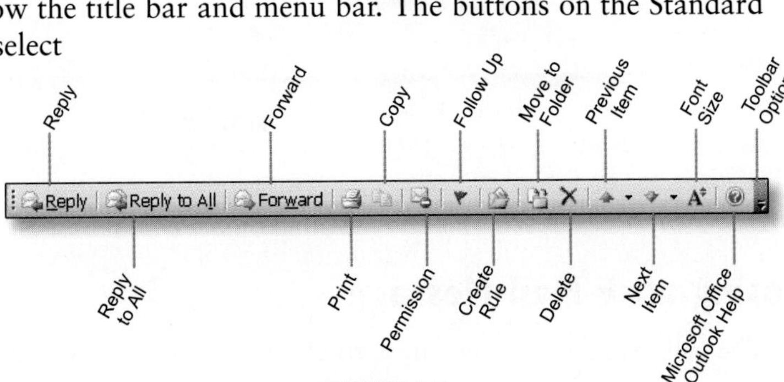

FIGURE 1-7

Printing an E-Mail Message

You can print the contents of an e-mail message before or after opening the message. The following steps describe how to print an opened e-mail message.

To Print an Opened E-Mail Message

1

- **Point to the Print button on the Standard toolbar (Figure 1-8).**

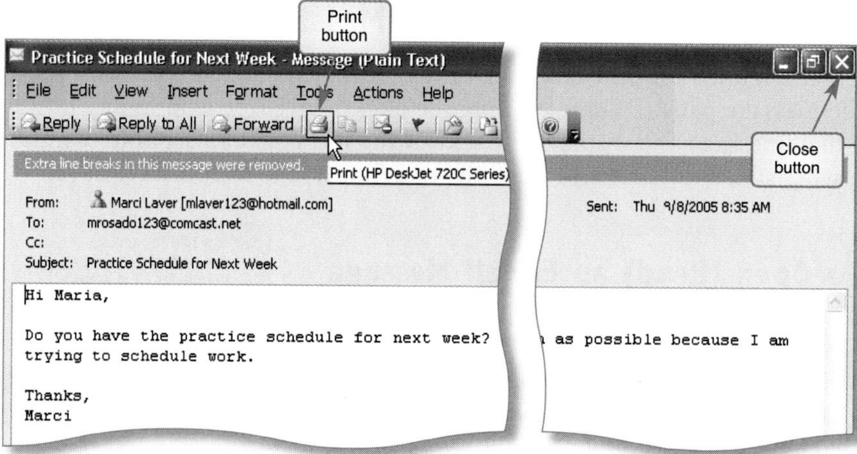

FIGURE 1-8

2

- **Click the Print button.**

Outlook prints the message (Figure 1-9). The printed message consists of a header at the top of the page, the recipient's name (Maria Rosado), and a horizontal line. Below the recipient's name are the From, Sent, To, and Subject entries, and the e-mail message. A footer at the bottom of the page contains the page number. The contents of the header and footer on your printout may be different.

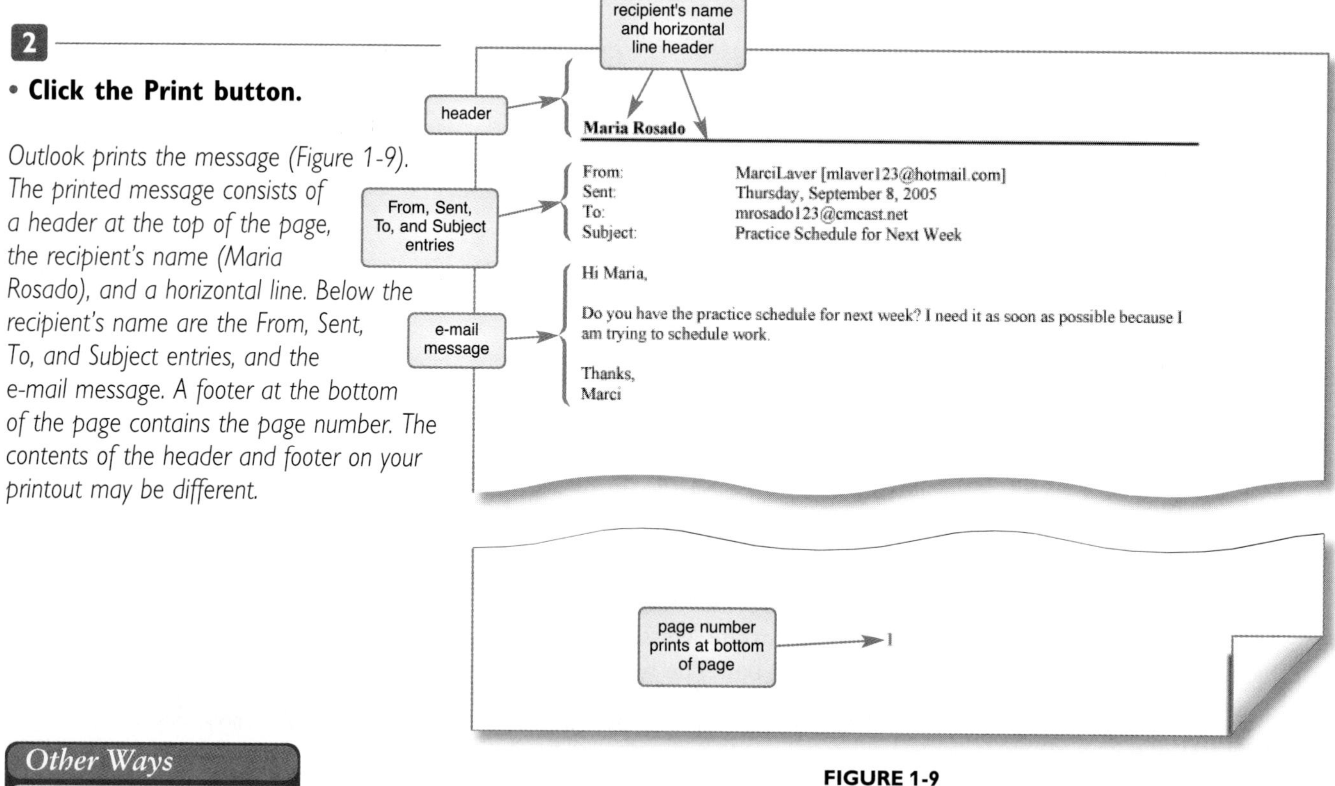

FIGURE 1-9

Other Ways

1. On File menu click Print, click OK button
2. Press ALT+F, press P, press ENTER
3. Press CTRL+P, press ENTER
4. In Voice Command mode, say "Print"

Closing an E-Mail Message

The following step shows how to close the Message window.

To Close an E-Mail Message

1

• **Click the Close button on the title bar (Figure 1-8).**

Outlook closes the Message window and displays the Inbox window (Figure 1-10).

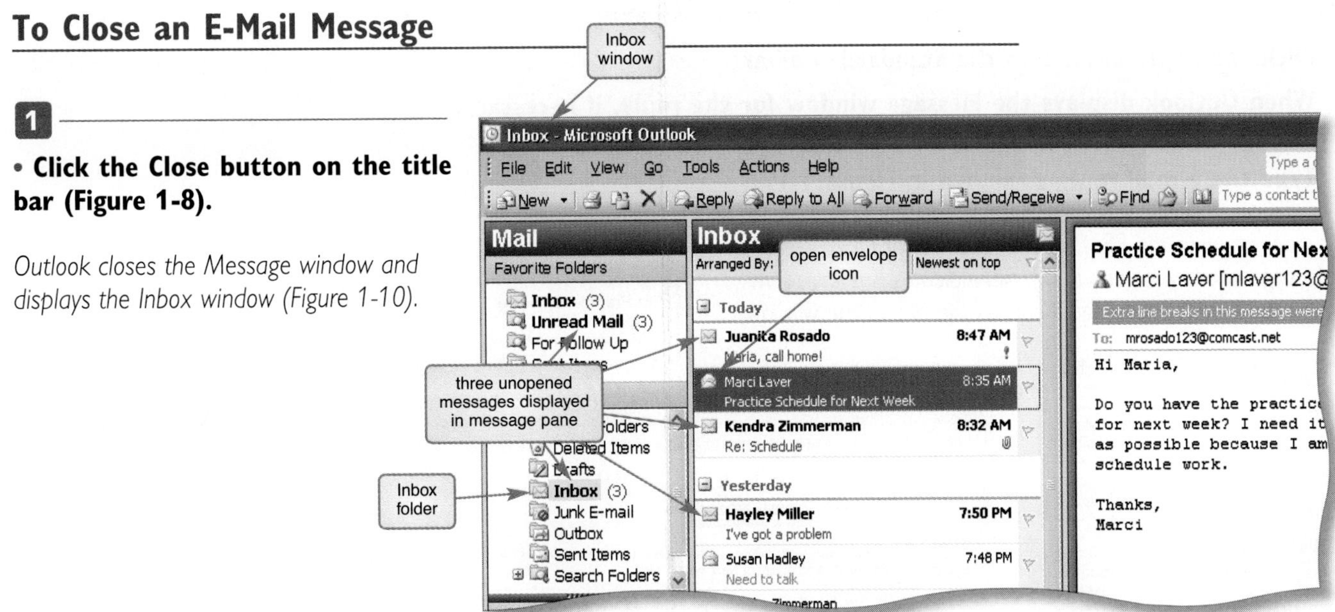

FIGURE 1-10

Other Ways

1. On File menu click Close
2. Press ALT+F4
3. In Voice Command, say "File, Close"

When you double-click a message heading with a closed envelope icon in the message pane, Outlook displays the corresponding message in the Message window. When you close the Message window, the Marci Laver message heading in the message pane no longer appears in bold type and the closed envelope icon changes to an open envelope icon to indicate the e-mail message has been opened. In addition, the Inbox folder in the All Mail Folders pane (Inbox (3)) indicates three e-mail messages remain unopened.

More About

Spam Filters

If an individual or company is not receiving e-mail from you, it is likely that the recipient's ISP spam filter is not allowing it through to their mailbox. Try sending the message in Plain Text format, because spam filters are less likely to drop an e-mail in Plain Text format.

Replying to an E-Mail Message

The next step is to reply to the e-mail message from Marci Laver. The Reply button on the Standard toolbar in the Inbox window allows you to reply quickly to an e-mail message using the sender's e-mail address as shown in the following steps.

To Reply to an E-Mail Message

1

• **If necessary, click the Marci Laver message heading in the message pane (Figure 1-11).**

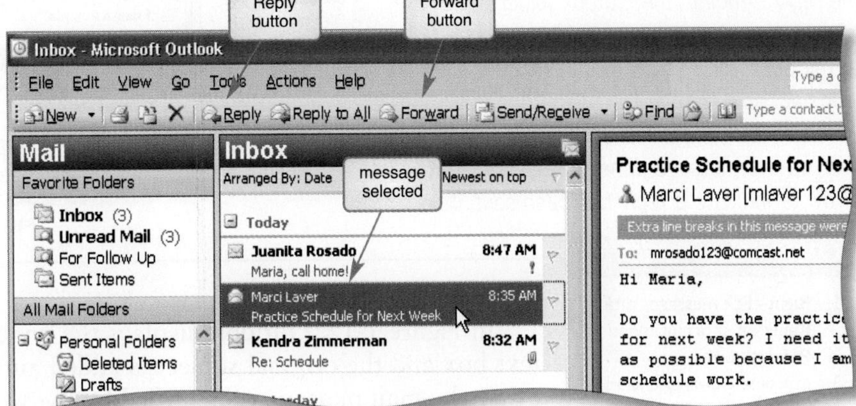

FIGURE 1-11

2

- **Click the Reply button on the Standard toolbar.**
- **When Outlook displays the Message window for the reply, if necessary, double-click the title bar to maximize the window.**
- **Type the e-mail reply as shown in Figure 1-12.**

Outlook displays the RE: Practice Schedule for Next Week - Message window (Figure 1-12). RE: indicates it is the reply, the subject of the message identifies the title of the window, and Message indicates it is the Message window. The menu, E-Mail toolbar, Mail toolbar, and three text boxes are displayed at the top of the window. The RE: entry and subject appear in the window title and Subject text box. The e-mail reply and original message appear in the message body.

RE: Practice Schedule for Next Week - Message window

Send button

Mail toolbar

recipient's name

carbon copy text box

E-Mail toolbar

e-mail reply

original e-mail message

subject entry

message body

RE: Practice Schedule for Next Week - Message

To... Marci Laver <mlaver123@hotmail.com>

Subject: RE: Practice Schedule for Next Week

Marci,

I just got done making up the schedule. I still have to go over it with Coach and get her approval. I will send it to you as soon as she says it is ok.

Maria

-----Original Message-----
From: Marci Laver [mailto:mlaver123@hotmail.com]
Sent: Thursday, September 8, 2005 8:35 AM
To: mrosado123@comcast.net
Subject: Practice Schedule for Next Week

Hi Maria,

Do you have the practice schedule for next week? I need it as soon as possible because I am trying to schedule work.

Thanks,
Marci

FIGURE 1-12

3

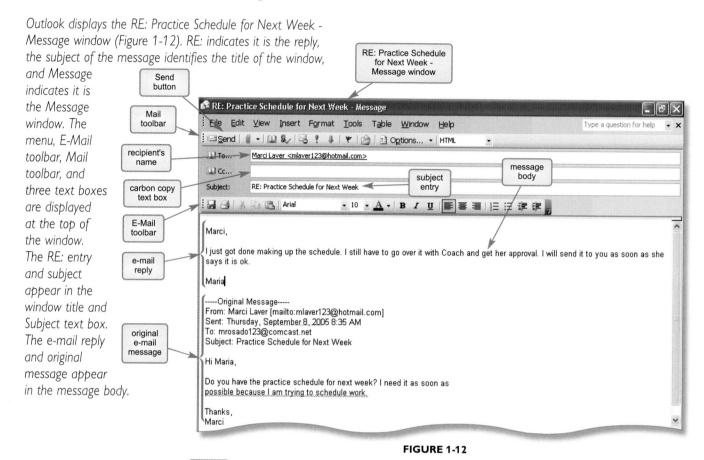

- **Click the Send button.**

Outlook closes the Message window, stores the reply e-mail in the Outbox folder while it sends the message, moves the message to the Sent Items folder, and displays the Inbox window (Figure 1-13). The opened envelope icon to the left of the Marci Laver entry in the message pane contains an arrow to indicate a reply has been sent.

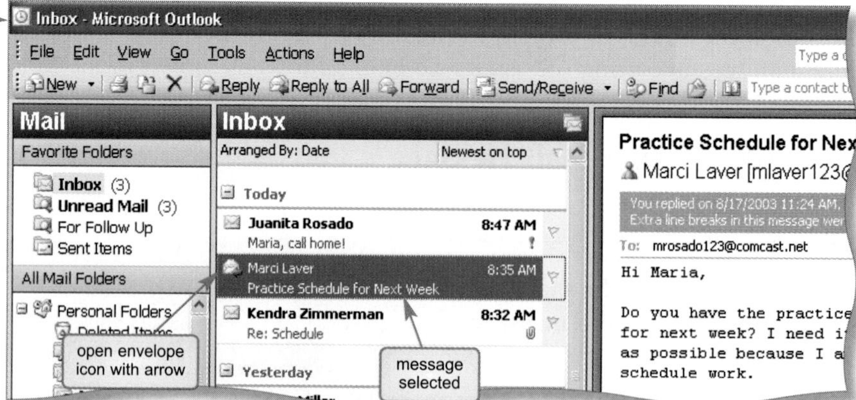

FIGURE 1-13

Other Ways

1. Right-click message, click Reply on shortcut menu
2. Press CTRL+R
3. In Voice Command mode, say "Message, Reply"

In Figure 1-12, Outlook displays the underlined Marci Laver name in the To text box and the original subject is added automatically to the Subject text box. The original e-mail message is identified by the words, Original Message, and the From, Sent, and To entries in the message body. In addition, the window

The E-Mail toolbar and Mail toolbar appear below the menu bar. The **E-Mail toolbar**, shown in Figure 1-14a, allows you to change the appearance, size, and color of text; bold, italicize, or underline text; create a numbered or bulleted list; change paragraph indentation or align text; and create a link or insert a picture in an e-mail message. Figure 1-14b illustrates the **Mail toolbar**, which includes buttons that are useful when replying to a message.

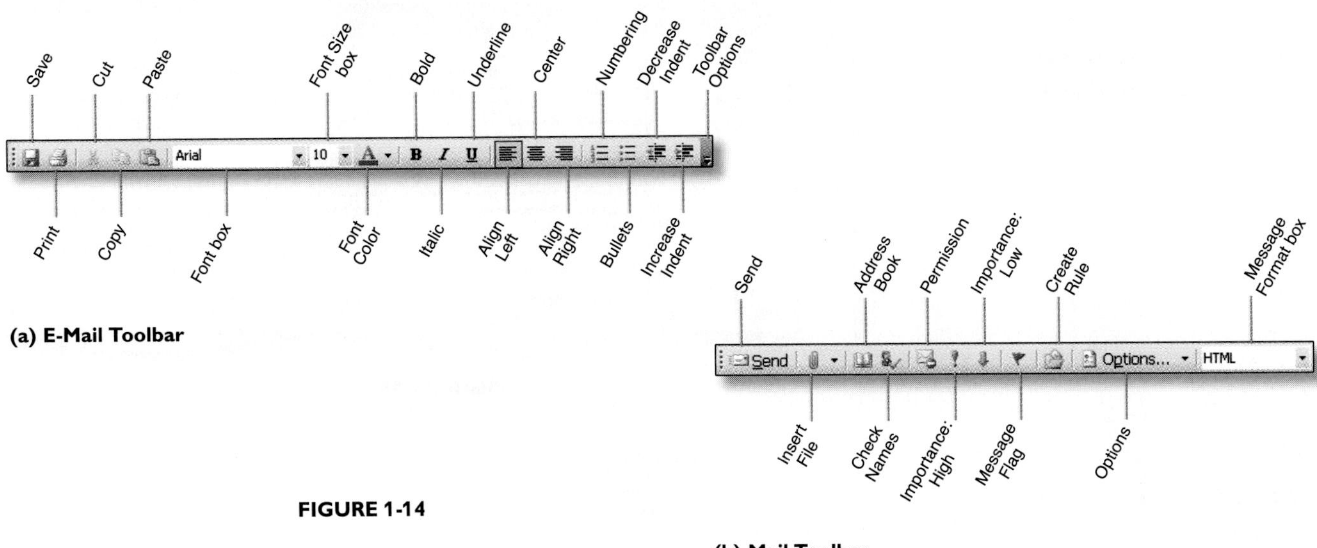

(a) E-Mail Toolbar

FIGURE 1-14

(b) Mail Toolbar

The Message Format box on the right side of the Mail toolbar is important because it allows you to change the format of the message. The options are HTML, Plain Text, and Rich Text and are summarized in Table 1-2. It is recommended that you use HTML format for your messages.

Table 1-2 Message Formats

MESSAGE FORMAT	DESCRIPTION
HTML	HTML format is the default format used when you create a message in Outlook. HTML supports the inclusion of pictures and basic formatting, such as text formatting, numbering, bullets, and alignment. HTML is the recommended format for Internet mail because the most popular e-mail programs use it.
Plain Text	Plain Text format is understood by all e-mail programs and is the most likely format to make it through a company's virus-filtering program. Plain text does not support basic formatting, such as bold, italic, colored fonts, or other text formatting. It also does not support pictures displayed directly in the message.
Rich Text	Rich Text Format (RTF) is a Microsoft format that only the latest versions of Microsoft Exchange Client and Outlook understand. RTF supports more formats than HTML or Plain Text, as well as linked objects and pictures.

More About

Replying to an E-Mail Message

Many e-mail users prefer to reply to a message without including the original e-mail message along with their response. To remove the original message from all e-mail replies, click Tools on the menu bar, click Options, and then click the E-mail Options button in the Preferences sheet of the Options dialog box. In the E-mail Options dialog box, select Do not include original message text in the When replying to a message list.

Forwarding an E-Mail Message

In addition to replying to a message, you also can forward the message to additional recipients with or without adding additional comments as shown in the steps on the next page.

To Forward an E-Mail Message

1

- **With the Inbox window active, click the Marci Laver message header in the message pane.**
- **Click the Forward button on the Standard toolbar (Figure 1-15).**

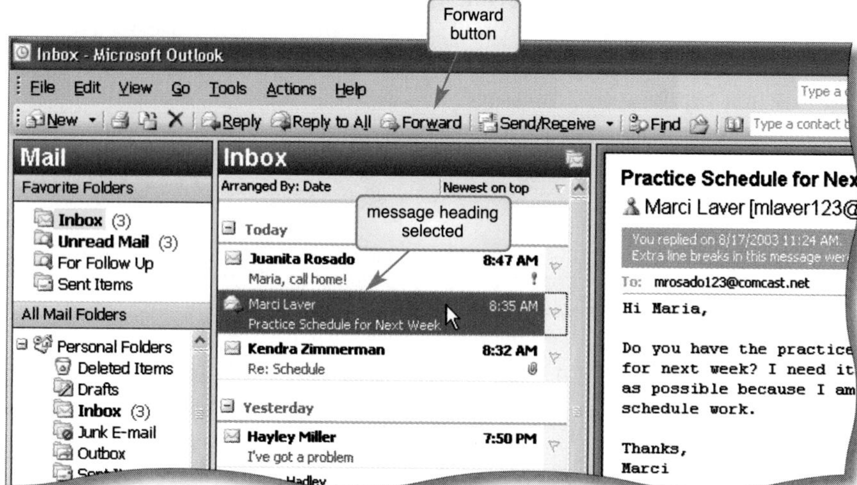

FIGURE 1-15

2

- **When Outlook displays the Message window for the forwarded message, type** kzimm123@hotmail.com **in the To text box as the recipient's e-mail address. (If you are stepping through this task, use an actual e-mail address in the To text box.)**
- **Enter the forwarding message in the message body as shown in Figure 1-16.**

Outlook displays the FW: Practice Schedule for Next Week - Message window as shown in Figure 1-16.

3

- **Click the Send button.**

Outlook closes the Message window, stores the reply e-mail in the Outbox folder while it sends the message, moves the message to the Sent Items folder, and displays the Inbox window.

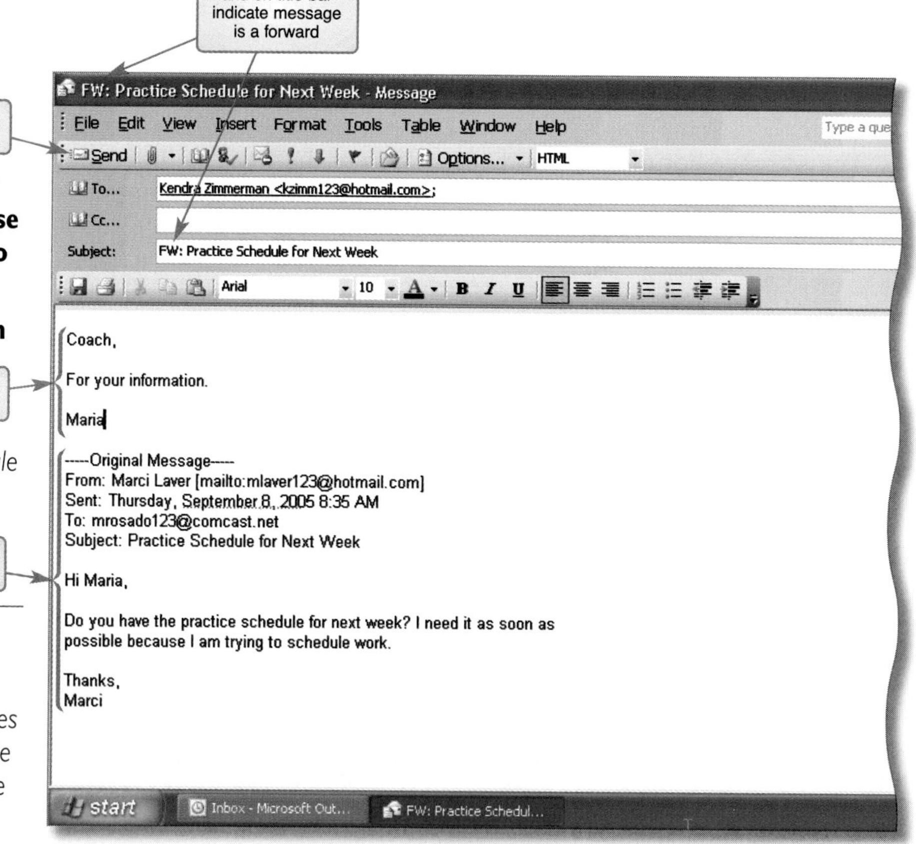

FIGURE 1-16

Other Ways

1. Right-click message heading, click Forward on shortcut menu
2. Press CTRL+F
3. In Voice Command mode, say "Message, Forward"

Deleting an E-Mail Message

After reading and replying to an e-mail message, you may want to delete the original e-mail message from the message list. Deleting a message removes the e-mail message from the Inbox folder. If you do not delete unwanted messages, large numbers of messages in the Inbox folder make it difficult to find and read new messages and wastes disk space. The following steps show how to delete the e-mail message from Marci Laver.

To Delete an E-Mail Message

1

- **With the Inbox window active, click the Marci Laver message heading in the message pane.**

The highlighted Marci Laver message heading appears in the message pane and the e-mail message appears in the Reading Pane (Figure 1-17). The open envelope icon contains an arrow to indicate you have replied to the message.

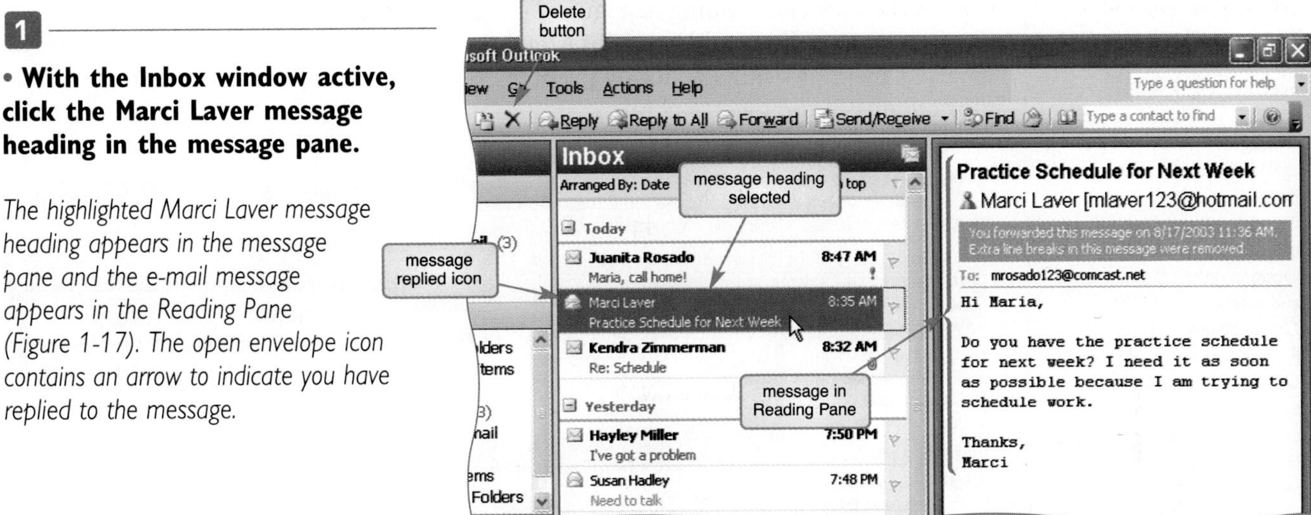

FIGURE 1-17

2

- **Click the Delete button on the Standard toolbar.**

Outlook moves the Marci Laver e-mail message from the Inbox folder to the Deleted Items folder and removes the e-mail entry from the message pane (Figure 1-18).

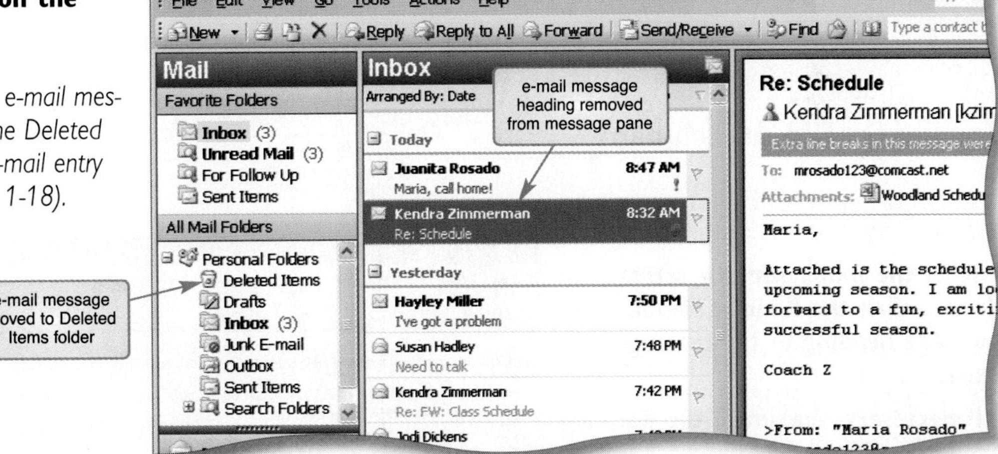

FIGURE 1-18

Other Ways

1. Drag e-mail message to Deleted Items folder in All Mail Folders pane
2. On Edit menu click Delete
3. Press CTRL+D
4. Click e-mail message, press DELETE key
5. In Voice Command mode, say "Edit, Delete"

As you delete messages from the Inbox or Sent Items folders, the number of messages in the Deleted Items folder increases. To delete an e-mail message from the Deleted Items folder, click the Deleted Items folder icon in the All Mail Folders pane, highlight the message in the Deleted Items message pane, click the Delete button, and then click the Yes button in the Microsoft Office Outlook dialog box. You also can delete multiple messages at one time by clicking the first message and then holding down the SHIFT key or CTRL key to click one or more messages. Use the SHIFT key to select a list of adjacent messages. Use the CTRL key to select nonadjacent messages. Once the messages are selected, click the Delete button on the Standard toolbar or press the DELETE key.

More About

Message Formatting

Changing the format of an e-mail message also can help prevent the possibility of virus infection. Many viruses are found in HTML formatted messages. To help protect against viruses, you can configure Outlook to display opened messages automatically in plain text. Click Options on the Tools menu and then click the E-mail Options button in the Preferences sheet of the Options dialog box. In the E-mail Options dialog box, select Read all standard mail in plain text in the Message handling area.

Viewing a File Attachment

The message from Kendra Zimmerman contains a file attachment. The paper clip icon in the message heading in Figure 1-19 indicates the e-mail message contains a file attachment (file or object). The Attachments line in the Reading Pane indicates an attachment as well. The following steps show how to open the message and view the contents of the file attachment.

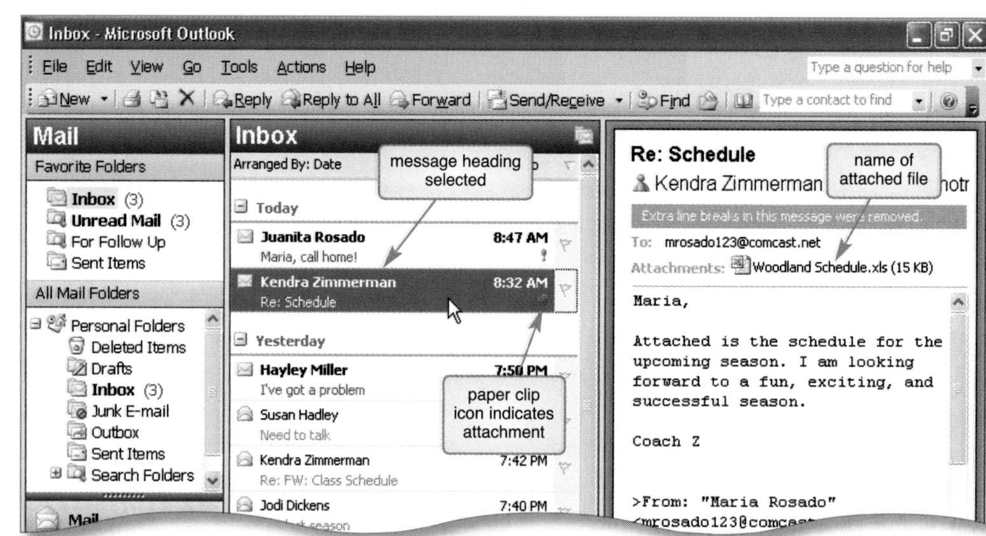

FIGURE 1-19

To View a File Attachment

1

- **With the Inbox window active, double-click the Kendra Zimmerman message heading in the message pane.**
- **If necessary, maximize the Re: Schedule - Message window.**

Outlook displays the Message window (Figure 1-20). The Attachments entry, containing an Excel icon, the file name (Woodland Schedule.xls), and the file size (15 KB) appear above the message body on the Attachments line.

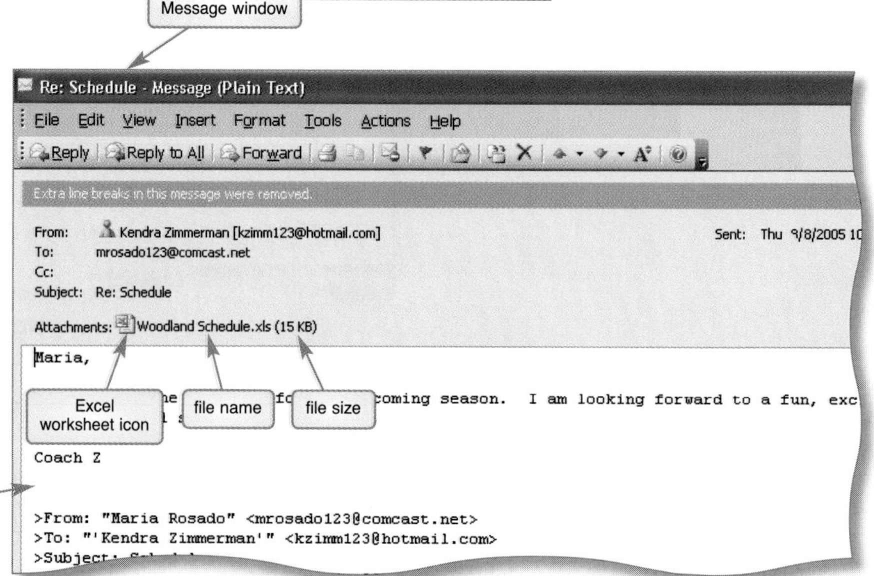

FIGURE 1-20

2

- **Double-click the Woodland Schedule.xls icon on the Attachments line.**
- **If Outlook displays the Opening Mail Attachment dialog box, click the Open button.**

The Microsoft Excel - Woodland Schedule window containing the schedule appears (Figure 1-21).

3

- **After viewing the worksheet, click the Close button on the right side of the title bar in the Excel window.**
- **Click the Close button in Message window.**

The Excel window and Message window close.

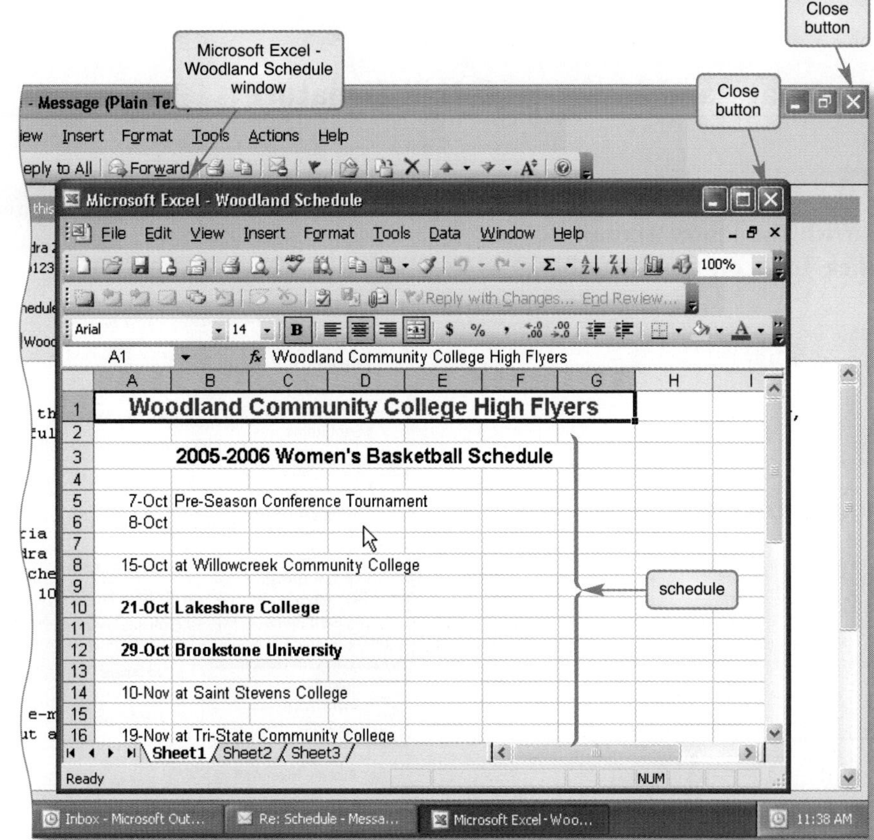

FIGURE 1-21

Other Ways

1. Double-click file attachment name in Reading Pane
2. Click Save button in Opening Mail Attachments dialog box to save attachment on disk
3. On File menu point to Save Attachments to save attachment on disk

File attachments can be any type of file from worksheets to documents to presentations to pictures. Files can be viewed only if your computer has the appropriate software. For example, if your computer does not have Excel installed, then you cannot view an Excel file attachment. The Opening Mail Attachment dialog box in Step 2 gives you the option of viewing the attachment as you read the e-mail or saving it on disk to view at another time.

Creating an E-Mail Signature

An **e-mail signature** is a unique message automatically added to the end of an outgoing e-mail message. An e-mail signature can be much more than adding your name to the end of a message. It can consist of text and/or pictures. The type of signature you add may depend on the recipient of the message. For messages to family and friends, a first name may be sufficient, while messages to business contacts may include your full name, address, telephone number, and other business information. Outlook allows you to create a different signature for each e-mail account created in Outlook. The steps on the next page create and insert an e-mail signature in an e-mail message.

To Create and Insert an E-Mail Signature

1

• **With the Inbox window active, click Tools on the menu bar.**

Outlook displays the Tools menu (Figure 1-22).

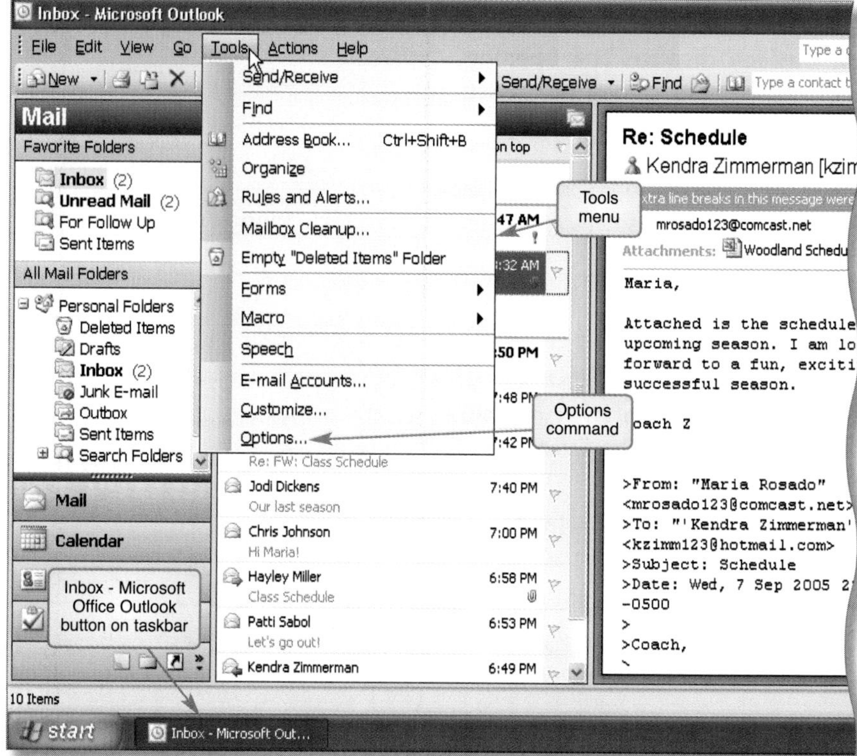

FIGURE 1-22

2

• **Click Options on the Tools menu.**

• **When Outlook displays the Options dialog box, click the Mail Format tab.**

Outlook displays the Mail Format sheet in the Options dialog box (Figure 1-23).

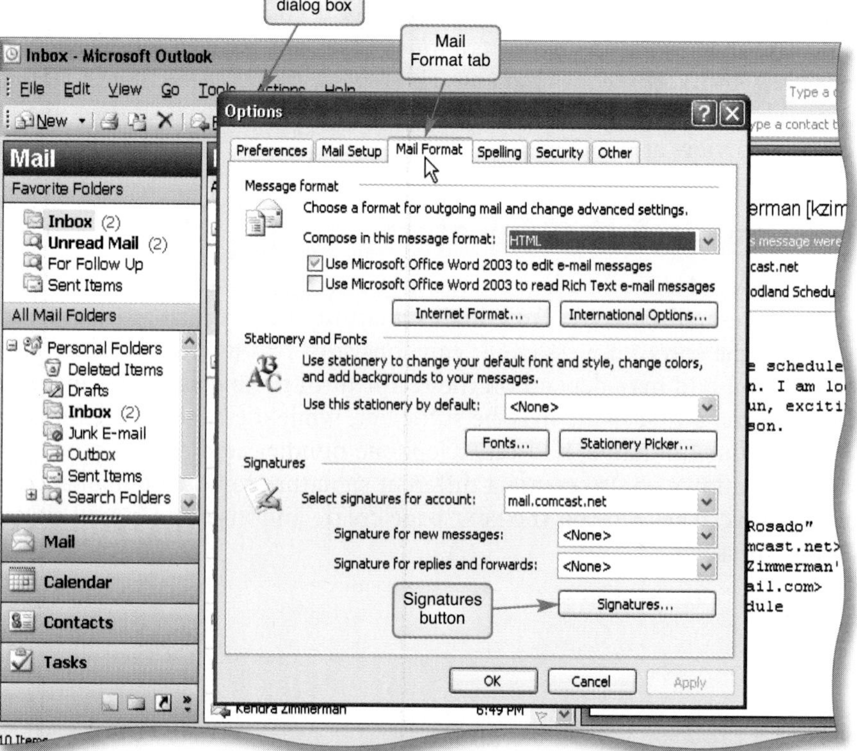

FIGURE 1-23

3

• **Click the Signatures button.**

Outlook displays the Create Signature dialog box (Figure 1-24).

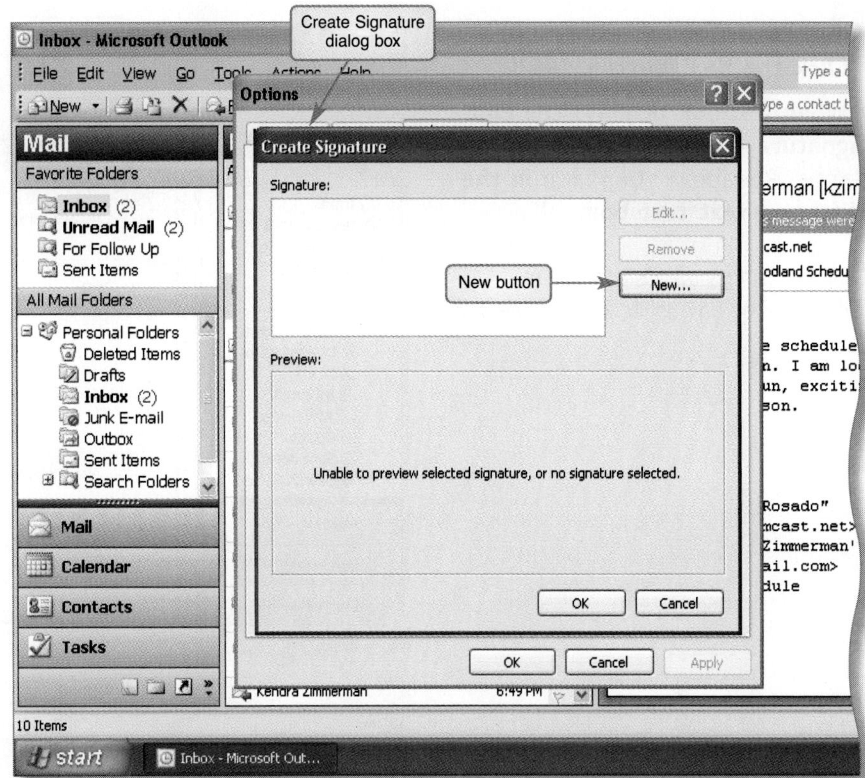

FIGURE 1-24

4

• **Click the New button.**

• **When Outlook displays the Create New Signature dialog box, type** `Team` **in the Enter a name for your new signature text box.**

Outlook displays the Create New Signature dialog box. Team is the name of the signature being created (Figure 1-25).

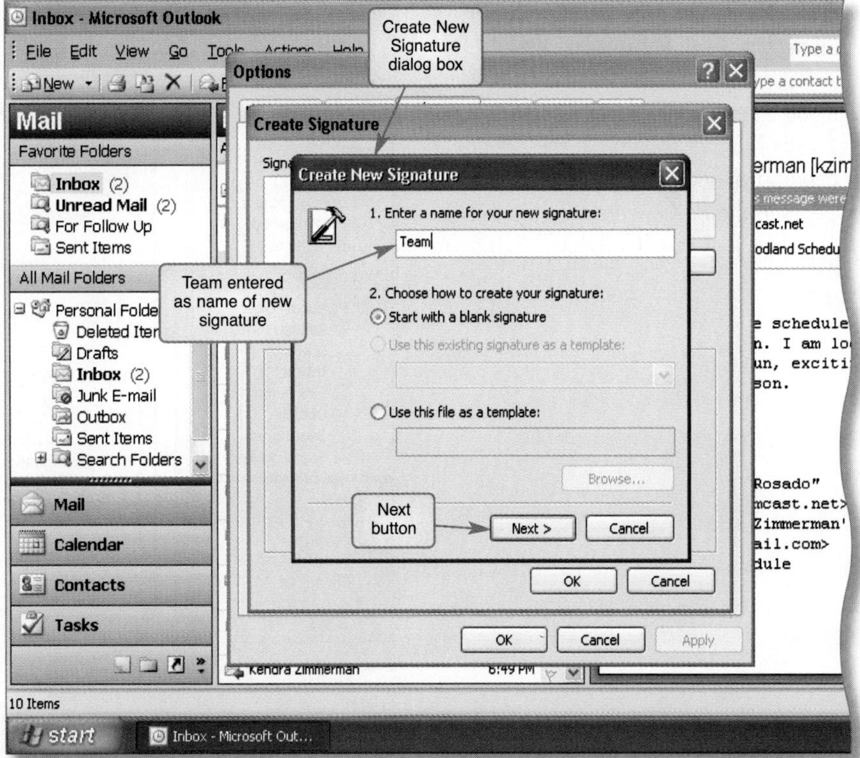

FIGURE 1-25

5

- **Click the Next button.**
- **When Outlook displays the Edit Signature – [Team] dialog box, type** `Maria Rosado - Captain` **in the Signature text text box.**

Outlook displays the Edit Signature – [Team] dialog box as shown in Figure 1-26.

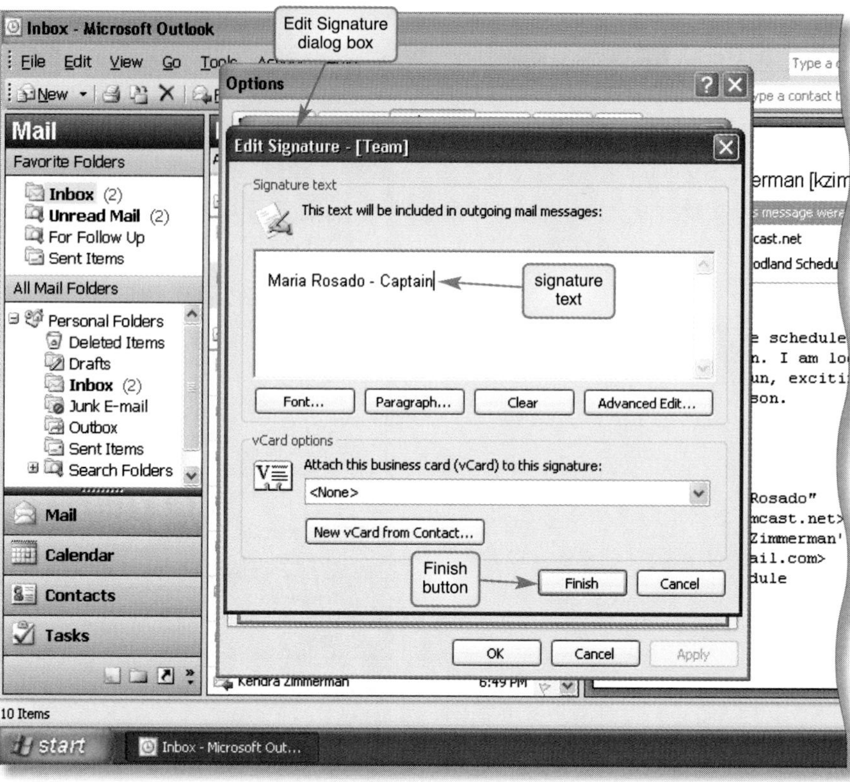

FIGURE 1-26

6

- **Click the Finish button.**

Outlook displays the Create Signature dialog box with Team highlighted in the Signature text box. The newly created signature appears in the Preview area (Figure 1-27).

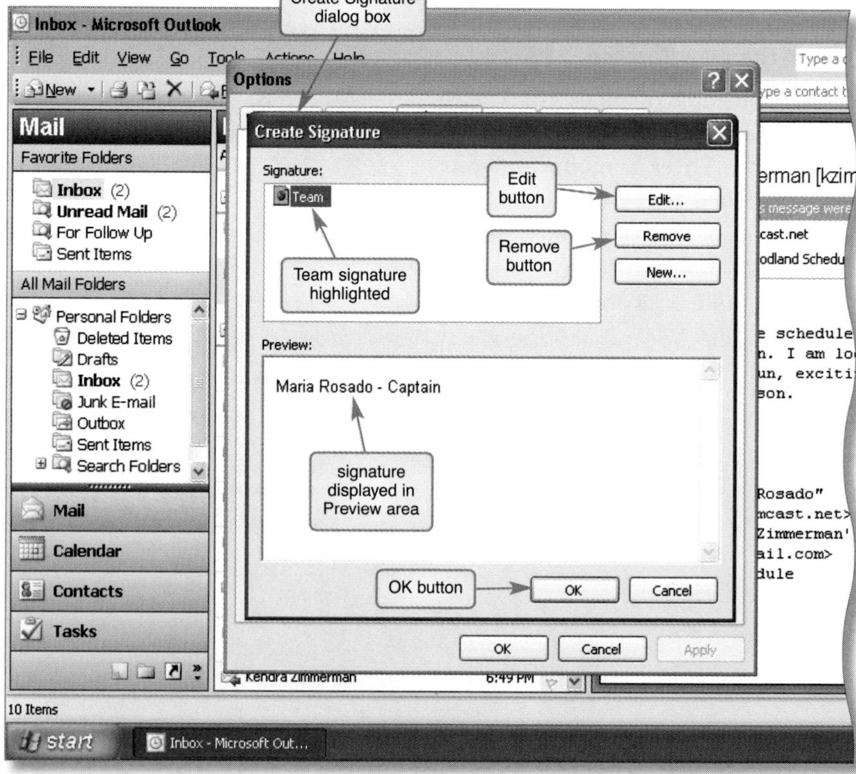

FIGURE 1-27

- **Click the OK button.**
- **In the Signatures area of the Options dialog box, select the appropriate e-mail account (if you are stepping through this project, ask your instructor for the appropriate e-mail account).**
- **If necessary, select Team in the Signature for new messages box and the Signature for replies and forwards box.**

Outlook displays the Options dialog box as shown in Figure 1-28. Team is selected as the signature for new messages and for replies and forwards.

8

- **Click the OK button.**

The signature settings are applied.

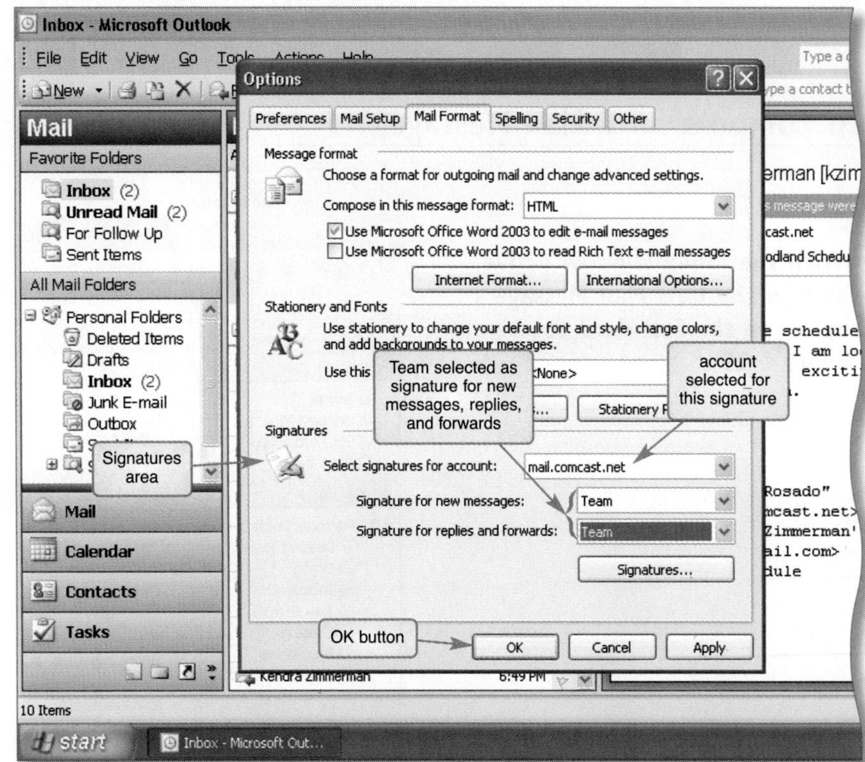

FIGURE 1-28

Other Ways

1. Press ALT+T, press O
2. In Voice Command mode, say "Tools, Options"

The signature Maria Rosado – Captain now will be inserted automatically in all new messages as well as reply messages and forward messages. Signatures can be modified or removed at anytime by clicking the Edit or Remove buttons in the Create Signature dialog box (Figure 1-27). You can add a variety of signatures to Outlook for different purposes that include any specific characteristics that you desire.

Creating Unique E-Mail Signatures for Multiple Accounts

You can create unique signatures for different accounts by adding new signatures and selecting a different account in the Signatures area of the Options dialog box (Figure 1-28). For one account, you may want to insert a personal signature. In another, you may want to include a business or professional signature with contact and other information.

More About

E-Mail Signatures

Outlook allows you to add signatures to your e-mail messages that you create in Word 2003. Some of the advantages to creating them in Word is the ability to insert pictures and hyperlinks into the signature.

Composing a New Mail Message

In addition to opening and reading, replying to, forwarding, and deleting e-mail messages, you will have many occasions to compose and send new e-mail messages. When you compose an e-mail message, you must know the e-mail address of the recipient of the message, enter a brief one-line subject that identifies the purpose or contents of the message, and then type the message in the message body.

You also can **format** an e-mail message to enhance the appearance of the message. Formatting attributes include changing the style, size, and color of the text in the document. As indicated earlier, Outlook allows you to choose from three formats: HTML, Plain Text, or Rich Text.

The following steps show how to compose a formatted e-mail message to Kendra Zimmerman with an attachment.

To Compose an E-Mail Message

1

• **With the Inbox window active, point to the New Mail Message button on the Standard toolbar (Figure 1-29).**

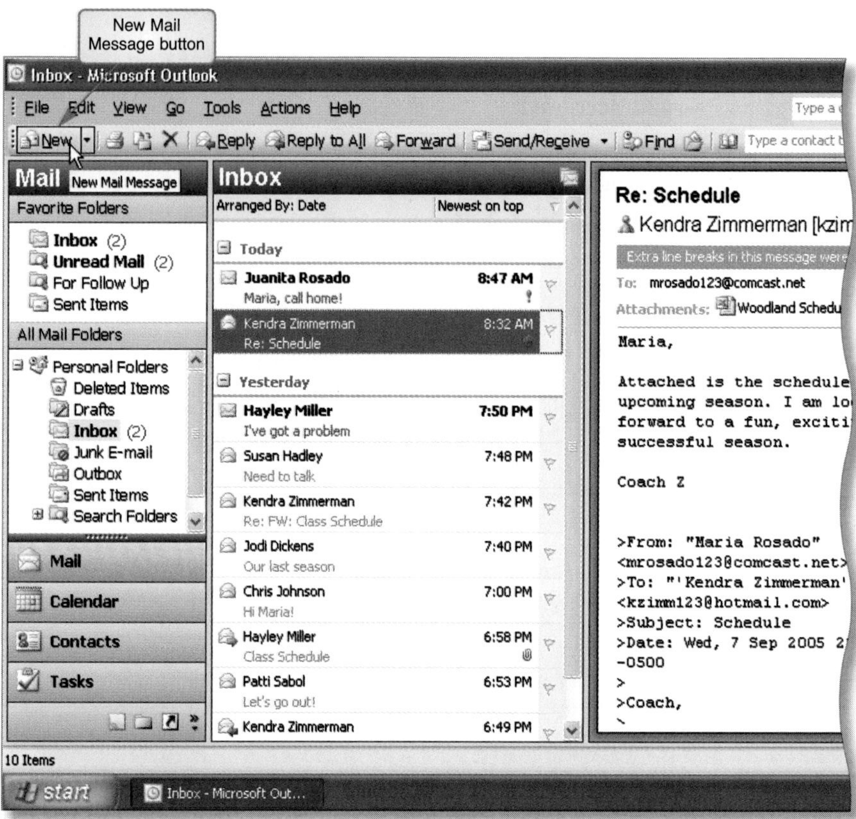

FIGURE 1-29

2

• **Click the New Mail Message button.**

Outlook displays the Untitled - Message window with the signature Maria Rosado - Captain (Figure 1-30). The Message window contains a menu bar, two toolbars, three text boxes, and the message body. Outlook positions the insertion point in the To text box.

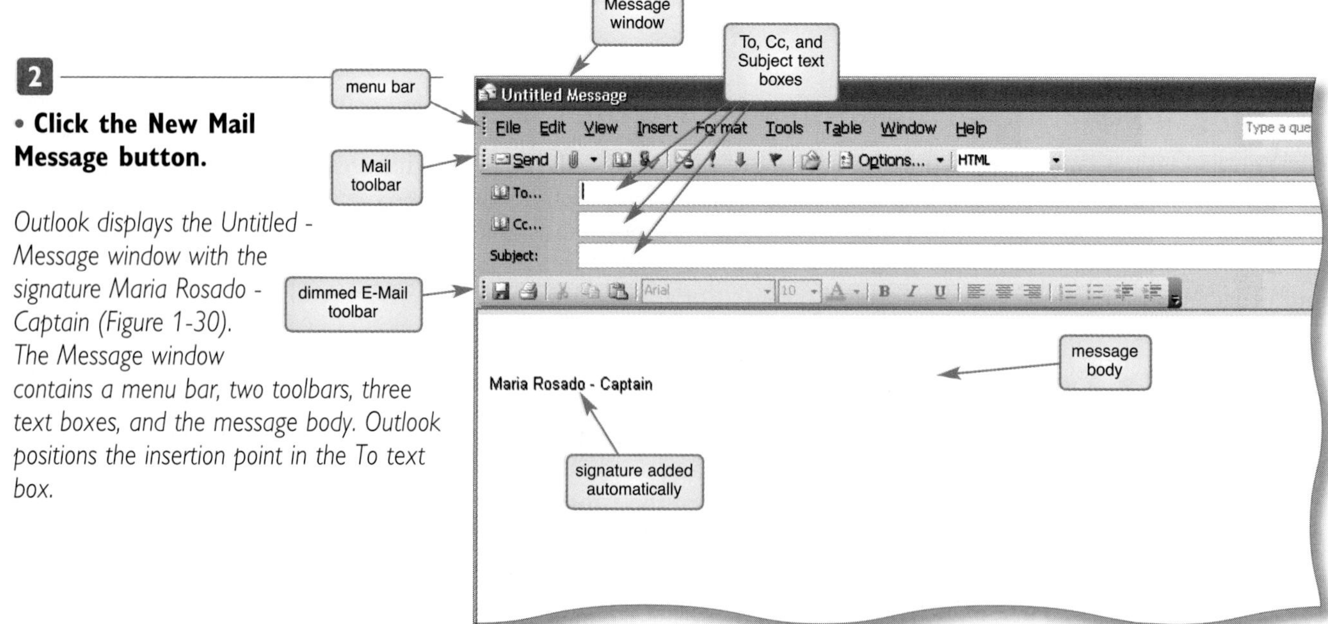

FIGURE 1-30

3

- **Type** kzimm123@hotmail.com **in the To text box, click the Subject text box, and then type** Updated Practice Schedule **in the Subject text box.**
- **Press the TAB key.**

The destination e-mail address appears in the To text box, and the subject of the message appears in the Subject text box (Figure 1-31). The title bar of the Untitled Message window now appears with the subject of the e-mail message (Updated Practice Schedule). The insertion point appears in the message body.

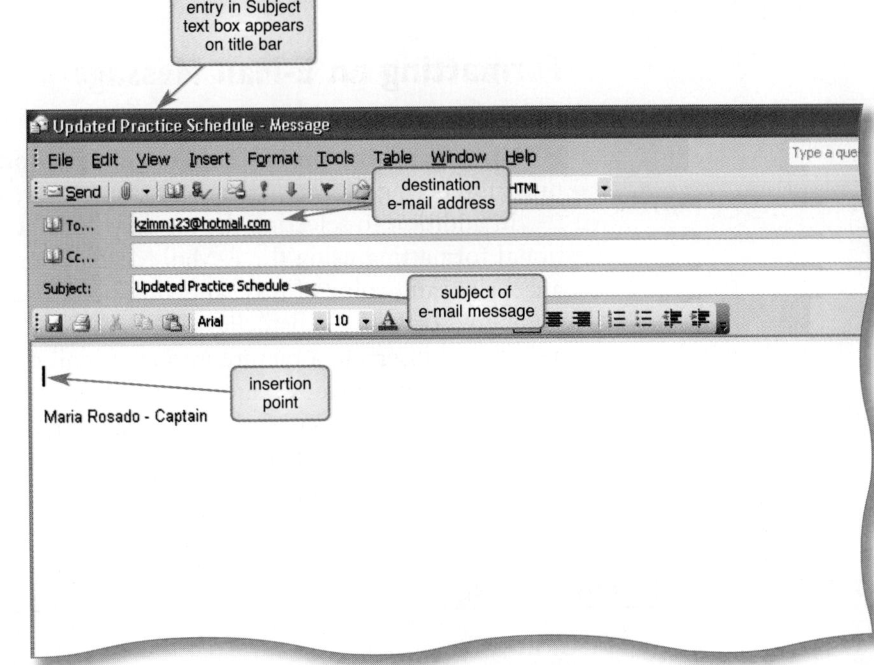

FIGURE 1-31

4

- **Type the e-mail message shown in Figure 1-32.**

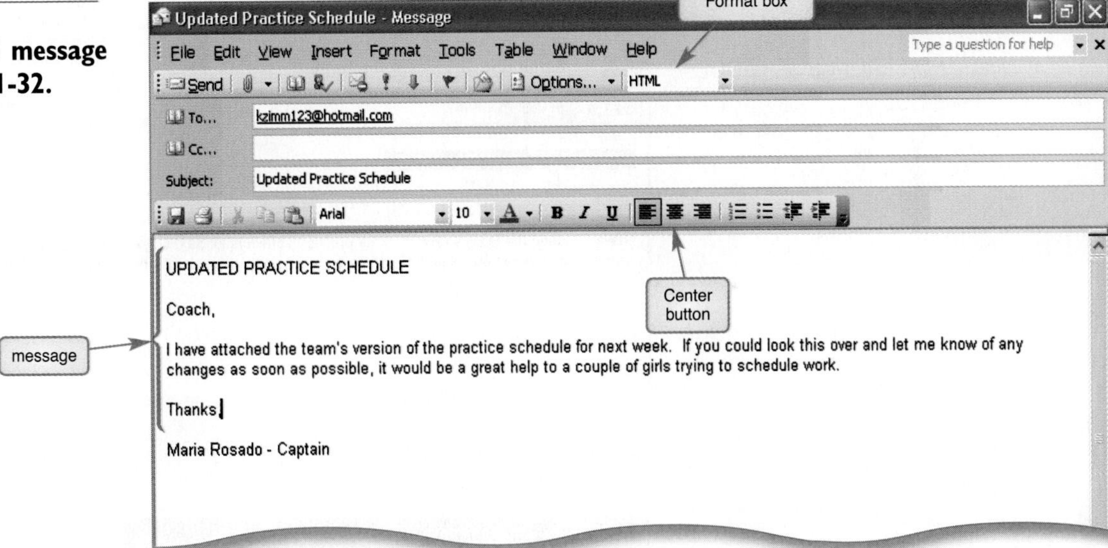

FIGURE 1-32

When you enter a message, you can use the DELETE key and BACKSPACE key to correct errors. Before pressing the DELETE key, select words, sentences, or paragraphs using the mouse. If you are using Microsoft Word as your e-mail editor and you have the appropriate Spelling options selected, then the spell checker will flag the misspelled words with a red wavy underline. Furthermore, the message will be spell checked before it is sent. To set the Spelling options, activate the Inbox window, click Tools on the menu bar, click Options on the Tools menu, and then click the Spelling tab in the Options dialog box.

Formatting an E-Mail Message

When you compose a message in Outlook, the default message format is **HTML** (**Hypertext Markup Language**). This format allows you to do text formatting, numbering, bullets, alignment, signatures, and linking to Web pages.

In addition to selecting the message format, Outlook allows you to apply additional formatting using the E-Mail toolbar. Formatting includes changing the appearance, size, and color of text; applying bold, italic, and underlines to text; creating a numbered or bulleted list, changing paragraph indentation or aligning text; creating a link, and inserting a picture into an e-mail message.

The following steps center the text, UPDATED PRACTICE SCHEDULE, and changes its font size to 36-point. A **font size** is measured in points. A **point** is equal to 1/72 of one inch in height. Thus, a font size of 36 points is approximately one-half inch in height.

To Format an E-Mail Message

1

- **Drag to select the text, UPDATED PRACTICE SCHEDULE, in the message body.**

The text, UPDATED PRACTICE SCHEDULE, is selected (Figure 1-33).

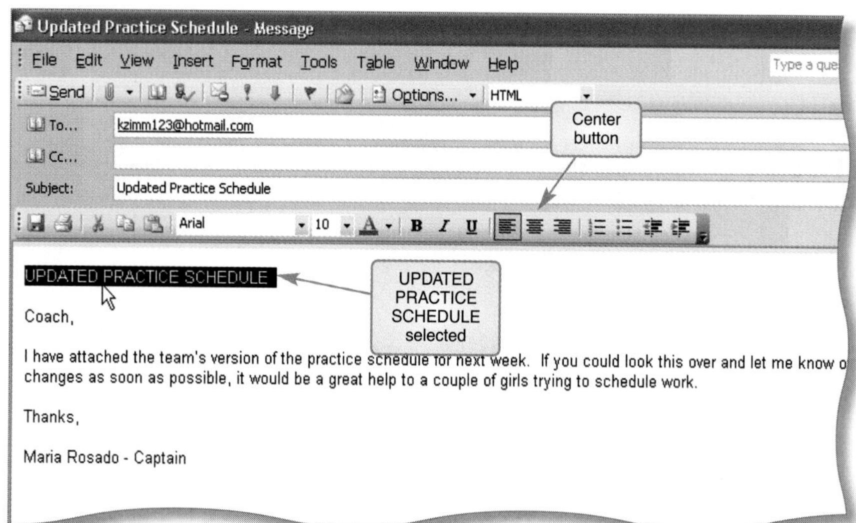

FIGURE 1-33

2

- **Click the Center button on the E-Mail toolbar.**

Outlook centers the text, UPDATED PRACTICE SCHEDULE, on the first line of the e-mail message (Figure 1-34). The current font size is the default 10-point.

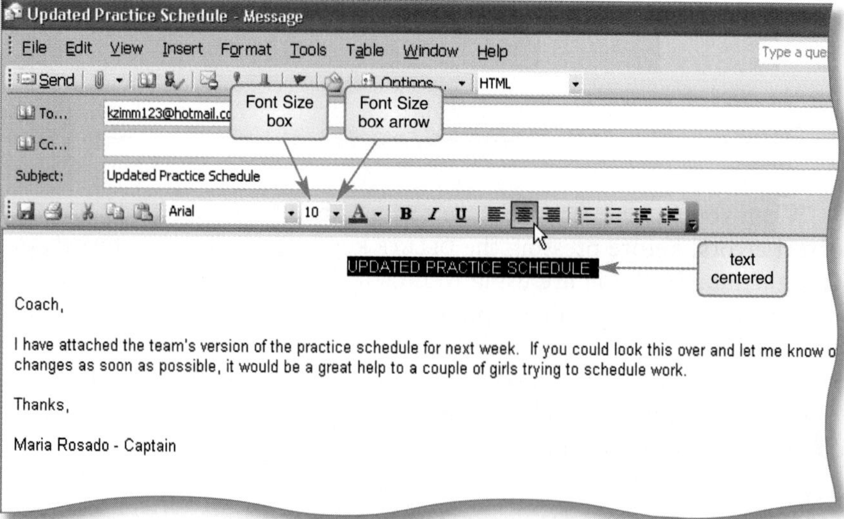

FIGURE 1-34

3

- **Click the Font Size box arrow on the E-Mail toolbar.**

Outlook displays the Font Size list (Figure 1-35).

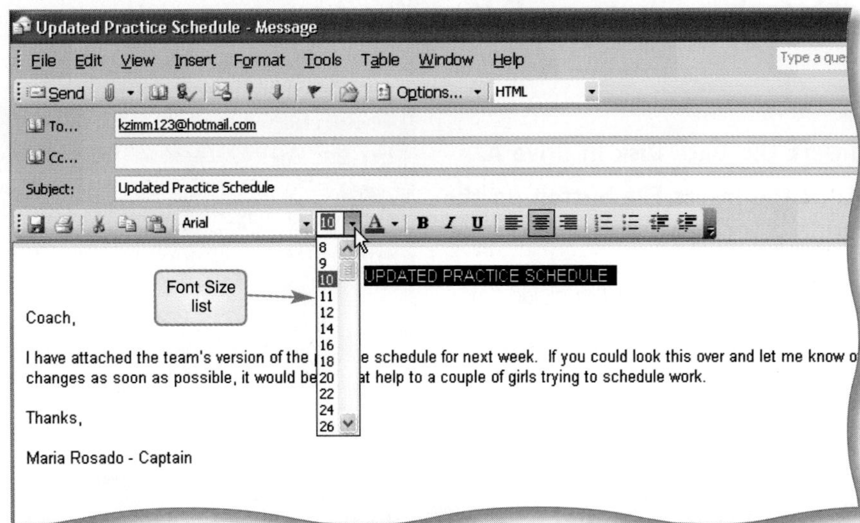

FIGURE 1-35

4

- **Scroll down the Font Size list, click 36, and then click the selected text to remove the selection.**

Outlook displays the text, UPDATED PRACTICE SCHEDULE, in 36-point font size (Figure 1-36).

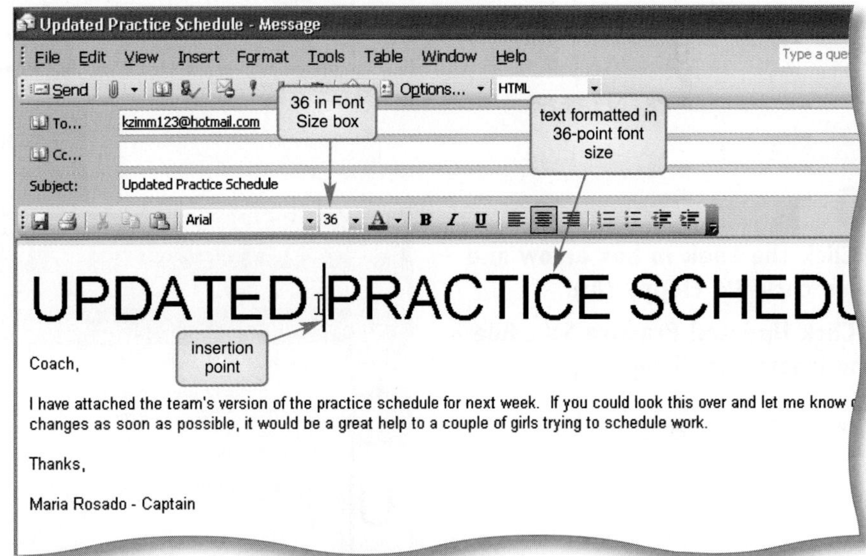

FIGURE 1-36

You do not have to select the text UPDATED PRACTICE SCHEDULE to center it on the line because centering is a paragraph format. All you have to do is click within the text, and then click the Center button on the E-Mail toolbar. Font size, however, is a character format; therefore, you must select all the characters in the text before you select the new font size.

> *More About*
>
> **File Attachments**
>
> Outlook allows other ways for a file to be inserted into a message. You can drag a file from any folder on your computer to a message, or you can copy and paste a file into a message as an attachment by right-clicking the file, clicking Copy on the shortcut menu, then in the Outlook message, clicking Paste on the Edit menu.

Attaching a File to an E-Mail Message

In some situations, a simple e-mail message is not sufficient to get the required information to the recipient. In these cases, you may want to attach a file to your e-mail message. Outlook allows you to attach almost any kind of file to your message. You may need to send a Word document, an Excel worksheet, a picture, or any number of file types. The steps on the next page show how to attach the Updated Practice Schedule.xls file to the e-mail message.

To Attach a File to an E-Mail Message

1

- **Insert the Data Disk in drive A.**
- **Click the Insert File button on the Standard toolbar.**

Outlook displays the Insert File dialog box (Figure 1-37).

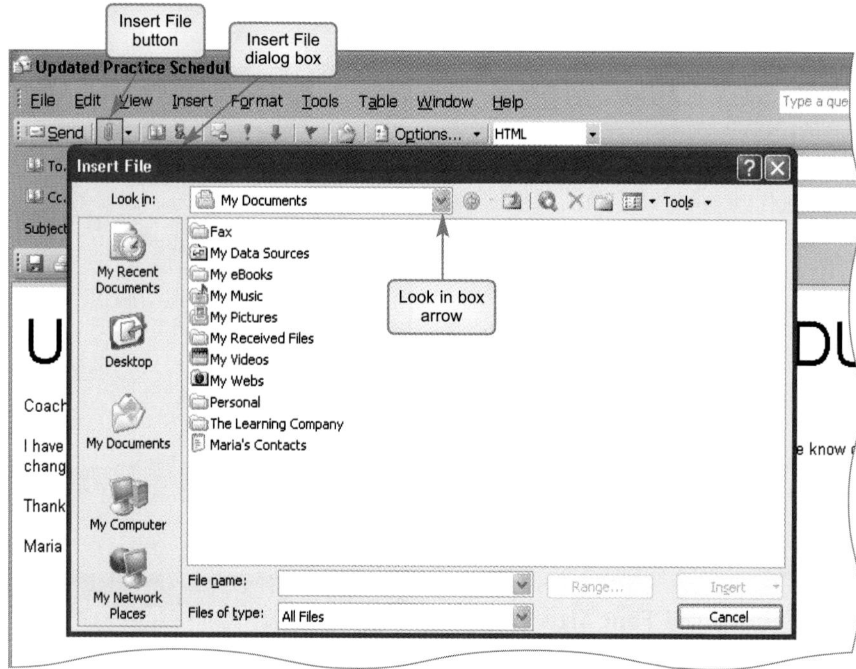

FIGURE 1-37

2

- **Click the Look in box arrow and then click 3½ Floppy (A:).**
- **Click Updated Practice Schedule in the Insert File dialog box.**

Updated Practice Schedule file is highlighted (Figure 1-38).

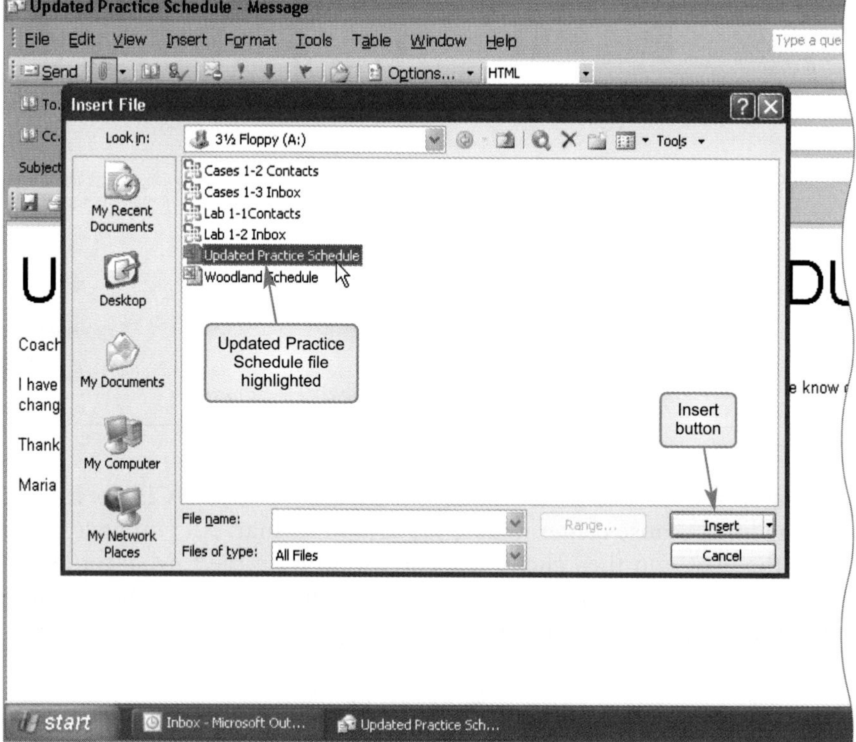

FIGURE 1-38

3

• **Click the Insert button in the Insert File dialog box.**

Outlook displays the name of the file, Updated Practice Schedule.xls, in the Attachment box, along with an Excel icon and file size (Figure 1-39).

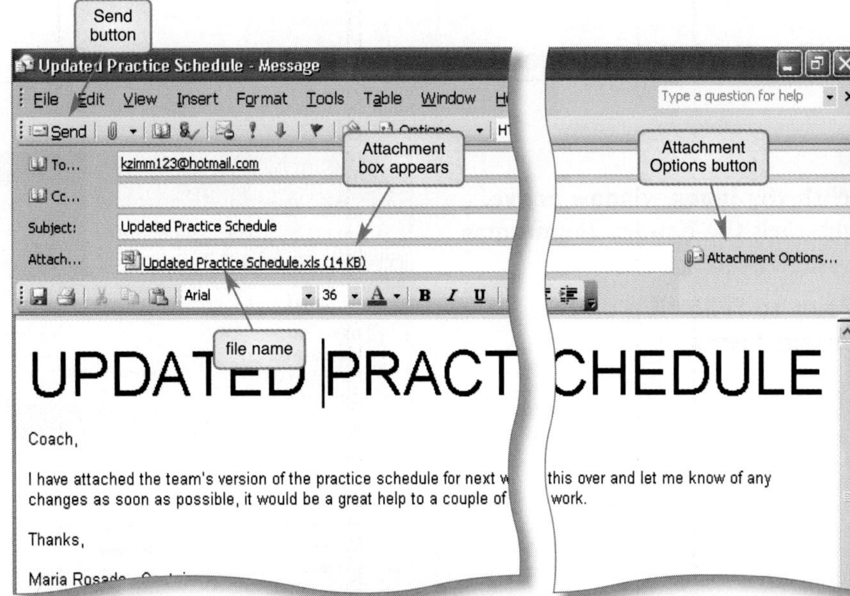

FIGURE 1-39

Other Ways

1. On Insert menu click File
2. Press ALT+I, press L
3. In Voice Command mode, say "Insert, File"

You can attach multiple documents to the same e-mail message. Simply perform the previous steps for each attachment. Keep in mind, however, that some Internet service providers have limits on the total size of e-mail messages they will accept. For example, if you attach pictures, which often are quite large, to an e-mail message, the recipient's service provider may not allow it to go through. In such cases, the sender is not informed that the e-mail message did not get through to the recipient. It is recommended that you keep the sum of the file sizes attached to an e-mail message less than 500 kilobytes.

More About

Junk E-Mail Filters

A new feature in Outlook is the Junk E-mail Filter. The filter is on by default. It automatically evaluates whether an unread message should be sent to the Junk E-mail folder. While you can configure the Junk E-mail Filter to your own personal settings, the default settings evaluate several factors, such as content, time the message was sent, and who sent the message. To change junk e-mail settings, click Options on the Tools menu, and then click the Junk E-mail button in the Preferences sheet of the Options dialog box. Make the preferred changes in the Junk E-mail Options dialog box. Note that the Junk E-mail folder is not available if you use an Exchange Server e-mail account.

Sending an E-Mail Message

After composing, formatting, and adding an attachment to an e-mail message, the next step is to send the message as illustrated in the following step.

To Send an E-Mail Message

1 **Click the Send button on the Standard toolbar.**

Outlook closes the Message window and temporarily stores the e-mail message in the Outbox folder while it sends the message, and then it moves the message to the Sent Items folder.

Flagging, Sorting, and Filtering E-Mail Messages

To the right of the message heading is the Flag Status column. The **Flag Status column** contains flags that can be assigned one of six different colors. One use for these flags could be to remind you to follow up on an issue. Color selection and the meaning of each color are entirely at the discretion of the user. For example, a red flag could mean the message needs immediate attention, a yellow flag may mean a response requires some information before you can reply, and a green flag simply may mean that the message requires a reply at your convenience (non-urgent). The steps on the next page show how to flag and sort e-mail messages.

To Flag E-Mail Messages

1

- **With the Inbox window active, right-click the Kendra Zimmerman message heading.**
- **Point to Follow Up on the shortcut menu.**

Outlook displays the message shortcut menu and the Follow Up submenu with the Flag commands (Figure 1-40).

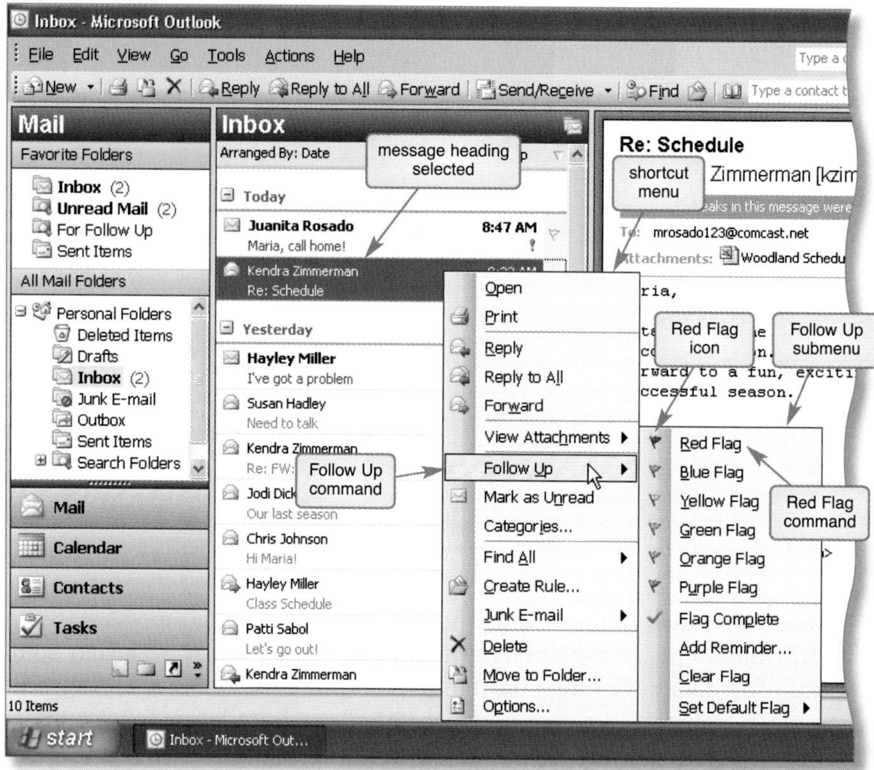

FIGURE 1-40

2

- **Click the Red Flag command on the Follow Up submenu.**
- **Repeat the Steps 1 and 2 to flag the remaining messages in the message pane.**
- **Select different colors as necessary.**

The Kendra Zimmerman message now displays a red flag icon in the Flag Status column (Figure 1-41). The remaining messages also display colored flag icons.

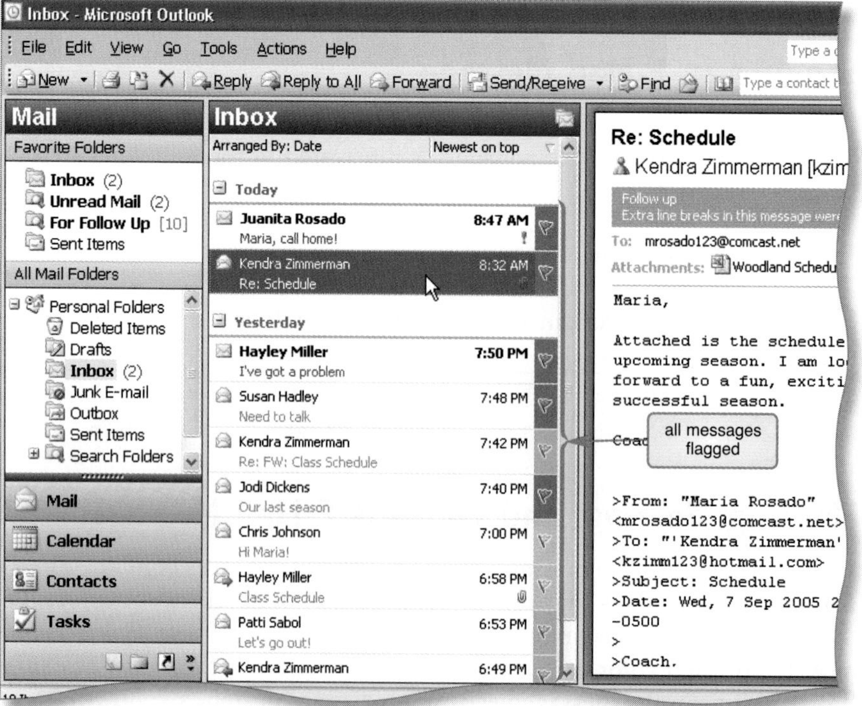

FIGURE 1-41

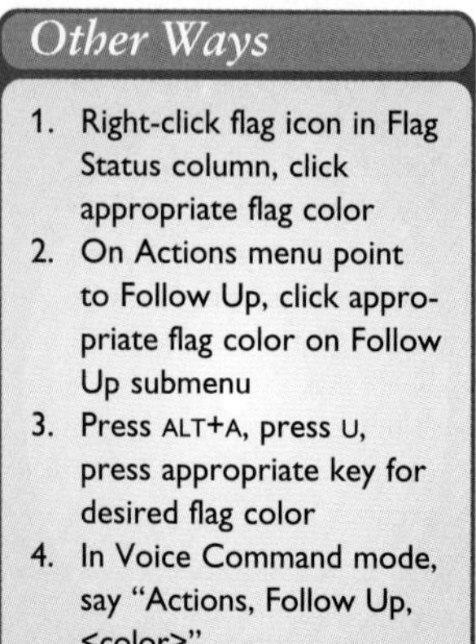

Other Ways

1. Right-click flag icon in Flag Status column, click appropriate flag color
2. On Actions menu point to Follow Up, click appropriate flag color on Follow Up submenu
3. Press ALT+A, press U, press appropriate key for desired flag color
4. In Voice Command mode, say "Actions, Follow Up, <color>"

After flagging the appropriate messages, you can sort the messages by flag color. This is useful for grouping all the messages that require immediate attention as opposed to those messages that can be replied to at your convenience. The following steps show how to sort the messages by flag color.

To Sort E-Mail Messages by Flag Color

1

• **With the Inbox window active, click View on the menu bar and then point to Arrange By.**

Outlook displays the View menu and the Arrange By submenu (Figure 1-42).

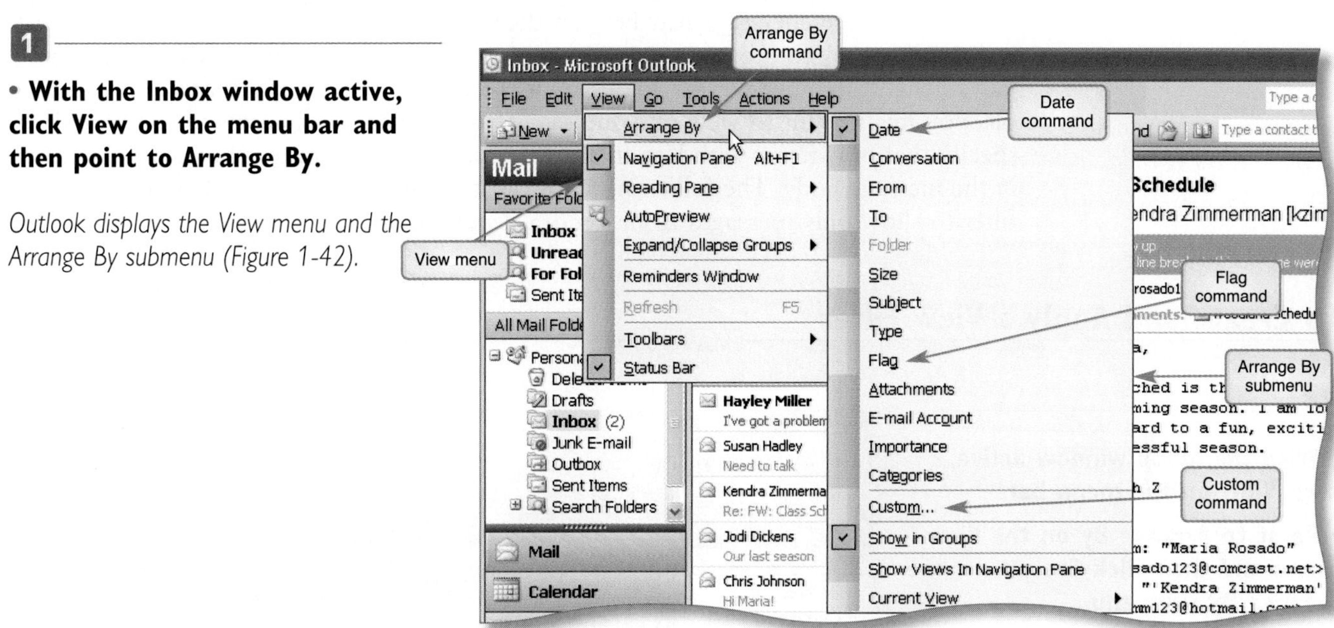

FIGURE 1-42

2

• **Click Flag on the Arrange By submenu.**

Outlook displays the Inbox window with messages arranged by flag and sorted by color (red on top) (Figure 1-43).

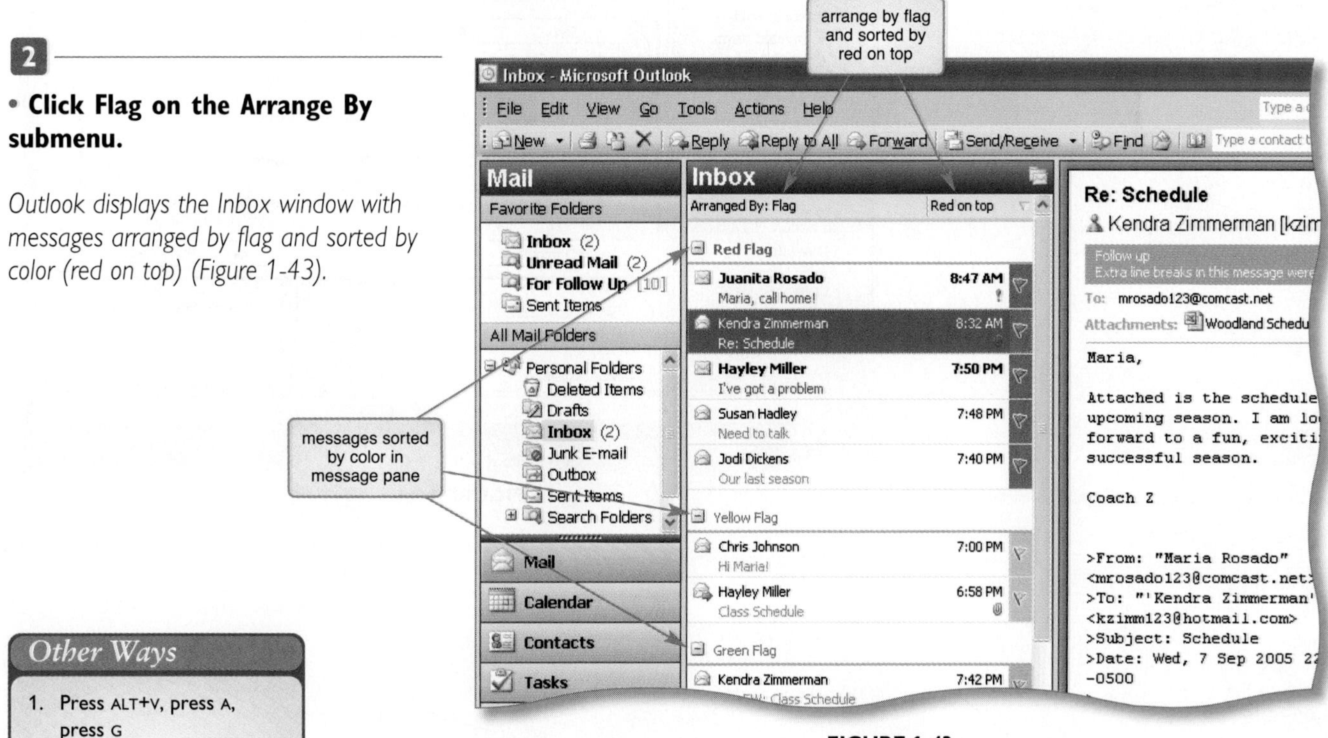

FIGURE 1-43

Other Ways

1. Press ALT+V, press A, press G
2. In Voice Command mode, say "View, Arrange By, Flag"

Outlook allows you to sort your messages several different ways using the Arrange By submenu (Figure 1-42 on the previous page). For example, you might want to see one particular person's messages. In this case, you would choose From on the Arrange By submenu. To return the messages to the default view, click Date on the Arrange By submenu.

After you have taken the appropriate action on a flagged message, you can indicate that no further action is required by changing the flag to a check mark by simply clicking the flag for that message. You also can remove the flag by right-clicking the flag and then clicking Clear Flag on the shortcut menu.

Another way to organize your messages is to use a view filter. A **view filter** displays items stored in Outlook folders that meet your specific conditions. For example, you might want to view only messages from Kendra Zimmerman. You would specify that only items with Kendra Zimmerman in the From text box should appear in the message body. The following steps illustrate how to create and apply a view filter to show only messages from Kendra Zimmerman.

To Create and Apply a View Filter

1

- **With the Inbox window active, click View on the menu bar.**
- **Point to Arrange By on the View menu and then click Custom on the Arrange By submenu.**

Outlook displays the Customize View: Messages dialog box (Figure 1-44).

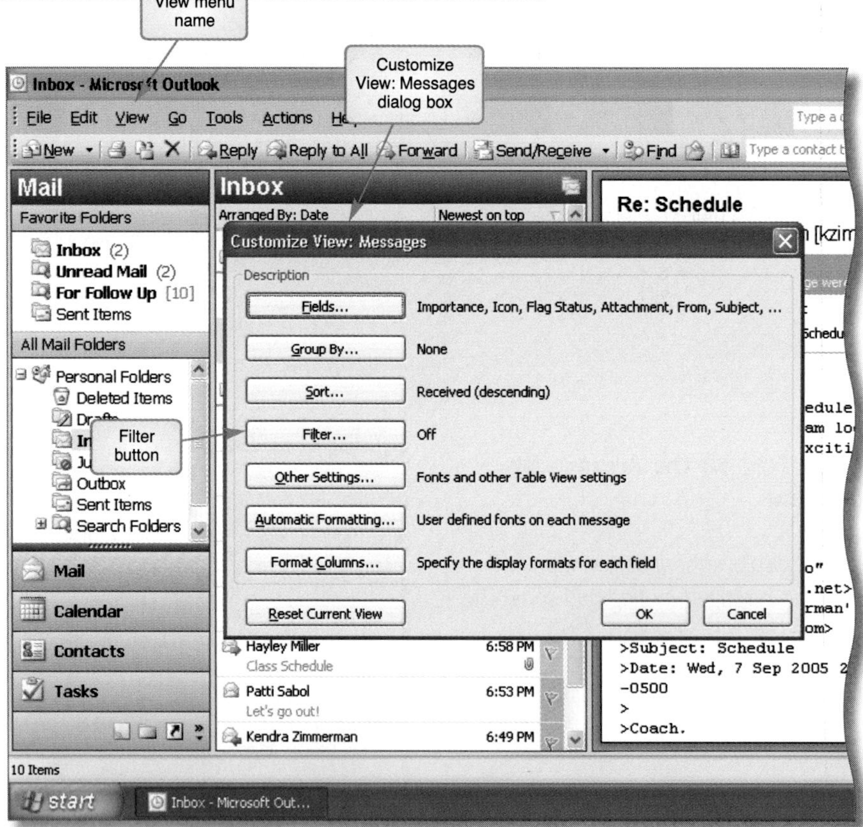

FIGURE 1-44

2

- **Click the Filter button.**
- **When Outlook displays the Filter dialog box, click the From text box.**
- **Type** `Kendra Zimmerman` **in the From text box.**

Outlook displays the Filter dialog box. The name, Kendra Zimmerman, appears in the From text box (Figure 1-45).

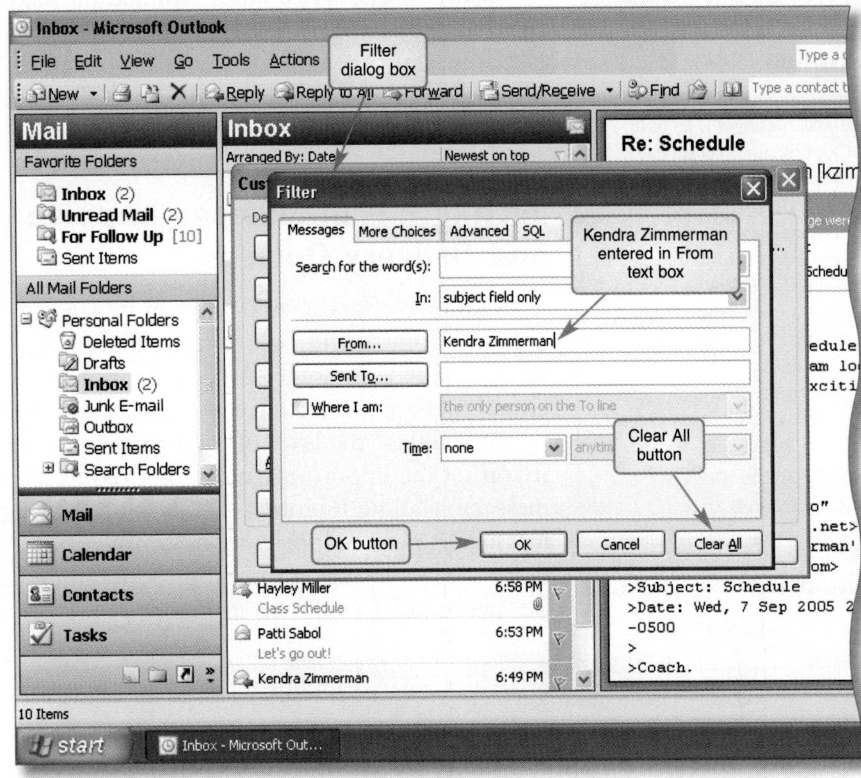

FIGURE 1-45

3

- **Click the OK button in the Filter dialog box and the Customize View: Messages dialog box.**

The Inbox window is redisplayed with only messages from Kendra Zimmerman showing in the message pane (Figure 1-46). The words, Filter Applied, appear on the status bar in the lower-left corner of the window.

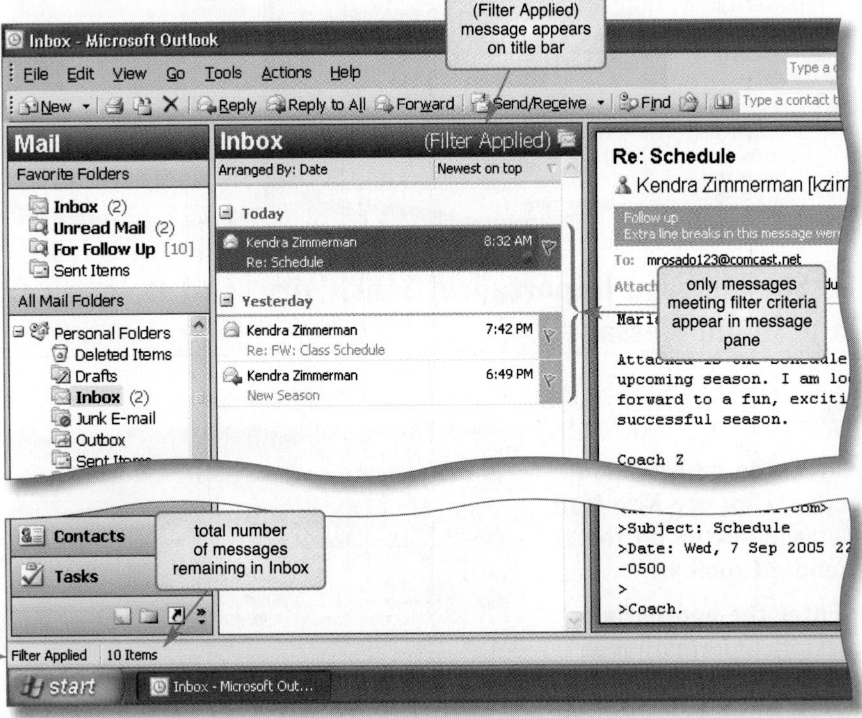

FIGURE 1-46

> *More About*
>
> **Rules**
>
> Another way to manage e-mail messages is to have Outlook apply rules when receiving and/or sending messages. Using rules, you can have messages automatically forwarded, categorized, or flagged for follow up, just to name a few of the available options. To create a rule, click Rules and Alerts on the Tools menu, and then click the New Rule button in the E-mail Rules sheet of the Rules and Alerts dialog box.

Outlook displays a Filter Applied message on the status bar and the Inbox pane title bar when a view filter is applied to a selected folder. It also shows the total number of messages remaining in the Inbox folder on the status bar. To remove a view filter, click the Clear All button in the Filter dialog box (Figure 1-45 on the previous page).

Setting E-Mail Message Importance, Sensitivity, and Delivery Options

Outlook offers several ways in which you can customize your e-mail. You can either customize Outlook to treat all messages in the same manner, or you can customize a single message. Among the options available through Outlook are setting e-mail message importance and sensitivity. Setting **message importance** will indicate to the recipient the level of importance you have given to the message. For example, if you set the importance at high, a red exclamation point icon will appear with the message heading (Figure 1-47). Setting **message sensitivity** indicates whether the message is personal, private, or confidential. A message banner indicating the sensitivity of the message appears in the Reading Pane below the sender's name in the message header as shown in Figure 1-47.

FIGURE 1-47

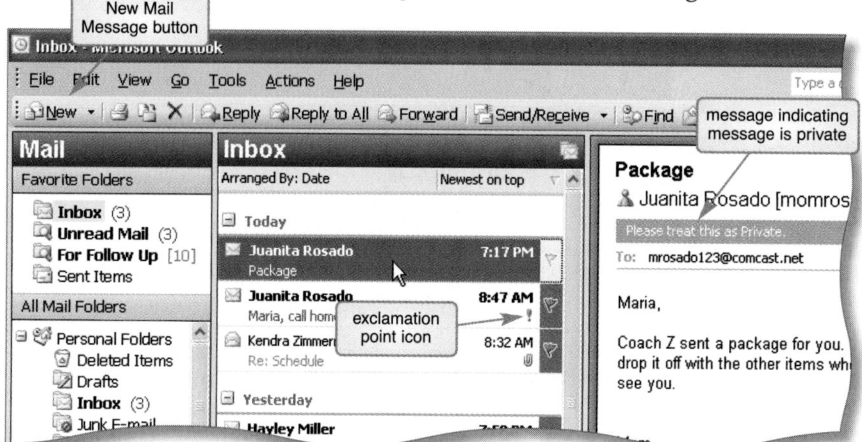

Along with setting importance and sensitivity, Outlook also offers several delivery options. You can have replies to your message automatically forwarded, save sent messages in a location of your choice (default is Sent Items folder), or delay delivering a message until a specified date and time.

The following steps illustrate how to set message importance, sensitivity, and delivery options in a single message.

To Set Message Importance, Sensitivity, and Delivery Options in a Single Message

1

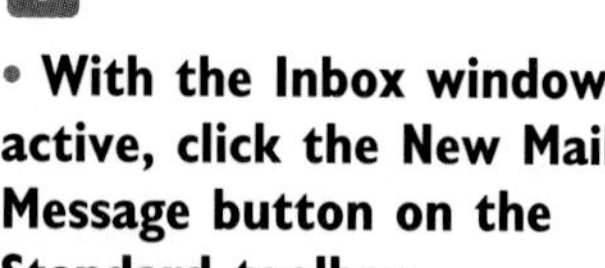

- **With the Inbox window active, click the New Mail Message button on the Standard toolbar.**
- **Enter the appropriate message information as shown in Figure 1-48.**

Outlook displays the Hayley Message window with the new message entered (Figure 1-48).

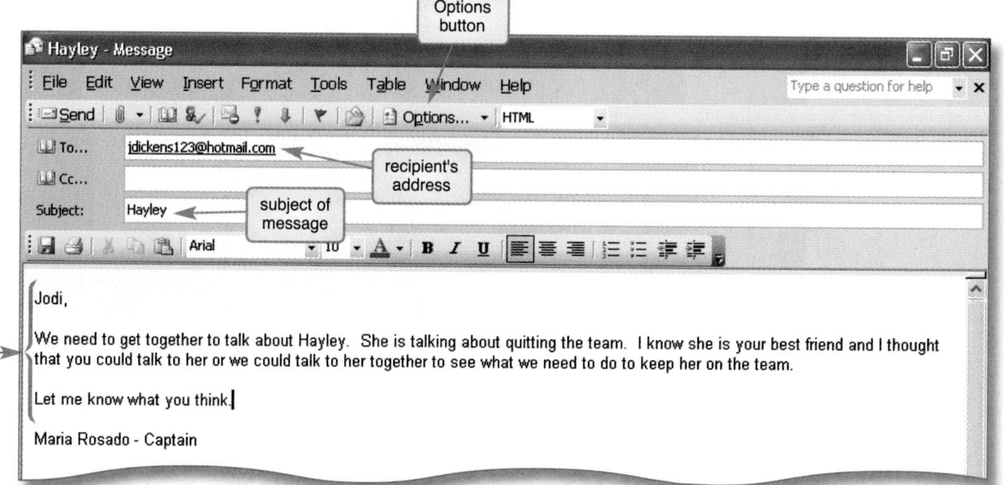

FIGURE 1-48

2

- **Click the Options button on the Mail toolbar (Figure 1-48).**

Outlook displays the Message Options dialog box (Figure 1-49).

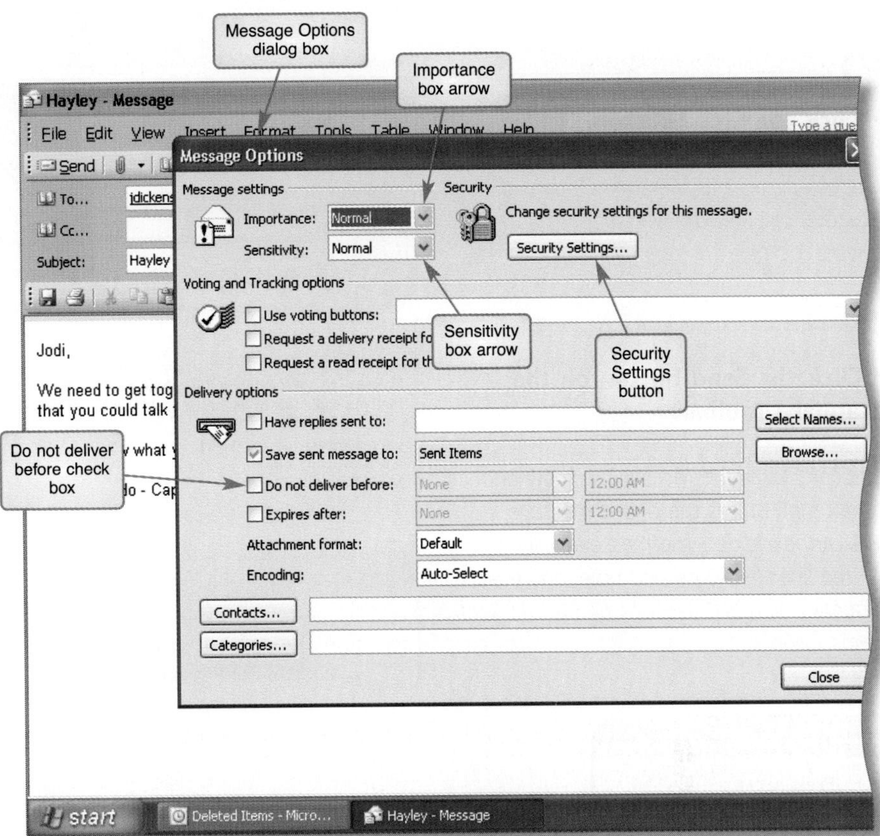

FIGURE 1-49

3

- **Click the Importance box arrow and then select High in the Importance list.**
- **Click the Sensitivity box arrow and then select Private in the Sensitivity list.**
- **Click Do not deliver before in the Delivery options area to select it.**
- **Select September 12, 2005 in the calendar and 12:00 PM as the time in the respective delivery boxes.**

Outlook displays the Message Options dialog box as shown in Figure 1-50. High is selected in the Importance box, Private is selected in the Sensitivity box, and the message delivery is set for 9/12/2005 at 12:00 PM in the date and time boxes.

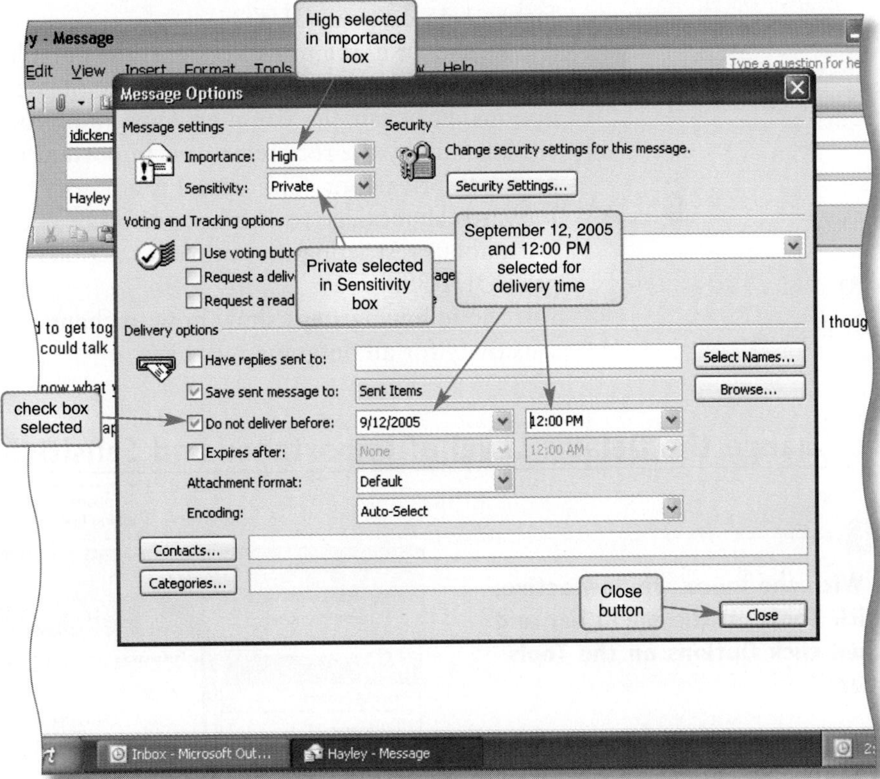

FIGURE 1-50

4

• **Click the Close button.**

Outlook closes the Message Options dialog box and displays the Message window (Figure 1-51).

5

• **Click the Send button on the Standard toolbar.**

Outlook closes the Message window and temporarily stores the e-mail message in the Outbox folder. The message will be sent on the specified date and time, and then Outlook will move the message to the Sent Items folder.

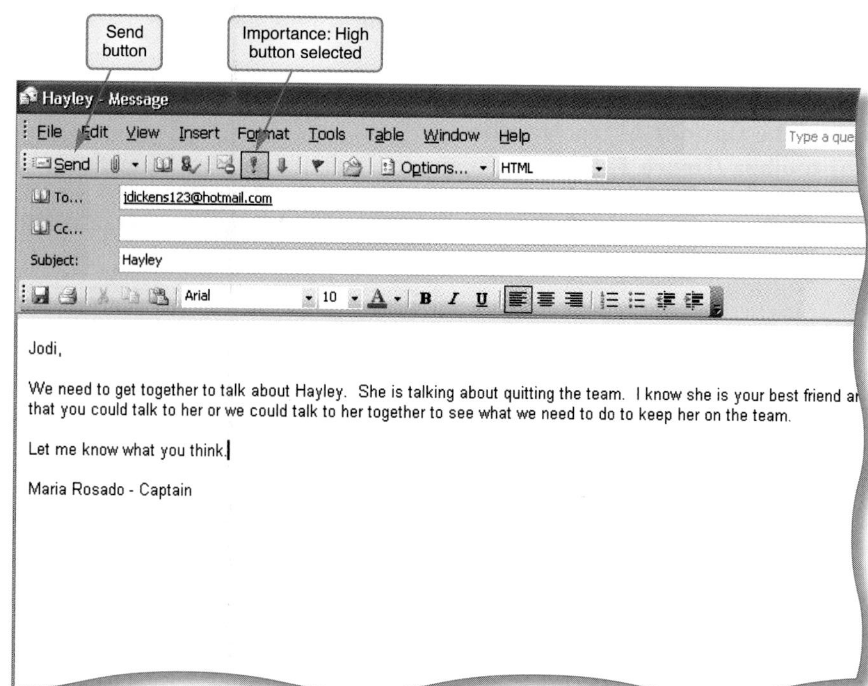

FIGURE 1-51

Other Ways

1. Press ALT+P
2. Right-click message heading in Inbox pane, click Options on submenu

The recipient of the message will receive the message with the red exclamation point icon and the message indicating the e-mail is private like the one shown in Figure 1-47 on page OUT 34.

As shown in the previous steps, the default level of importance and sensitivity is Normal. Outlook allows you to change the default level for either or both of these options. For example, you may want all of your outgoing messages to be treated as confidential by the recipients. It is important to know that marking an e-mail as personal, private, or confidential is advisory only. The recipient will still be able to forward the message to another person or copy the message into another e-mail. To learn about restricting the recipient's actions on a message, see the More About on page OUT 38.

The following steps show how to change the default level of importance and sensitivity for all outgoing messages.

To Change the Default Level of Importance and Sensitivity

1

• **With the Inbox window active, click Tools on the menu bar and then click Options on the Tools menu.**

Outlook displays the Options dialog box (Figure 1-52).

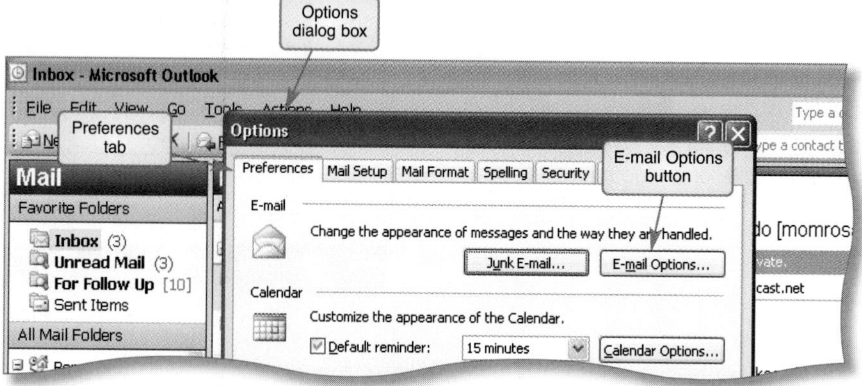

FIGURE 1-52

2

• **In the Preferences sheet, click the E-mail Options button.**

Outlook displays the E-mail Options dialog box (Figure 1-53).

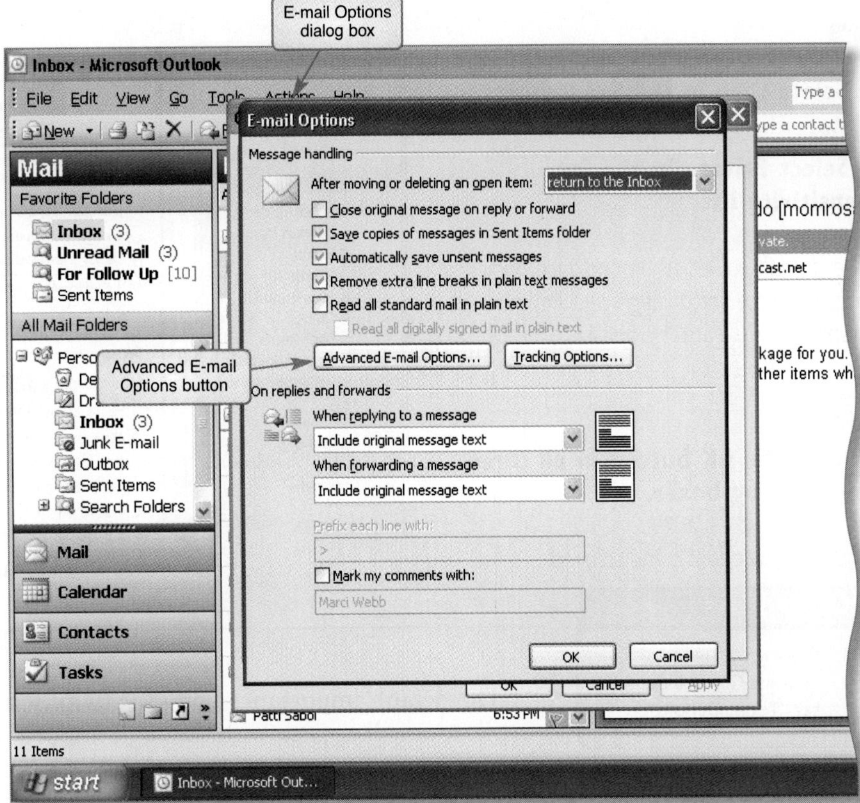

FIGURE 1-53

3

• **Click the Advanced E-mail Options button.**

• **When Outlook displays the Advanced E-mail Options dialog box, click the Set importance box arrow.**

Outlook displays the Advance E-mail Options dialog box with the Set importance list showing the available importance settings (Figure 1-54).

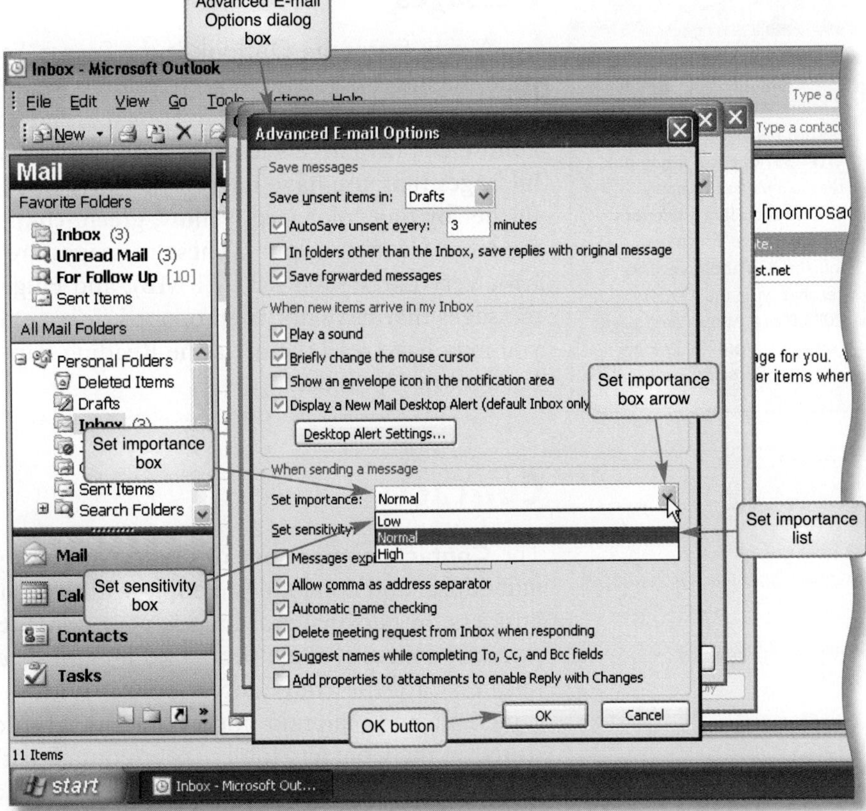

FIGURE 1-54

4

• **Select High in the Set importance list.**

• **Select Private in the Set sensitivity list.**

The default values for importance and sensitivity are set at High and Private, respectively (Figure 1-55).

5

• **Click the OK button in all three open dialog boxes.**

The Inbox window is redisplayed.

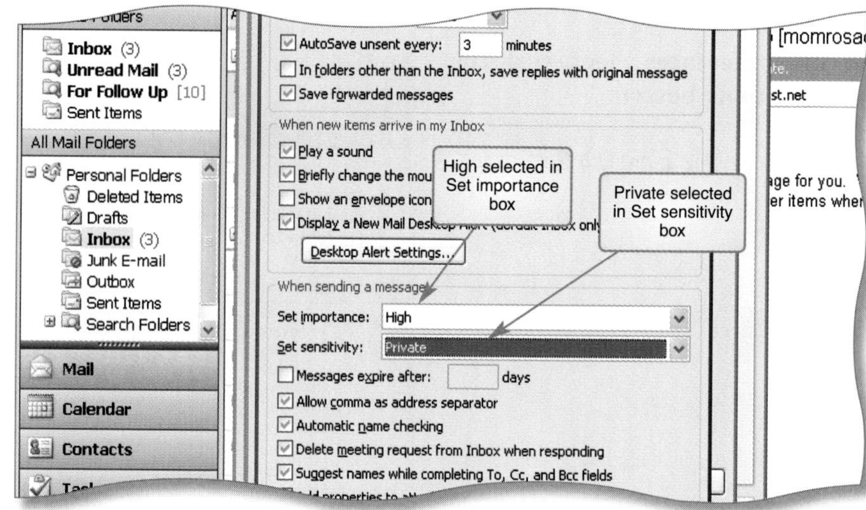

FIGURE 1-55

Other Ways

1. Press ALT+T, press O
2. In Voice Command mode, say "Tools, Options"

The default importance and sensitivity settings have been changed. Any outgoing e-mail now will appear with the high importance icon and the message indicating the message is private in the recipient's Inbox.

Using Search Folders to Display Categories of E-Mail Messages

More About

Security Settings

Clicking the Security Settings button (Figure 1-49 on page OUT 35) opens a dialog box that allows you to apply certain security restrictions on a message. For more information about security settings, visit the Outlook 2003 More About Web page (scsite.com/out2003/more) and click Security Settings.

A new feature in Outlook is the Search Folders folder in the All Mail Folders pane (Figure 1-56). The **Search Folders folder** includes a group of folders that allows you to group and view your messages quickly in one of three ways: (1) For Follow Up, (2) Large Messages, and (3) Unread Mail. **For Follow Up** messages are messages that you have flagged but have not taken action. These messages are sorted further by flag color (red, yellow, green, etc.). **Large Messages** are messages containing large file attachments. These messages are grouped by size: Large (100 to 500 KB), Very Large (500 KB to 1 MB), and Huge (1 to 5 MB). **Unread Mail** comprises messages that have not been opened or have not been marked as read even though you may have read them via the Reading Pane. Figure 1-56 shows messages in the For Follow Up folder.

Contacts

The **Contacts component** of Outlook allows you to store information about individuals and companies. People with whom you communicate for school, business, or personal reasons are your **contacts**. To help organize information about personal contacts, some people keep names, addresses, and telephone numbers in business-card files and address books. With the Outlook Contacts component, you can create and maintain important contact information in a **contact list**, which is stored in the Contacts folder. Your contact list is like an electronic address book that allows you to store names, addresses, e-mail addresses, and more. Once the information has been entered, your contact list can be retrieved, sorted, edited, organized, or printed. Outlook also includes a **Find option** that lets you search for a contact name in your address book while you are using the Calendar, Inbox, or other Outlook components.

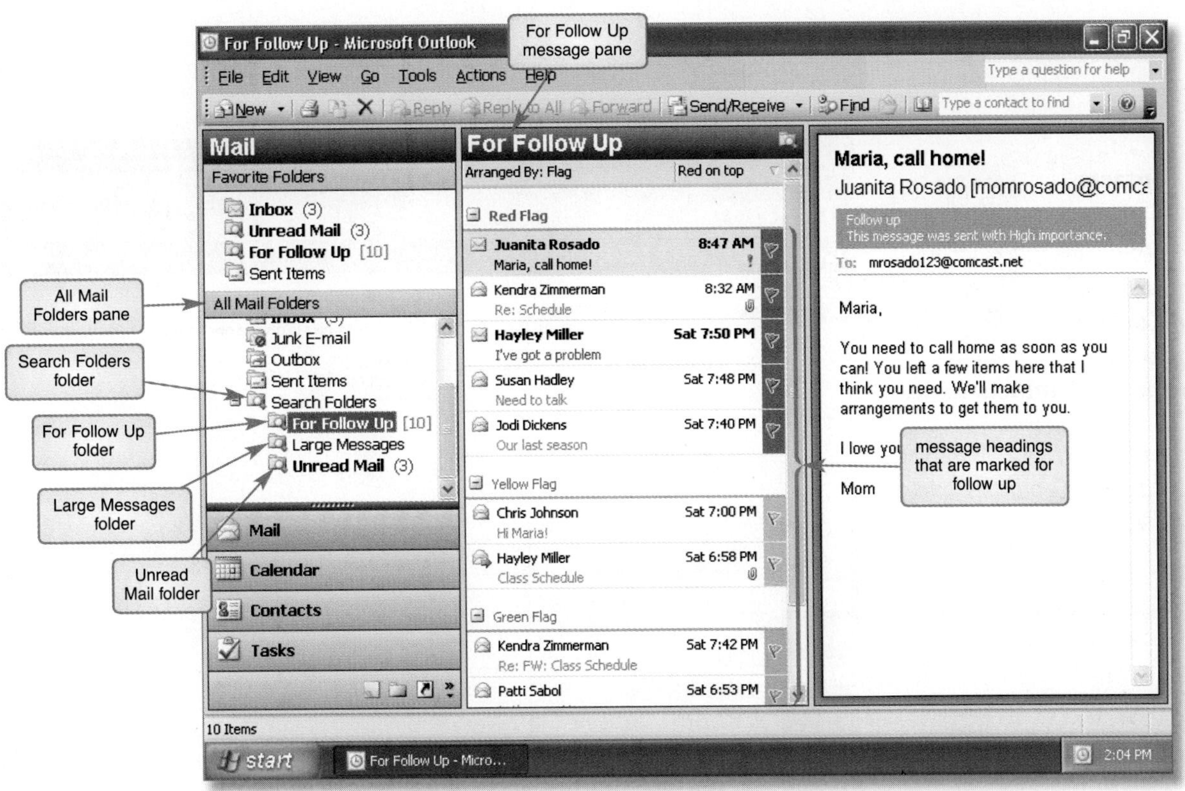

FIGURE 1-56

When the Contacts folder is open, information about each contact appears on an address card in the default **Address Cards view**. Each address card includes fields such as name, address, and various telephone numbers, as well as e-mail and Web page addresses. Choose which fields are displayed on the cards using the View menu.

Previously, an e-mail message was composed, signed, formatted, and sent to Kendra Zimmerman. Kendra's e-mail address was typed into the To text box (see Figure 1-31 on page OUT 25). The following sections show how to (1) create a personal folder; (2) create a contact list; (3) edit contact information; (4) print contact information; (5) send an e-mail to a contact; and (6) delete a contact.

Q: Can I create my own Search Folders to meet my personal specifications?

A: Yes. Besides the three default Search Folders that Outlook provides, you also can create your own personal Search Folders using search criteria that you specify. To create a personal Search Folder, right-click Search Folders in the All Mail Folders pane, click New Search Folder on the shortcut menu, scroll down to the Custom category in the New Search Folder dialog box, and then select Create a custom Search Folder. Click the OK button. From this point on, you select criteria to meet your particular needs.

Creating a Personal Folder

The first step in creating the contact list is to create a personal folder in which the contact list will be stored. When only one person is working on a computer, a contact list can be stored in Outlook's Contacts folder. If you share your computer with a roommate, lab partner, or coworker, you likely will want to store your contact list in a personal folder, which usually is added as a subfolder within the Contacts folder. The steps on the next page create a personal folder for Maria Rosado.

To Create a Personal Folder

1

- **Click the Contacts button in the Navigation Pane.**
- **When Outlook displays the Contacts window, right-click Contacts in the My Contacts pane.**

Outlook displays the Contacts - Microsoft Outlook window and the Contacts shortcut menu (Figure 1-57).

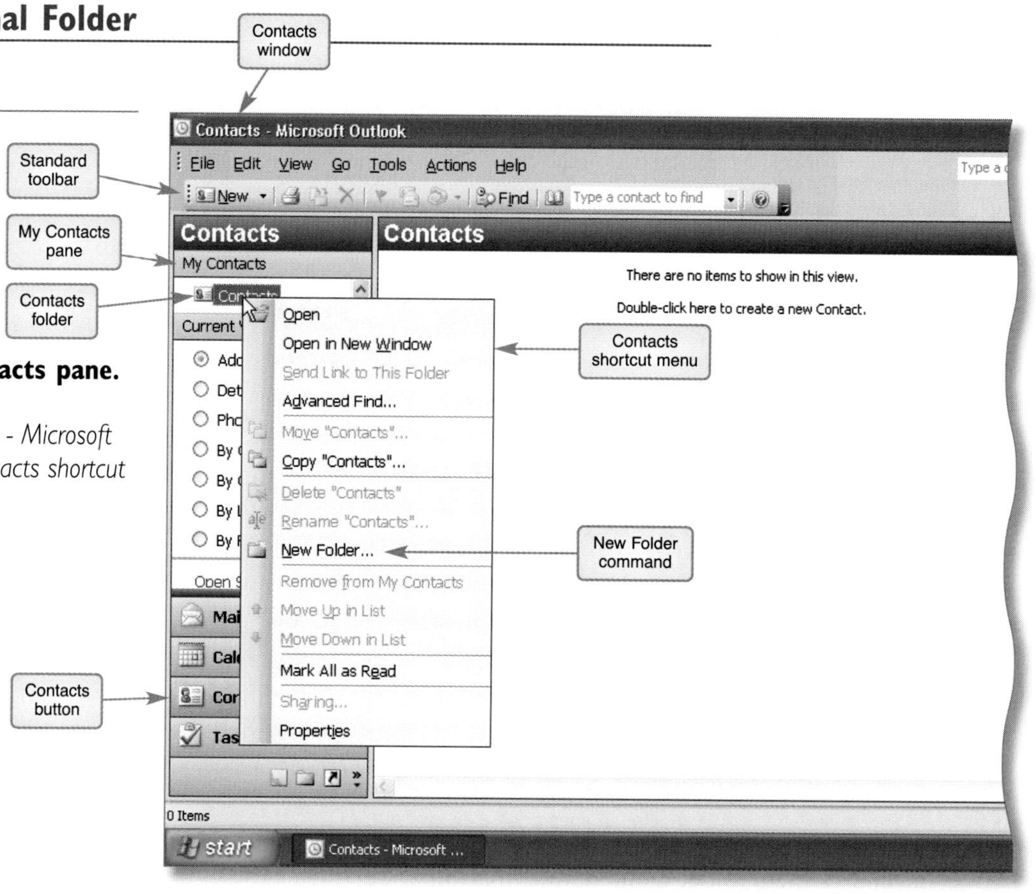

FIGURE 1-57

2

- **Click New Folder on the My Contacts shortcut menu.**
- **When Outlook displays the Create New Folder dialog box, type** `Maria's Contacts` **in the Name text box.**
- **If necessary, select Contact Items in the Folder contains list.**
- **Click Contacts in the Select where to place the folder list.**

The new folder, Maria's Contacts becomes a subfolder of the Contacts folder (Figure 1-58). Maria's Contacts appears in the Name text box.

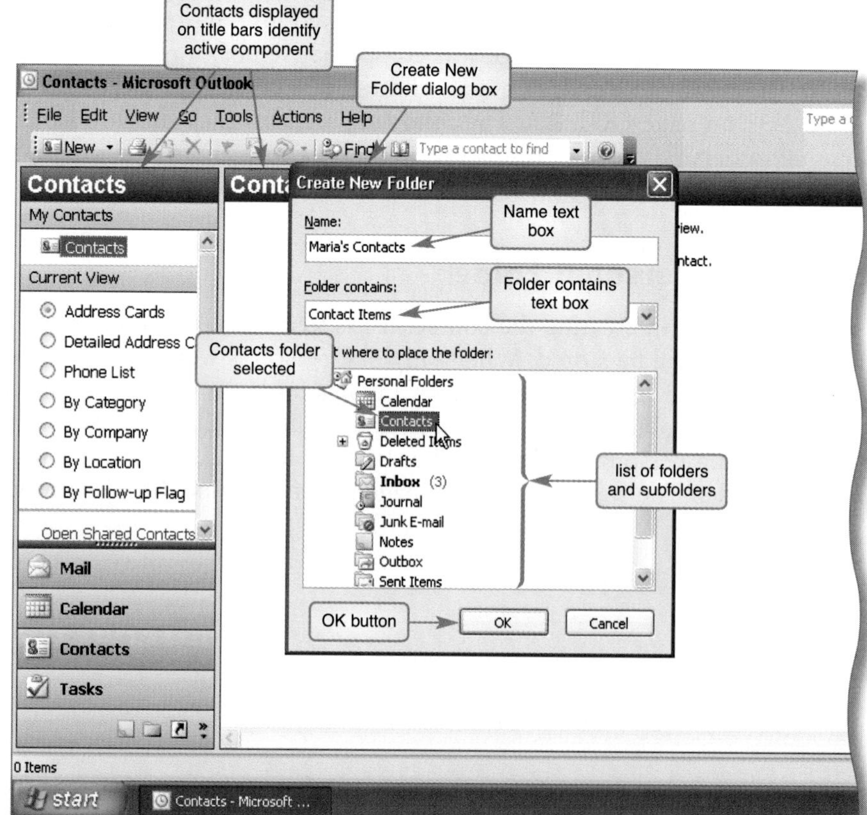

FIGURE 1-58

3

- **Click the OK button.**
- **Click Maria's Contacts in the My Contacts list.**

Outlook displays a list of available folders in the My Contacts pane and displays an empty Contacts pane (Figure 1-59).

New Contact button
Contacts pane titled Maria's Contacts
My Contacts pane
Maria's Contacts folder
double-click Contacts pane to create new contact
Contacts pane blank except for Outlook message

FIGURE 1-59

Other Ways

1. On File menu point to New, click Folder on New submenu
2. On File menu, point to Folder, click New Folder on Folder submenu
3. Press CTRL+SHIFT+E
4. In Voice Command mode, say "File, New Folder"

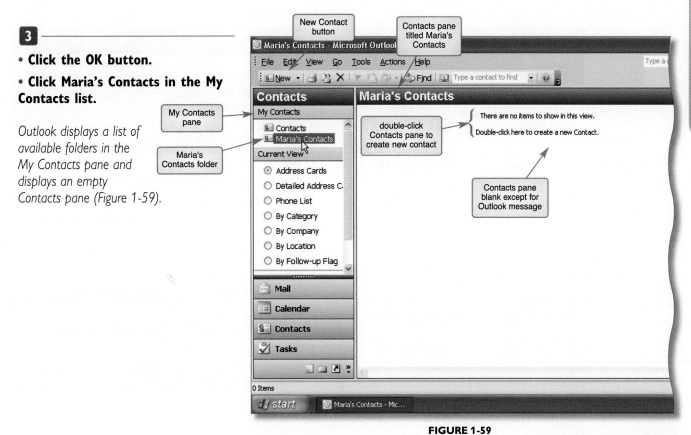

As indicated in the previous steps, it is relatively easy to create folders for your contacts. Most Outlook users have one folder for all their contacts. But you can create a folder for your family, another for friends, another for business associates, and so on. The number of folders you use for your contacts will depend on what works best for you.

Figure 1-60 illustrates the Standard toolbar located below the menu bar in the Contacts window.

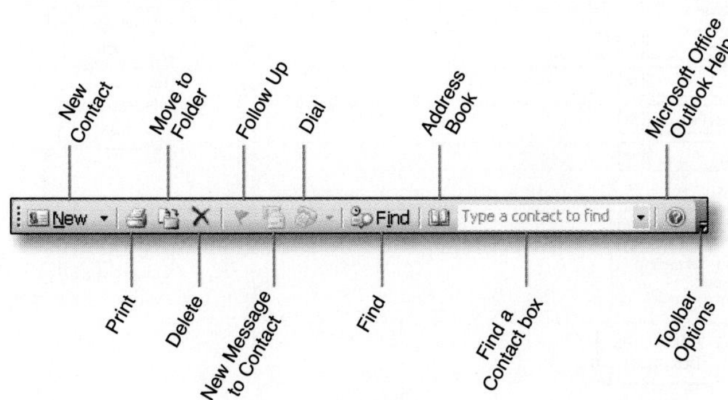

FIGURE 1-60

Creating a Contact List

The steps on the next page describe how to enter the contact information in Table 1-3 on the next page into the contact list.

Table 1-3 Contact Information

NAME	TELEPHONE	ADDRESS	E-MAIL ADDRESS
Kendra Zimmerman	Business: (219) 555-8520 Home: (219) 555-6547	188 Hohman Ave. Hammond, IN 46327	kzimm123@hotmail.com
Marci Laver	(219) 555-0547	1097 Whitcomb St. Merrillville, IN 46410	mlaver123@hotmail.com
Susan Hadley	(219) 555-6387	9873 Porter Ave. Chesterton, IN 46304	shadley101@hotmail.com
Patti Sabol	(219) 555-7964	1631 Columbia Ave. Hammond, IN 46327	psabol123@hotmail.com
Jodi Dickens	(219) 555-3060	845 Meridian St. Valparaiso, IN 46385	jdickens123@hotmail.com
Courtney Craig	(219) 555-7015	3287 Southport Rd. Portage, IN 46368	ccraig101@hotmail.com
Hayley Miller	(708) 555-5204	732 Burnham Ave. Calumet City, IL 60409	hmiller101@hotmail.com
Chris Johnson	(219) 555-8041	1786 61st Ave. Hobart, IN 46342	cjohnson123@hotmail.com

To Create a Contact List

1

- **With the Contacts window active and Maria's Contacts folder selected, click the New button on the Standard toolbar (Figure 1-59 on the previous page).**
- **When Outlook displays the Untitled - Contact window, if necessary, maximize the window.**
- **Type** `Kendra Zimmerman` **in the Full Name text box.**
- **Click the Business text box in the Phone numbers area.**

Notice that Outlook automatically fills in the File as box, last name first (Figure 1-61). The name on the title bar of the Contact window changes to the Kendra Zimmerman - Contact window.

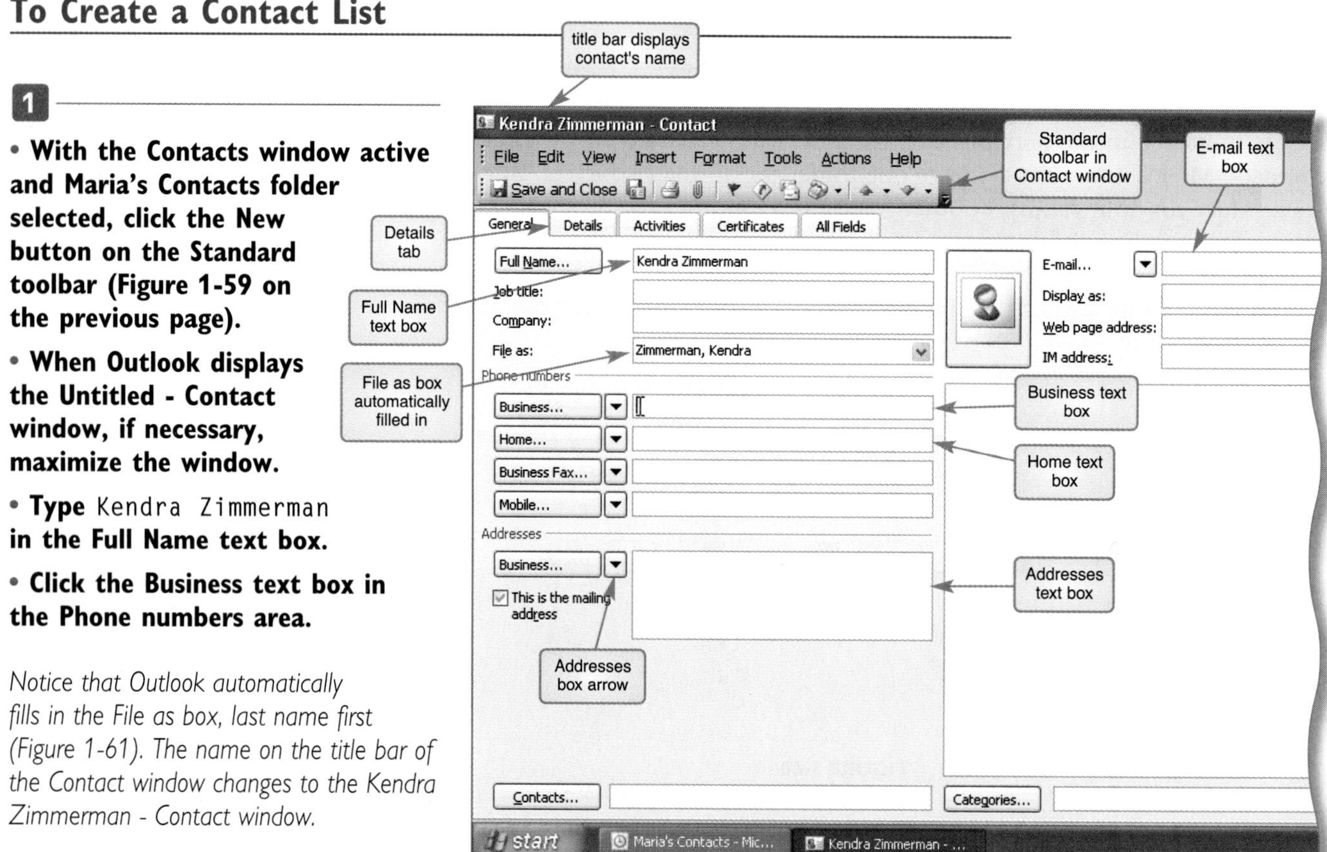

FIGURE 1-61

2

- **Type** 2195558520 **as the business telephone number and then click the Home text box.**
- **Type** 2195556547 **as the Home telephone number.**
- **Click the Addresses box arrow and select Home.**
- **Click the text box in the Addresses area, type** 188 Hohman Ave. **and then press the ENTER key.**
- **Type** Hammond, IN 46327 **to complete the address entry.**
- **Click the E-mail text box.**
- **Type** kzimm123@hotmail.com **as the e-mail address.**

Outlook displays the Kendra Zimmerman - Contact window as shown in Figure 1-62.

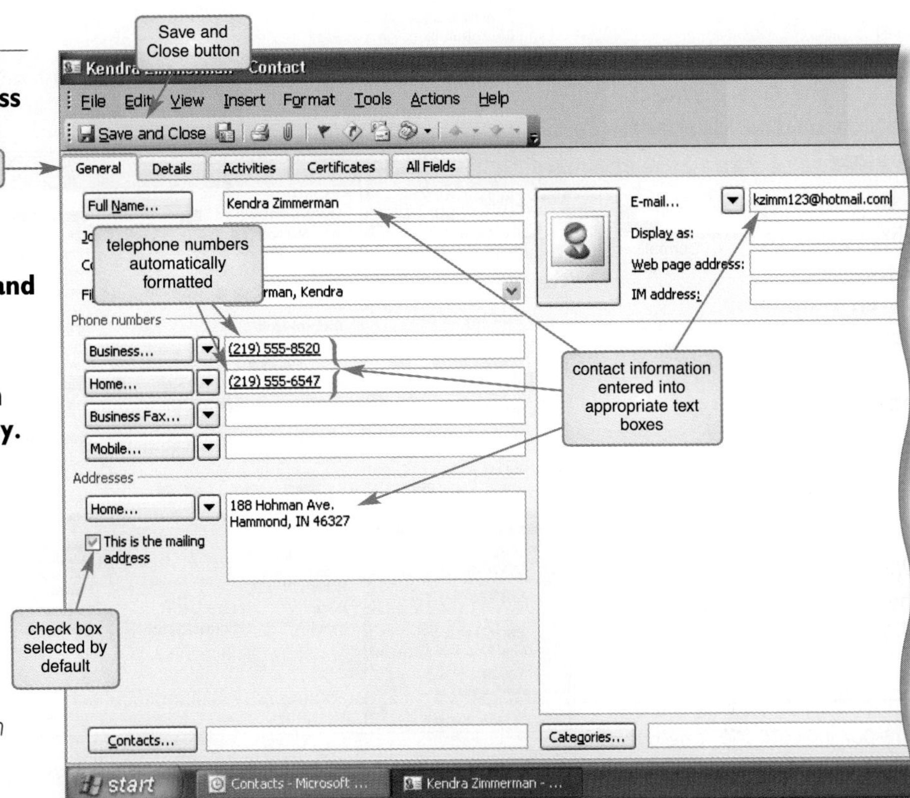

FIGURE 1-62

3

- **Click the Save and Close button on the Standard toolbar.**

Outlook displays the Kendra Zimmerman address card in Address Cards view in the Maria's Contacts pane (Figure 1-63). Address Cards is the current view by default.

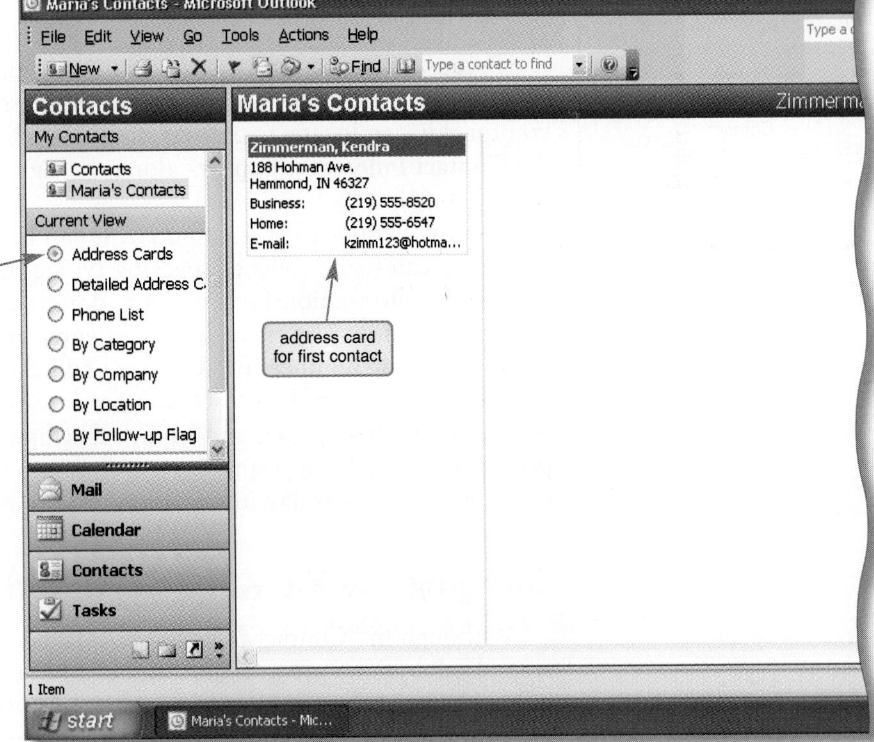

FIGURE 1-63

4

- **Click the New Contact button on the Standard toolbar.**
- **Repeat Steps 2 through 4 to enter the seven remaining contacts in Table 1-3 on page OUT 42.**

Outlook displays the contact list as shown in Figure 1-64. Outlook automatically lists the contacts in alphabetical order. The letters, Cra – Zim, that appear on the right side of the Maria's Contacts pane title bar indicate the range of contacts currently displayed (Craig to Zimmerman).

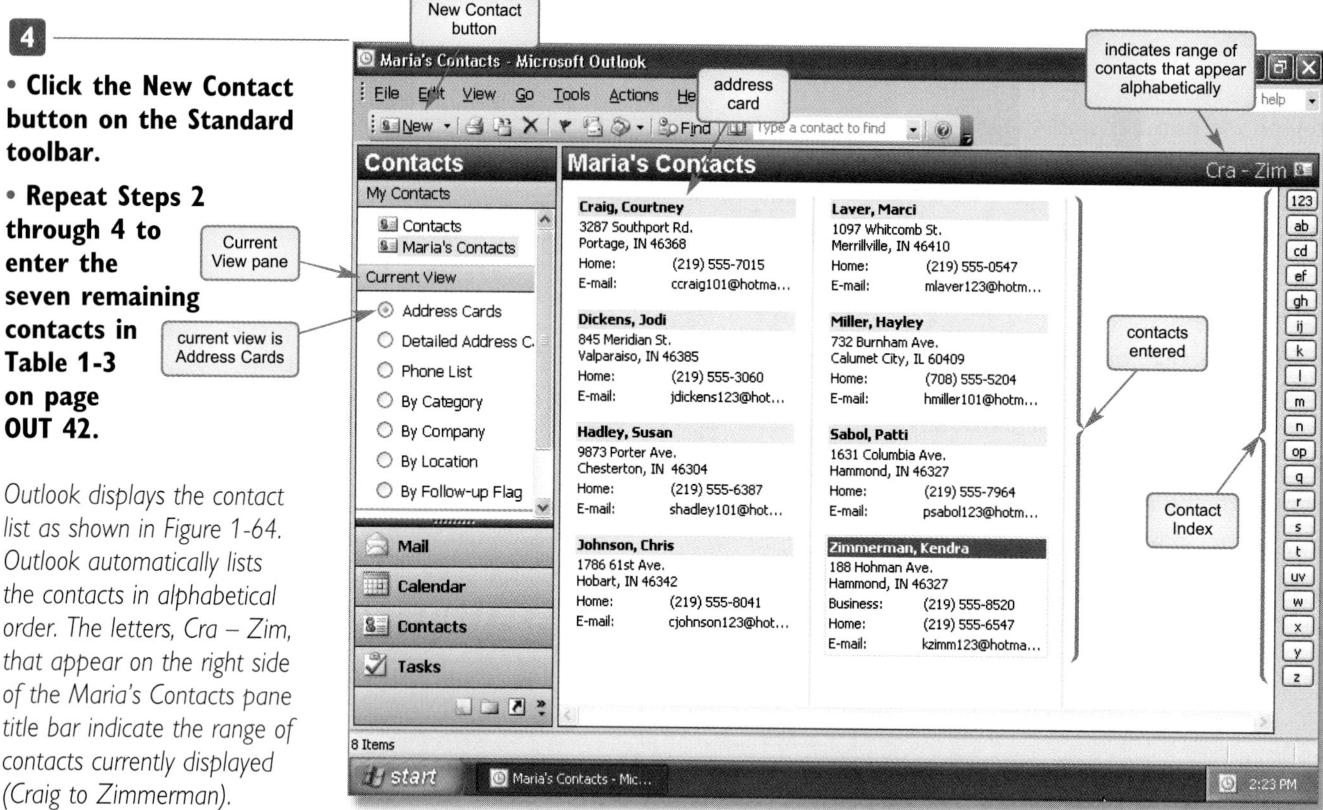

FIGURE 1-64

Other Ways

1. On File menu point to New, click Contact on New submenu
2. On Actions menu click New Contact
3. Press CTRL+SHIFT+C
4. In Voice Command mode, say "File, New, Contact"

Because this contact list consists of only eight names, Outlook displays all of the contact names. The default view is Address Cards. With longer lists, however, you quickly can locate a specific contact by clicking a letters or numbers button on the **Contact Index** that appears along the right side of the Contacts window (Figure 1-64).

After the contact list is complete, it can be viewed, edited, or updated at any time. You can make some changes by typing inside the card itself. To display and edit all the information for a contact, double-click the address card to display the Contacts window. Use this window to enter information about a contact, such as home telephone numbers or Web page addresses. Up to 19 different telephone numbers can be stored for each contact categorized by location and type (business, home, fax, mobile, pager, and so on). Clicking the Details tab (Figure 1-62 on the previous page) allows you to enter a contact's department, manager's name, nickname, and even birthday information.

Changing the View and Sorting the Contacts List

Although the Contacts folder is displayed in Address Cards view by default, several other views are available and can be selected in the Navigation Pane. The following steps show how to change the view from Address Cards to Phone List, sort the contact list in descending sequence, and then change back to Address Cards view.

To Change the View and Sort the Contact List

1

- **With the Maria's Contacts - Microsoft Outlook window active, click Phone List in the Current View pane of the Navigation Pane.**
- **With the Phone List in ascending sequence by the File As field, click the File As column heading in the Contacts pane.**

Outlook changes the contact list view from Address Cards to Phone List and displays the contact list in descending sequence by last name (Figure 1-65). Notice the direction of the small arrow in the File As column heading.

2

- **After reviewing the contact list in Phone List view, click Address Cards in the Current View pane in the Navigation Pane.**

Outlook displays the contact list in ascending sequence in Address Cards view (Figure 1-64).

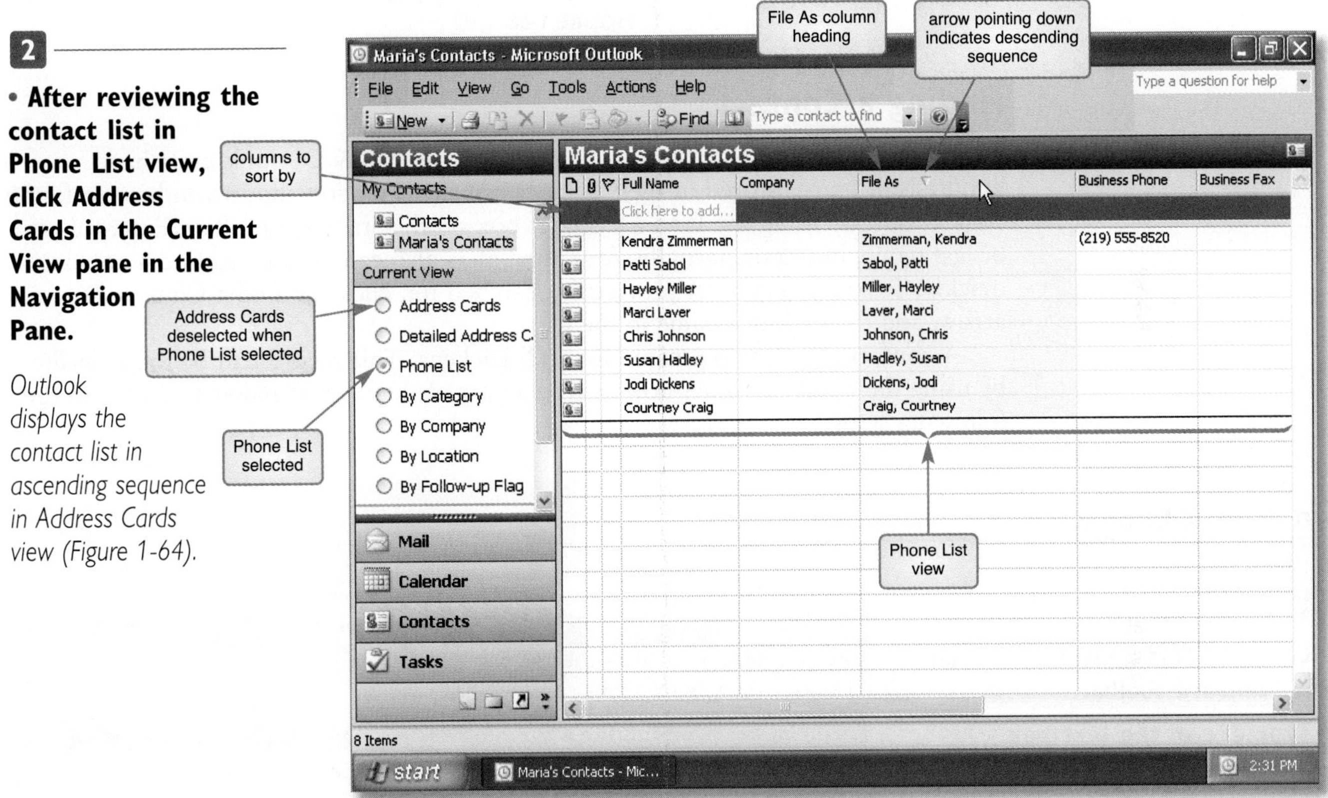

FIGURE 1-65

To see how easy it is to change views of the contact list, click one of the view options in the Current View pane in the Navigation Pane. You also can sort by any one of the column headings in the Contacts pane (Icon, Attachment, Flag Status, Full Name, Company, File As, Business Phone, etc.) just by clicking the column heading (see Figure 1-65). Click a column heading once and Outlook sorts the contacts list into descending sequence. Click the same column heading again and Outlook sorts the contact list into ascending sequence. The arrow in the middle of the column heading indicates whether the contact list is in ascending sequence or descending sequence. When you switch from one view to another, the sequence of the contact list reverts back to what it was the last time the view was used.

You can sort the views of the contact list, e-mail messages, and other Outlook information in many different ways. If you right-click a column heading in any Outlook component and point to the Arrange By command on the shortcut menu (Figure 1-66 on the next page) you can see the Arrange By commands.

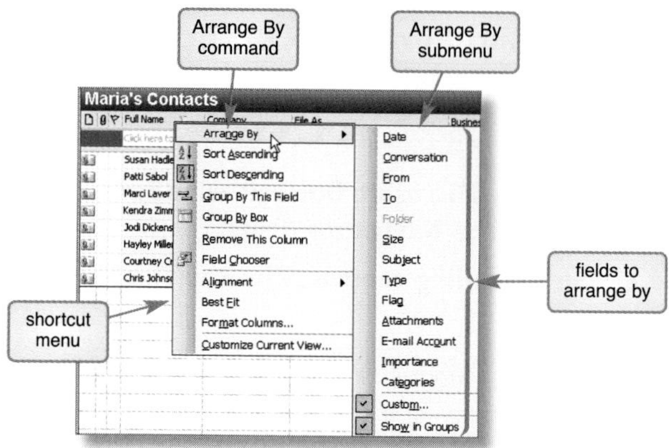

FIGURE 1-66

Finding a Contact

The contact list created in this project is small. Many Outlook users have hundreds of names stored in their contact lists. This section shows you how to find a contact quickly using the Find a Contact box on the Standard toolbar. Enter a first or last name, in full or partially. An e-mail alias also can be used to find a contact quickly. To locate a contact previously searched for, click the find a Contact box arrow, and then select a name in the list.

A contact record was created for Jodi Dickens. This record can be found easily by using the Find a Contact box to type a part of the contact name as shown in the following steps.

To Find a Contact

1

- **Click the Find a Contact box on the Standard toolbar.**
- **Type** `dic` **in the text box.**

The letters appear in the Find a Contact box (Figure 1-67). The letters, dic, are used to find the contact beginning with those letters.

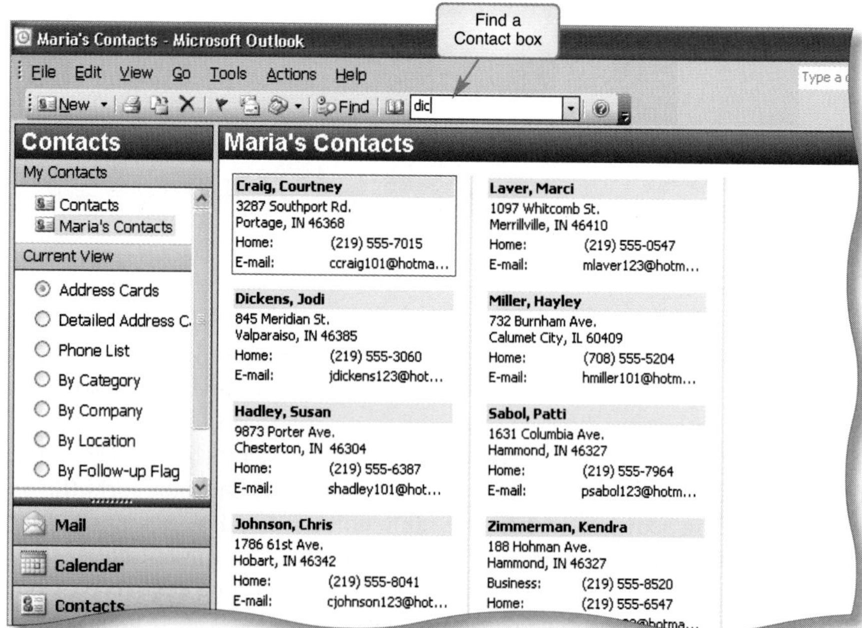

FIGURE 1-67

2

• **Press the ENTER key.**

Outlook opens the Contact window (Figure 1-68). Currently, only one contact exists with the letters dic in its name.

3

• **Click the Close button on the right side of the title bar in the Contact window.**

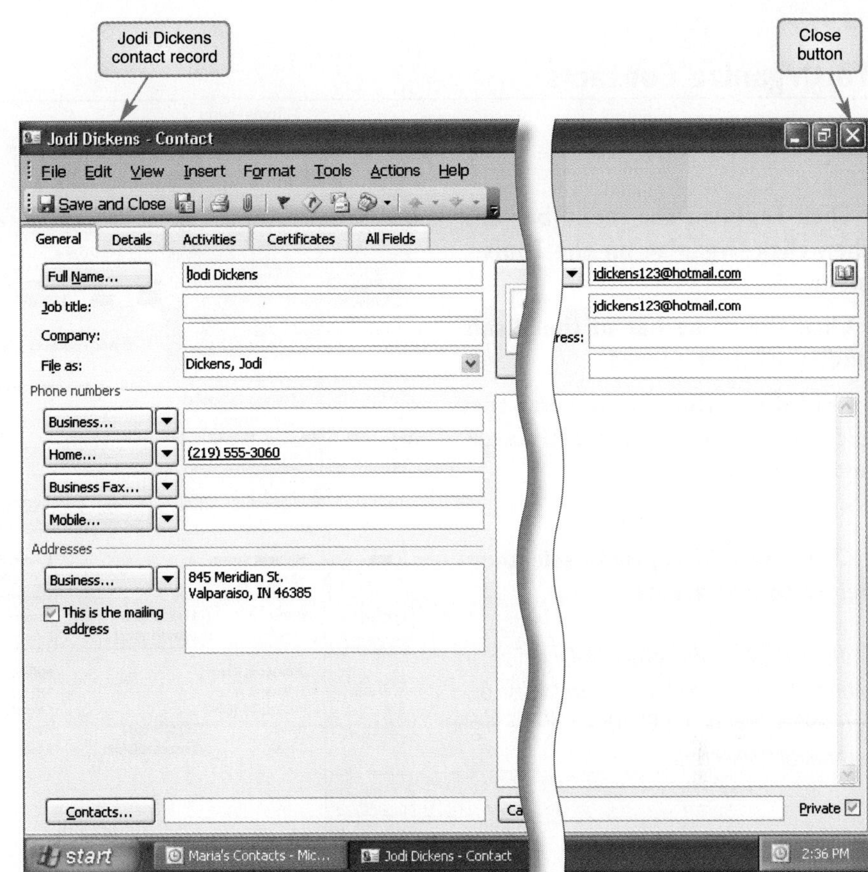

FIGURE 1-68

If more than one contact with the starting letters, dic, exists, Outlook displays a Choose Contact dialog box with the list of all contacts beginning with the string, dic. You then can select the appropriate contact from the Choose Contact dialog box.

Other Ways

1. On Tools menu point to Find, click Find on Find submenu
2. Click Find button on Standard toolbar
3. Press CTRL+SHIFT+F
4. In Voice Command mode, say "Tools, Find"

Organizing Contacts

To help manage your contacts further, the contact list can be categorized and sorted in several ways. For example, you can group contacts into categories such as Key Customer, Business, Hot Contact, or even Ideas, Competition, and Strategies. In addition, you may want to create your own categories to group contacts by company, department, a particular project, a specific class, and so on. You also can sort by any part of the address; for example, you can sort by postal code for bulk mailings.

For the contact list created in this project, it is appropriate to organize the contacts in a personal category. You can do this by selecting the contacts and then adding them to the personal category of the contact list. The steps on the next page illustrate this procedure.

More About

Contacts

You can organize contacts from one or more Contacts folders in a personal distribution list. Outlook also detects duplicates and provides the option to merge the new information with the existing contact entry. You also can filter your contact list and then use the filtered list to begin a mail merge from Outlook.

To Organize Contacts

1

- **Click Tools on the menu bar and then click Organize on the Tools menu.**
- **Click the name bar of the Susan Hadley contact record.**
- **Hold down the CTRL key and then click the name bar of Marci Laver and Patti Sabol.**
- **Release the CTRL key.**
- **Click the Add contacts selected below to box arrow.**

Outlook displays the Ways to Organize Maria's Contacts dialog box and a list of categories (Figure 1-69). Three of the eight records are selected.

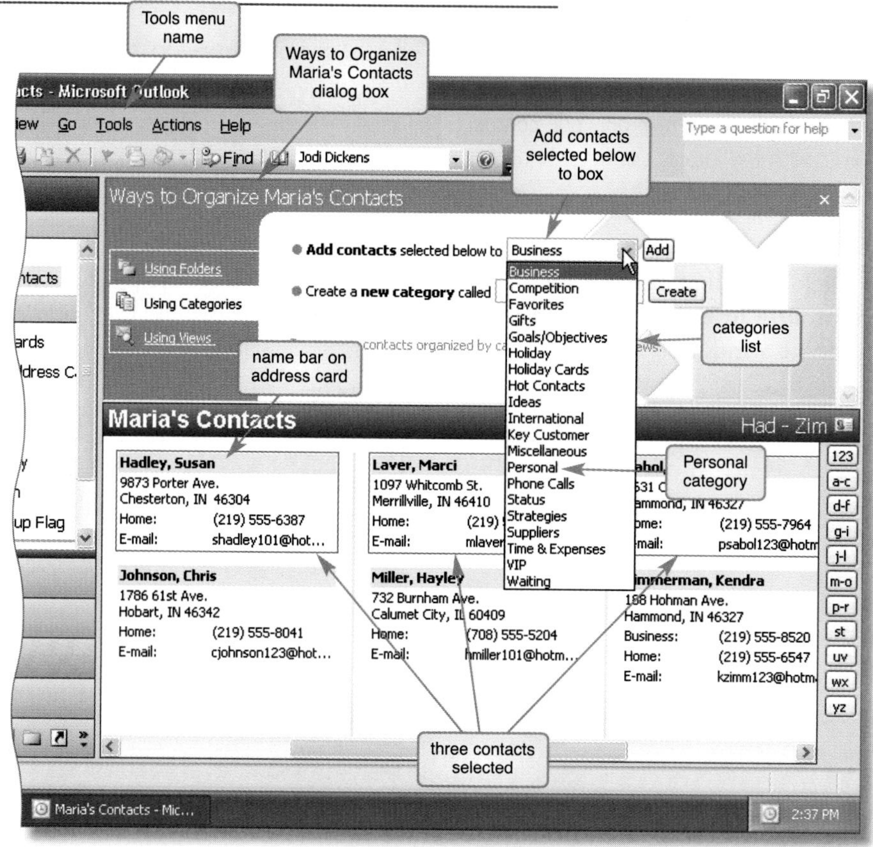

FIGURE 1-69

2

- **Click Personal in the list.**
- **Click the Add button.**

Outlook adds the selected records to the Personal category and the word Done! appears next to the Add button (Figure 1-70).

3

- **Click the Close button on the Ways to Organize Maria's Contacts dialog box.**

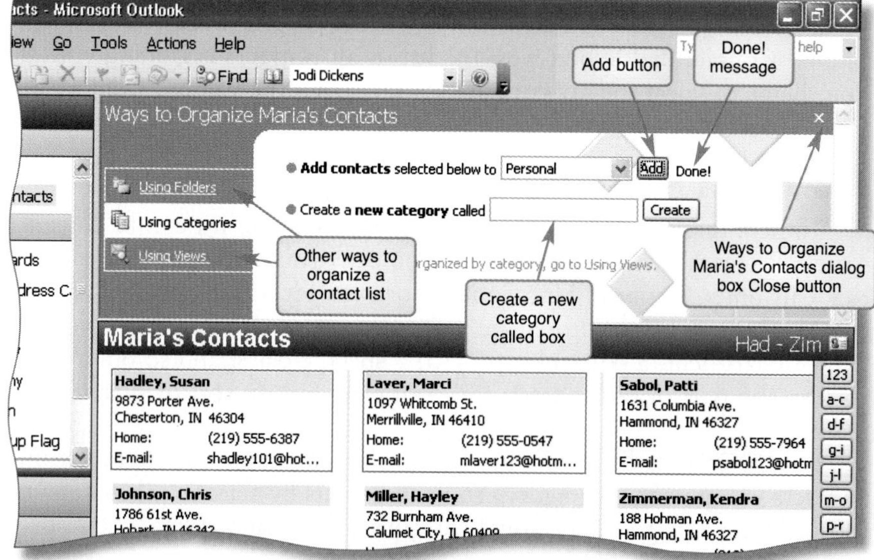

FIGURE 1-70

Other Ways

1. Press ALT+T, press Z
2. In Voice Command mode, say "Tools, Organize"

The three contacts are organized into a category called Personal. Organizing contacts in different categories helps make searching for groups of names easier.

Displaying the Contacts in a Category

By assigning the three contacts to a personal category, you can instruct Outlook to display only those contacts that belong to the category shown in the following steps.

To Display the Contacts in a Category

1

- **With the Contacts window active, click the Find button on the Standard toolbar.**
- **When Outlook displays the Find toolbar above the Contacts pane, type** `Personal` **in the Look for box.**
- **If necessary, click Maria's Contacts in the My Contacts pane so it appears in the Search In box.**
- **Click the Find Now button on the Find toolbar.**

Outlook displays the three contacts that belong in the Personal category (Figure 1-71).

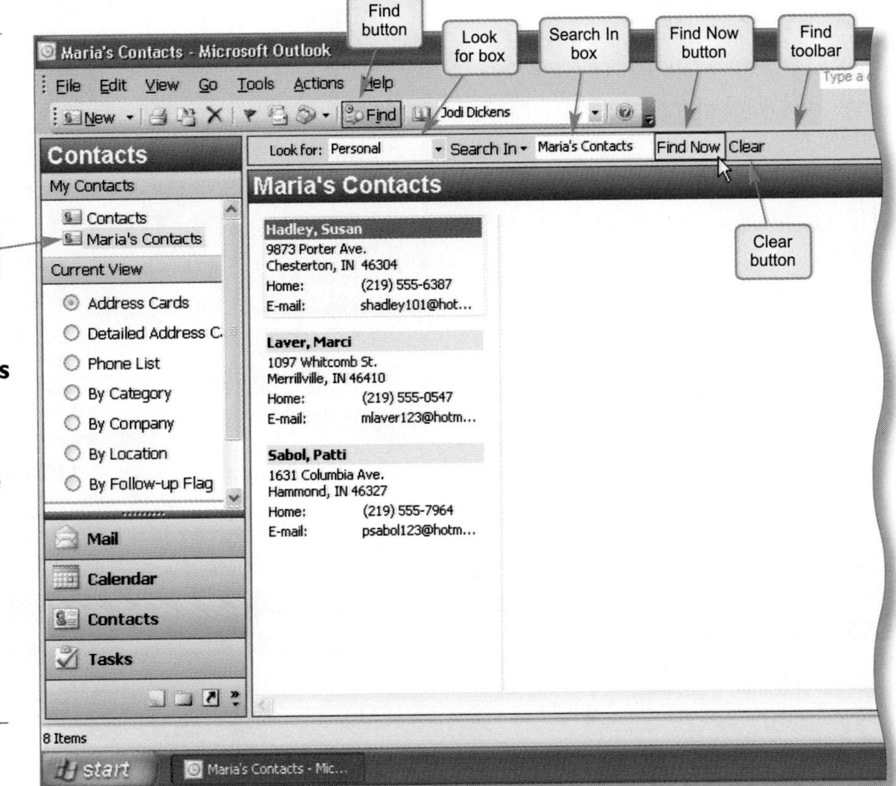

FIGURE 1-71

2

- **After viewing the contacts in the Personal category, click the Find button on the Standard toolbar.**

Outlook displays all the contacts in the Maria's Contacts folder.

Other Ways

1. On Tools menu point to Find, click Find on Find submenu
2. Press CTRL+E
3. For advanced search, press CTRL+SHIFT+F
4. In Voice Command mode, say "Tools, Find, Find"

You can use the Find button on the Standard toolbar to find contacts when the Contacts component is active, messages when the Mail component is active, appointments when the Calendar component is active, and tasks when the Tasks component is active.

Previewing and Printing the Contact List

Printing the contact list is an easy way to obtain a listing of people you frequently contact. Previewing the contact list before you print it helps ensure the printed list can be used for business mailings, invitations to social gatherings, or even a telephone or Christmas card list. The step on the next page describes how to preview and print the contact list.

To Preview and Print the Contact List

1

- **With the Contacts window active, click the Print button on the Standard toolbar.**

Outlook displays the Print dialog box (Figure 1-72). In the Print dialog box you can select a format for the printout, print range, and number of copies. You can also change the orientation from portrait to landscape through the use of the Page Setup button.

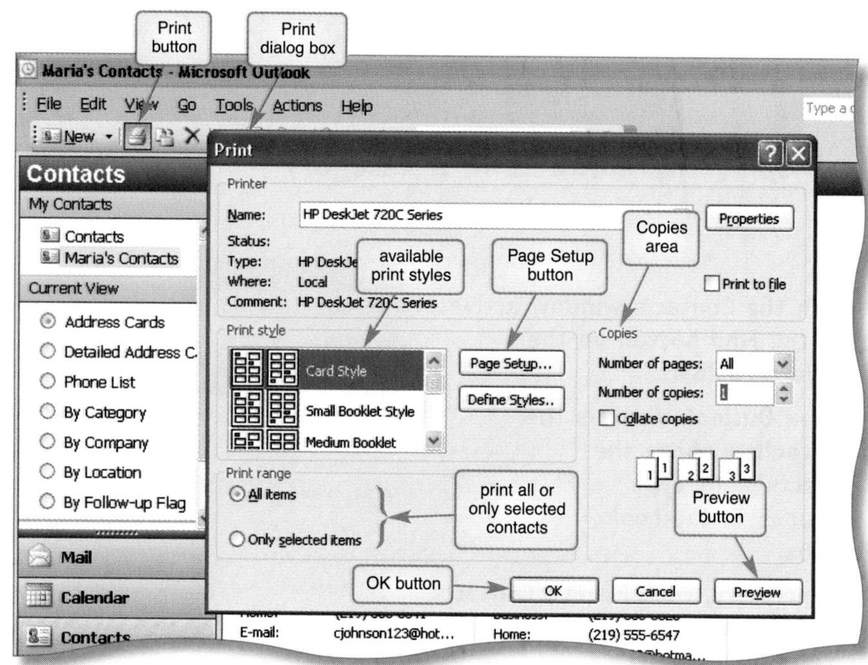

FIGURE 1-72

2

- **Click the Preview button.**

Outlook displays a preview of the printout (Figure 1-73).

3

- **After viewing the preview of the printed contacts list, click the Close button.**
- **If the preview is acceptable, ready the printer.**
- **Click the Print button on the Standard toolbar.**
- **When Outlook displays the Print dialog box, click the OK button.**

Outlook prints the contact list. The printout should resemble the preview in Figure 1-73.

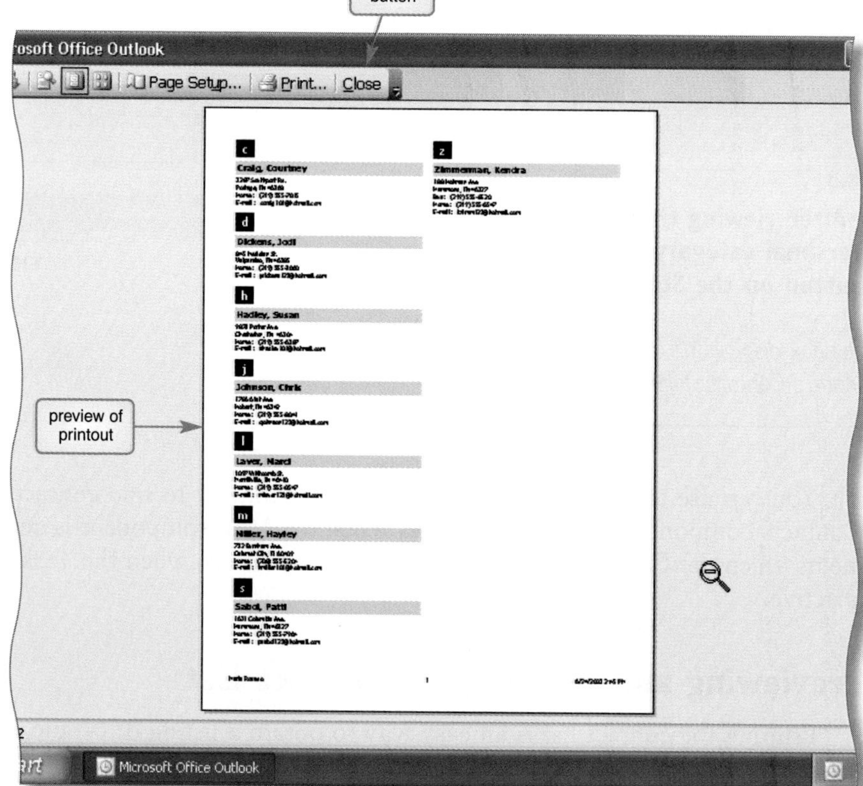

FIGURE 1-73

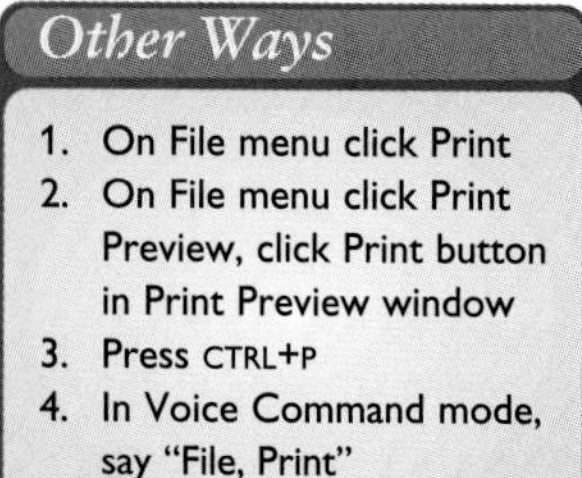

Other Ways

1. On File menu click Print
2. On File menu click Print Preview, click Print button in Print Preview window
3. Press CTRL+P
4. In Voice Command mode, say "File, Print"

If you display a category of contacts and then click the Print button, Outlook will print only the contacts in that category. A printout can be customized by changing the Print style in the Print dialog box. These styles let you choose from a variety of formats along with choices for paper orientation and size.

More About

Contacts

Outlook allows you to add contact information in any of the Contacts current views except Address Cards view. Simply click in the first row below the column headings and then enter the appropriate information.

Using the Contact List to Address an E-Mail Message

When you address an e-mail message, you must know the e-mail address of the recipient of the message. Previously, when an e-mail message was addressed, the e-mail address was typed in the To text box in the Message window (see Figure 1-31 on page OUT 25). In addition to entering the e-mail address by typing the e-mail address, an e-mail address can be entered using the contact list. The following steps show how to use the contact list to address an e-mail message to Patti Sabol.

To Use the Contact List to Address an E-Mail Message

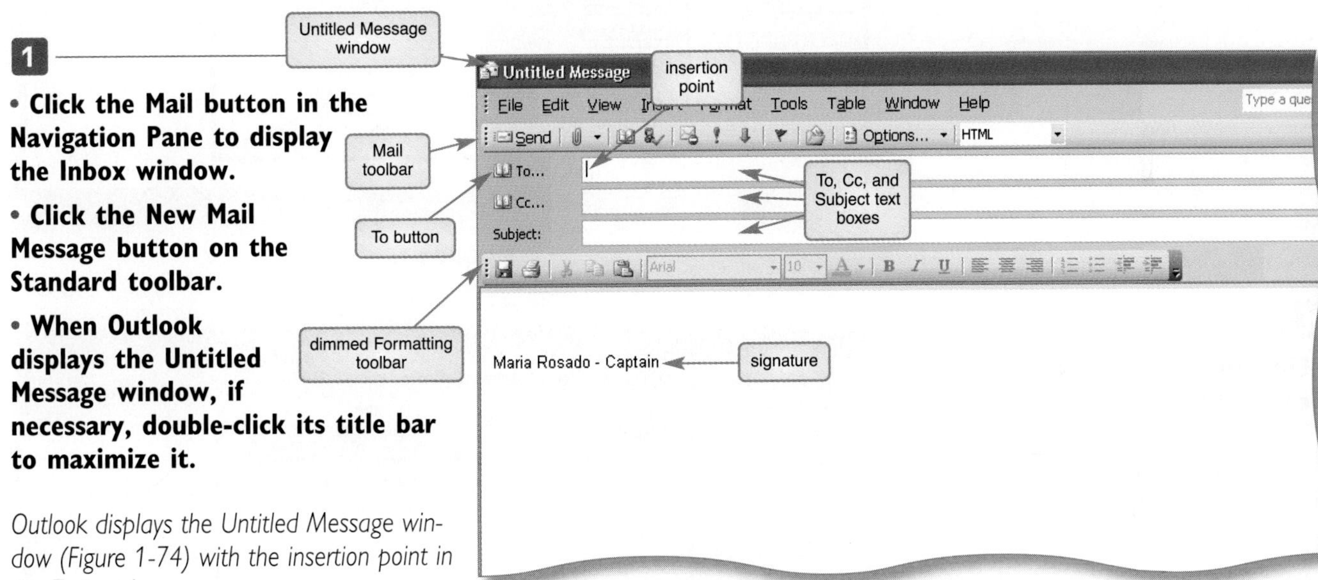

1

- **Click the Mail button in the Navigation Pane to display the Inbox window.**
- **Click the New Mail Message button on the Standard toolbar.**
- **When Outlook displays the Untitled Message window, if necessary, double-click its title bar to maximize it.**

Outlook displays the Untitled Message window (Figure 1-74) with the insertion point in the To text box.

FIGURE 1-74

2

- **Click the To button on the left side of the Message window.**
- **When Outlook displays the Select Names dialog box, click the Show Names from the box arrow.**

Outlook displays the Select Names dialog box (Figure 1-75). The Show Names from the list displays the available contact lists from which to choose.

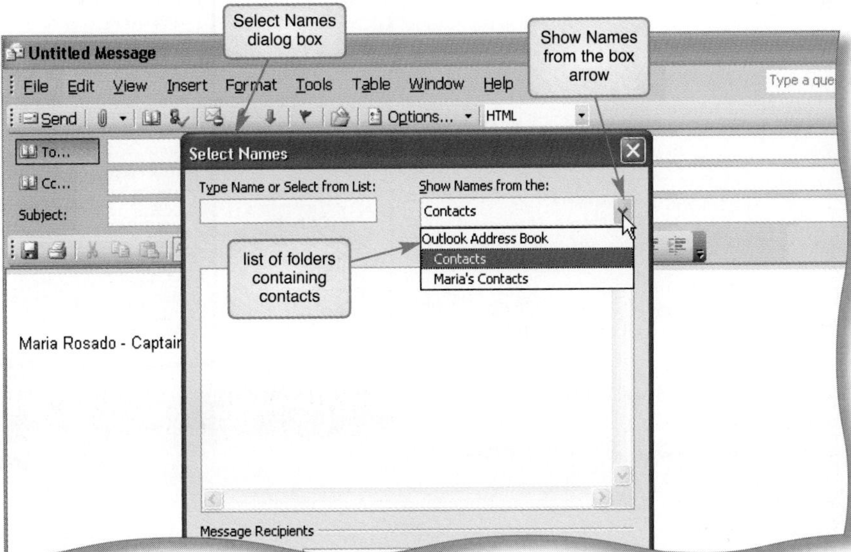

FIGURE 1-75

3

• **Click Maria's Contacts in the list.**

• **Click the Patti Sabol entry in the E-mail Address list box.**

The Patti Sabol entry in the E-mail Address list box is selected (Figure 1-76).

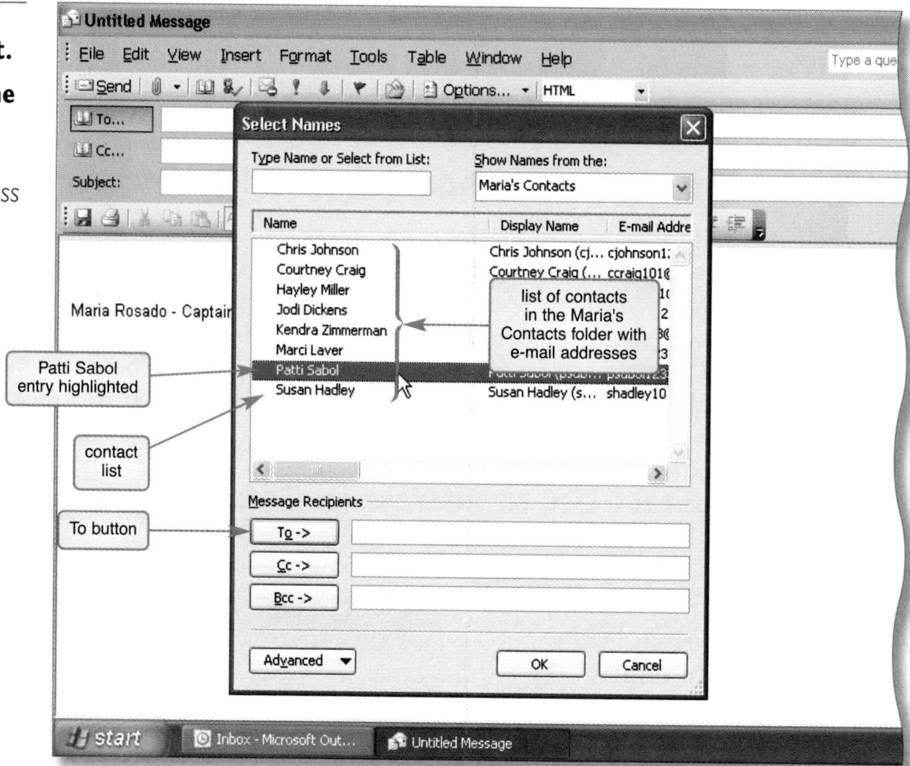

FIGURE 1-76

4

• **Click the To button in the Message Recipients area.**

Outlook displays the Patti Sabol entry in the To text box (Figure 1-77).

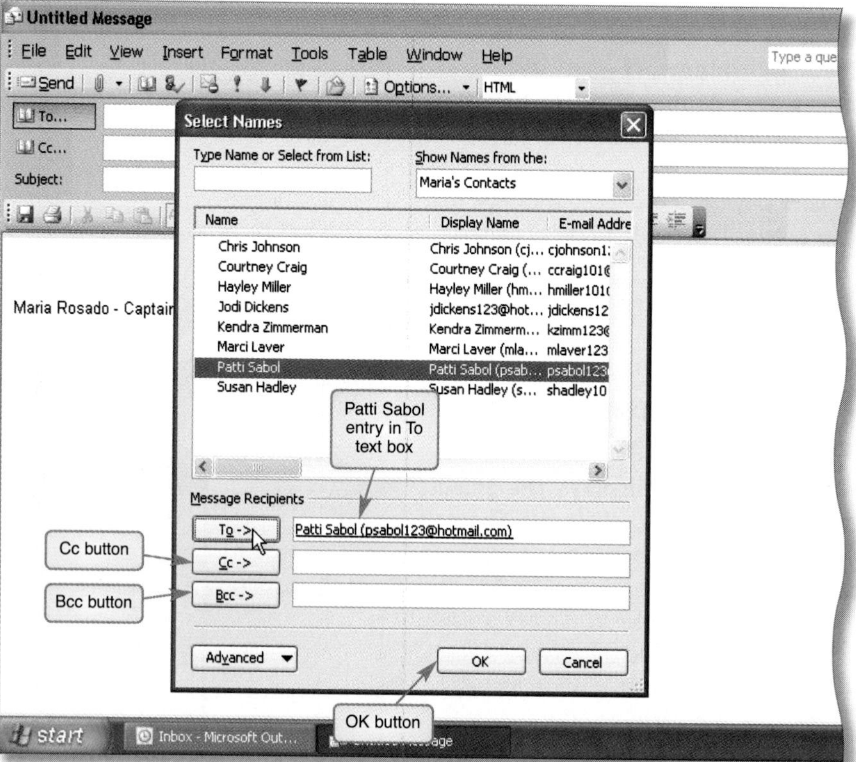

FIGURE 1-77

5

- **Click the OK button.**
- **Click the Subject text box and then type** `Fund-raiser T-Shirts` **as the entry.**
- **Press the TAB key.**

Outlook closes the Select Names dialog box, and displays the Patti Sabol entry in the To text box in the Message window (Figure 1-78).

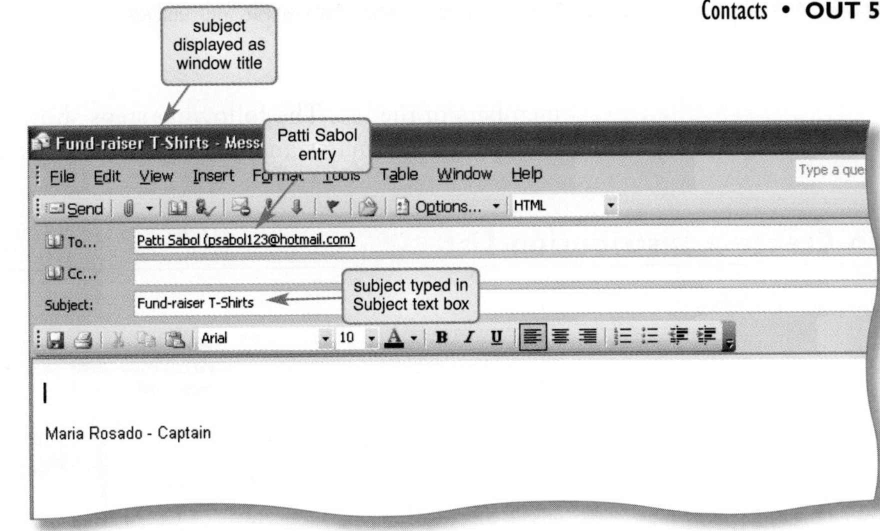

FIGURE 1-78

6

- **Type** `Patti, I need help!` **and then press the ENTER key twice.**
- **Type** `The T-shirts for the team fund-raiser will be ready at 2:00 p.m. on Friday. I will be in class at that time, so I will need you to pick them up.`

Outlook displays the e-mail message in the message body (Figure 1-79).

7

- **Click the Send button.**

Outlook closes the Message window, displays the Inbox window, stores the e-mail message in the Outbox folder temporarily while it sends the message, and then moves the message to the Sent Items folder.

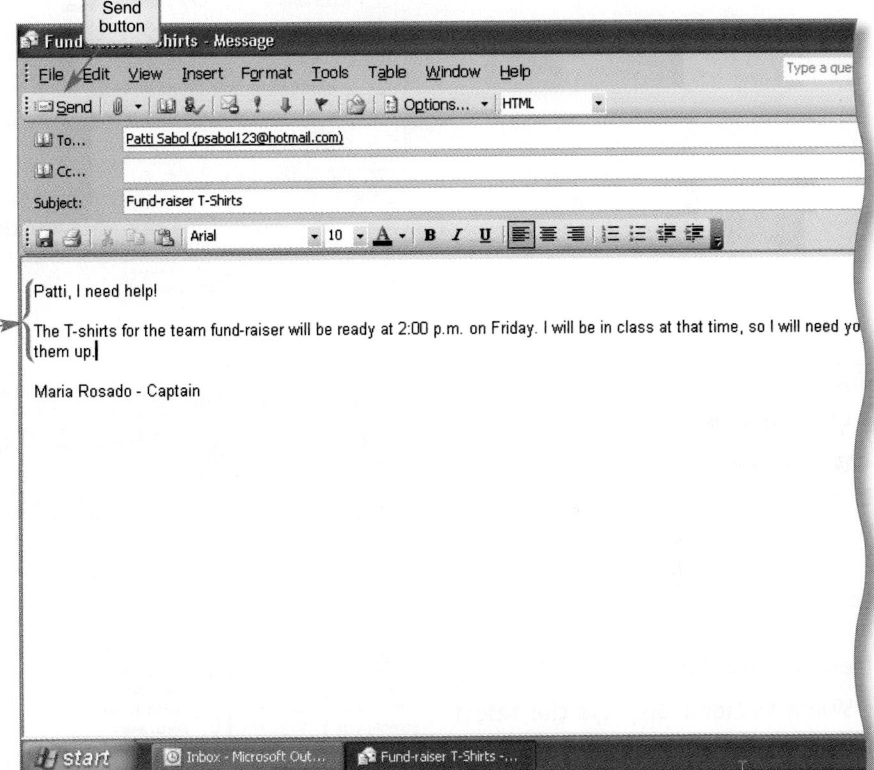

FIGURE 1-79

Other Ways

1. Click Address Book button on Mail toolbar

You can add as many names as you want to the To text box in Figure 1-77. You also can add names to the Cc text box. If you do not want those listed in the To text box or Cc text box to know you sent a copy to someone else, send a **blind copy** by adding the name to the Bcc text box.

Creating and Modifying a Distribution List

If you find yourself sending e-mail messages to the same group of people over and over, then you should consider creating a distribution list. A **distribution list** is similar to a category of contacts in that when you select the name of the distribution list as the recipient of an e-mail message, Outlook will send the message to all the members of the list. The following steps show how to create a distribution list titled Computer Classmates and add three members from the Maria's Contacts list.

To Create a Distribution List

1

- **With the Inbox window active, click the New Mail Message button arrow on the Standard toolbar.**

Outlook displays the New Mail Message menu (Figure 1-80).

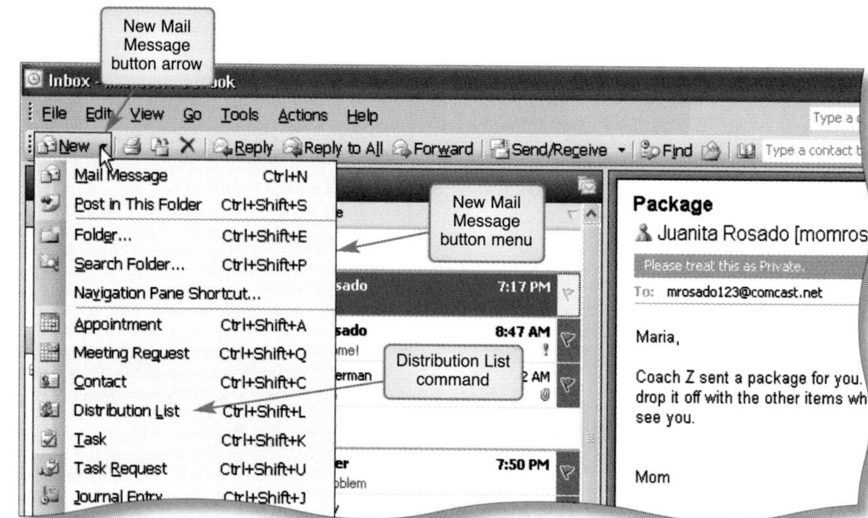

FIGURE 1-80

2

- **Click Distribution List.**
- **When Outlook displays the Untitled - Distribution List window, type** `Computer Classmates` **in the Name text box, and then click the Select Members button.**
- **When Outlook displays the Select Members dialog box, click the Show Names from the box arrow and click Maria's Contacts.**
- **Select Chris Johnson and then click the Members button.**
- **Add Hayley Miller and Susan Hadley in the same manner to the Members list in the Add to distribution list area.**

Outlook displays the three members to add to the Computer Classmates Members list (Figure 1-81). The Members list is displayed in the Add to distribution list area at the bottom of the Select Members dialog box.

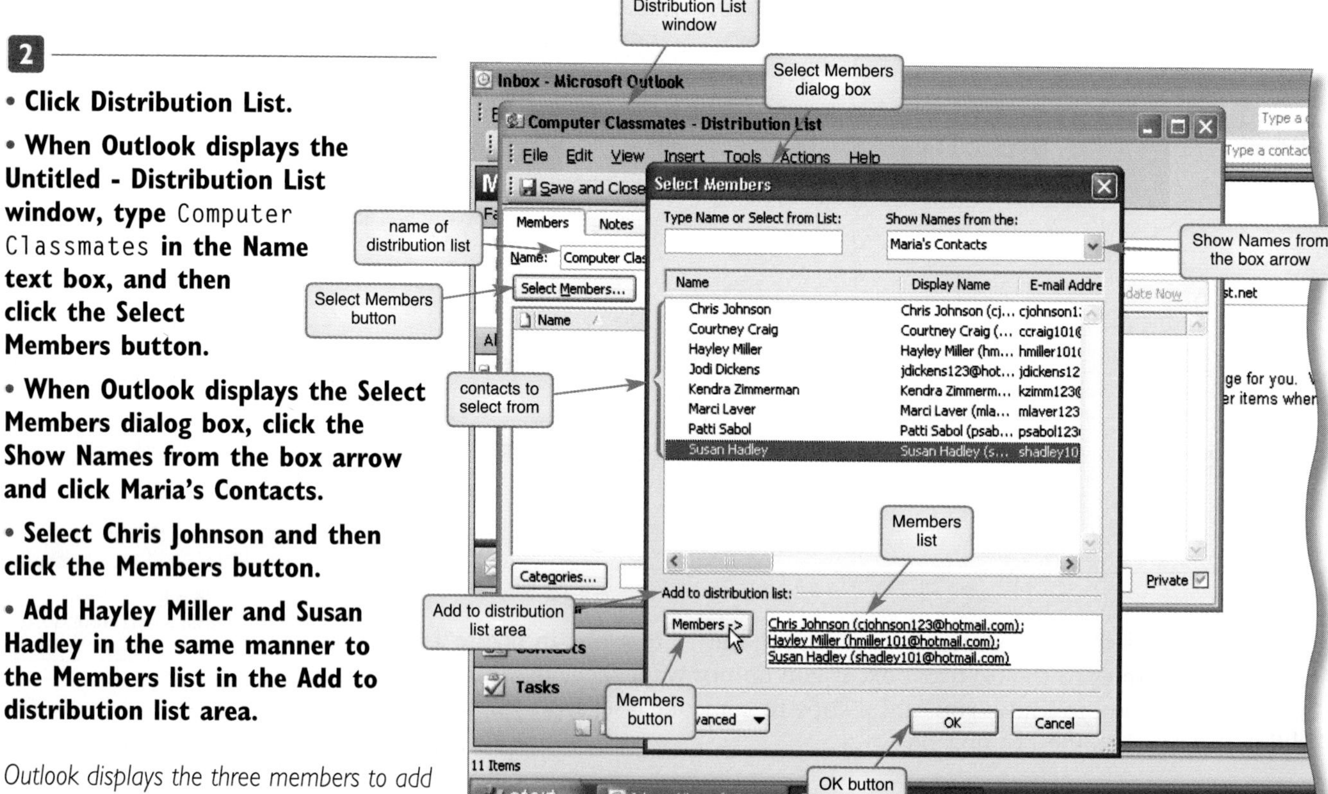

FIGURE 1-81

3

• **Click the OK button.**

Outlook displays the members of the Computer Classmates distribution list in the Untitled - Distribution List window (Figure 1-82).

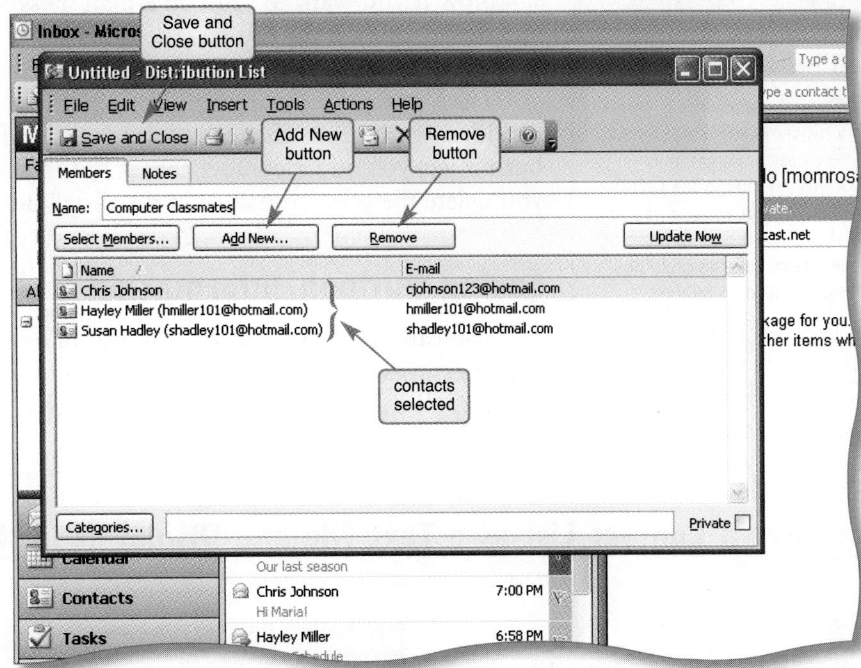

FIGURE 1-82

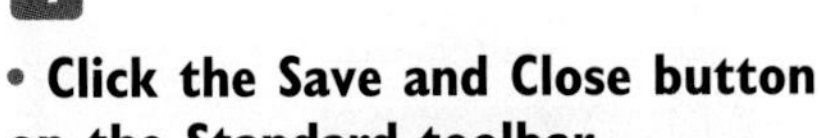

4

• **Click the Save and Close button on the Standard toolbar.**

Outlook closes the Untitled - Distribution List window, adds the new distribution list to the contact list, and activates the Inbox window.

5

• **Click the Address Book button on the Standard toolbar.**

Outlook displays the Address Book window, which includes the Computer Classmates distribution list (Figure 1-83).

6

• **Click the Close button on the right side of the title bar in the Address Book window.**

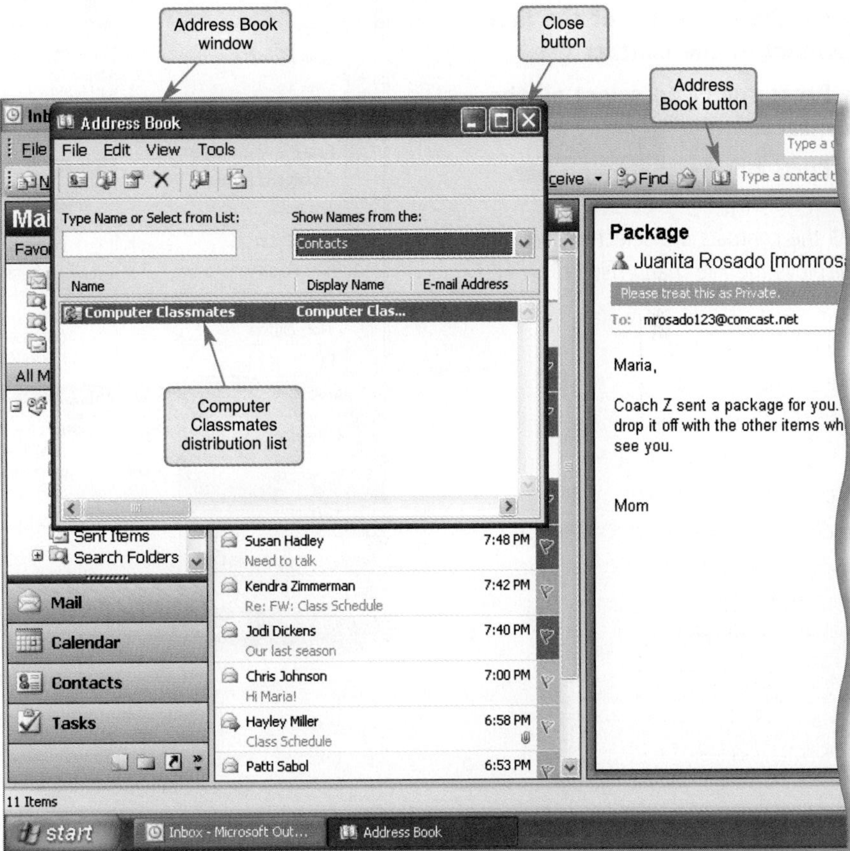

FIGURE 1-83

More About

The Internet

Outlook automatically creates a hyperlink when you type a Web page address or an e-mail address in the text box of a Contact window. If you are connected to an Internet browser, you can click the hyperlink to go to the destination quickly or send an e-mail message.

Now if you want to send an e-mail message to Chris Johnson, Hayley Miller, and Susan Dudley, all you have to do is select the distribution list Computer Classmates as the recipient of the e-mail message.

The Untitled - Distribution List window in Figure 1-82 on the previous page includes two buttons that are useful for modifying a distribution list. The Add New button lets you add a contact that is not in the contact list. The Remove button lets you delete the selected names in the distribution list.

Saving Outlook Information in Different Formats

You can save Outlook files on disk in a several formats. For example, you can save messages and contact lists in text format, which can be read or copied into other applications. The following steps show how to save a contact list on disk as a text file and display it in Notepad.

To Save a Contact List as a Text File and Display It in Notepad

1

- **Insert the Data Disk in drive A.**
- **With the Contacts window active, click the name bar of the first contact in the contact list.**
- **Press CTRL+A to select all the contacts.**
- **Click File on the menu bar.**

All the contacts are selected and Outlook displays the File menu (Figure 1-84).

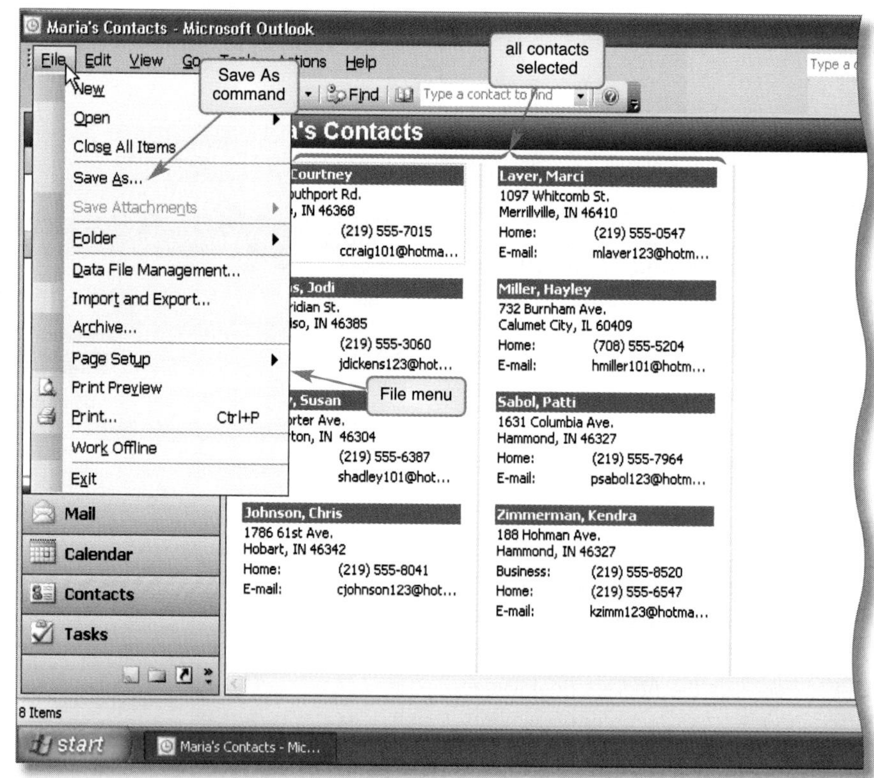

FIGURE 1-84

- **Click Save As on the File menu.**
- **When Outlook displays the Save As dialog box, type `Maria's Contacts` in the File name text box.**
- **If necessary, select Text Only in the Save as type box.**
- **Click the Save in box arrow and then select 3½ Floppy (A:).**

Outlook displays the Save As dialog box as shown in Figure 1-85.

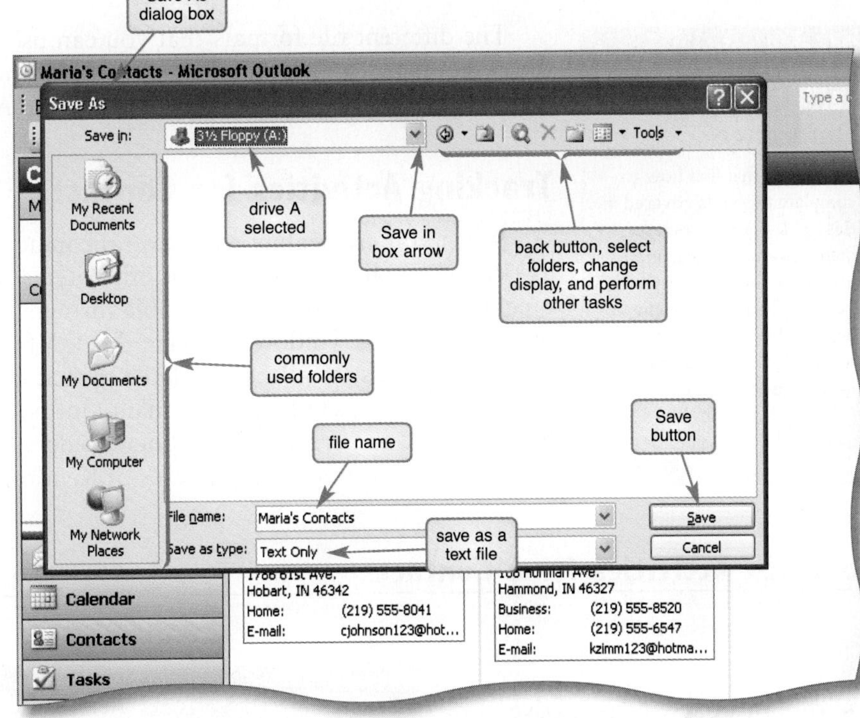

FIGURE 1-85

3

- **Click the Save button in the Save As dialog box.**
- **Click the Start button on the Windows taskbar, point to All Programs on the Start menu, point to Accessories on the All Programs submenu, and then click Notepad on the Accessories submenu.**
- **When Notepad starts, click the Maximize button on the title bar, click File on the menu bar, and then click Open.**
- **When Outlook displays the Open dialog box, click the Files of type box arrow, click All Files, click the Look in box arrow, and then click 3½ Floppy (A:) in the Look in list.**
- **Double-click Maria's Contacts.**

Notepad displays Maria's Contacts as a text file (Figure 1-86).

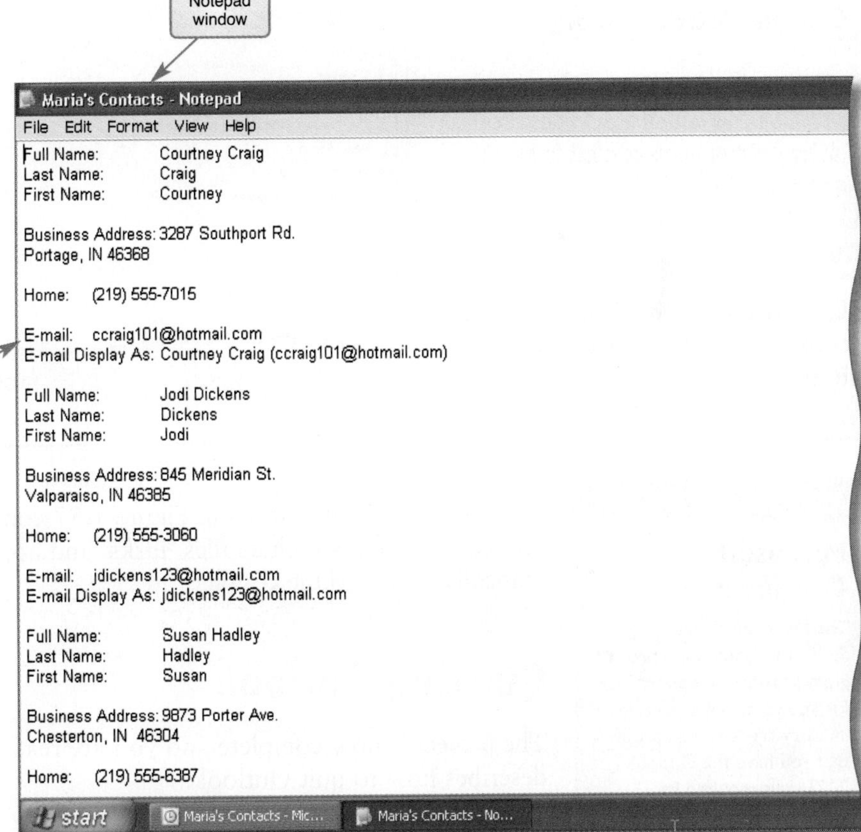

FIGURE 1-86

- **After viewing the text file, click the Close button on the right side of the Notepad title bar.**

More About

The Quick Reference

For a table that lists how to complete the tasks covered in this book using the mouse, menu, shortcut menu, and keyboard, see the Quick Reference Summary at the back of this book, or visit the Outlook 2003 Quick Reference Web page (scsite.com/out2003/qr).

The different file formats that you can use to save information is dependent on the component you are working in. To view the different file formats for a component, click the Save as type arrow in the Save As dialog box.

Tracking Activities for Contacts

When you are dealing with several contacts, it can be useful to have all associated e-mails, documents, or other items related to the contact available quickly. Outlook makes this possible through the use of the Activities tab in the selected contact's window. Clicking this tab for any contact in your contact list will provide you a list of all items related to that contact. Outlook searches for items linked only to the contact in the main Outlook folders (Contacts, Calendar, etc.); however, you can create and add new folders to be searched. The following steps illustrate how to track the activities of Kendra Zimmerman.

To Track Activities for a Contact

1

- **With Contacts window active, double-click the Kendra Zimmerman contact heading.**
- **Click the Activities tab.**

Outlook displays the Kendra Zimmerman – Contact window with the Activities sheet showing a list of items related to Kendra Zimmerman (Figure 1-87).

2

- **Click the Close button on the Kendra Zimmerman – Contact window.**

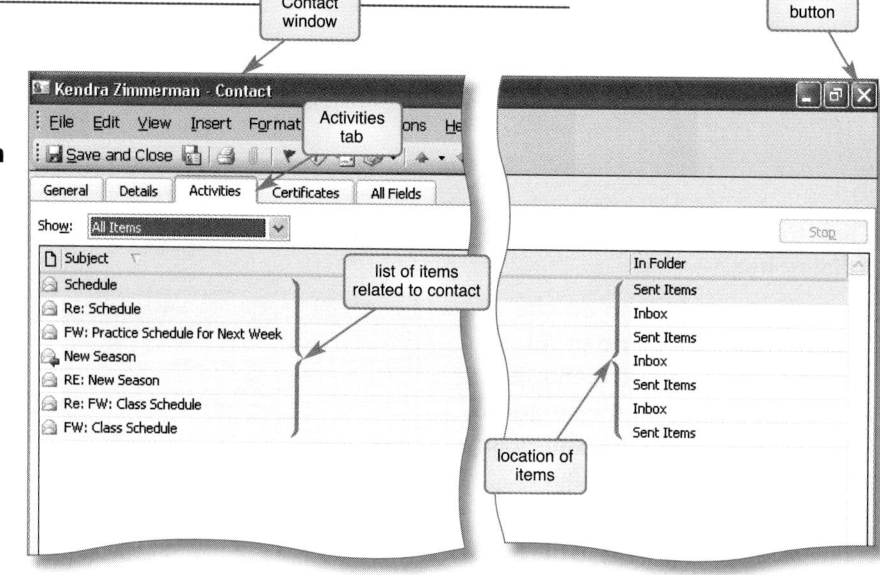

FIGURE 1-87

More About

Microsoft Certification

The Microsoft Office Specialist Certification program provides an opportunity for you to obtain a valuable industry credential — proof that you have the Outlook 2003 skills required by employers. For more information, see Appendix E or visit the Outlook 2003 Certification Web page (scsite.com/out2003/cert).

The list of items shown in Figure 1-87 consists entirely of e-mail messages. You also can link items such as files, tasks, and appointments. E-mail messages are automatically linked to the contact.

Quitting Outlook

The project is now complete and you are ready to quit Outlook. The following step describes how to quit Outlook.

To Quit Outlook

1 **Click the Close button on the Outlook title bar.**

Outlook is closed, and the Windows desktop appears.

Project Summary

In this project, you learned to use Outlook to open, read, print, reply to, forward, delete, sign, compose, format, and send e-mail messages. You opened and viewed file attachments as well as attached a file to an e-mail message. You learned how to flag, sort, and set importance and delivery options to e-mail messages. You added and deleted contacts to a contact list. Finally, you used the contact list to create a distribution list and track activities of a contact.

What You Should Know

Having completed this project, you should be able to perform the tasks below. The tasks are listed in the same order they were presented in this project. For a list of the buttons, menus, toolbars, and commands introduced in this project, see the Quick Reference Summary at the back of this book and refer to the Page Number column.

1. Start and Customize Outlook (OUT 6)
2. Open (Read) an E-Mail Message (OUT 11)
3. Print an Opened E-Mail Message (OUT 12)
4. Close an E-Mail Message (OUT 13)
5. Reply to an E-Mail Message (OUT 13)
6. Forward an E-Mail Message (OUT 16)
7. Delete an E-Mail Message (OUT 17)
8. View a File Attachment (OUT 18)
9. Create and Insert an E-Mail Signature (OUT 20)
10. Compose an E-Mail Message (OUT 24)
11. Format an E-Mail Message (OUT 26)
12. Attach a File to an E-Mail Message (OUT 28)
13. Send an E-Mail Message (OUT 29)
14. Flag E-Mail Messages (OUT 30)
15. Sort E-Mail Messages by Flag Color (OUT 31)
16. Create and Apply a View Filter (OUT 32)
17. Set Message Importance, Sensitivity, and Delivery Options in a Single Message (OUT 34)
18. Change the Default Level of Importance and Sensitivity (OUT 36)
19. Create a Personal Folder (OUT 40)
20. Create a Contact List (OUT 42)
21. Change the View and Sort the Contact List (OUT 45)
22. Find a Contact (OUT 46)
23. Organize Contacts (OUT 48)
24. Display the Contacts in a Category (OUT 49)
25. Preview and Print the Contact List (OUT 50)
26. Use the Contact List to Address an E-Mail Message (OUT 51)
27. Create a Distribution List (OUT 54)
28. Save a Contact List as a Text File and Display It in Notepad (OUT 56)
29. Track Activities for a Contact (OUT 58)
30. Quit Outlook (OUT 58)

Learn It Online

Instructions: To complete the Learn It Online exercises, start your browser, click the Address bar, and then enter the Web address scsite.com/out2003/learn. When the Outlook 2003 Learn It Online page is displayed, follow the instructions in the exercises below. Each exercise has instructions for printing your results, either for your own records or for submission to your instructor.

1 Project Reinforcement TF, MC, and SA

Below Outlook Project 1, click the Project Reinforcement link. Print the quiz by clicking Print on the File menu for each page. Answer each question.

2 Flash Cards

Below Outlook Project 1, click the Flash Cards link and read the instructions. Type 20 (or a number specified by your instructor) in the Number of playing cards text box, type your name in the Enter your Name text box, and then click the Flip Card button. When the flash card is displayed, read the question and then click the ANSWER box arrow to select an answer. Flip through Flash Cards. If your score is 15 (75%) correct or greater, click Print on the File menu to print your results. If your score is less than 15 (75%) correct, then redo this exercise by clicking the Replay button.

3 Practice Test

Below Outlook Project 1, click the Practice Test link. Answer each question, enter your first and last name at the bottom of the page, and then click the Grade Test button. When the graded practice test is displayed on your screen, click Print on the File menu to print a hard copy. Continue to take practice tests until you score 80% or better.

4 Who Wants To Be a Computer Genius?

Below Outlook Project 1, click the Computer Genius link. Read the instructions, enter your first and last name at the bottom of the page, and then click the PLAY button. When your score is displayed, click the PRINT RESULTS link to print a hard copy.

5 Wheel of Terms

Below Outlook Project 1, click the Wheel of Terms link. Read the instructions, and then enter your first and last name and your school name. Click the PLAY button. When your score is displayed, right-click the score and then click Print on the shortcut menu to print a hard copy.

6 Crossword Puzzle Challenge

Below Outlook Project 1, click the Crossword Puzzle Challenge link. Read the instructions, and then enter your first and last name. Click the SUBMIT button. Work the crossword puzzle. When you are finished, click the Submit button. When the crossword puzzle is redisplayed, click the Print Puzzle button to print a hard copy.

7 Tips and Tricks

Below Outlook Project 1, click the Tips and Tricks link. Click a topic that pertains to Project 1. Right-click the information and then click Print on the shortcut menu. Construct a brief example of what the information relates to in Outlook to confirm you understand how to use the tip or trick.

8 Newsgroups

Below Outlook Project 1, click the Newsgroups link. Click a topic that pertains to Project 1. Print three comments.

9 Expanding Your Horizons

Below Outlook Project 1, click the Expanding Your Horizons link. Click a topic that pertains to Project 1. Print the information. Construct a brief example of what the information relates to in Outlook to confirm you understand the contents of the article.

10 Search Sleuth

Below Outlook Project 1, click the Search Sleuth link. To search for a term that pertains to this project, select a term below the Project 1 title and then use the Google search engine at google.com (or any major search engine) to display and print two Web pages that present information on the term.

11 Outlook Online Training

Below Outlook Project 1, click the Outlook Online Training link. When your browser displays the Microsoft Office Online Web page, click the Outlook link. Click one of the Outlook courses that covers one or more of the objectives listed at the beginning of the project on page OUT 4. Print the first page of the course before stepping through it.

12 Office Marketplace

Below Outlook Project 1, click the Office Marketplace link. When your browser displays the Microsoft Office Online Web page, click the Office Marketplace link. Click a topic that relates to Outlook. Print the first page.

Apply Your Knowledge

1 Creating a Contact List

Instructions: Start Outlook. Create a Contacts folder using your name as the name of the new folder. Create a contact list using the people listed in Table 1-4. Use the Department text box in the Details sheet to enter the student's grade level. Create a distribution list consisting of freshmen and sophomores. Sort the list by last name in descending sequence. When the list is complete, print the list in Card Style view and submit to your instructor.

Table 1-4 Contact Information

NAME	TELEPHONE	ADDRESS	E-MAIL ADDRESS	GRADE LEVEL
Beth Thomas	(219) 555-6434	9865 Wexford	bthomas@isp.com	Sophomore
Jose Tinoco	(219) 555-6374	846 W. 5th	jtinoco@isp.com	Senior
David Price	(219) 555-1470	752 Calumet	dprice@isp.com	Senior
Kris Clark	(219) 555-0560	1853 Colonial	kclark@isp.com	Freshman
Judy Watson	(219) 555-5431	1548 Clay	jwatson@isp.com	Sophomore
Walter Stern	(219) 555-5415	2187 Porter	wstern@isp.com	Junior

Importing Subfolders for the In the Lab Exercises — Follow these steps to import subfolders for the following In the Lab Exercises:

1. Insert the Data Disk into drive A.
2. Click File on the Outlook menu bar and then click Import and Export.
3. In the Import and Export Wizard dialog box, click Import from another program or file and then click the Next button.
4. In the Import a File dialog box, click Personal Folder File (.pst) and then click the Next button.
5. In the Import Personal Folders dialog box, click the Browse button to access drive A, select the appropriate subfolder, click Open, and then click the Next button.
6. In the Import Personal Folders dialog box, select the appropriate folder to import from and then click the Finish button.

1 Creating a Distribution List and Sending E-Mail

Problem: You are the volunteer campaign chairperson of a friend's campaign for state senator. Part of your responsibilities is to solicit and organize campaign donations. To do so, you need to maintain and contact a list of past and potential donors.

Instructions Part 1: Import the Lab 1-1 Contacts folder (Figure 1-88 on the next page) into Outlook. Create two distribution lists; one consisting of past donors, the other consisting of potential donors. The status of each contact can be found in the Job Title text box. Print each distribution list and submit to your instructor.

(continued)

Creating a Distribution List and Sending E-Mail *(continued)*

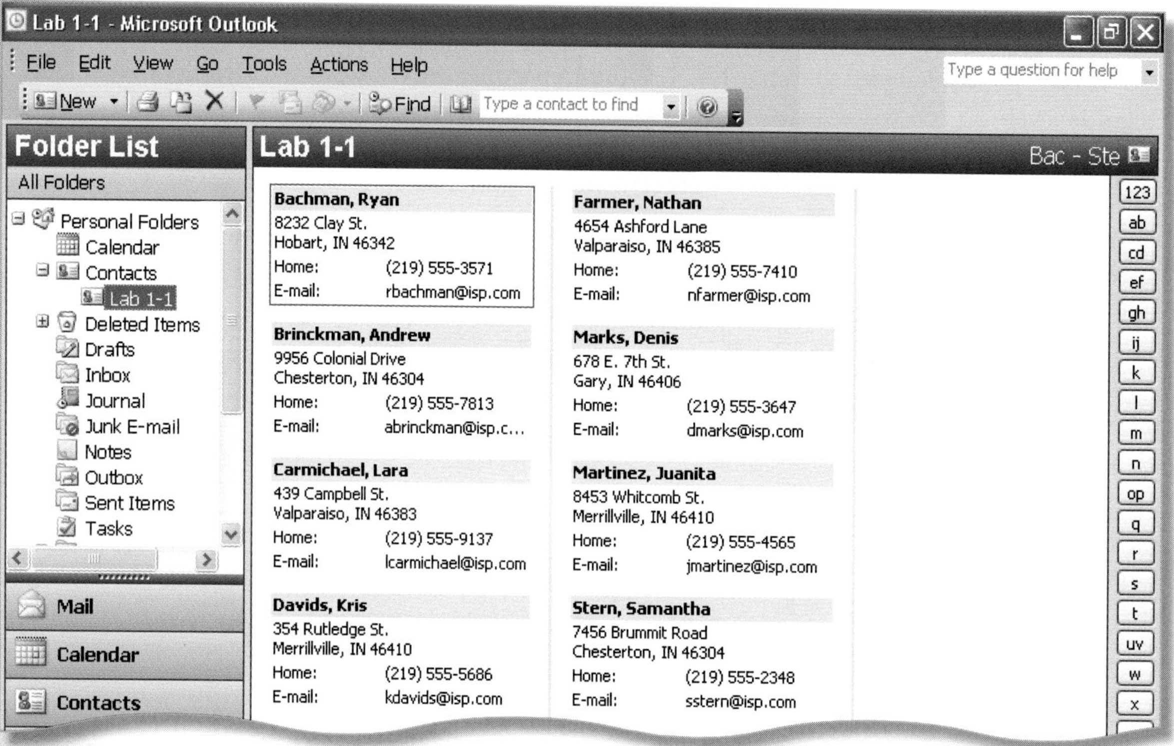

FIGURE 1-88

Instructions Part 2: Do the following:

1. Compose a message to each group created in Part 1. The message to past donors should thank them for their past support and request donations for this year's campaign. The message to potential donors should include a few reasons why it would be beneficial to have your candidate in office.
2. Set the sensitivity for each message as confidential.
3. Using Microsoft Word, create a document called Campaign Platform, and include this file as an attachment with your e-mail messages.
4. Set the delivery for each message to November 1, 2005 at 9:00 a.m.
5. Format your messages to past donors as Plain Text and your messages to potential donors as HTML.
6. Print each e-mail message and hand them in to your instructor.

Instructions Part 3: Save the Lab 1-1 contact list as a text file. Open the file using Notepad. Print the contact list from Notepad and hand it in to your instructor.

2 Flagging and Sorting Messages

Problem: As student director of the Computer Help Center, you are responsible for responding to questions received via e-mail. Some questions require a more timely response than others do, so you need a way to sort the questions first by urgency and then by when they were received. At that point, you will be able to address the questions in an orderly manner.

In the Lab

Instructions: Import the Lab 1-2 Inbox folder (Figure 1-89) into Outlook. Read through each message and appropriately flag each one. Use a red flag for messages requiring immediate attention, yellow for messages requiring information before you can respond and green for non-urgent, general questions. After you have flagged each message, sort the messages based on flag color.

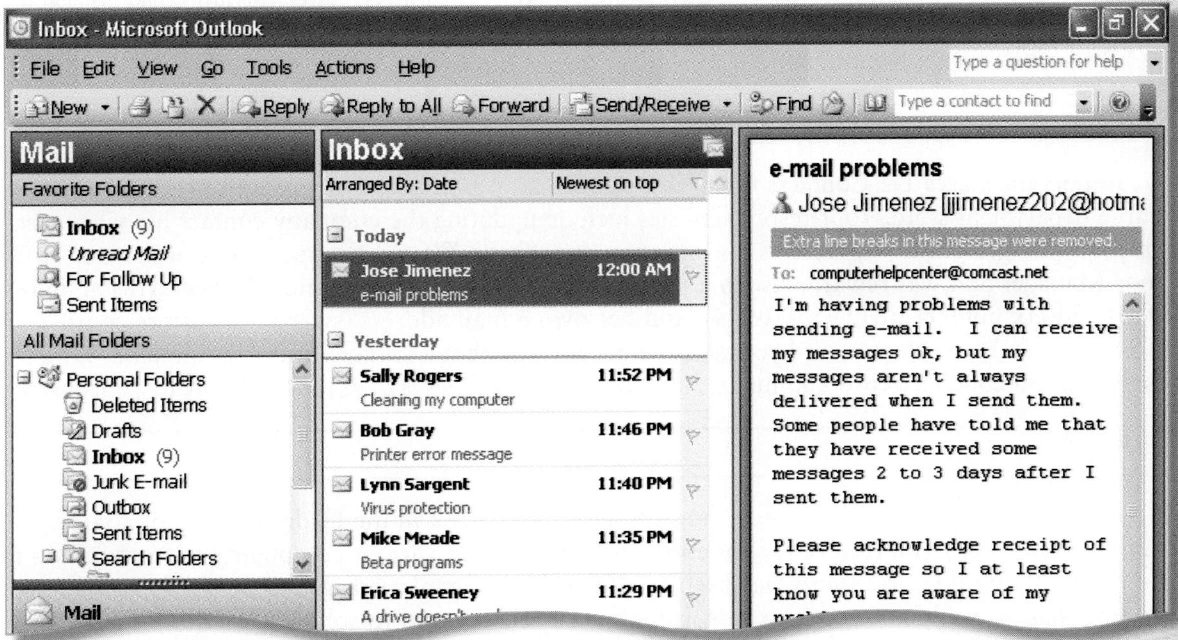

FIGURE 1-89

3 Creating an E-Mail Signature, Replying To, and Forwarding Messages

Problem: With all the messages sorted and flagged, you now have to respond to the messages. You need to perform this task in an efficient manner as it is the Computer Center's policy to respond to questions within 24 hours. It is also required that the name of the person responding, the Computer Center's telephone number, and its hours of operation appear on every reply.

Instructions Part 1: Create an e-mail signature consisting of your name, title (Director), a telephone number (555-1234), and hours of operation (8:00 a.m. – 8:00 p.m.). Click the New Message button on the Standard toolbar. Print the blank message containing the signature and hand it in to your instructor.

Instructions Part 2: Send a reply with the importance set at high to the messages flagged red. Forward the messages flagged yellow. You may use fictitious e-mail addresses for this exercise as the messages will not actually be sent. Hand in printouts of the replies and forwards to your instructor.

Instructions Part 3: Do the following:

1. Clear all the green flags from the non-urgent messages. Use Search Folders to display only the messages flagged for follow up. Make a list of the sender's name, subject, and flag color and hand it in to your instructor.
2. Using information from Microsoft Outlook Help, create a unique signature for a separate e-mail account. See your instructor about setting up a separate e-mail account.
3. Print a blank message containing the signature and hand it in to your instructor.

Cases and Places

The difficulty of these case studies varies:
■ are the least difficult and ■■ are more difficult. The last exercise is a group exercise.

1 ■ Create a contact list of your family, friends, and colleagues. Include their names, addresses, telephone numbers, e-mail addresses (if any), and IM address (if any). Enter the employer for each one, if appropriate. For family members, use the Detail sheet to list birthdays and wedding anniversaries (if any). Print the contact list and hand it in to your instructor.

2 ■ Import the Cases 1-2 Contacts folder into Outlook. You are the Human Resources Director for a large department store. Your responsibilities include updating the company contact list whenever someone changes positions, receives a promotion, etc. Sheila Weston has received a promotion to 3rd Floor Manager and was rewarded with a private office (Room 301), private telephone ((815) 555-0943) and fax number ((815) 555-0944), and her own e-mail address (sweston@bigstore.com). The information in her current record contains the general telephone number and store's e-mail. Find the Sheila Weston contact record and make the appropriate changes. Hand in a printout to your instructor.

3 ■ Import the Cases 1-3 Inbox folder into Outlook. You work in the IT department of a large company. Every day you receive several e-mail messages about various computer problems within the company. A coworker, Joe Smith, has been sending several e-mail messages to the IT department complaining that his problem has yet to be solved. You have been told to solve his problem. Apply a filter to the Cases 1-3 Inbox folder to display only the messages from Joe Smith. Respond to his latest e-mail message while sending a copy to your boss to show that you have found a resolution to Joe's problem. Hand in a printout of your reply to your instructor. Add Joe Smith to your contact list. Track the activities of Joe Smith. List the first five entries from the Activities list and hand it in to your instructor. After printing your reply message, delete all the messages from Joe Smith and remove the filter.

4 ■■ You recently accepted a position with an international construction company. Your first assignment is to make the main telephone and address file available to everyone in the firm. The file, which currently is maintained in a three-ring binder, contains names, addresses, telephone numbers, fax numbers, e-mail addresses, and Web site addresses of your company's subcontractors and vendors. You decide to create a contact list using Outlook so everyone can access the same information and automatically dial and send e-mail and access Web sites. Create a contact list that includes at least the names, addresses, and Web site URLs of seven construction companies. Use fictitious company names and addresses or look up construction companies on the Web using an Internet search engine. Create a Contacts subfolder in which to store the contact list. Categorize the contacts by subcontractor or vendor. Print the contact list and submit to your instructor.

5 ■■ **Working Together** Have each member of your team submit a design of a form for collecting contact information. Have them base the form on the available fields in the General and Details sheets in the Contact window. Have the team select the best form design. After selecting a form, Xerox copies for the entire class. Have your classmates fill out the form. Collect the forms and create a contact list from the collected information. Hand in printouts of the final contact list.

MICROSOFT Office Outlook 2003

Schedule Management and Instant Messaging Using Outlook

PROJECT

2

CASE PERSPECTIVE

Maria Rosado is a student-athlete at Woodland Community College. Her busy schedule includes classes, working part-time in the registrar's office, as well as being captain of the Woodland Community College High Flyers championship women's basketball team. As a busy college student, she is concerned about scheduling her school and work activities so they do not interfere with her basketball games and practice schedule. As captain, she is responsible for scheduling team meetings and she would like a simple way to plan future team meetings. She recently read an article about Outlook and thinks it would be the perfect tool to maintain her personal schedule and help with planning team meetings. She also read that she could use instant messaging with Outlook, and knows how easy it would be to communicate with team members and co-workers using this Outlook feature. She is unfamiliar with Outlook, however, and needs some direction.

You work part-time at the Help desk in the school's computer lab and are quite familiar with Outlook and its features. Maria has visited the Help desk requesting that you help her set up her calendar. She would like to use Outlook to schedule her classes, practices, games, work schedule, and other events. She read that Outlook allows you to create a single calendar event and set a weekly recurrence pattern, which will help her with this task. Maria feels that having her time scheduled should help her coordinate her school activities and her extracurricular activities more efficiently. She also would like for you to show her how to set up a team meeting, including inviting attendees and organizing any resources she may need. Finally, Maria would like you to help her set up instant messaging using Outlook. With your help, she can accomplish this goal.

MICROSOFT Office Outlook 2003

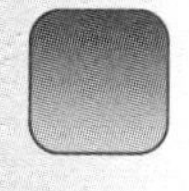

Schedule Management and Instant Messaging Using Outlook

PROJECT

Objectives

You will have mastered the material in this project when you can:

- Start Outlook and open the Calendar folder
- Describe the components of the Calendar - Microsoft Outlook window and understand the elements of the Outlook Navigation Pane
- Enter, move, and edit one-time and recurring appointments
- Create an event
- Display the calendar in Day, Work Week, Week, and Month views
- Create and customize a task list and move it to a new folder
- Import, export, and delete personal subfolders
- Delegate tasks
- Schedule a meeting
- Customize the calendar
- Print the calendar in Daily Style, Weekly Style, and Monthly Style
- Enable and start instant messaging in Outlook
- Add an instant messaging address in the contact list
- Send an instant message and send a file with instant messaging

Introduction

Whether you are CEO of a major company or president of an extracurricular activity group in school, Outlook has all the features you need for scheduling and managing appointments, meetings, and tasks (top of Figure 2-1). Using Outlook's Calendar component, managers can schedule meetings and appointments, and assign tasks for the other members of the group and even keep track of meeting attendance and task progression. Outlook also allows you to store miscellaneous information using Notes.

In addition to the contact related capabilities, Outlook is a great tool for scheduling and managing your own time. Most individuals have multiple appointments to keep and tasks to accomplish in a day, week, or month. Outlook assists in maintaining a full schedule such as this, organizing the information in a structured, readable manner.

Outlook also has an instant messaging feature (bottom of Figure 2-1) that works in conjunction with Windows Messenger or MSN Messenger. This allows you to communicate instantaneously with people in your contact list who also use one of these instant messenger services.

OUTLOOK CALENDAR

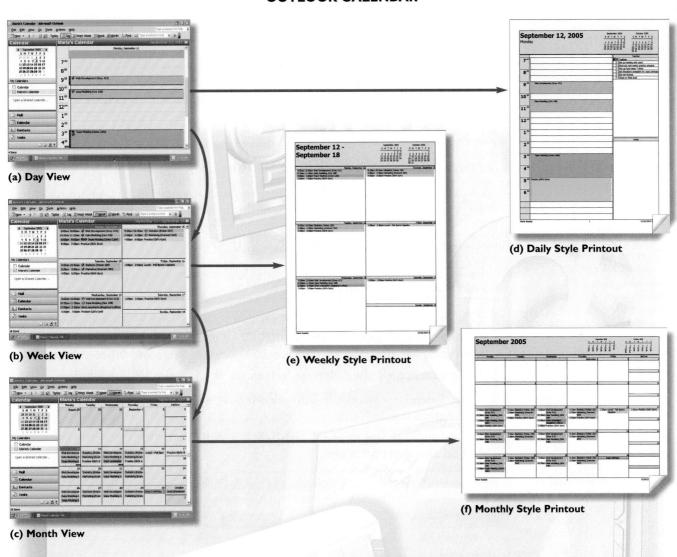

(a) Day View

(b) Week View

(c) Month View

(d) Daily Style Printout

(e) Weekly Style Printout

(f) Monthly Style Printout

INSTANT MESSAGING VIA OUTLOOK

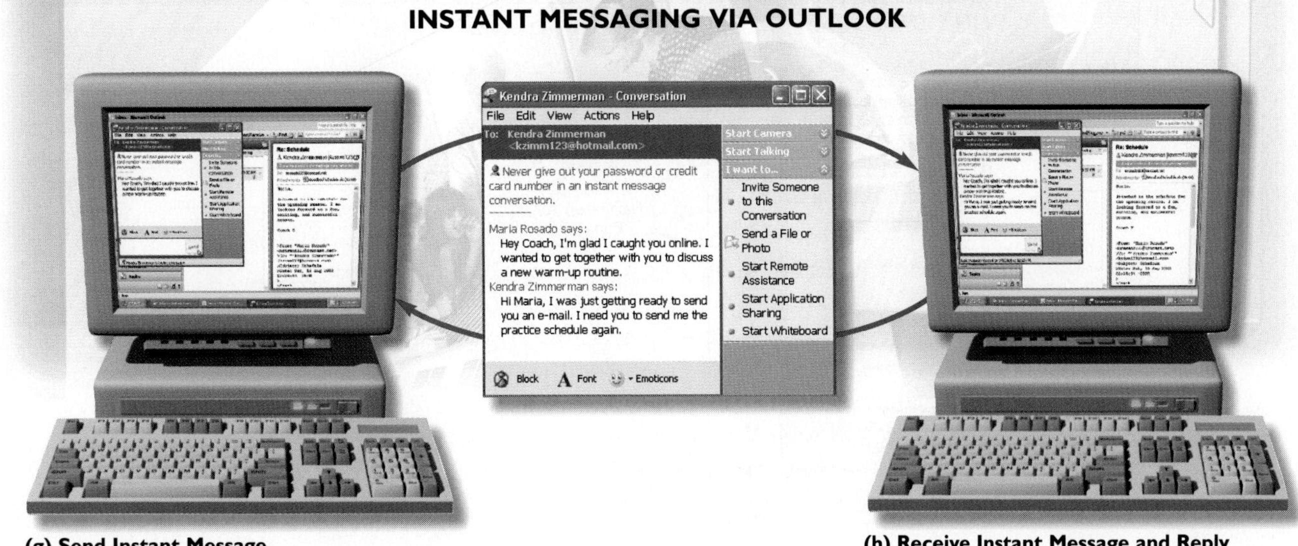

(g) Send Instant Message

(h) Receive Instant Message and Reply

FIGURE 2-1

More About

The Outlook 2003 Help System

Need Help? It is no further than the Type a question for help box on the menu bar in the upper-right corner of the window. Click the box that contains the text, Type a question for help (Figure 2-2), type `help`, and then press the ENTER key. Outlook responds with a list of topics you can click to learn about obtaining help on any Outlook -related topic. To find out what is new in Outlook 2003, type `what is new in Outlook` in the Type a question for help box.

Project Two — Personal Information Manager

In Project 2, the basic features of Outlook are illustrated while creating a calendar of classes, work schedules, and extra-curricular activities for Maria Rosado. Scheduling meetings is illustrated. In addition to creating the calendar, the project shows how to print it in three views: Day, Week, and Month. Figures 2-1d, 2-1e, and 2-1f on the previous page show the resulting printouts. The project also shows how to create a task list and delegate those tasks. Finally, the project presents using Windows Messenger with Outlook.

Starting and Customizing Outlook

To start and customize Outlook, Windows must be running. If you are stepping through this project on a computer and you want your screen to agree with the figures in this book, then you should set your computer's resolution to 800 × 600. The following steps start Outlook and customize its window.

To Start and Customize Outlook

1. **Click the Start button on the Windows taskbar, point to All Programs on the Start menu, point to Microsoft Office on the All Programs submenu, and then click Microsoft Office Outlook 2003 on the Microsoft Office submenu.**
2. **If necessary, click the Calendar button on the left side of the window.**
3. **If the Calendar - Microsoft Outlook window is not maximized, double-click its title bar to maximize it.**
4. **If the Language bar appears, right-click it and then click Close the Language bar on the shortcut menu.**

Outlook is started and displays the Calendar - Microsoft Outlook window as shown in Figure 2-2.

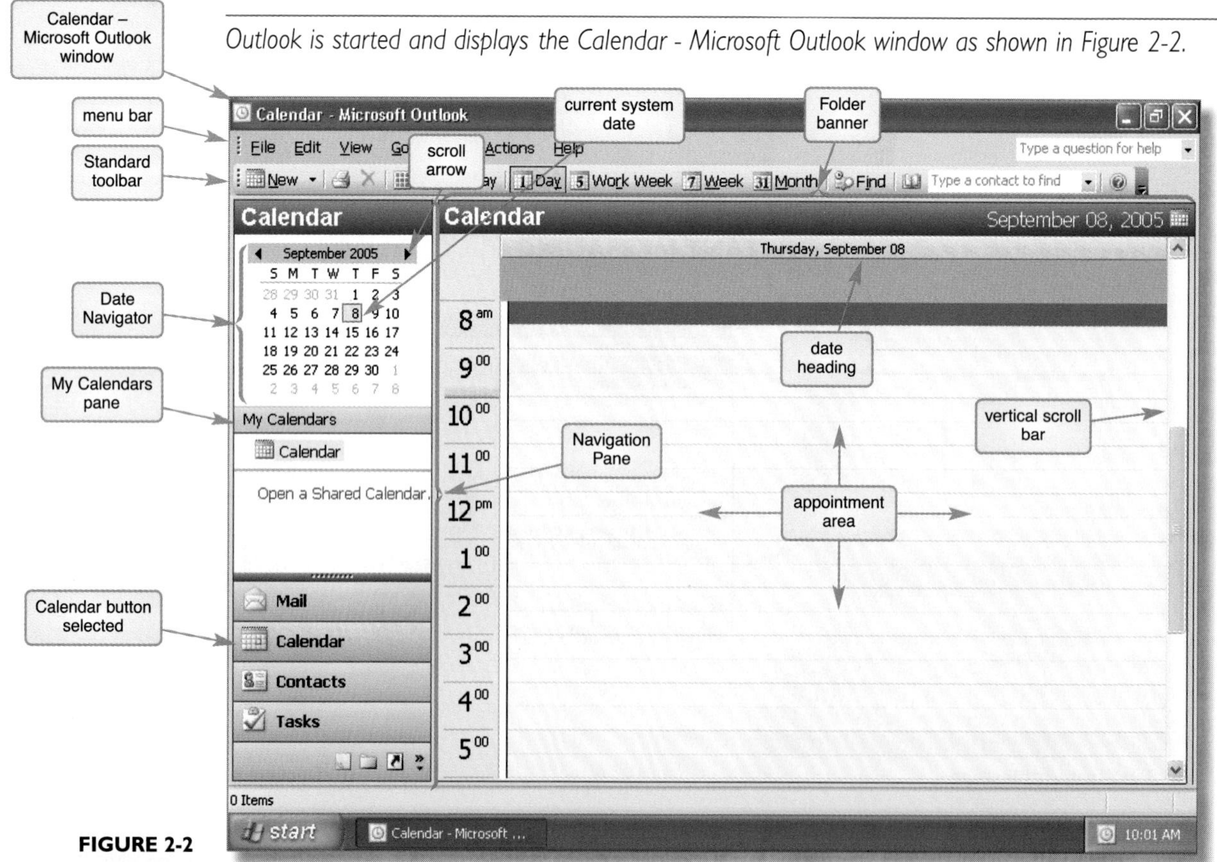

FIGURE 2-2

The Calendar - Microsoft Outlook Window

The **Calendar - Microsoft Outlook window** (Figure 2-2) includes a variety of features to help you work efficiently. It contains many elements similar to the windows in other Office applications, as well as some that are unique to Outlook. The main elements of the Calendar window are the Navigation Pane, the Standard toolbar, and the appointment area. The following paragraphs explain some of the features of the Calendar window.

FOLDER BANNER The **Folder banner** (Figure 2-2) is the horizontal bar just below the Standard toolbar. The name of the active folder, the selected date, and an icon for the active folder display in the Folder banner.

NAVIGATION PANE The **Navigation Pane** (Figure 2-2) includes two sets of buttons and two panes: the Date Navigator pane and My Calendars pane. The **Date Navigator** includes a calendar for the current month and scroll arrows. When you click the scroll arrows to move to a new date, Calendar displays the name of the month, week, or day in the current view in the appointment area. The current system date has a square around it in the Date Navigator. Dates displayed in bold in the Date Navigator indicate days on which an item is scheduled.

Below the Date Navigator, the My Calendars pane includes a list of available calendars on your computer. In this pane, you can select a single calendar to view, or view other calendars side-by-side with your calendar.

On the lower portion of the Navigation Pane are two groups of buttons (Figure 2-3). The first group of buttons are shortcuts representing the standard items that are part of Microsoft Outlook: Mail, Calendar, Contacts, and Tasks. The second group of buttons are shortcuts to other functions of Outlook: Notes, Folder List, Shortcuts, and Configure buttons. When you click a shortcut, Outlook opens the corresponding folder. The function performed when you click each folder is illustrated in Figure 2-3.

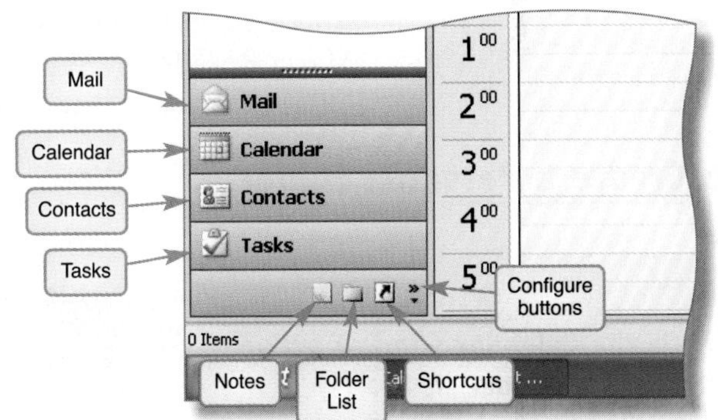

FIGURE 2-3

APPOINTMENT AREA The **appointment area** (Figure 2-2) contains a date heading and, under the date heading, time slots for the current view. The date currently selected in the Date Navigator appears in the date heading. By default, workday time slots are set from 8:00 a.m. to 5:00 p.m. in one hour increments. Time slots outside this period are shaded. A vertical scroll bar allows backward or forward movement through the time slots.

Scheduled items, such as appointments, meetings, or events, display in the appointment area. An **appointment** is an activity that does not involve other resources or people. The term **resources** refers to meeting rooms, audio visual equipment, and other items that may be used with an appointment or in a meeting. Resources are discussed in more detail later in this project. A **meeting**, by contrast, is an appointment to which other resources or people are invited. Outlook's Calendar can be used to schedule several people to attend a meeting or only one person to attend an appointment (such as a class). An **event** is an activity that lasts 24 hours or longer, such as a seminar, birthday, or vacation. Scheduled events do not occupy time slots in the appointment area; instead, they display in a banner below the date heading.

STANDARD TOOLBAR Figure 2-4 shows the Standard toolbar in the Calendar window. The button names indicate their functions. Each button can be clicked to perform a frequently used task, such as creating a new appointment, printing, or changing the current view.

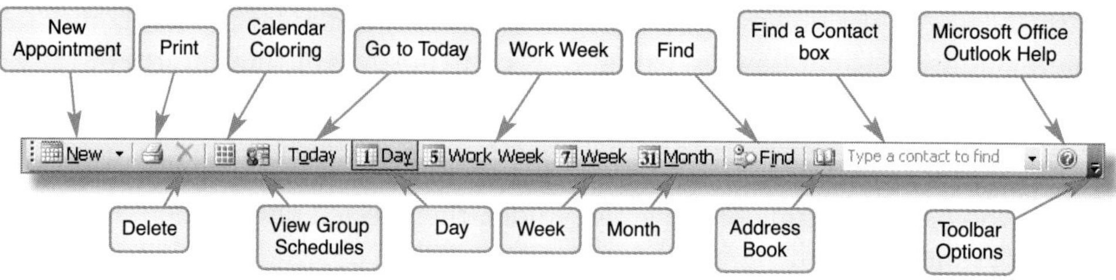

FIGURE 2-4

Creating a Personal Folder

If you were the only person using Outlook on a computer, you could enter appointments and events directly into the main Calendar folder, creating a daily, weekly, and monthly schedule. In many office and school situations, however, several people share one computer and therefore need to create separate folders in which to store appointments and events. The following steps create a personal folder for Maria Rosado.

To Create a Personal Folder

1

• **With the Calendar window active, right-click Calendar in the My Calendars pane.**

Outlook displays the Calendar shortcut menu (Figure 2-5).

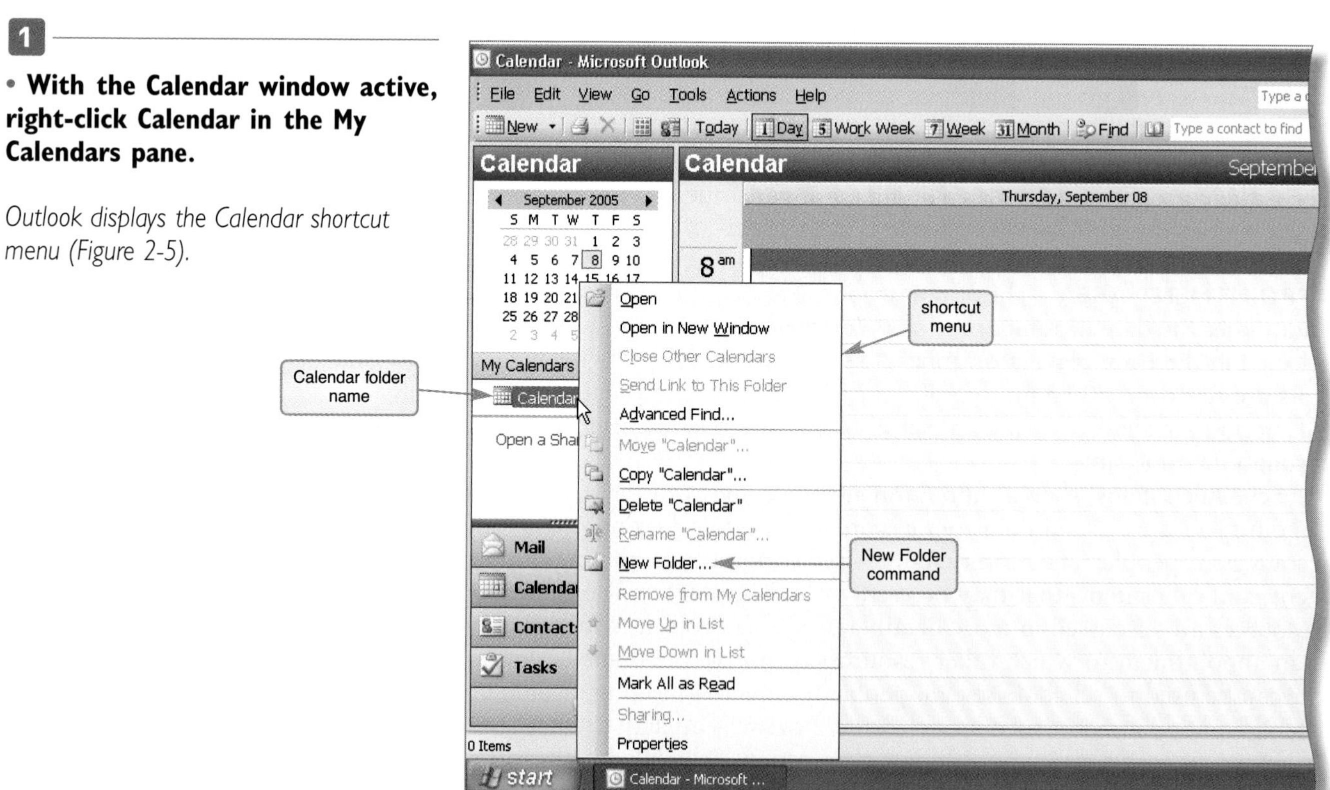

FIGURE 2-5

2

- **Click New Folder on the Calendar shortcut menu.**
- **When Outlook displays the Create New Folder dialog box, type** `Maria's Calendar` **in the Name text box.**
- **Select Calendar Items in the Folder contains text box.**
- **Click Calendar in the Select where to place the folder list box.**

The new folder, Maria's Calendar, becomes a subfolder of the Calendar folder (Figure 2-6). Maria's Calendar appears in the Name text box.

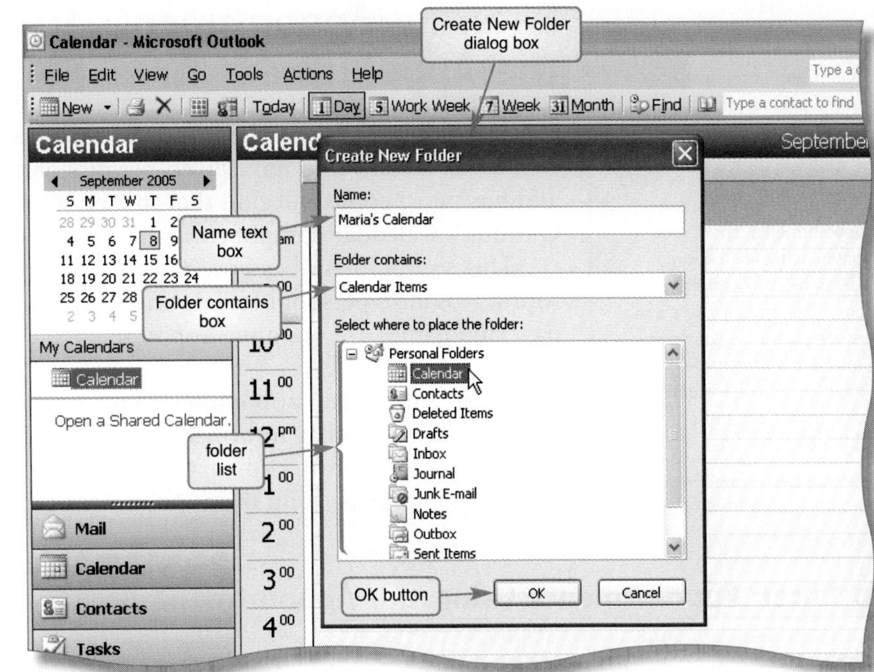

FIGURE 2-6

3

- **Click the OK button.**
- **Click the check box next to Maria's Calendar in the My Calendars list. Click the check box next to Calendar to remove the existing check mark.**

Outlook displays a list of available folders in the My Calendars pane and displays an empty appointment area (Figure 2-7).

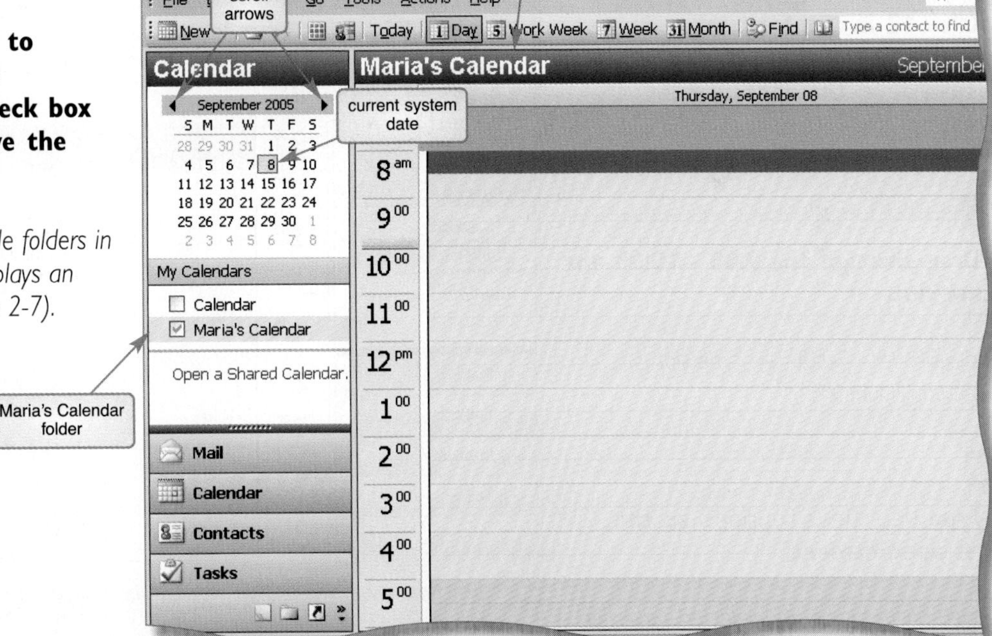

FIGURE 2-7

Figure 2-7 shows the default view for Calendar. If this view does not appear on your computer, click View on the menu bar, point to Arrange By, point to Current View, and then make sure the Day/Week/Month option is selected.

Other Ways

1. On File menu point to Folder, click New Folder on Folder submenu
2. Press CTRL+SHIFT+E
3. In Voice Command mode, say "File, New Folder"

Q: Can I access other users' calendars?

A: Yes. Other users can give you access to their calendars. This allows you to make appointments, check free times, schedule meetings, check or copy contacts, or any other tasks that you can accomplish with your own calendar. This is useful if you need to schedule meetings or events that depend on other people's schedules.

Entering Appointments Using the Appointment Area

Calendar allows you to schedule appointments, meetings, and events for yourself as well as for others who have given permission to open their personal folders. Students and business people will find that it is easy to schedule resources and people with Outlook's Calendar component.

This section describes how to enter appointments, or in this case, classes into Maria Rosado's personal folder, starting with classes for September 12, 2005. Work days and games are one-time appointments; classes and team meetings are recurring appointments.

When entering an appointment into a time slot that is not visible in the current view, use the scroll bar to bring the time slot into view. Once you enter an appointment, you can perform ordinary editing actions. The following steps show how to enter appointments using the appointment area.

To Enter Appointments Using the Appointment Area

1

- **If necessary, click the scroll arrows in the Date Navigator to display September 2005.**
- **Click 12 in the September calendar in the Date Navigator to display it in the appointment area.**

2

- **Drag through the 9:00 - 10:00 am time slot.**

The 9:00 am - 10:00 am time slot is selected (Figure 2-8).

3

- **Type** `Web Development` **as the first appointment.**

As you begin typing, the selected time slot changes to a text box with blue top and bottom borders.

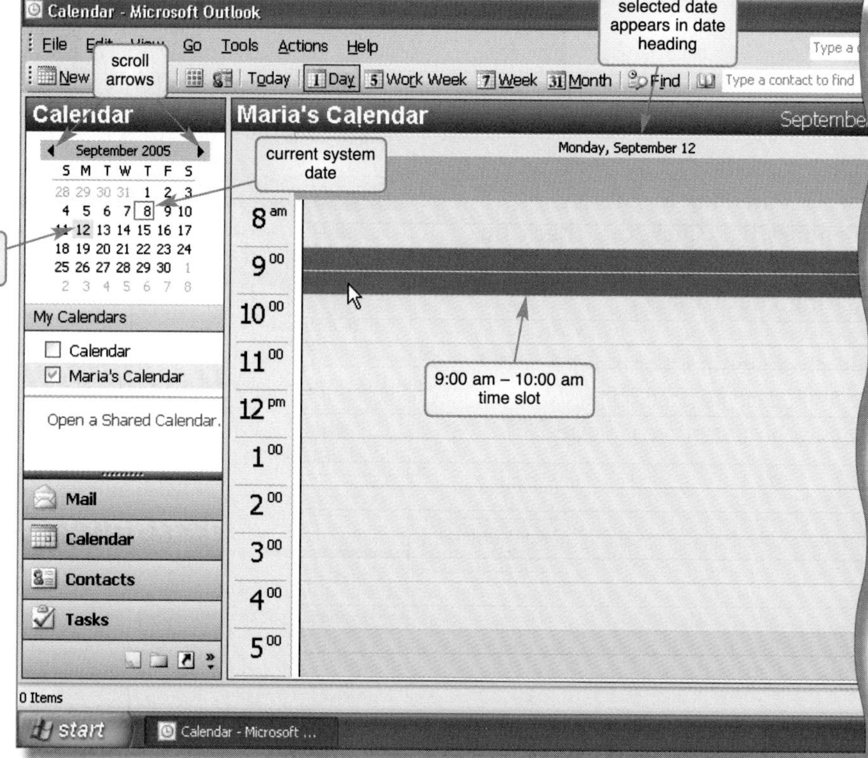

FIGURE 2-8

4

- **Drag through the 10:30 am - 11:30 am time slot.**
- **Type** `Data Modeling` **as the second appointment.**

5

- **Drag through the 12 pm - 1:00 pm time slot.**
- **Type** `Lunch - Fall Sports Captains` **as the third appointment and then press the ENTER key.**

The three appointments display in the appointment area (Figure 2-9).

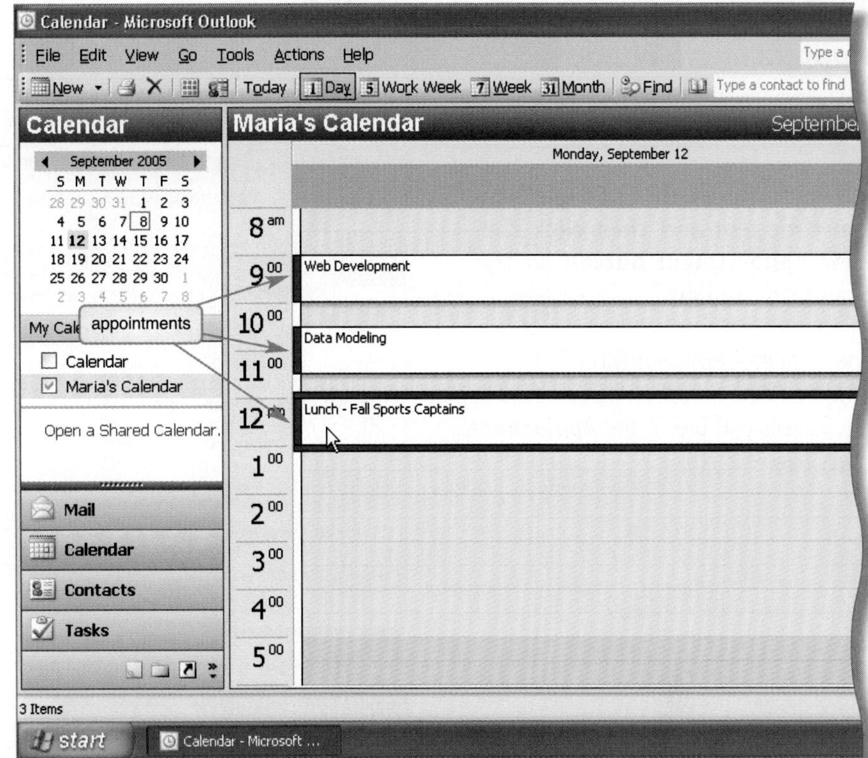

FIGURE 2-9

If you make a mistake while typing and notice the error before clicking outside the appointment time slot or pressing the ENTER key, use the BACKSPACE key to erase all the characters back to and including the error. To cancel the entire entry before clicking outside the appointment time slot or pressing the ENTER key, press the ESC key. If you discover an error in an appointment after clicking outside the appointment or pressing the ENTER key, click the appointment and retype the entry. Later in this project, additional editing techniques are discussed.

Entering Appointments Using the Appointment Window

You can enter appointments either by typing them directly into the appointment area as shown in the previous section, or you can enter them using the **Appointment window**. Using the Appointment window is a slightly more involved process, but it allows the specification of more details about the appointment. The steps on the next page describe how to enter an appointment at 3:00 p.m. to 5:00 p.m. using the appointment window.

More About

Appointments

Appointments can be designated as busy, free, tentative, or out of office. The Private check box in the Appointment window allows you to designate as private any appointments, tasks, meetings, or contacts. The private designation prevents viewing by other users with access to your calendar. Private calendar elements are identified with a key symbol.

To Enter and Save Appointments Using the Appointment Window

1

• **Drag through the 3:00 pm - 5:00 pm time slot and then click the New Appointment button on the Standard toolbar.**

The Untitled - Appointment window opens with the insertion point in the Subject text box in the Appointment sheet (Figure 2-10).

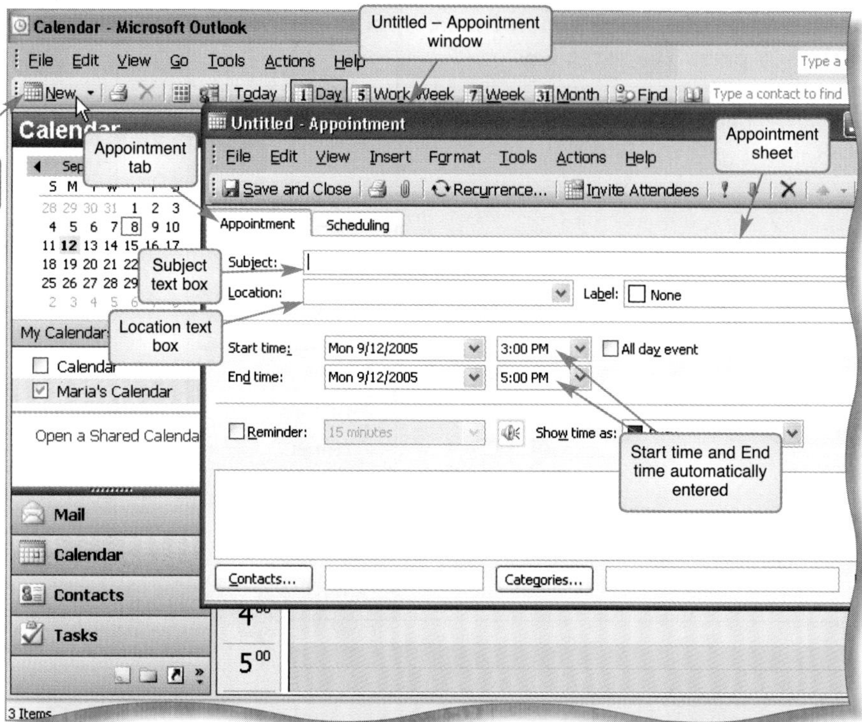

FIGURE 2-10

2

• **Type** `Team meeting` **in the Subject text box and then press the TAB key to move the insertion point to the Location text box.**

• **Type** `Union Cafe` **in the Location text box.**

Both the subject and location of the appointment appear in the appropriate text boxes. Once typed, the appointment subject appears on the Team Meeting - Appointment window title bar and on the taskbar (Figure 2-11).

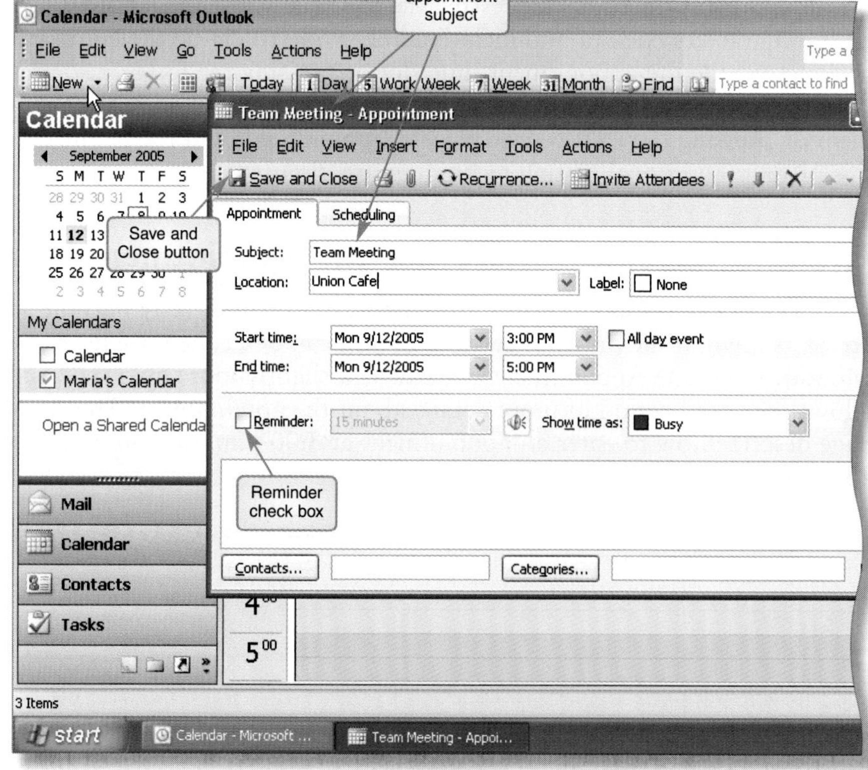

FIGURE 2-11

3

• **Click the Save and Close button on the Standard toolbar.**

Outlook saves the appointment and closes the Appointment window. The schedule for Monday, September 12 appears in the appointment area with the four new appointments entered (Figure 2-12).

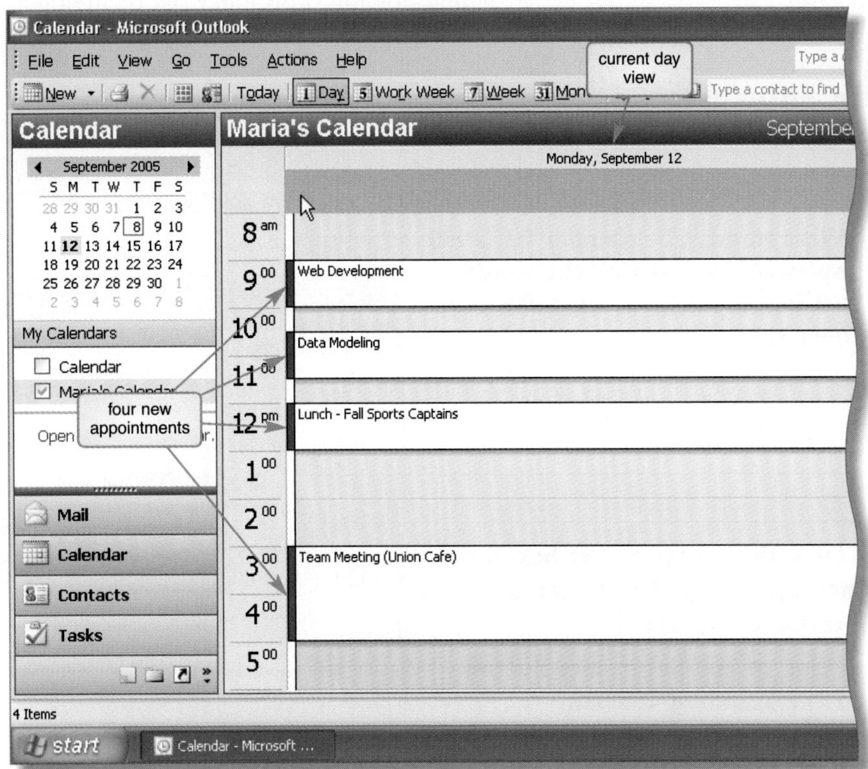

FIGURE 2-12

Other Ways

1. Double-click time slot, enter appointment
2. On Actions menu click New Appointment
3. Right-click time slot, click New Appointment on shortcut menu
4. Press CTRL+N
5. Press ALT+A, type O
6. In Voice Command mode, say "Actions, New Appointment"

The Reminder check box (Figure 2-11) can be checked to instruct your computer to play a reminder sound before an appointment time. A bell icon, called the **Reminder symbol**, appears next to appointments with reminders.

Press the TAB key to move through the fields in the Appointment window (Figure 2-11), or click any text or list box to make a change. Normal editing techniques also can be used to make changes.

Recurring Appointments

Many appointments are **recurring**, or occur at regular intervals. For example, a class held every Monday and Wednesday from 9:00 a.m. to 10:00 a.m. is a recurring appointment. In this project, Maria Rosado's college classes and team meetings occur at regular, weekly intervals. Typing these recurring appointments for each occurrence would be very time-consuming. By designating an appointment as recurring, the appointment needs to be added only once and then recurrence is specified for the days on which it occurs. Table 2-1 lists Maria's recurring appointments.

Table 2-1 Recurring Appointments

TIME	APPOINTMENT	OCCURRENCE
9:00 am - 10:00 am	Web Development (Knoy 412)	Every Monday and Wednesday (30 times)
10:30 am - 11:30 am	Data Modeling (Gris 108)	Every Monday and Wednesday (30 times)
3:00 pm - 5:00 pm	Team Meeting (Union Cafe)	Every other Monday (15 times)

The following steps enter the recurring appointments.

To Enter Recurring Appointments

1

- **With Monday, September 12, 2005 displayed, double-click the words Web Development in the 9:00 – 10:00 time slot.**

The Web Development - Appointment window opens.

2

- **Click the Location text box and then type** `Knoy 412` **to set the location of the class.**
- **Point to the Recurrence button on the Standard toolbar.**

The symbol on the Recurrence button (Figure 2-13) will become the Recurrence symbol that appears beside the appointment in the appointment area.

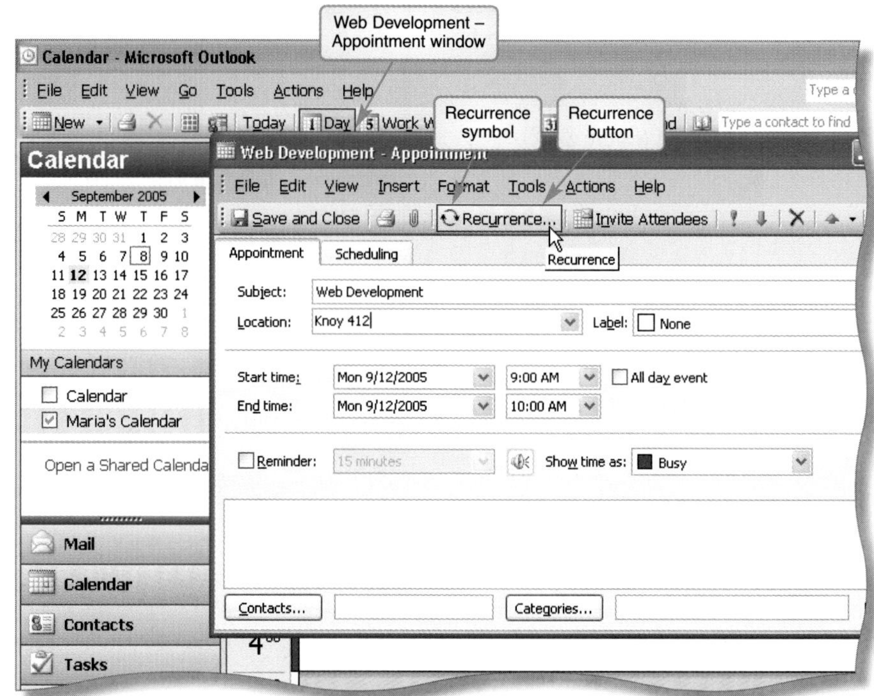

FIGURE 2-13

3

- **Click the Recurrence button.**
- **When the Appointment Recurrence dialog box is displayed, click the Wednesday check box to select the days this appointment will recur.**
- **Click End after in the Range of recurrence area, double-click the End after text box, and then type** 30 **as the number of occurrences.**

Outlook displays the Appointment Recurrence dialog box (Figure 2-14). The Web Development appointment is set to recur on Mondays (selected as the default) and Wednesday (selected in the step) and end after 30 occurrences.

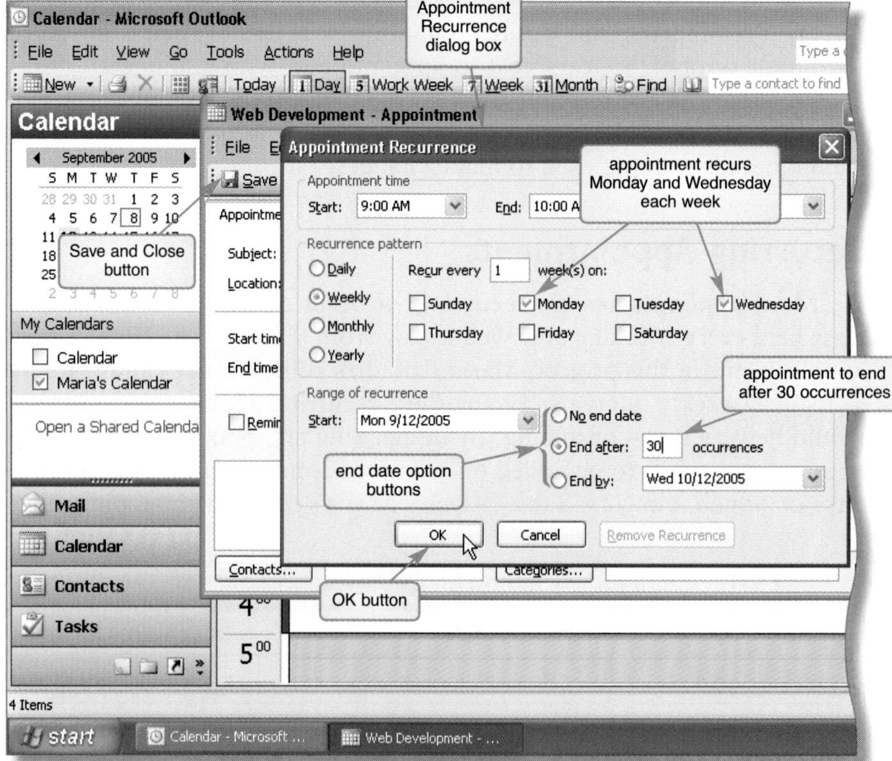

FIGURE 2-14

4

- **Click the OK button.**
- **Click the Save and Close button on the Standard toolbar in the Web Development - Appointment window.**

5

- **Repeat Steps 1 through 4 to make the Data Modeling and Team Meeting appointments recurring. Refer to Table 2-1 on page OUT 75 for the location, range, and ending dates.**

The Monday, September 12 schedule is complete (Figure 2-15). A Recurrence symbol appears beside each recurring appointment.

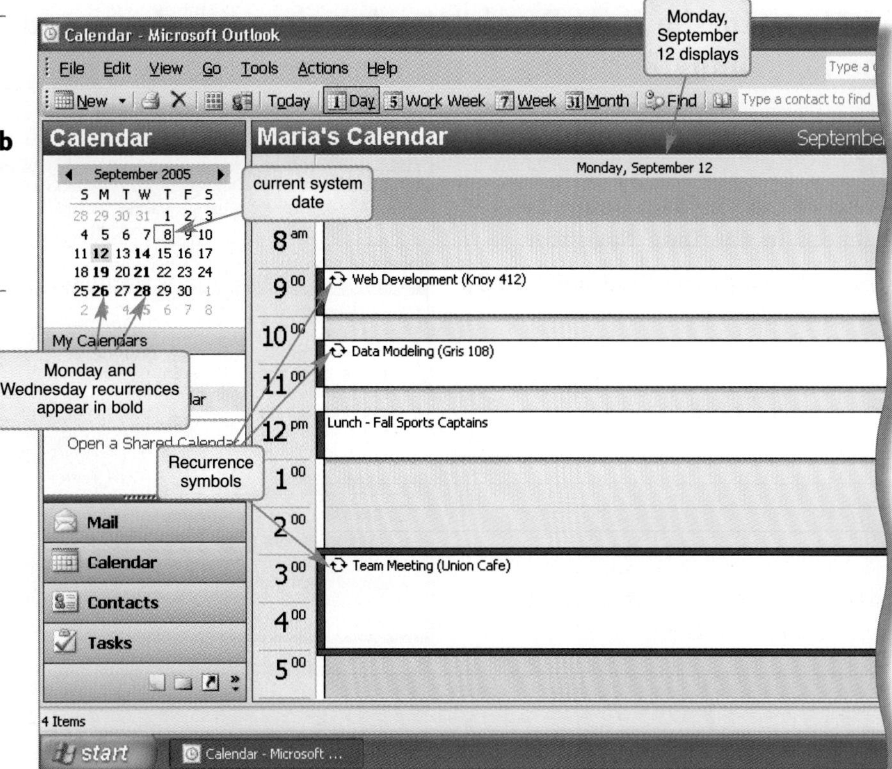

FIGURE 2-15

The Date Navigator serves several purposes when creating appointments. Recurring appointments are assigned to their appropriate dates automatically. After an appointment is assigned to a date, it appears bold in the Date Navigator (Figure 2-15). You can change these features using the Customize Current View command on the Current View submenu of the Arrange By menu accessed by clicking View on the menu bar.

The Date Navigator also allows easy movement and display of a specific date in the appointment area. This allows appointment to be entered on that date.

More About

The Recurrence Symbol

The Recurrence symbol can be applied to appointments, events, meetings, and tasks. Double-click the item to open its dialog box and then click the Recurrence button.

Moving to the Next Day in Calendar and Entering the Remaining Recurring Appointments

With the Monday schedule entered, the next step is to move to the next day in the appointment area and complete the recurring appointments for every Tuesday and Thursday using the appointment information in Table 2-2. Because the recurring appointments start on Tuesday, Tuesday must be displayed in the appointment area. The steps on the next page show how to move to the next day using the Date Navigator and then enter the remaining recurring appointments.

Table 2-2 Additional Recurring Appointments

TIME	APPOINTMENT	OCCURRENCE
9:30 am - 10:30 am	Statistics (Potter 205)	Every Tuesday and Thursday (30 times)
2:30 pm - 3:30 pm	Marketing (Krannert 504)	Every Tuesday and Thursday (30 times)

To Move to the Next Day in the Appointment Area, and Enter the Remaining Recurring Appointments

1

• **Click 13 in the September 2005 calendar in the Date Navigator.**

• **Drag through the 9:30 am - 10:30 am time slot.**

Tuesday, September 13 appears in the appointment area (Figure 2-16).

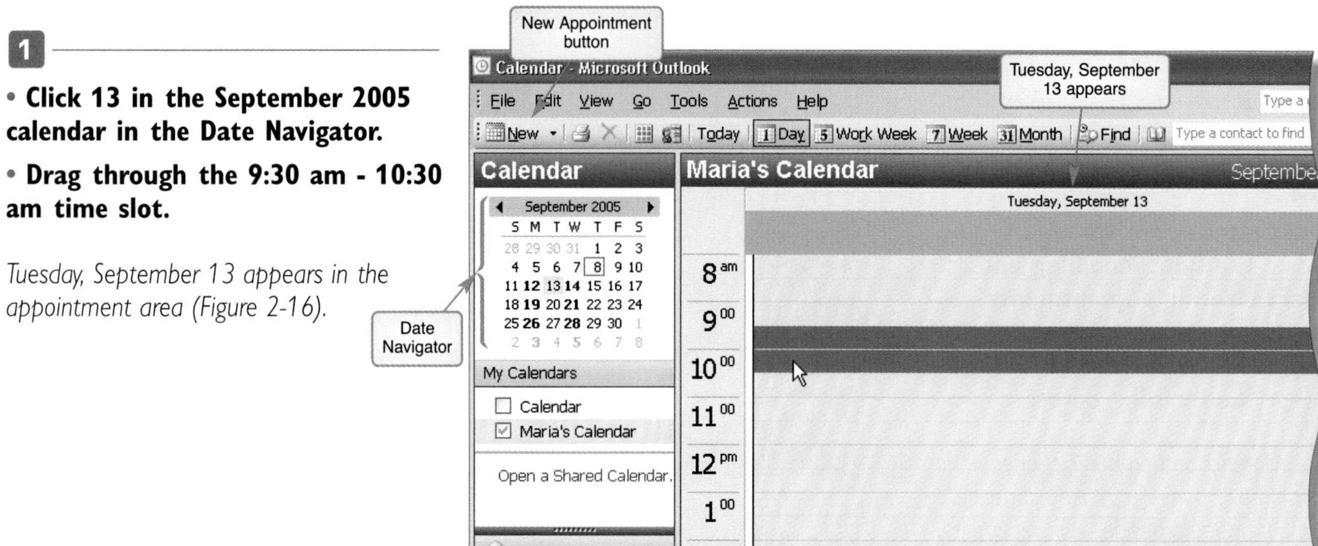

FIGURE 2-16

2

• **Click the New Appointment button on the Standard toolbar.**

3

• **Enter the recurring appointments provided in Table 2-2 on the previous page.**

• **Click the Save and Close button in the Appointment window.**

The appointments for Tuesday, September 13 are displayed (Figure 2-17). These appointments are scheduled to recur on Tuesdays and Thursdays and appear in bold on the calendar in the Date Navigator.

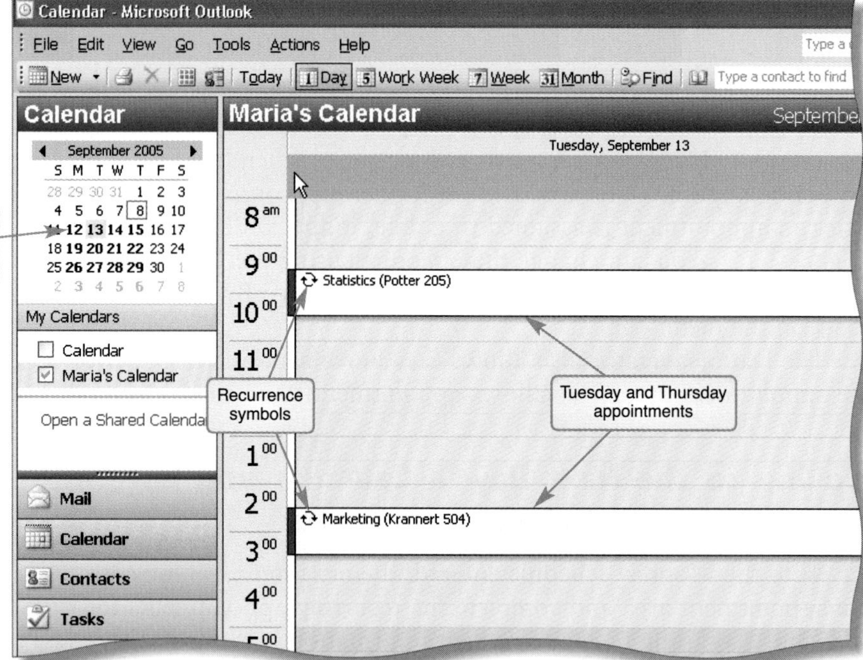

FIGURE 2-17

Other Ways

1. On Actions menu click New Recurring Appointment
2. Press ALT+A, type A
3. In Voice Command Mode, say "Actions, New Recurring Appointment"

Daily, weekly, monthly, or yearly recurrence patterns are possible in the Appointment Recurrence options. Outlook also provides three options for the range of recurrence. Appointments can recur every week or choice of weeks for one or multiple days. An appointment can be set to occur a certain number of times or up to a certain date. If the recurring appointment is ongoing, such as office hours, you can select the No end date option button (Figure 2-14 on page OUT 76).An appointment can be set as recurring when it first is entered, or, if you decide to make a one-time appointment recurring later, double-click the appointment and then click the Recurrence button. You can edit recurring appointments to add new days, omit certain days, or change other recurrence details. Editing recurring appointments is covered in more detail later in this project.

> *More About*
>
> **Moving a Recurring Appointment**
>
> If a recurring appointment is moved, only the selected instance of the appointment is moved. If all instances of an appointment need to be moved, open the appointment, click Recurrence on the Appointment menu, and then change the recurrence pattern.

Using Natural Language Phrases to Enter Appointment Dates and Times

In the steps just completed, dates and times were entered in the Appointment window using standard numeric entries. Outlook's **AutoDate function**, however, provides the capability of specifying appointment dates and times using **natural language phrases**. For example, you can type phrases such as, next Tuesday, two weeks from yesterday, or midnight, and Outlook will calculate the correct date and/or time.

This example schedules working at the registrar's office next Wednesday, September 14, 2005 from noon to 2:45 p.m., and one week from Saturday on September 24, 2005 from 8:00 a.m. to noon. The following steps describe how to enter the date and time for the work schedule using natural language phrases.

Note: If you are stepping through this project on a computer, then you should set your system clock to September 8, 2005 or the steps in the next section will not work properly.

To Enter Appointment Dates and Times Using Natural Language Phrases

1

- **With Tuesday, September 13 displayed in the appointment area, click the New Appointment button on the Standard toolbar.**

2

- **Type** `Work orientation` **in the Subject text box and then press the TAB key.**
- **Type** `Registrar's office` **in the Location text box and then press the TAB key twice.**
- **Type** `next Wednesday` **in the Start time date box for the date.**

The appointment information is entered in the Appointment window. Next Wednesday is entered in the Start time date box (Figure 2-18).

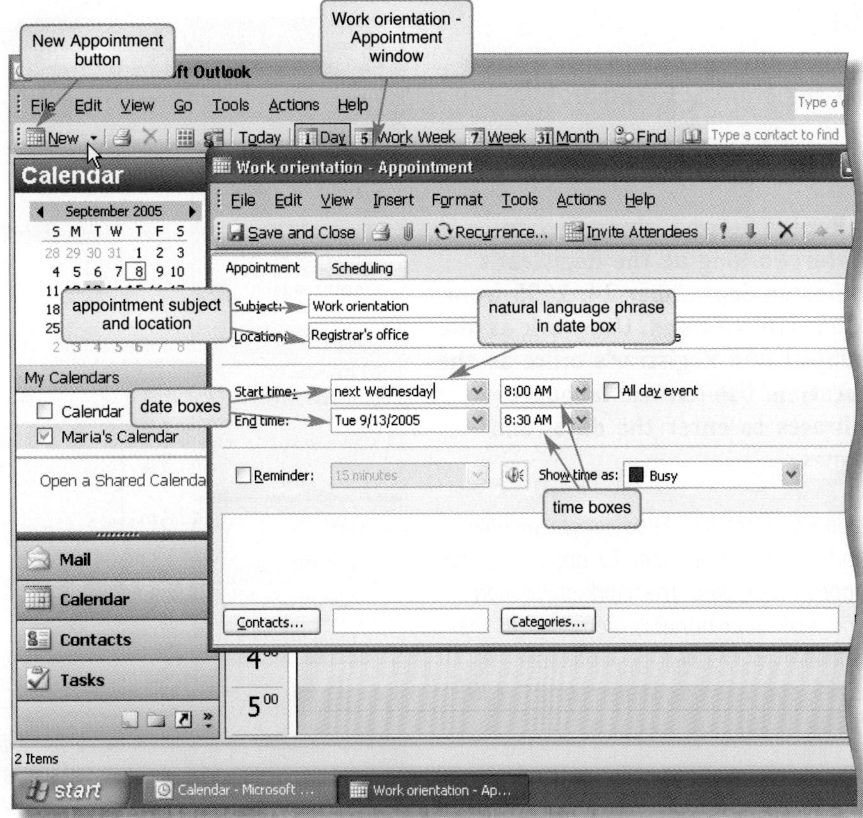

FIGURE 2-18

3

- **Press the TAB key.**
- **Type** noon **in the Start time box.**
- **Press the TAB key twice.**

Outlook automatically converts the phrase, next Wednesday, into the date, Wed 9/14/2005, in both the Start time date and End time date boxes. It also converts the word, noon, into 12:00 PM in the time box (Figure 2-19).

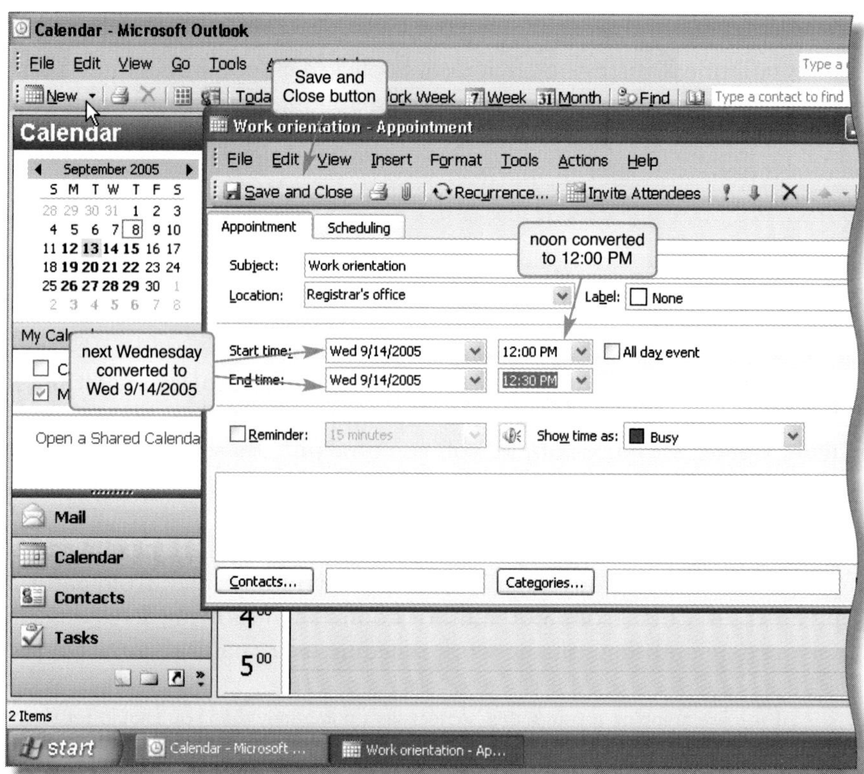

FIGURE 2-19

4

- **Type** two forty five **in the End time time box and then press the ENTER key.**

Outlook automatically converts the words, two forty five, to 2:45 PM and sets the appointment end time for 2:45 PM. Outlook sets appointments for 30 minutes unless you enter a new end time or drag through a longer time slot in the appointment area before clicking the New Appointment button or changing the default setting.

5

- **Click the Save and Close button on the Standard toolbar.**

6

- **Repeat Steps 1 through 5 to enter working at the Registrar's office on September 24, 2005 from 8:00 a.m. to noon. Use work as the subject and Registrar's office as the location. Use natural language phrases to enter the dates and times.**

Outlook closes the Appointment window and Tuesday, September 13 appears in the appointment area. The Work orientation and work appointments are added to the calendar on Wednesday, September 14, 2005, and Saturday, September 24, 2005 (Figure 2-20).

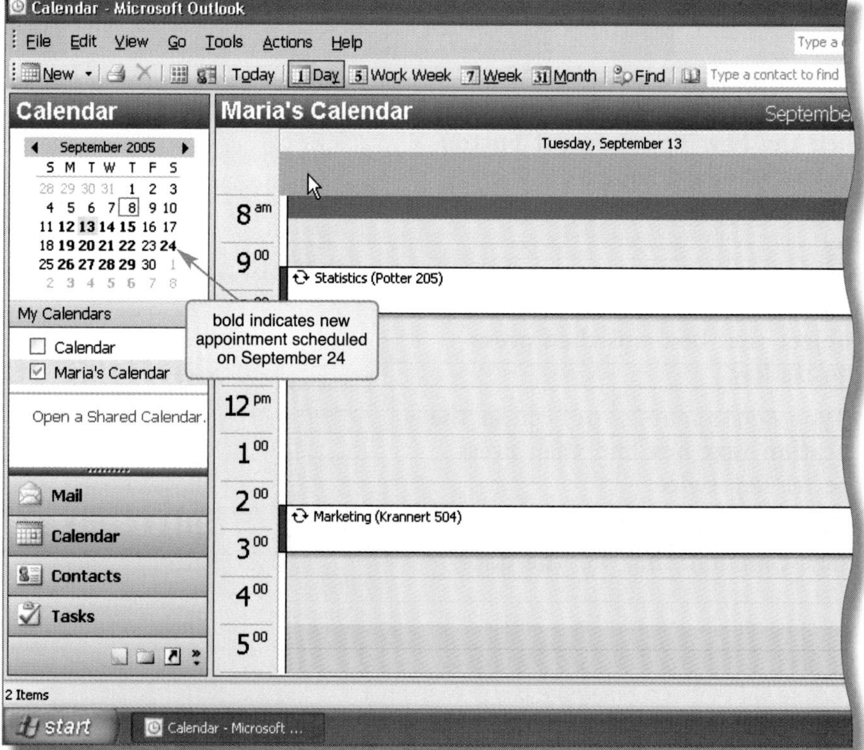

FIGURE 2-20

In addition to these natural language phrases, Outlook can convert abbreviations and ordinal numbers into complete words and dates. For example, you can type Feb instead of February or the first of September instead of 9/1. Outlook's Calendar application also will convert words such as yesterday, tomorrow, and the names of holidays that occur only once each year, such as Valentine's Day. Table 2-3 lists various AutoDate options.

Table 2-3 AutoDate Options

CATEGORY	EXAMPLES
Dates Spelled Out	• July twenty-third, March 29th, first of December • this Fri, next Sat, two days from now • three weeks ago, next week • one month from today
Times Spelled Out	• noon, midnight • nine o'clock a.m., five twenty • 7 pm
Descriptions of Times and Dates	• now • yesterday, today, tomorrow • next, last • ago, before, after, ending, following • for, from, that, this, till, through, until
Holidays	• Cinco de Mayo • Christmas, Christmas Day, Christmas Eve • Halloween • Independence Day • New Year's Day, New Year's Eve • St. Patrick's Day • Valentine's Day • Veterans Day

Entering the Remaining One-Time Appointments

Table 2-4 contains the current week's practice schedule along with the game schedule for the first two months of the upcoming season. The following steps show how to enter the remaining one-time appointments.

Table 2-4 Additional One-Time Appointments

DATE	TIME	APPOINTMENT	LOCATION
9/12/2005	5:00 p.m. - 7:00 p.m.	Practice	Girl's Gym
9/13/2005	4:00 p.m. - 6:00 p.m.	Practice	Girl's Gym
9/14/2005	5:00 p.m. - 7:00 p.m.	Practice	Girl's Gym
9/15/2005	4:00 p.m. - 6:00 p.m.	Practice	Girl's Gym
9/17/2005	1:00 p.m. - 3:00 p.m.	Practice	Girl's Gym
10/7/2005	7:30 p.m. - 9:30 p.m.	Game	City Arena
10/8/2005	5:00 p.m. - 7:00 p.m.	Game	City Arena
10/15/2005	6:30 p.m. - 8:30 p.m.	Game	Willowcreek
10/21/2005	6:30 p.m. - 8:30 p.m.	Game	Woodland Arena
10/29/2005	7:00 p.m. - 9:00 p.m.	Game	Woodland Arena
11/10/2005	5:30 p.m. - 7:30 p.m.	Game	Saint Stevens
11/19/2005	3:00 p.m. - 5:00 p.m.	Game	Tri-State

To Enter the Remaining One-Time Appointments

1. **With the Calendar window active, click September 12, 2005 in the Date Navigator.**
2. **Click the New Appointment button on the Standard toolbar.**
3. **Type** `Practice` **in the Subject text box, and then press the TAB key.**
4. **Type** `Girl's Gym` **in the Location text box, and then press the TAB key three times.**
5. **Type** `5 pm` **in the Start time time box, press the TAB key two times, and then type** `7 pm` **in the End time time box.**
6. **Click the Save and Close button on the Standard toolbar.**
7. **Using techniques demonstrated in this project, repeat Steps 1 through 6 to enter the remaining one-time appointments in Table 2-4.**

Editing Appointments

Because schedules often need to be rearranged, Outlook provides several ways of editing appointments. Edit the subject and location of an appointment by clicking the appointment and editing the information directly in the appointment area, or double-click the appointment and make corrections using the Appointment window. All occurrences in a series of recurring appointments can be changed, or a single occurrence can be altered.

Deleting Appointments

Appointments sometimes are canceled and must be deleted from the schedule. For example, the schedule created thus far in this project contains an appointment on Thursday, November 24, 2005. Because November 24 is Thanksgiving Day, however, no classes will meet and the scheduled appointment needs to be deleted. The following steps describe how to delete an appointment from the calendar.

To Delete an Appointment

1

- **Click the scroll arrows in the Date Navigator to display November 2005.**
- **Click 24 in the November 2005 calendar.**
- **Click the first appointment to be deleted, Statistics, and then point to the Delete button on the Standard toolbar.**

Thursday, November 24 appears at the top of the appointment area (Figure 2-21). The blue top and bottom borders indicate the Statistics appointment is selected.

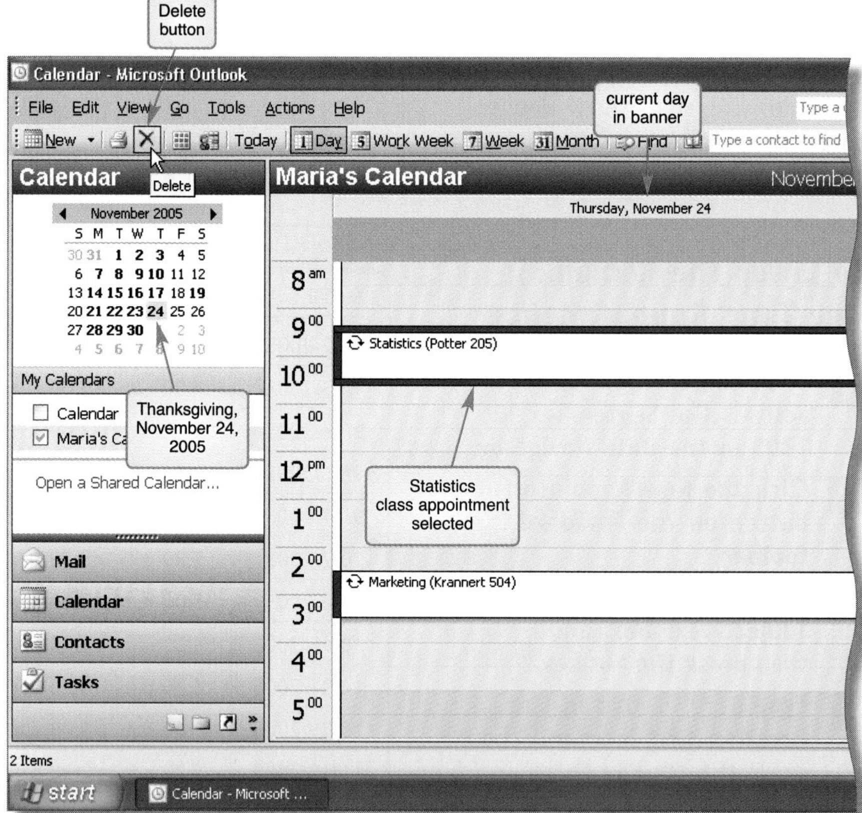

FIGURE 2-21

• **Click the Delete button.**

Because the appointment selected is a recurring appointment, Outlook displays a Confirm Delete dialog box providing the option of deleting all occurrences of the recurring appointment or just this one (Figure 2-22). The Delete this occurrence option button is selected by default.

• **Click the OK button.**

The Statistics appointment is deleted from Thursday, November 24, 2005. All other occurrences of the appointment remain in the schedule.

4

• **Repeat Steps 1 through 3 to delete the Marketing appointment from Thursday, November 24, 2005.**

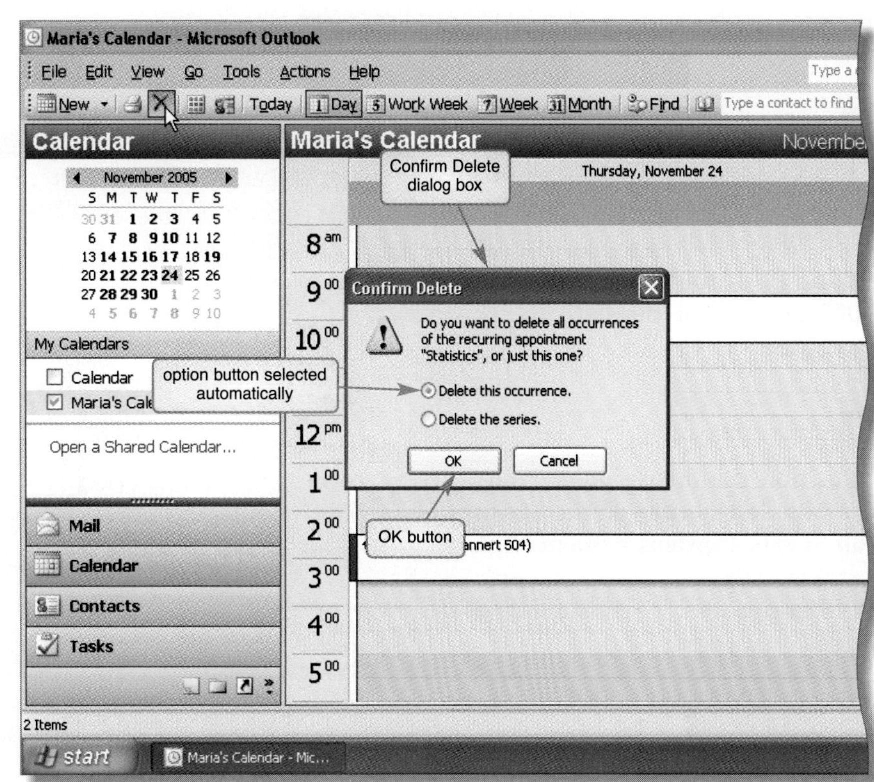

FIGURE 2-22

> ***Other Ways***
>
> 1. Right-click appointment to be deleted, click Delete on shortcut menu
> 2. Click blue border of appointment, press Delete

Appointments also can be deleted using the DELETE key. First, select the entire appointment by clicking the blue left border and then press the DELETE key. If the entire appointment is not selected, pressing the DELETE key (or the BACKSPACE key) will not delete the entry; it will delete only individual characters of the appointment subject. Even if all the characters are deleted, the time slot remains active and any symbols remain in place.

Moving Appointments to a New Time

Outlook also provides several ways to move appointments. Suppose for instance, that some team captains cannot make if for lunch at noon on Monday, September 12, 2005. The appointment needs to be rescheduled to 1:00 p.m. to 2:00 p.m. Instead of deleting and then retyping the appointment, simply drag it to the new time slot. The steps on the next page describe how to move an appointment to a new time.

> ***More About***
>
> **Editing Appointments**
>
> If you cannot remember the details about a specific appointment, you easily can check it. Click Tools on the menu bar, point to Find, and then click Advanced Find to locate the appointment in question. In the Look for box, click Appointments and Meetings. You then may search for any word or subject.

To Move an Appointment to a New Time

1

- **If necessary, click the scroll arrow in the Date Navigator to display September 2005.**
- **Click 12 in the September 2005 calendar in the Date Navigator.**

2

- **Position the mouse pointer on the blue left border of the Lunch - Fall Sports Captains appointment.**

The mouse pointer changes to a four-headed arrow (Figure 2-23).

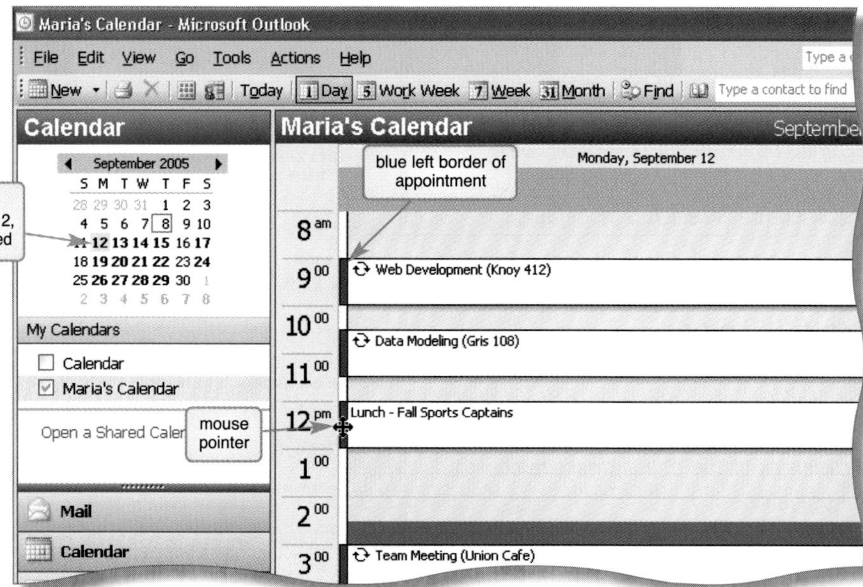

FIGURE 2-23

3

- **Drag the appointment down to the 1:00 pm - 2:00 pm time slot. Do not release the mouse button.**

As the appointment is dragged, the mouse pointer changes to a pointer with a small dotted box below it, called the ***drag icon****.*

4

- **Release the mouse button to drop the appointment in the new time slot.**

The appointment is placed in the 1:00 pm - 2:00 pm time slot (Figure 2-24). Outlook automatically allows adequate time for the moved appointment, in this case, one hour.

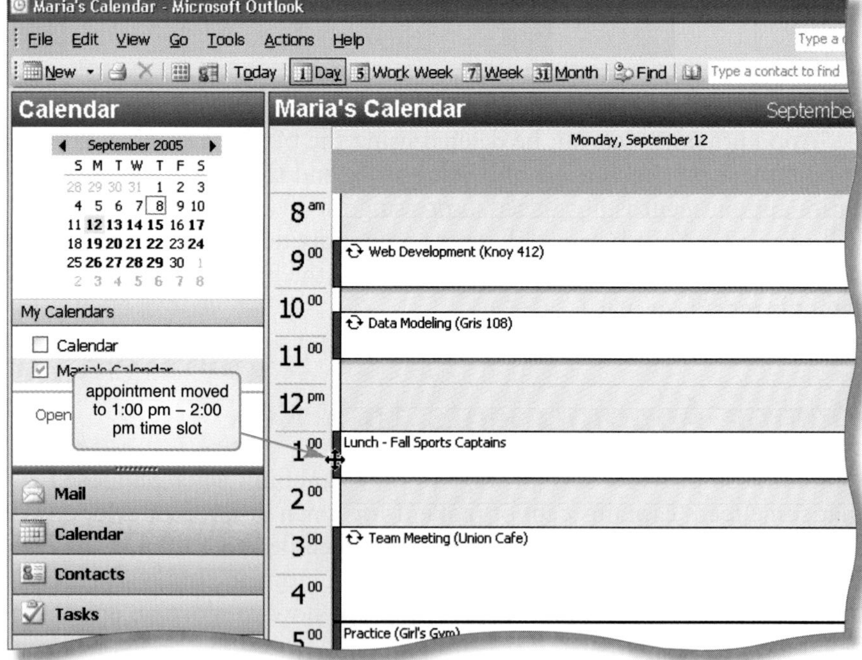

FIGURE 2-24

Other Ways

1. Double-click appointment, edit date in Start date date box in Appointment window
2. Click left border of appointment, press CTRL+X, click new date in Date Navigator, click new time slot in appointment

An appointment can be moved to a new time using the Appointment window, as well. Simply type a different time in the Start time or End time time boxes or click one of the time box arrows and select a different time in the list. Natural language phrases also can be used in the time box, which Outlook converts to the appropriate times.

Moving Appointments to a New Date

If an appointment is being moved to a new date but remaining in the same time slot, simply drag the appointment to the new date in the Date Navigator. Using this method allows the movement of an appointment quickly and easily to a new date, as shown in the following steps.

To Move an Appointment to a New Date

1

- **Click 12 in the September 2005 calendar in the Date Navigator.**
- **Click the blue left border of the Lunch - Fall Sports Captains appointment to select it.**
- **Drag the appointment from the appointment area to the 16 in the September 2005 calendar. Do not release the mouse button.**

Dragging outside the appointment area causes the mouse pointer to change to the drag icon. A black border appears around the 16 in the September 2005 calendar in the Date Navigator (Figure 2-25).

FIGURE 2-25

2

- **Release the mouse button.**

The appointment moves from Monday, September 12, 2005 to Friday, September 16, 2005 (Figure 2-26).

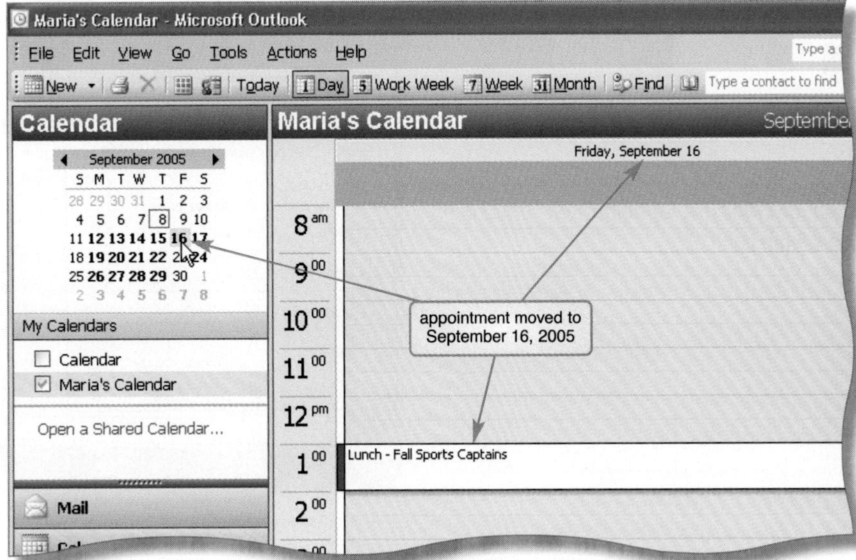

FIGURE 2-26

Outlook provides several ways to move appointments to new dates in addition to the drag and drop method used in the previous steps. Appointments can be moved to new dates by making changes in the Appointment window or by using the cut and paste method.

More About

Moving Appointments

To send an appointment to a coworker or classmate, right-click the appointment and click Forward on the shortcut menu.

Moving an Appointment to a New Month

If an appointment is being moved to a month not displayed in the Date Navigator, it cannot be dragged to a date not displayed. In this case, cutting and pasting the appointment to a new date can be used.

When you cut an item in most other Office 2003 applications, the item that you cut disappears from the screen. In Outlook, the item remains on the screen until it is pasted to another location.

The registrar's office has decided to reschedule the Saturday time slot to a date in October. The new work date is moved from Saturday, September 24, 2005 to Saturday, October 1, 2005. The following steps describe how to move an appointment to a new month using the cut and paste method.

To Move an Appointment to a New Month

1

- **Click 24 in the September 2005 calendar in the Date Navigator.**
- **Click the blue left border of the work appointment to select it.**
- **Click Edit on the menu bar.**

The Edit menu appears (Figure 2-27).

2

- **Click Cut on the Edit menu.**

The appointment is copied to the Office Clipboard, and the appointment remains on the screen.

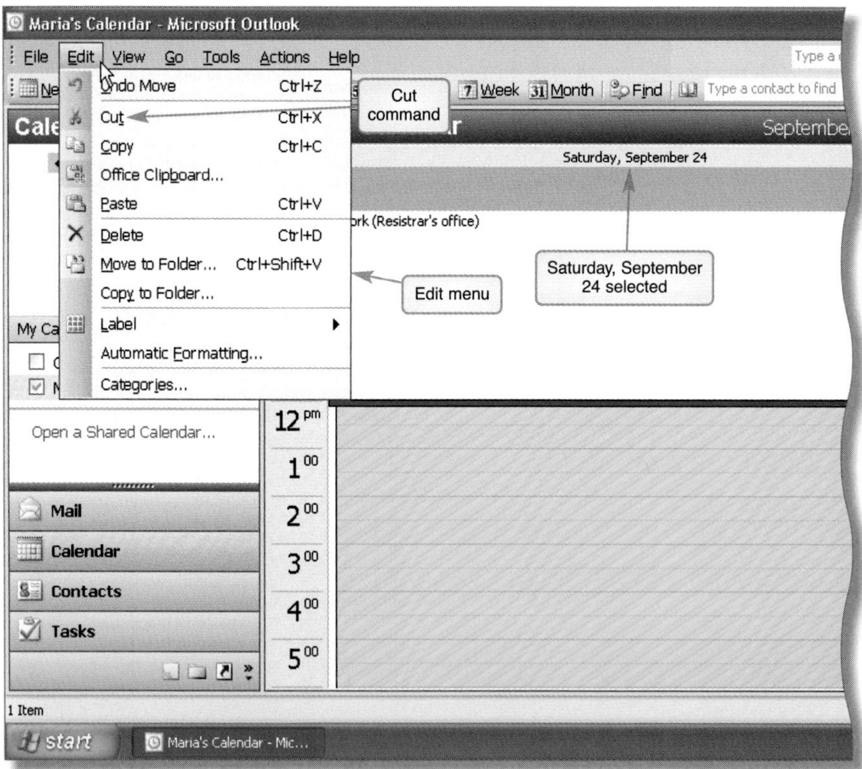

FIGURE 2-27

3

- **Click the right scroll arrow in the Date Navigator to display October 2005.**
- **Click 1 in the October 2005 calendar in the Date Navigator.**

Outlook displays Saturday, October 1 in the appointment area. The 8:00 am - 12:00 pm time slot is automatically selected (Figure 2-28) because this was the size of the time slot cut from September 24, 2005.

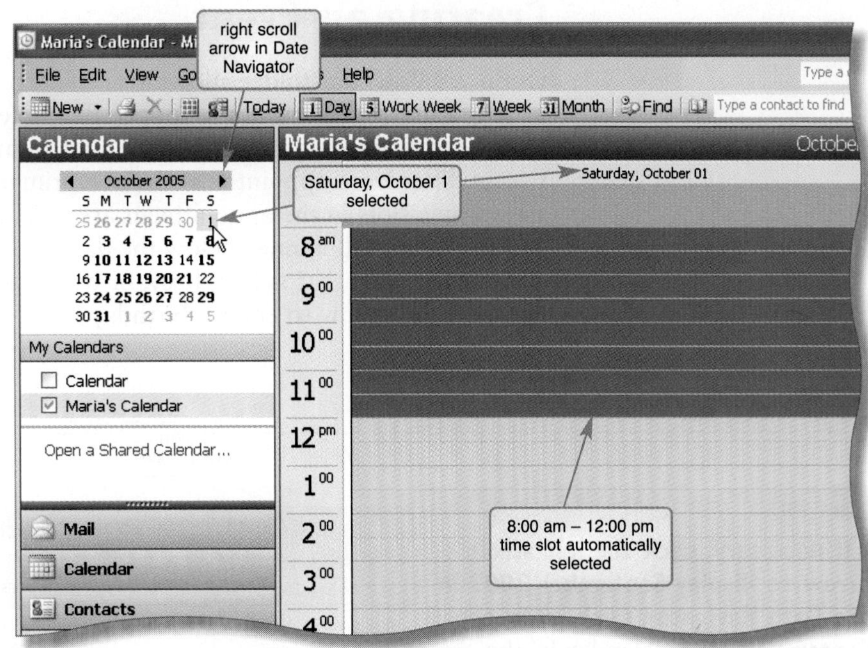

FIGURE 2-28

4

- **Click Edit on the menu bar and then click Paste.**

The appointment now appears in the 8:00 am - 12:00 pm time slot in the appointment area for Saturday, October 1 (Figure 2-29).

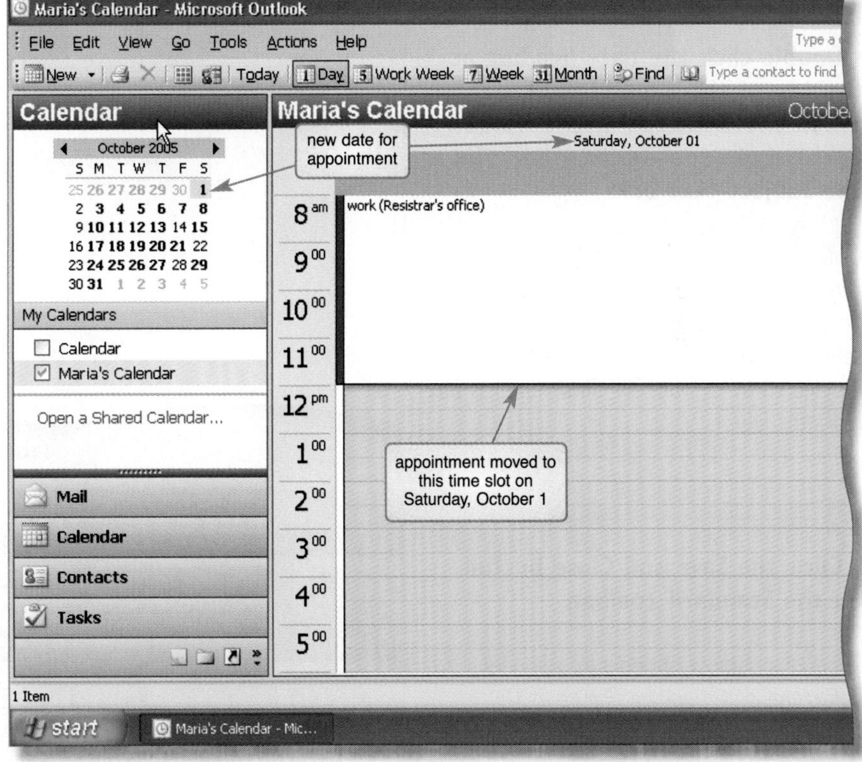

FIGURE 2-29

Either the drag-and-drop method or the cut and paste method is available for appointment movement. Regardless of the method, the results are the same. An appointment can be moved to a different time on the same day, to a different day, or an entirely different month.

Creating an Event

Outlook's Calendar folder allows you to keep track of important events. **Events** are activities that last 24 hours or longer. Examples of events include birthdays, conferences, weddings, vacations, holidays, and so on and can be one-time or recurring. Events differ from appointments in one primary way — they do not display in individual time slots in the appointment area. When an event is scheduled, its description appears in a small **banner** below the date heading. The details of the event can be indicated as time that is free, busy, or out of the office during the event. The following steps show how to enter a birthday as an event.

To Create an Event

1

• **If necessary, click the left scroll arrow to display September 2005 in the Date Navigator. Click 30 in the September 2005 calendar in the Date Navigator.**

2

• **Double-click the date heading at the top of the appointment area. When the Untitled - Event window opens, type** `Jose's birthday` **in the Subject text box.**

Outlook displays the Untitled - Event window (Figure 2-30). Double-clicking the date heading allows all day events to be scheduled. The All day event check box thus is selected by default. The Show time as box indicates Free.

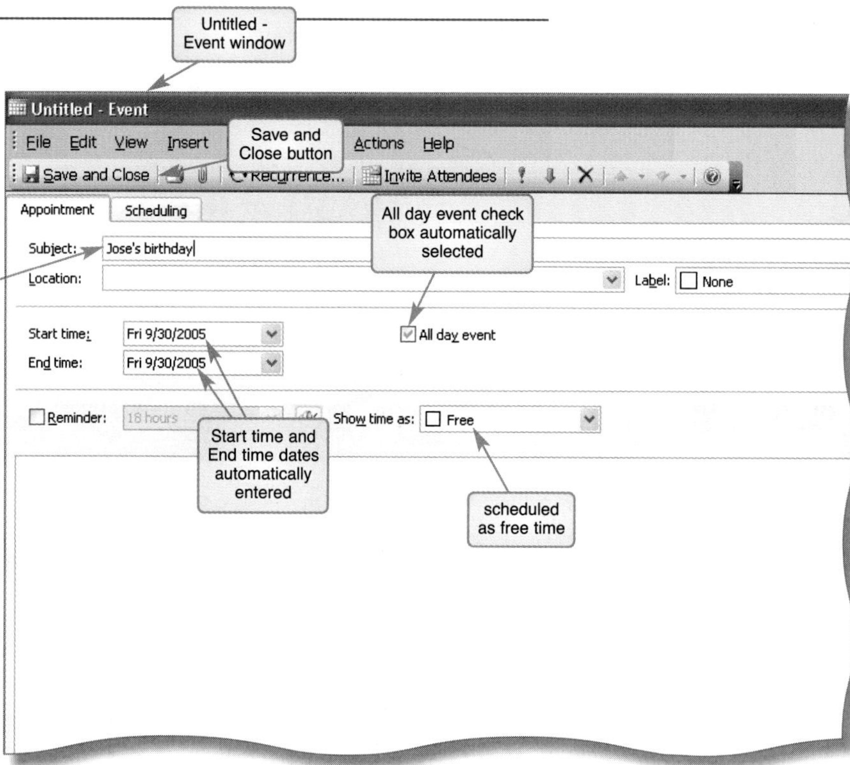

FIGURE 2-30

3

• **Click the Save and Close button on the Standard toolbar.**

The Event subject appears in a banner below the date heading (Figure 2-31).

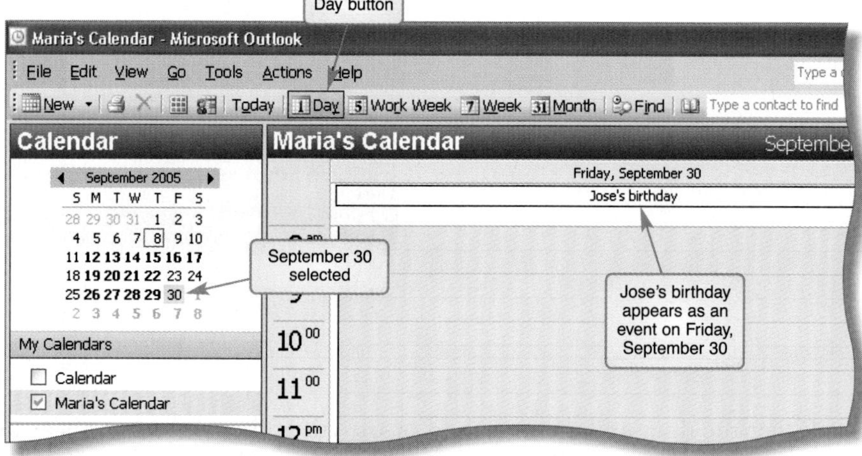

FIGURE 2-31

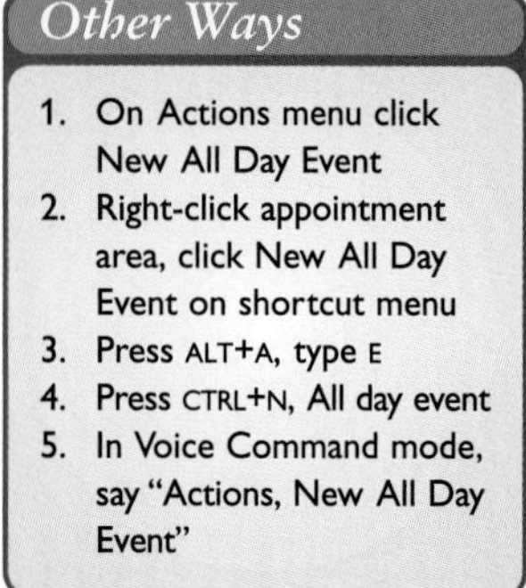

Other Ways

1. On Actions menu click New All Day Event
2. Right-click appointment area, click New All Day Event on shortcut menu
3. Press ALT+A, type E
4. Press CTRL+N, All day event
5. In Voice Command mode, say "Actions, New All Day Event"

You could use the same steps to enter holidays as annual events; however, Outlook has a folder of typical holidays for various countries that can be added to your calendar automatically. To do this, click Options on the Tools menu. Click Calendar Options, and then click Add Holidays in the Calendar Option sheet.

More About

Locations

As appointments or events are entered with specific locations, the locations automatically are accumulated in a list. To access this list, open the appointment and click the Location box arrow. Frequently used locations can be selected from this list, thereby saving typing time.

Displaying the Calendar in Week and Month Views

The default view type of the Calendar folder is the Day/Week/Month view. While in **Day/Week/Month view**, Outlook can display calendars in four different views: Day, Work Week, Week, and Month. So far in this project, you have used only the Day view, which is indicated by the selected Day button on the Standard toolbar (Figure 2-31).

Now that the schedule is complete, it also can be displayed in Week or Month view. Although the screen appears quite differently in Week and Month views, the same tasks can be performed as in Day view: appointments and events can be added, edited, or deleted, and reminders can be set or removed.

Work Week View

The **Work Week view** shows five work days (Monday through Friday) in columnar style. The advantage of displaying a calendar in this view is the ability to see how many appointments are scheduled for the Monday through Friday time frame, eliminating the weekends. The following step changes the Calendar view to Work Week view.

Other Ways

1. On View menu click Work Week
2. Press ALT+V, type R
3. In Voice Command mode, say "Work Week"

To Change to Work Week View

1

- **Click Tuesday, September 13 in the Date Navigator.**
- **Click the Work Week button on the Standard toolbar.**
- **If necessary, scroll up in the appointment area until the 8:00 am time slot appears.**

The calendar is displayed in Work Week view (Figure 2-32). Notice that September 12 through September 16 all are highlighted in the Date Navigator.

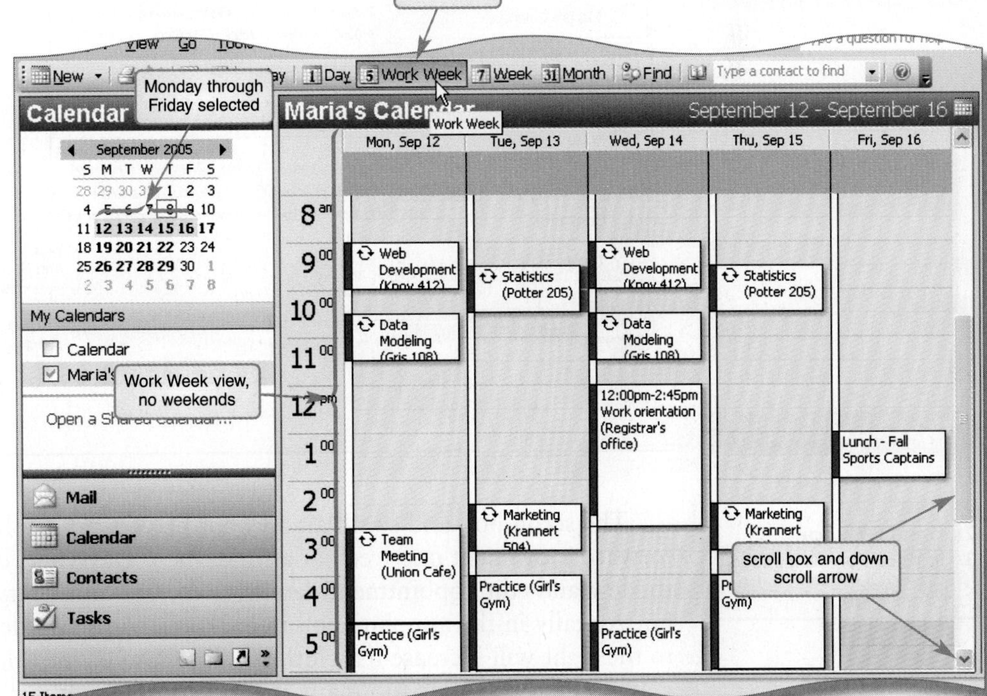

FIGURE 2-32

More About

Holidays and Observances

For more information about holidays and observances, visit the Outlook 2003 More About Web page (scsite.com/out2003/more) and click Calendar.

The scroll box and scroll arrows on the vertical scroll bar allow backward or forward movement within the selected week. An individual appointment can be selected by double-clicking it. As shown in Figure 2-32 on the previous page, some appointments may be too long to display horizontally in the appointment area. Dragging the border of the appointment area to the right will increase its width so that more of the appointment text appears.

Week View

The advantage of displaying a calendar in **Week view** is to see how many appointments are scheduled for any given week. In Week view, the seven days of the selected week display in the appointment area. The five days of the work week (Monday through Friday) display in individual frames, while Saturday and Sunday share a single frame. The following step describes how to display the calendar in Week view.

To Change to Week View

1

- **Click the Week button on the Standard toolbar.**

The calendar appears in Week view (Figure 2-33).

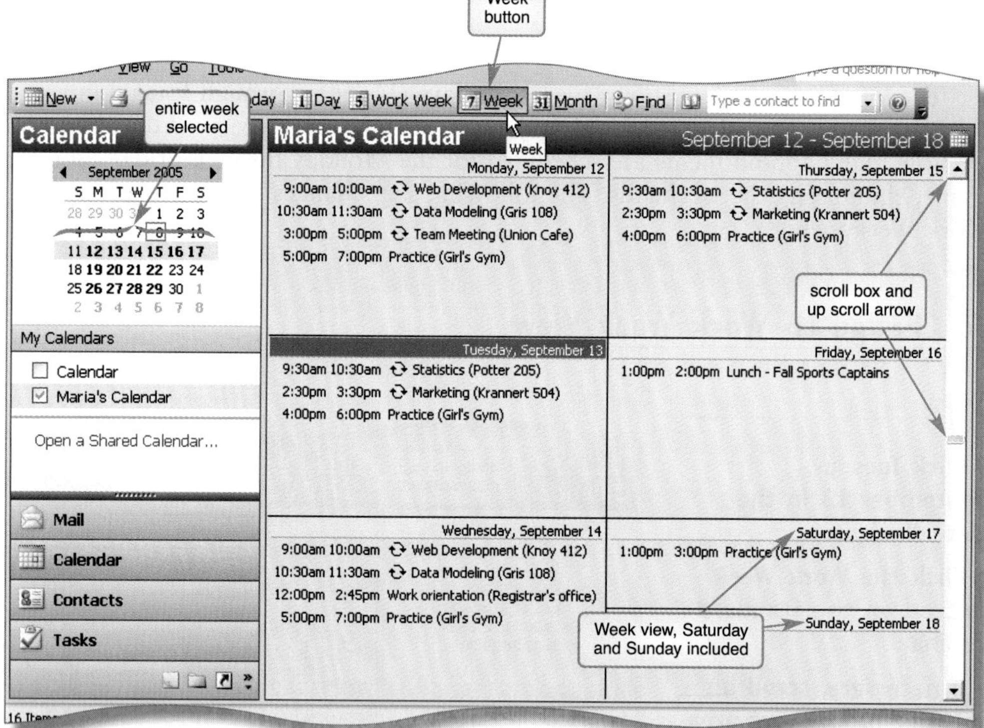

FIGURE 2-33

Other Ways

1. On View menu click Week
2. Press ALT+V, type W
3. In Voice Command mode, say "Week"

The scroll box and scroll arrows on the vertical scroll bar allow backward or forward movement one week at a time. As in Day view, double-click an appointment to view and edit appointment details. Some appointments may be too long to display horizontally in the appointment area. Dragging the border of the appointment area to the right will increase its width so that more of the appointment descriptions display. If a day contains too many items to display vertically, Outlook will display a down arrow in the lower-right corner of the day frame. Clicking the down arrow returns the calendar to Day view so you can view the rest of the appointments for the day.

Month View

The **Month view** resembles a standard monthly calendar page and displays a schedule for an entire month. Appointments are listed in each date frame in the calendar. The following steps illustrate how to display the calendar in Month view.

To Change to Month View

1

- **Click the Month button on the Standard toolbar.**

Outlook displays the calendar in Month view (Figure 2-34).

2

- **Click the Day button to return to Day view.**

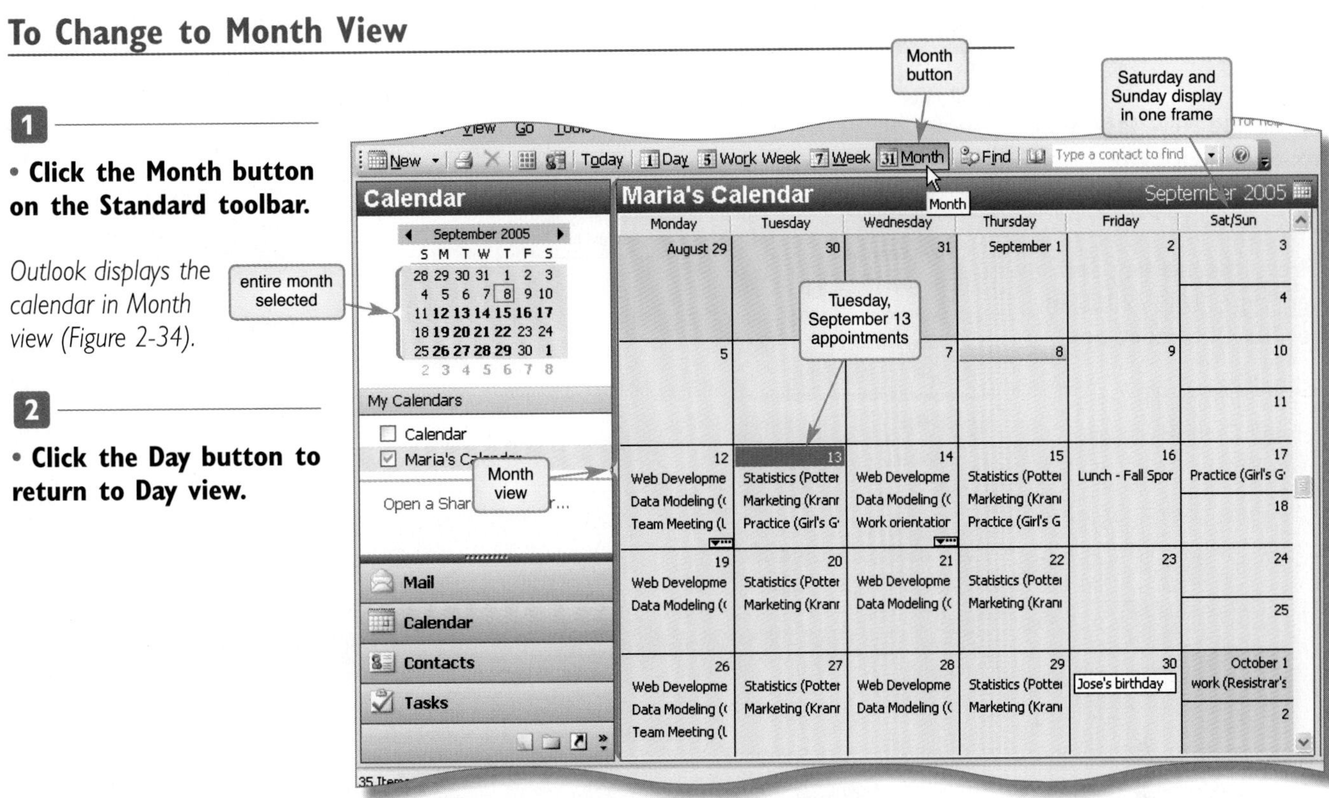

FIGURE 2-34

Use the vertical scroll box and scroll arrows on the vertical scroll bar to move the Month view forward and backward one week at a time. As you drag the scroll box, Outlook displays the first day of the week in a ScreenTip beside the scroll box. As with Day and Week views, you can add, edit, or delete appointments in Month view. Because the appointments are abbreviated considerably in Month view, however, it is easier to switch back to Day view to make changes.

Other Ways

1. On View menu click Month
2. Press ALT+V, type M
3. In Voice Command mode, say "Month"

Using Tasks to Create a Task List

With the daily appointments organized, you can use Tasks to organize the many duties and projects for each day. Tasks allows creation of a **task list** of items that need to be tracked through completion. **Tasks** can be simple to do items, daily reminders, assignments with due dates, or business responsibilities. In this project, Table 2-5 contains tasks that occur once and will be later made into group tasks, assigned, or forwarded. The steps on the next page show how to create a task list.

Table 2-5 Task List

TASK	DUE DATE
Check on Web book	9/14/2005
Get new license	9/30/2005
Pick up fund-raiser T-shirts	9/9/2005
Send out next week's practice schedule	9/11/2005
Set up meeting with Coach	9/11/2005

To Create a Task List

1

- **Click the Tasks button in the Navigation Pane.**

2

- **Click the New Task text box and then type** `Check on Web book` **as the first task.**
- **Press the TAB key and then type** `9/11/2005` **in the Due Date text box.**

Outlook displays the Tasks - Microsoft Outlook window (Figure 2-35).

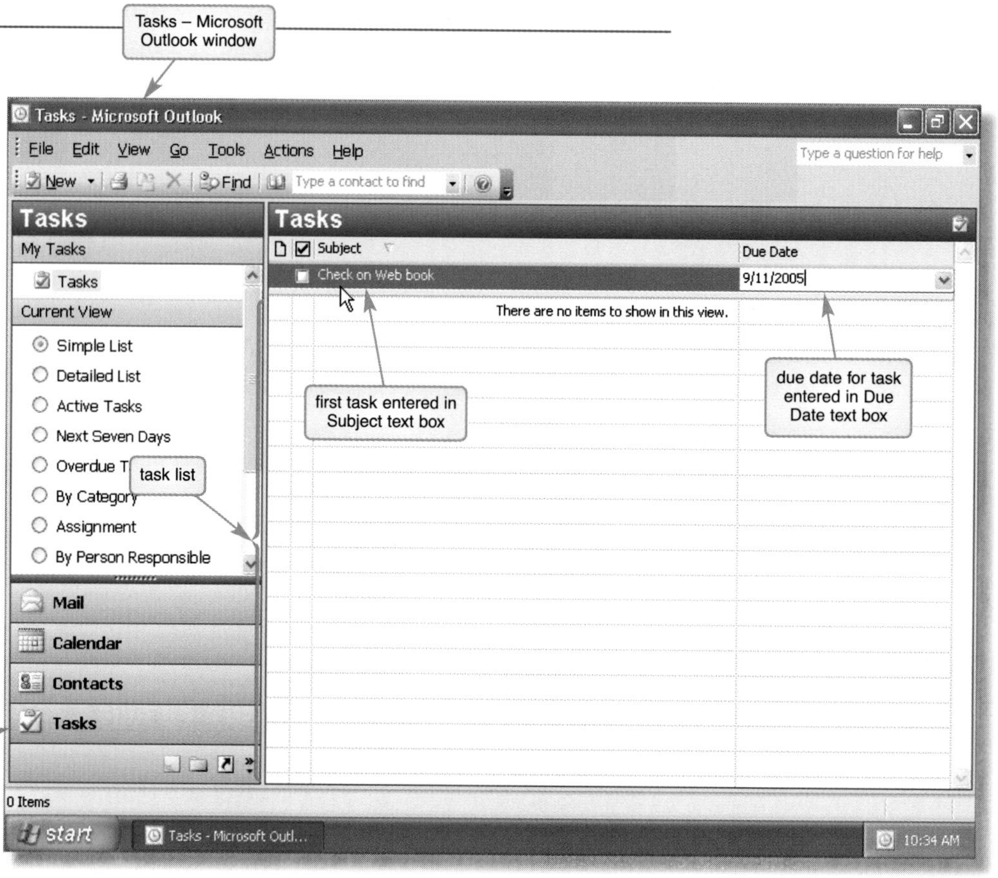

FIGURE 2-35

3

- **Press the ENTER key.**
- **Repeat Steps 1 and 2 to enter the remaining tasks in Table 2-5 on the previous page.**

The task icon appears to the right of each task. As each task is entered, the previous task moves down the list.

4

- **Click outside the task list.**

The Task window is displayed with all the tasks entered in the task list as shown in Figure 2-36.

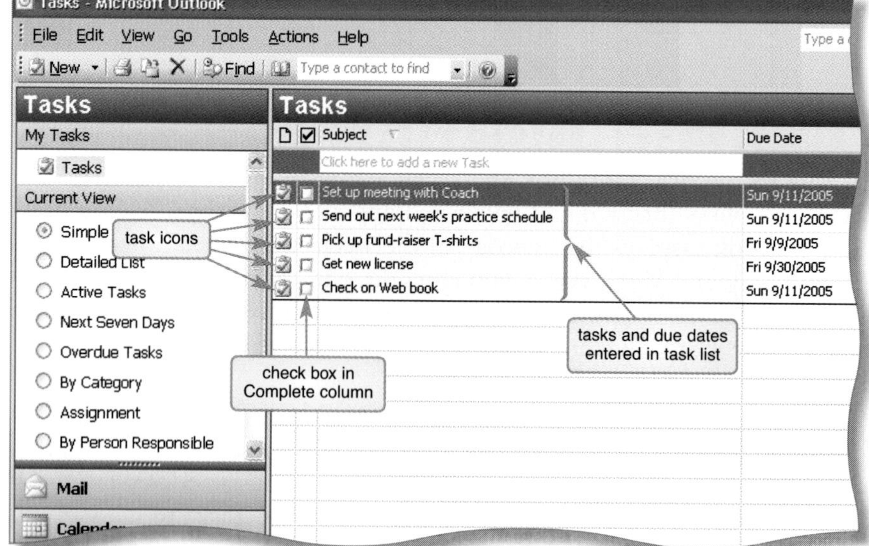

FIGURE 2-36

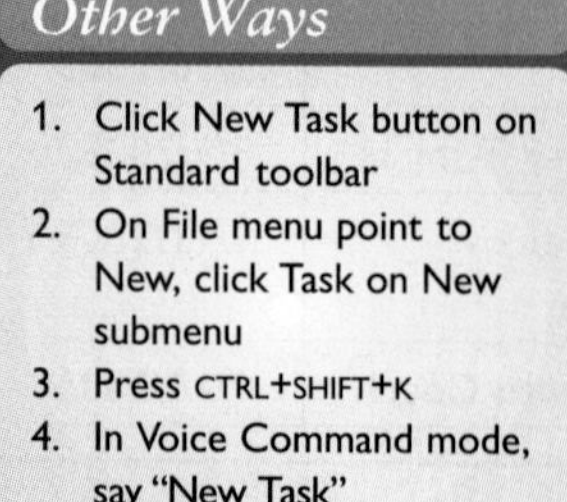

Other Ways

1. Click New Task button on Standard toolbar
2. On File menu point to New, click Task on New submenu
3. Press CTRL+SHIFT+K
4. In Voice Command mode, say "New Task"

To add details to tasks, such as start dates, status, and priority, double-click a task in the task list to open a Task window.

When a task is complete, click the check box in the Sort by: Complete column to the left of the task's subject. A check mark called a **Completed icon** will appear in the Complete column and a line will be placed through the task indicating it is complete. To delete a task entirely from the task list, select the task and then click the Delete button on Standard toolbar.

If you have many tasks on various days, or if you delegate tasks, it is advisable to create a personal Tasks folder for your task list. This also is true if you are working in a lab situation or on a shared computer.

More About

Tasks

You can add a task to your Outlook task list from within Word. This is helpful if you have a Word document that must be reviewed, and you want a reminder to do so.

Exporting, Deleting, and Importing Subfolders

The calendar is now ready to be saved on a floppy disk. Saving your work on a floppy disk allows you to take your schedule to another computer.

With many application software packages, a single file, such as a letter or spreadsheet, can be saved directly on a floppy disk. With Outlook, however, each appointment, task, or contact is a file in itself. Thus, rather than saving numerous individual files, Outlook uses an **Import and Export Wizard** to guide you through the process of saving an entire subfolder. Transferring a subfolder to a floppy disk is called **exporting**. Moving a subfolder back to a computer is called **importing**. Subfolders can be imported and exported from any Outlook application. Outlook then saves the subfolder on a floppy disk, adding the extension **.pst**.

More About

Editing Tasks

You can drag a task from the Task list to the Calendar button in the Navigation Pane, thereby making the task an appointment.

Exporting Subfolders

The following steps show how to export Maria's Calendar subfolder to a floppy disk.

To Export a Subfolder to a Floppy Disk

1

- **Insert a floppy disk in drive A.**
- **Click File on the menu bar and then click Import and Export.**

2

- **When the Import and Export Wizard dialog box is displayed, click Export to a file in the Choose an action to perform list.**

Outlook displays the Import and Export Wizard dialog box (Figure 2-37). Using this Wizard allows you to perform one of six import and export options available with Outlook.

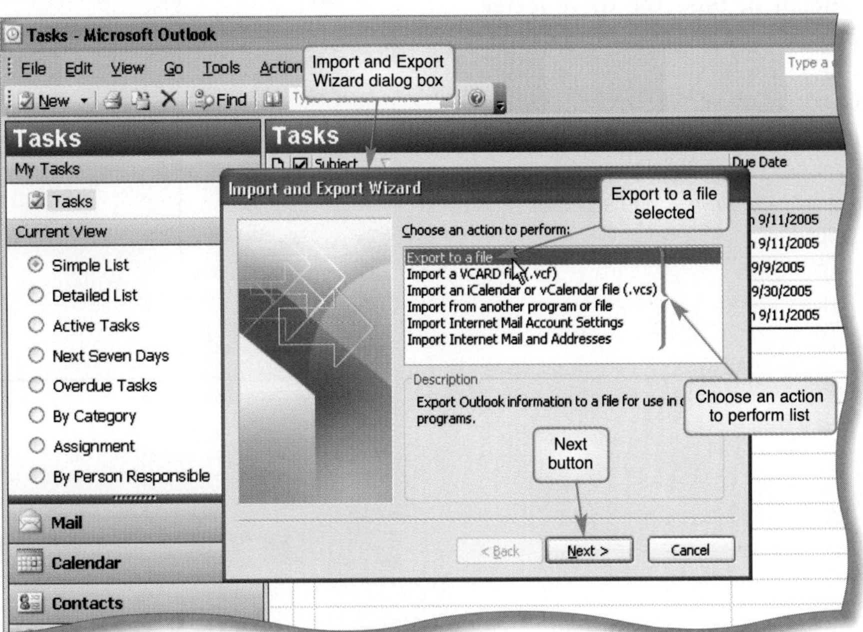

FIGURE 2-37

3

- **Click the Next button.**
- **In the Export to a File dialog box, click Personal Folder File (.pst) and then click the Next button.**
- **If necessary, click the plus sign (+) to the left of the Calendar icon in the Select a folder to export from list.**
- **Click Maria's Calendar.**

Outlook displays the Export Personal Folders dialog box (Figure 2-38). The Maria's Calendar subfolder is selected as the folder from which to export.

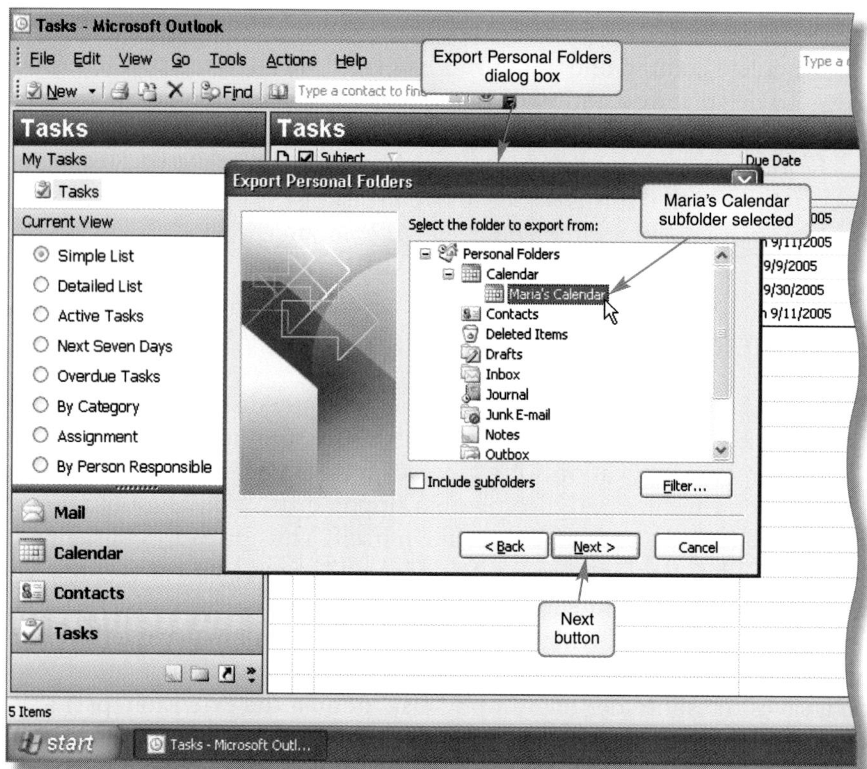

FIGURE 2-38

4

- **Click the Next button.**
- **Type** `a:\Maria's Calendar.pst` **in the Save exported file as text box. (If your floppy drive is not labeled A, type the drive letter accordingly.)**

Outlook displays the Export Personal Folders dialog box with the new subfolder name (Figure 2-39). The subfolder will be exported to drive A and saved as Maria's Calendar.

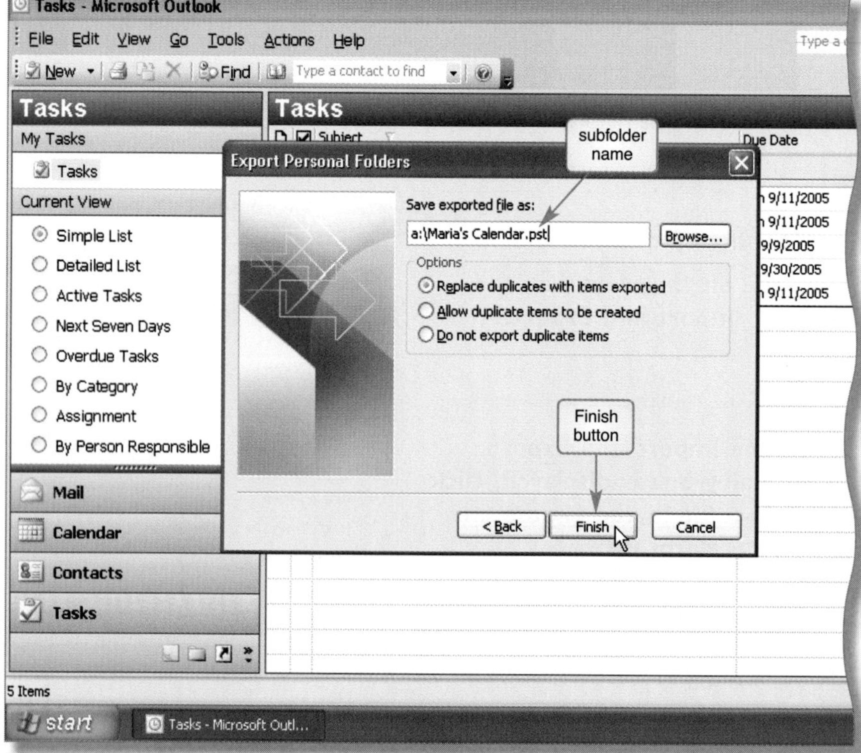

FIGURE 2-39

5

• **Click the Finish button.**

Outlook displays the Create Microsoft Personal Folders dialog box (Figure 2-40) as the folder is exported. The subfolder is saved on the floppy disk.

6

• **Click the OK button.**

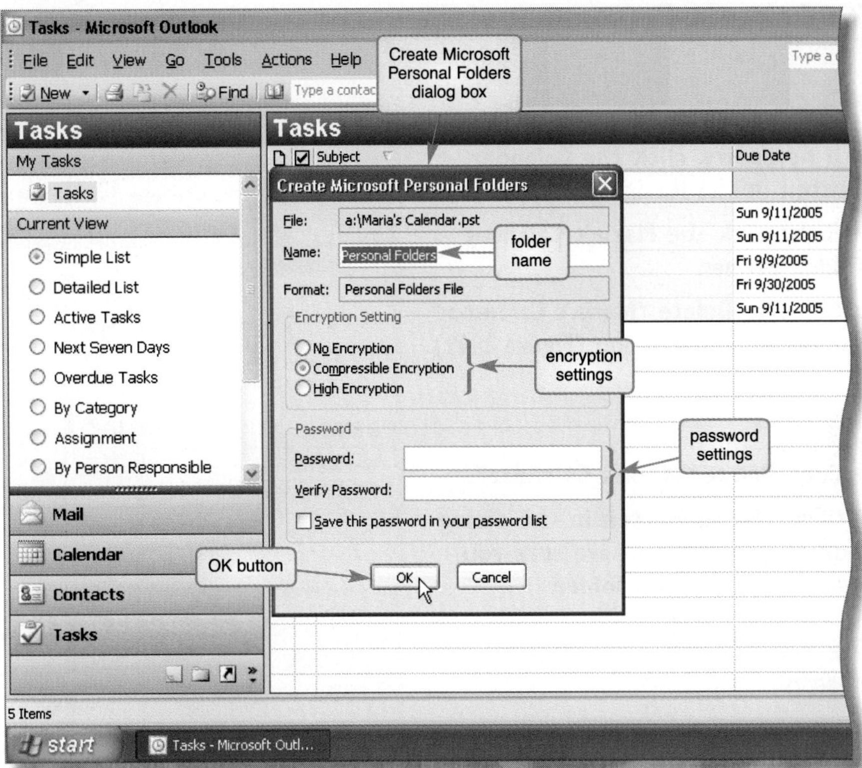

FIGURE 2-40

To export a folder, you do not have to have that particular Outlook application open. For example, if you were to export a Contact subfolder, the Contact window would not have to be open. Instead, when the Export Personal Folders dialog box is displayed, click the plus sign (+) next to the Contacts icon and then click the appropriate subfolder.

Subfolders can be exported to a personal folder file, which can be viewed only in Outlook or saved as another file type, such as a text file, which then can be imported into other programs. Importing and exporting folders allows Outlook items to be shared easily. For example, a company Calendar subfolder may be imported to publicize a company meeting, a group Contacts subfolder may be imported to make information about the people who work on a project available to every one, or a team Tasks subfolder may be imported to help everyone track work on a project.

More About

Saving

All appointments, events, meetings, and tasks are saved as separate files on your disk. As such, they can be edited, moved, copied, or deleted. These items can be saved as a group using the Import and Export Wizard on the File menu.

Deleting Subfolders

The Maria's Calendar subfolder now has been exported onto a floppy disk. A copy of it is still present on the hard disk of your computer, however, and appears in Outlook's Folder List. To delete a subfolder from the computer entirely, use the Delete command. The steps on the next page illustrate how to delete a personal subfolder.

To Delete a Personal Subfolder

1

- **If necessary, click the Calendar button in the Navigation Pane.**
- **Right-click the Maria's Calendar folder banner.**
- **Point to Delete "Maria's Calendar" on the shortcut menu (Figure 2-41).**

2

- **Click Delete "Maria's Calendar".**
- **Click the Yes button in the dialog box that asks if you are sure you want to delete the folder.**

The Maria's Calendar folder no longer appears.

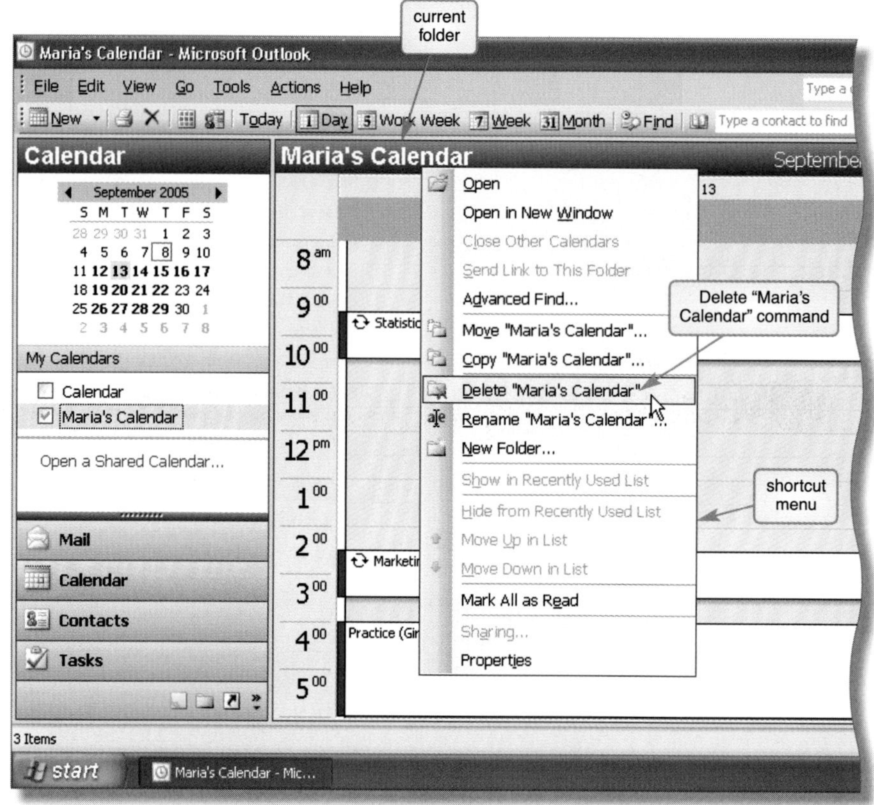

FIGURE 2-41

Other Ways

1. On File menu point to Folders, click Delete on Folders submenu
2. Press ALT+F, press F, press D
3. In Voice Command mode, say "File, Folders, Delete"

Outlook sends the deleted subfolder to a special folder in the Folder List called **Deleted Items**. If you accidentally delete a subfolder without first exporting it to a floppy disk, you still can open the subfolder by double-clicking it in the Deleted Items folder in the Folder List. To display the subfolder, you may need to click the plus sign (+) next to the Deleted Items folder.

Once a subfolder is no longer needed, right-click the subfolder in the Deleted Items folder in the Folder List and then click Delete on the shortcut menu. Deleting a subfolder from the Deleted Items folder permanently removes it from the hard disk. You can delete only subfolders; Outlook's main component folders, such as Calendar, Mail, and Contacts, cannot be deleted.

Thus far, a schedule and a task list have been created and the schedule has been exported to a personal subfolder on a floppy disk. Once a subfolder is created and exported, often it will need to be imported, or retrieved, from the disk. For example, you might want to revise office hours, add exam dates to the schedule, or use the schedule on a different computer. To do so, the schedule must be imported from the subfolder on the floppy disk.

Importing Subfolders

Earlier, the Calendar subfolder containing appointment and event files was exported to a floppy disk. The following steps illustrate how to import the same Calendar subfolder from the floppy disk. To import a subfolder, Outlook must be running. Any type of subfolder then can be imported from any application within Outlook. The following steps import a subfolder.

To Import a Subfolder

1

- **Insert the floppy disk containing the calendar in drive A.**
- **If necessary, click the Calendar button in the Navigation Pane.**

2

- **Click File on the menu bar and then click Import and Export.**
- **When the Import and Export Wizard dialog box is displayed, click Import from another program or file and then click the Next button.**
- **When the Import a File dialog box is displayed, click Personal Folder File (.pst) and then click the Next button.**

3

- **In the Import Personal Folders dialog box, type** `a:\Maria's Calendar.pst` **in the File to Import text box or click the Browse button to access the floppy drive and select the Maria's Calendar subfolder.**

The drive, subfolder name, and extension for the subfolder display in the File to import text box (Figure 2-42).

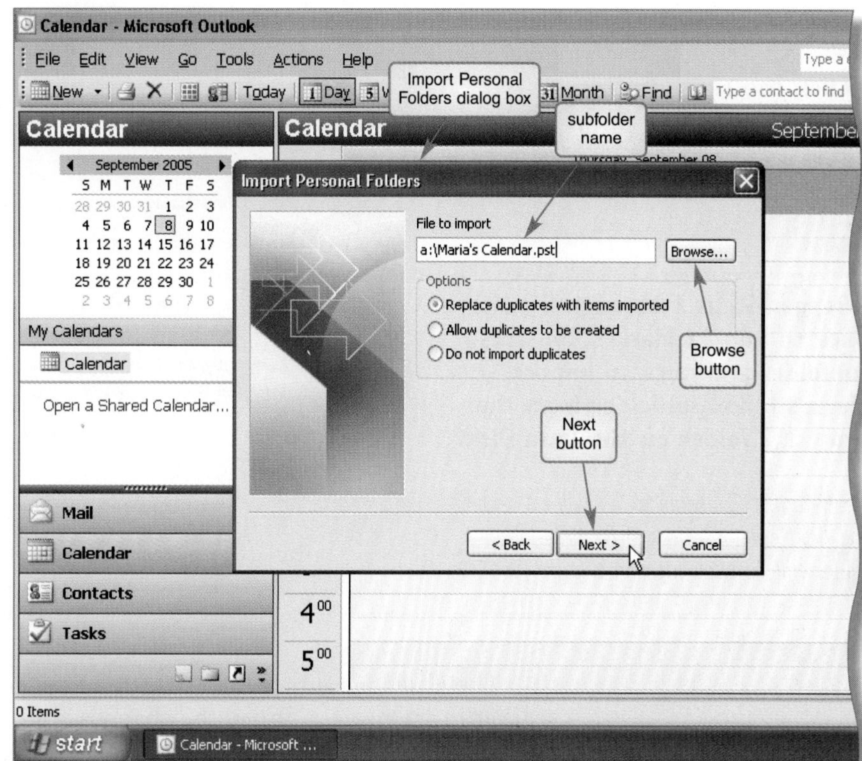

FIGURE 2-42

4

• **Click the Next button.**

• **When the Import Personal Folders dialog box is displayed, click Calendar in the Select the folder to import from list.**

In the Import Personal folders dialog box, you can choose the Outlook folder to import from (Figure 2-43).

5

• **Click the Finish button.**

The subfolder is imported into Outlook as a subfolder of Calendar.

6

• **Repeat Steps 1 through 5 twice, once to import Maria's Contacts subfolder and once to import Maria's Inbox subfolder from the Project 2 folder on the Data Disk.**

The Maria's Contacts folder will be used in the next section and the Maria's Inbox folder will be used later in this project.

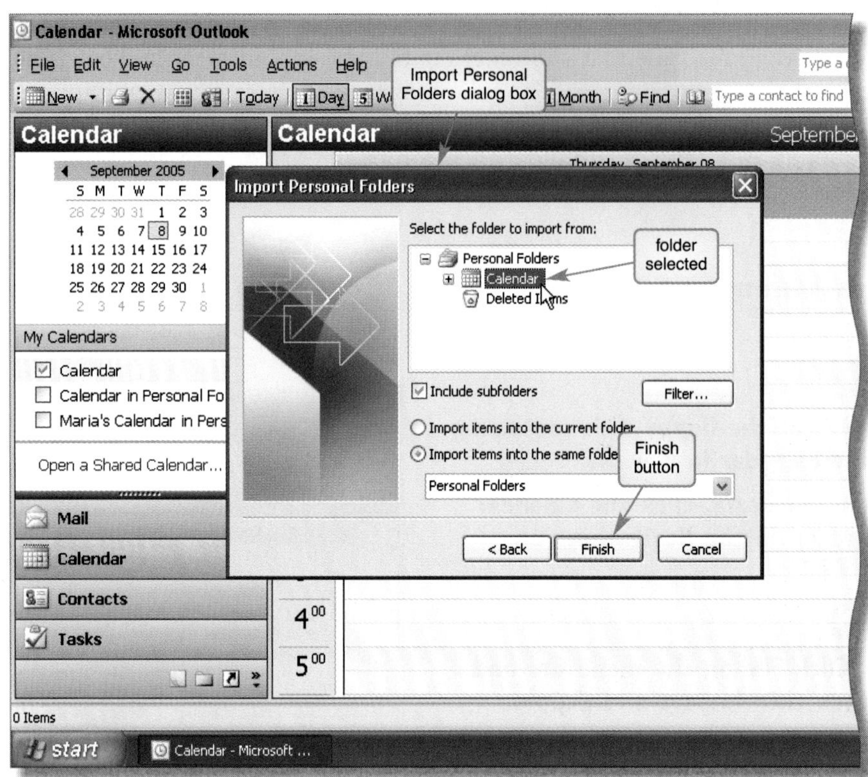

FIGURE 2-43

The Calendar subfolder now can be opened, edited, and printed as described earlier in the project. When the changes are complete, the subfolder again can be exported and deleted from the hard disk. In addition to Outlook subfolders, Outlook's Import and Export Wizard allows the import of a Personal Address Book with contact names, addresses and telephone numbers, or existing information to be brought in from other programs, such as Microsoft Mail or Schedule +.

> *More About*
>
> **Importing**
>
> Other contact information can be imported through the Import and Export Wizard on the File menu. This wizard allows you to copy information that was created and saved in other applications to Outlook.

Meeting and Task Management Using Outlook

If you are a person in charge of an organization or group, you are likely to encounter times when you will have to schedule meetings and delegate, or assign, tasks to other members of the group. Using your contact list, Outlook allows you easily to perform these functions. The following sections illustrate how to assign tasks and schedule meetings with individuals in the Maria's Contacts list.

Assigning Tasks

Sometimes, a person's personal schedule becomes so busy that it is necessary to assign certain tasks to other individuals. Using the task list, Outlook allows you to assign any task to any individual in your contact list. Using the task list previously created in this project and the imported Maria's Contacts contact list, the following steps show how to assign a task to an individual in the Maria's Contacts contact list.

To Assign a Task to Another Person

1

- **Click the Contacts button in the Navigation pane and then click Maria's Contacts in the My Contacts list.**
- **Click the Tasks button in the Navigation Pane.**
- **Double-click the Pick up fund-raiser T-shirts task.**
- **When the Pick up fund-raiser T-shirts - Task window is displayed, double-click the title bar to maximize the window.**

Outlook displays the Pick up fund-raiser T-shirts - Task window (Figure 2-44).

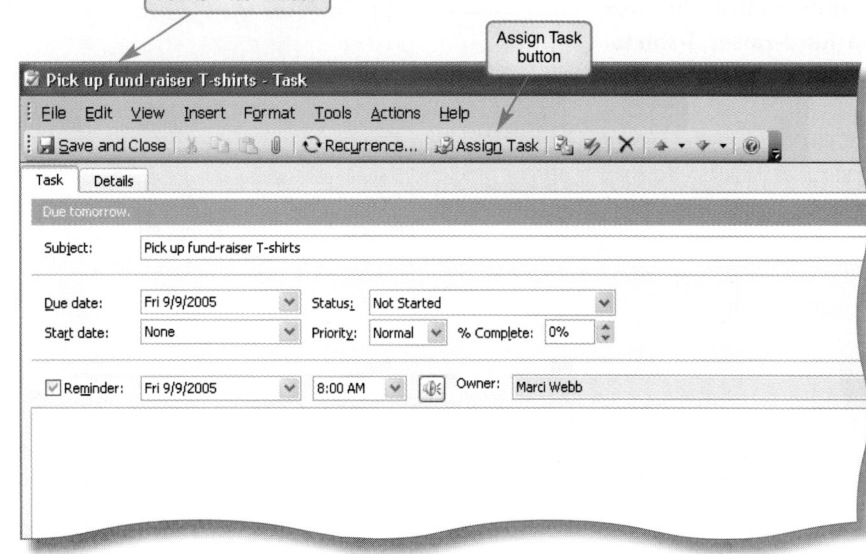

FIGURE 2-44

2

- **Click the Assign Task button on the Standard toolbar.**
- **Type** `Patti Sabol` **in the To text box.**

The Pick up fund-raiser T-shirts - Task window changes into a window similar to an e-mail message window. Patti Sabol is entered as the recipient for this task (Figure 2-45).

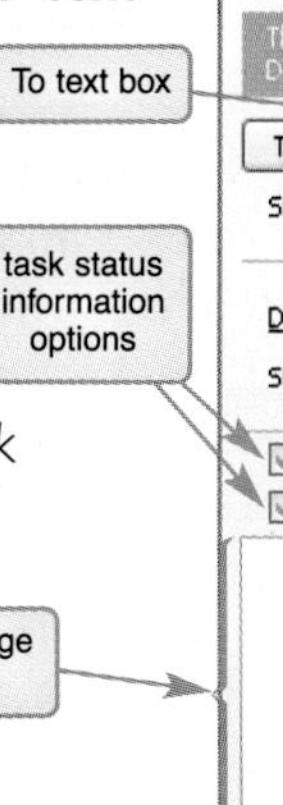

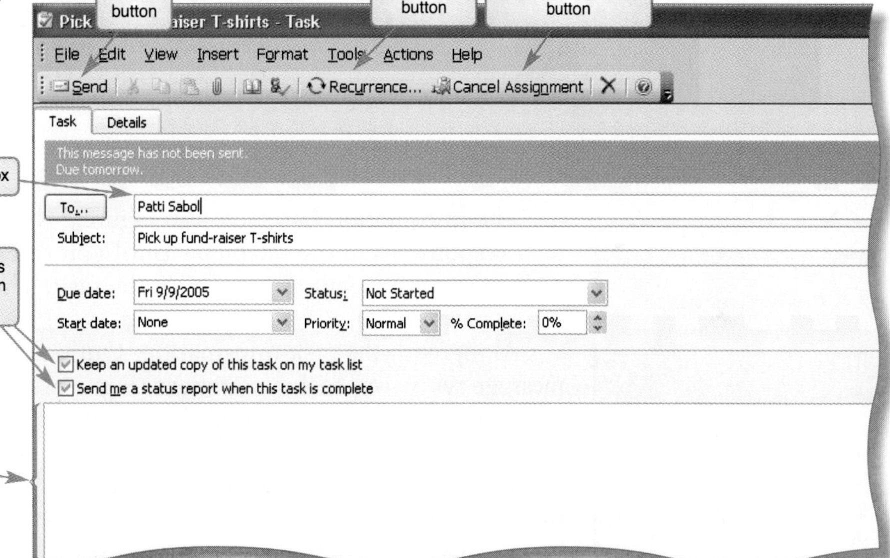

FIGURE 2-45

3

- **Click the Send button on the Standard toolbar.**
- **If necessary, click the OK button when the Microsoft Office Outlook dialog box appears.**

Outlook closes the Pick up fund-raiser T-shirts - Task window, stores the task request in the Outbox folder while it e-mails the request, moves the request to the Sent Items folder, and displays the Tasks - Microsoft Outlook window (Figure 2-46).

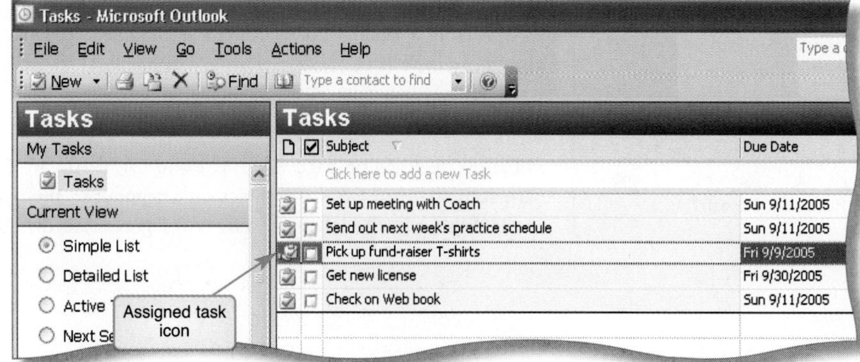

FIGURE 2-46

4

• **Double-click the Pick up fund-raiser T-shirts task.**

Outlook displays the Pick up fund-raiser T-shirts - Task window. Outlook has added an information bar indicating you are waiting for a response from the recipient (Figure 2-47).

5

• **Click the Close button on the Pick up fund-raiser T-shirts - Task window.**

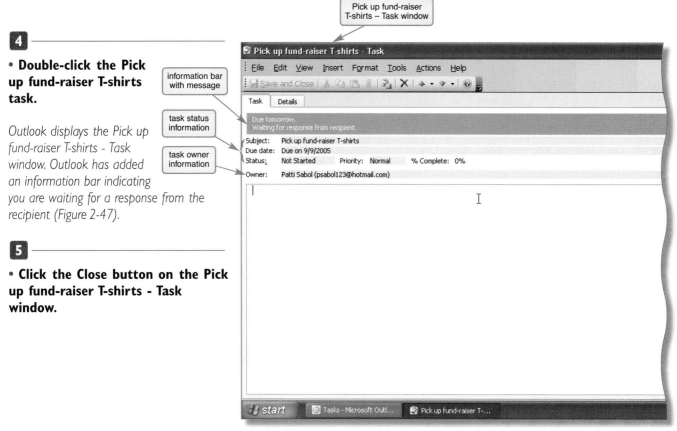

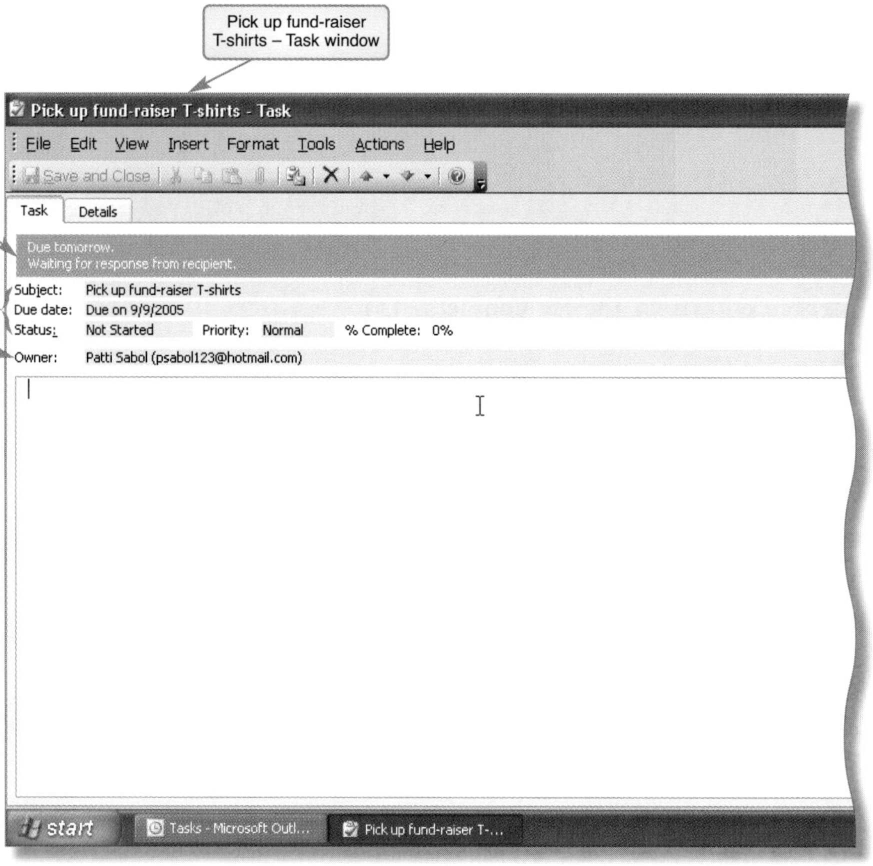

FIGURE 2-47

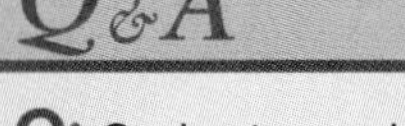

Q: Can I assign a task to more than one person at a time?

A: Yes, Outlook does allow you to assign a task to more than one person at a time; however, in order to have Outlook keep you up to date on the progress of the task, you must divide the work into separate tasks, and then assign each task individually. For example, if you wanted to assign a research project to three researchers, you would have to create three separate tasks named Research: Researcher 1, Research: Researcher 2, and Research: Researcher 3.

The information bar shown in Figure 2-47 indicates that the sender is waiting on a response from the recipient. Until you receive an acceptance from the task recipient, you are still the owner of the task. That means that you are responsible for its progression.

Along with the task information, Outlook provides you with an area to type a message with your task assignment (Figure 2-45 on the previous page). Two check boxes are included: Keep an updated copy of this task on my task list, and Send me a status report when this task is complete (Figure 2-45). These boxes are checked by default. These boxes allow you to see the task progression as the recipient updates the task in their task list.

Accepting a Task Assignment

When a recipient receives a task assignment, it appears in his or her Inbox. Then, the recipient has the option to accept or decline the task. The following steps show how to accept a task assignment.

Note: The steps on page OUT 101 and OUT 102 are for demonstration purposes only. Thus, if you are stepping through this project on a computer, then you must have someone send you a task request so it displays in the Inbox as shown in Figure 2-48 on the next page.

To Accept a Task Assignment

1

- **If necessary, click the Mail button in the Navigation Pane.**
- **Click the plus sign (+) next to the Inbox folder in the All Mail Folders list, and then select the Maria's Inbox folder.**
- **Click the Juanita Rosado Task Request to highlight it.**

Outlook displays the Inbox folder with the task request highlighted (Figure 2-48). All the information for the request appears in the Reading Pane along with the Accept and Decline buttons.

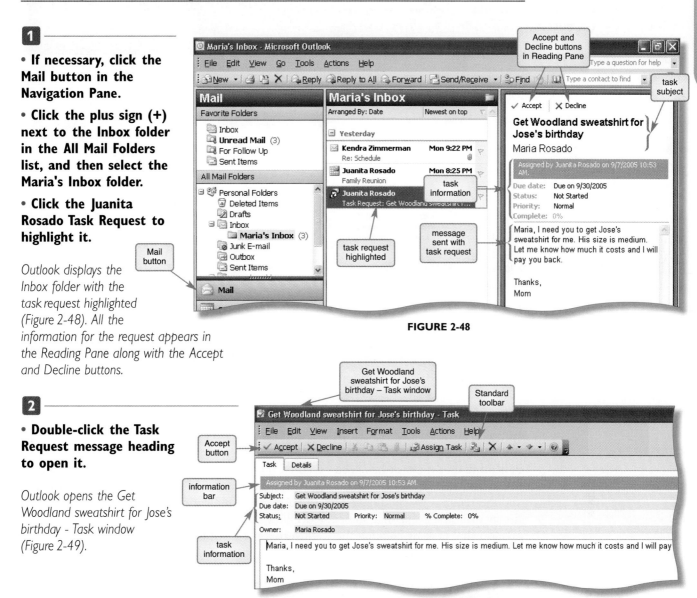

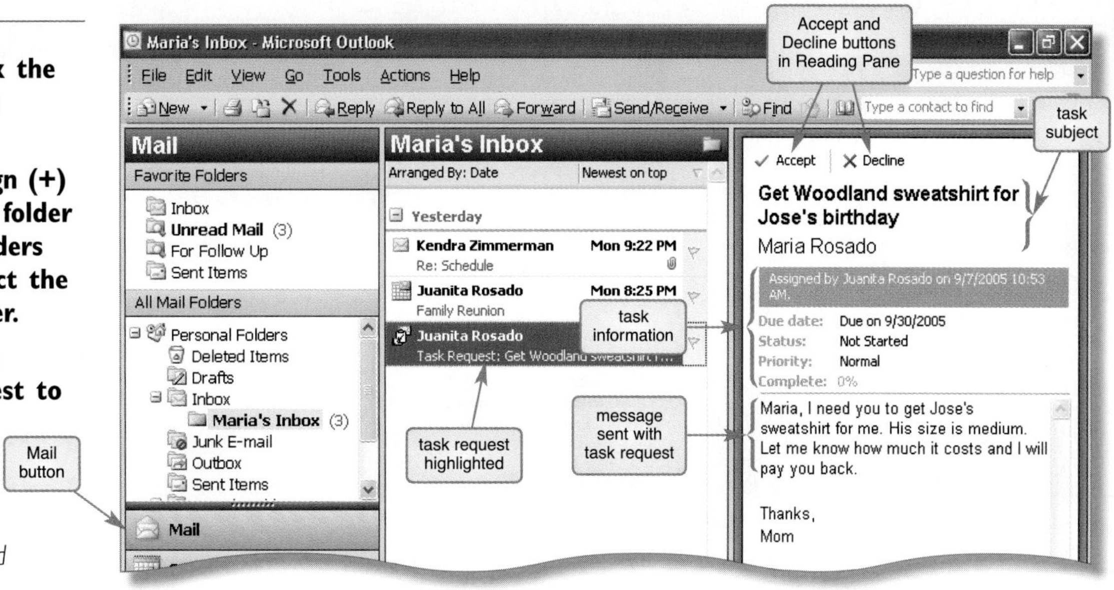

FIGURE 2-48

2

- **Double-click the Task Request message heading to open it.**

Outlook opens the Get Woodland sweatshirt for Jose's birthday - Task window (Figure 2-49).

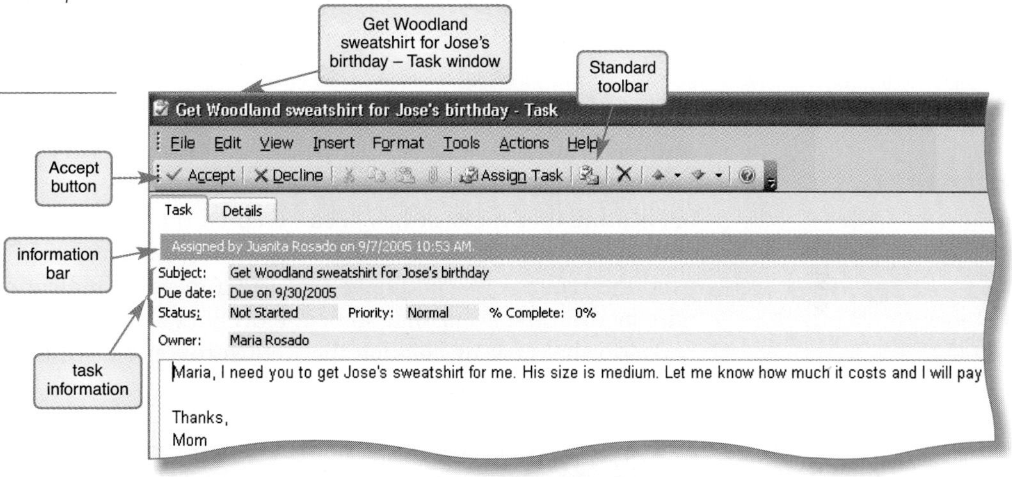

FIGURE 2-49

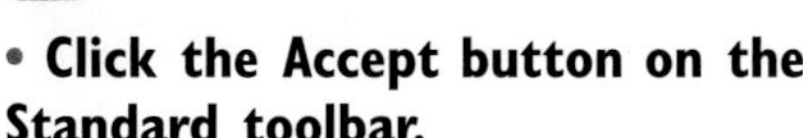

3

- **Click the Accept button on the Standard toolbar.**

Outlook displays the Accepting Task dialog box (Figure 2-50).

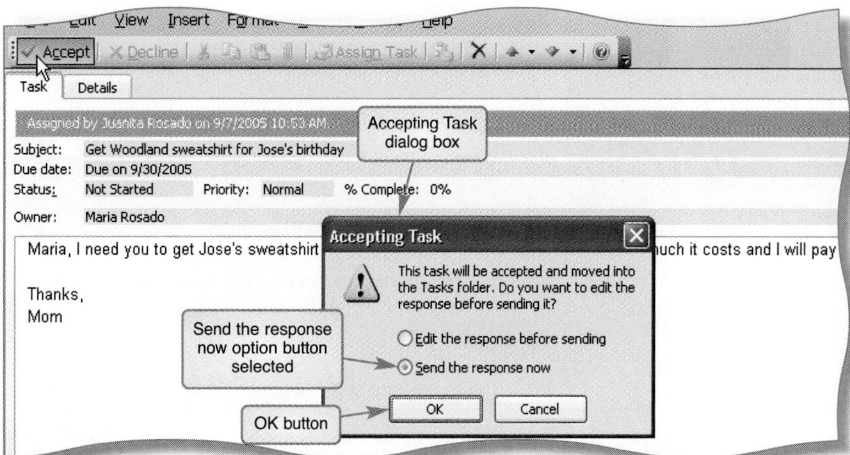

FIGURE 2-50

4

• **Click Send the response now, and then click the OK button.**

Outlook closes the Get Woodland sweatshirt for Jose's birthday - Task window and the Inbox - Microsoft Outlook window appears.

5

• **Click the Task button in the Navigation Pane.**

The Tasks - Microsoft Outlook window is displayed (Figure 2-51). The task request has been removed from the Inbox folder and placed in the Tasks folder as a new task. An Accepted Task icon appears to the left of the Get Woodland sweatshirt for Jose's birthday task.

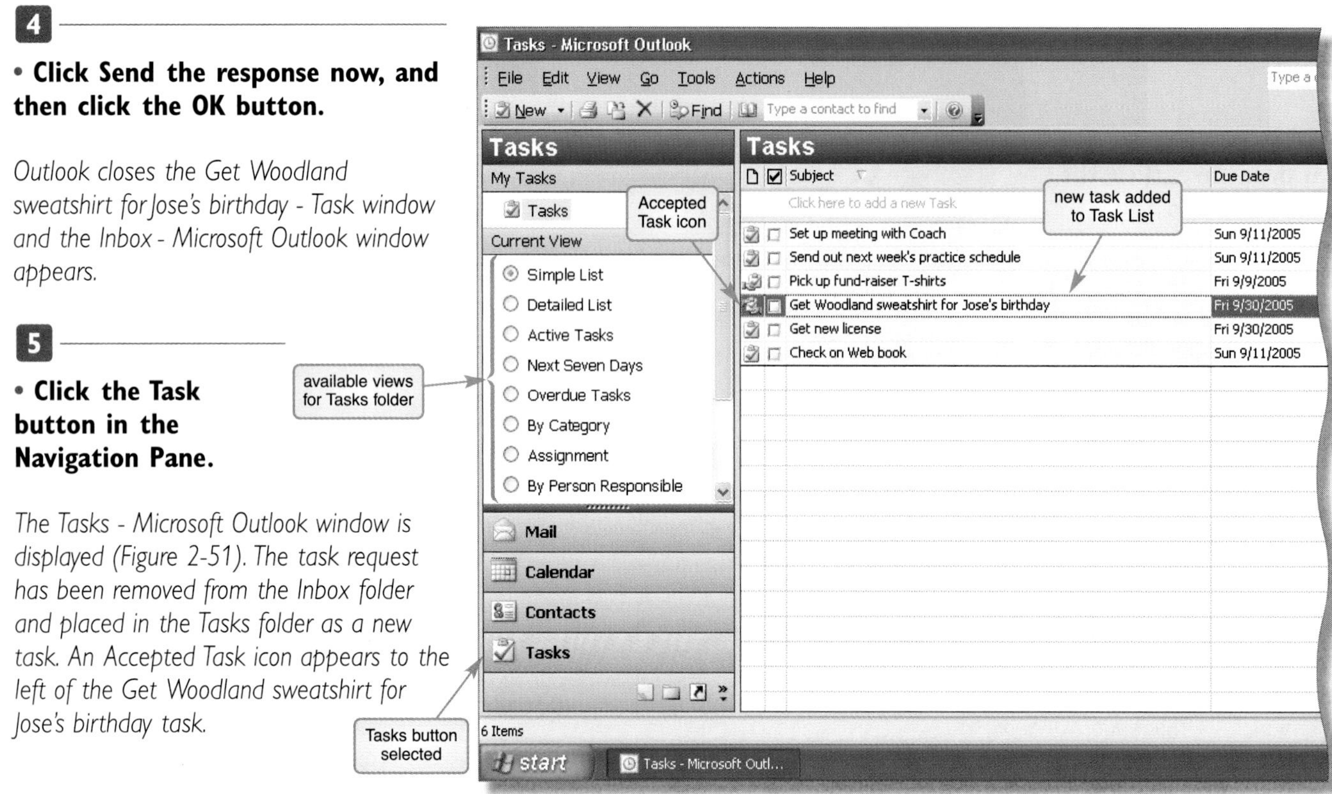

FIGURE 2-51

When a recipient accepts a task request, the requestor receives a message indicating that the task has been accepted (Figure 2-52). If the recipient had chosen to decline the task, the task request would have been moved to the Deleted Items folder, and the requestor would have received a message indicating that the request was declined. In the event that someone declines a task request, the requester can either take on that task by clicking the Return to Task List button, or attempt to assign the task to someone else.

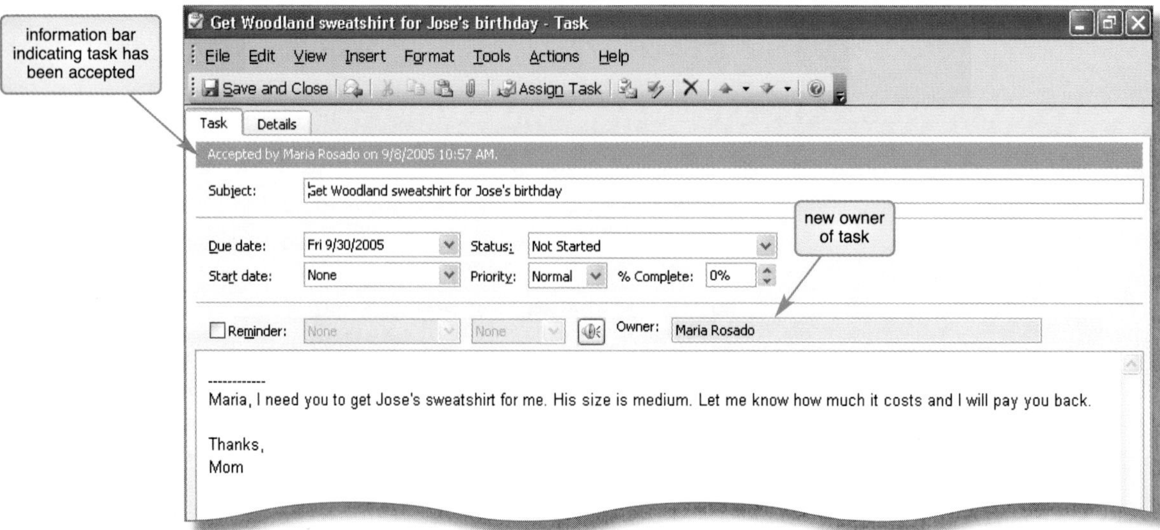

FIGURE 2-52

Customizing the Tasks Window and Moving Tasks to a Personal Folder

The default view for the task list is shown in Figure 2-51. This view contains the Task icon, the completed task check box, the task description, and the due date. Outlook allows to you add or delete columns, or **fields**, so you can display only the information that you want to view. To modify the current view of the task list, you would follow these steps.

To Add or Delete Fields in a View

1. On the View menu, point to Arrange By, point to Current View, and then click Customize Current View on the Current View submenu.
2. When the Customize View: Simple List dialog box is displayed, click the Fields button.
3. To add a new field, select a field in the Available fields list, and then click the Add button.
4. To delete a field, select a field in the Show these fields in this order list, and then click the Remove button.
5. When you are finished customizing the view, click the OK buttons in both open dialog boxes.

More About

Updating Tasks

To send a status report for a task on which you are working, open the task. On the Actions menu, click Send Status Report. If the task was assigned to you, the person who sent the task request automatically will be added to the update list.

For the same reason you created a separate folder for calendar items, you may want to create a separate folder for tasks and move the current task list to that folder. The following steps describe how to create a personal tasks folder and move the current task list to that folder.

To Move Tasks to a New Personal Folder

1. With the Tasks window active, right-click the Tasks title bar above the task list.
2. Click New folder on the shortcut menu.
3. When the Create New Folder dialog box is displayed, type Maria's Tasks in the Name text box and select Tasks in the select where to place the folder list. Click the OK button.
4. Click the first task in the task list, then, while holding the SHIFT key, click the last task in the task list to select all the tasks in the task list.
5. Right-click the task list. Click Move to Folder on the shortcut menu.
6. When the Move Items dialog box is displayed, select Maria's Tasks in the Move the selected items to the folder list. Click the OK button.

More About

Tasks

You can customize the Calendar window to include the task list. When you export the Calendar folder, however, the task list is not included. The task list is kept in the Tasks folder and is kept separate from the Calendar folder.

Scheduling a Meeting with Outlook

Earlier in this project an appointment was added for a team meeting. Outlook allows you to invite multiple attendees to a meeting by sending a single invitation. The sections on the next page will show how to invite attendees and schedule resources for that meeting.

To Invite Attendees to a Meeting

1

- **With the Calendar window active, click September 12 in the Date Navigator.**
- **Double-click the Team Meeting appointment to open the Team Meeting - Recurring Appointment window.**
- **When the Open Recurring Item dialog box is displayed, click Open this occurrence, and then click the OK button.**
- **Double-click the title bar to maximize the window.**
- **Click the Scheduling tab.**

Outlook opens the Team Meeting - Recurring Appointment window (Figure 2-53).

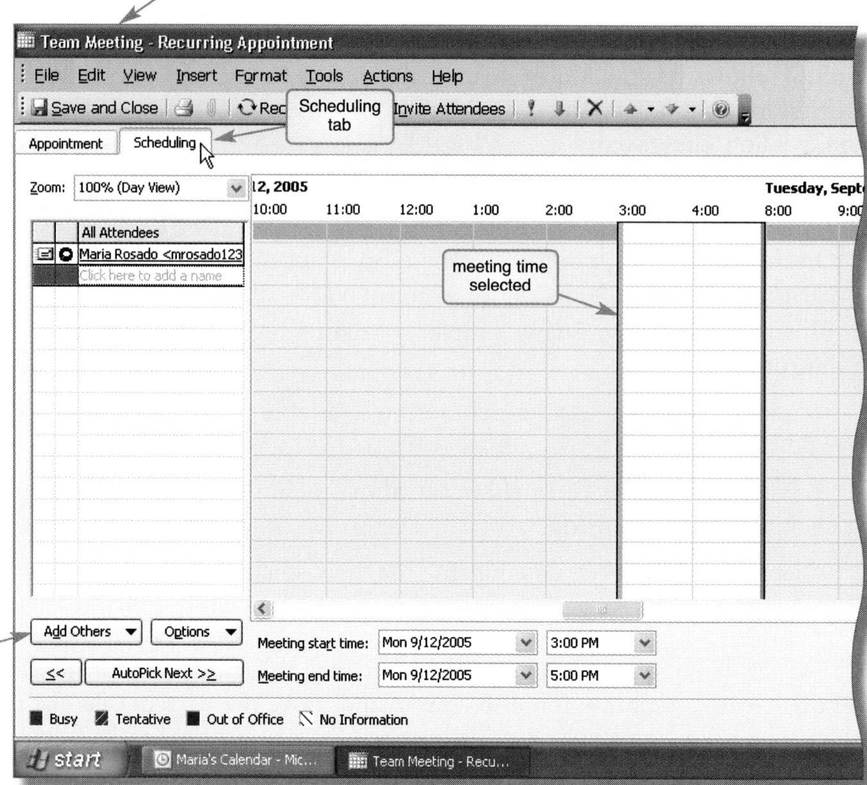

FIGURE 2-53

2

- **Click the Add Others button, and then click Add From Address Book.**

Outlook displays the Select Attendees and Resources dialog box (Figure 2-54).

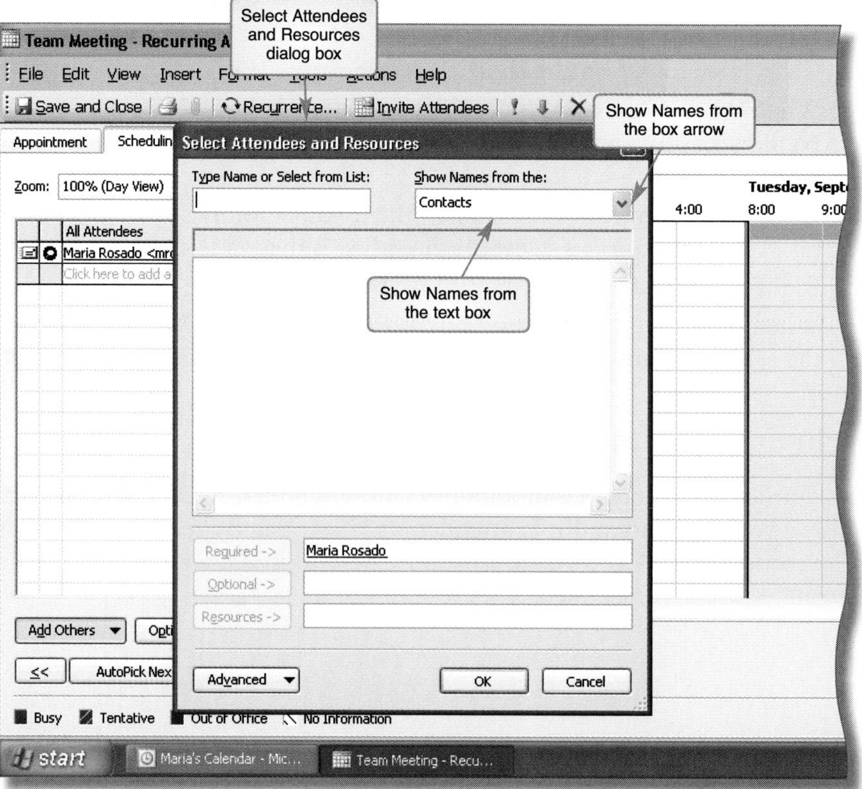

FIGURE 2-54

3

- **Click the Show Names from the box arrow, and then click Maria's Contacts.**
- **While holding the SHIFT key, click Susan Hadley to select the entire list.**
- **Click the Required button.**

The selected names from the contact list are added to the Required text box (Figure 2-55).

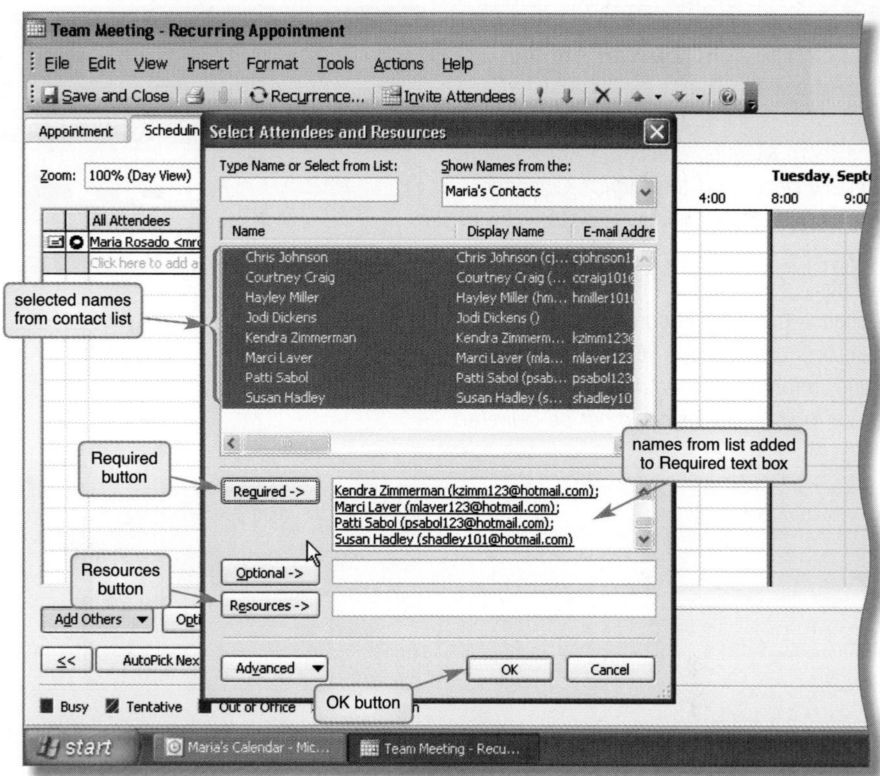

FIGURE 2-55

4

- **Click the OK button.**
- **If the Microsoft Office Internet Free/Busy dialog box displays, click the Cancel button.**

The Select Attendees and Resources dialog box closes and the Team Meeting - Recurring Appointment window is displayed with selected attendees in the All Attendees list (Figure 2-56).

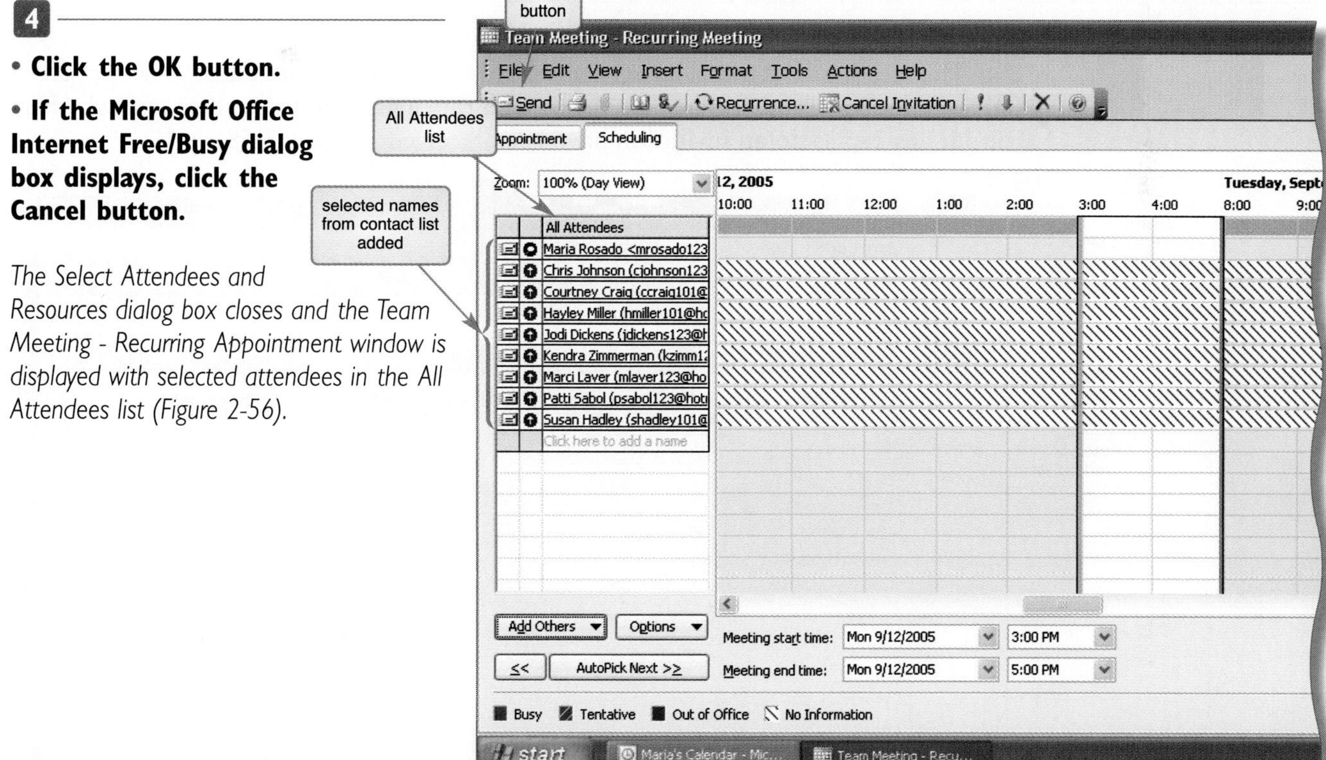

FIGURE 2-56

5

• **Click the Send button on the Standard toolbar.**

The Team Meeting -Recurring Appointment window closes and the Maria's Calendar - Microsoft Outlook window is displayed with a meeting icon displaying next to the Team Meeting appointment (Figure 2-57). Because the e-mail addresses in Maria's Contacts are fictitious, you may get messages returned to your inbox indicating that the e-mail messages could not be delivered.

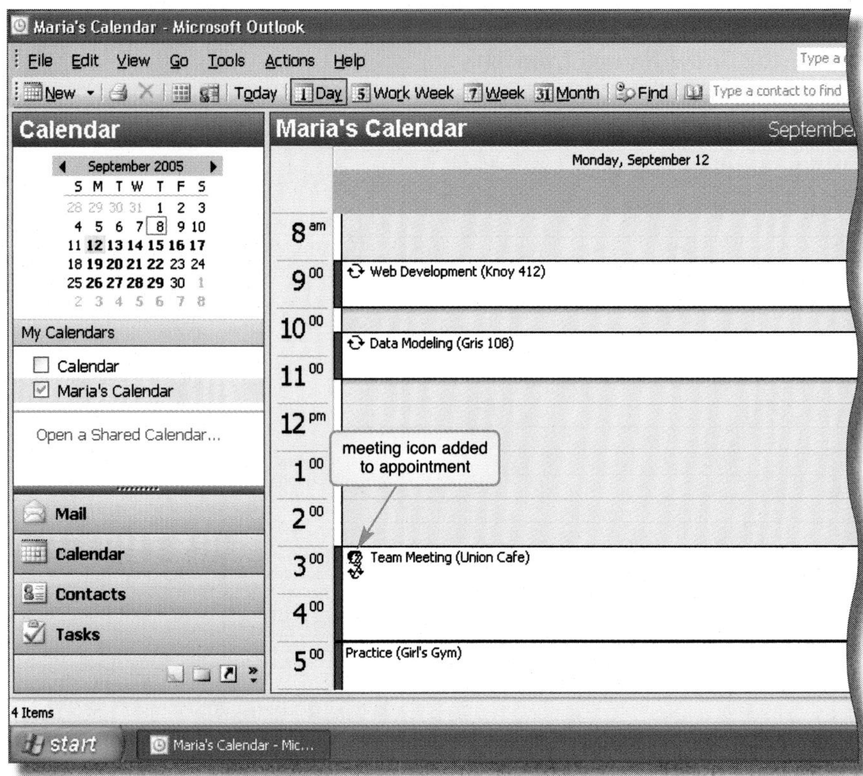

FIGURE 2-57

The meeting invitations have been sent to the respective attendees. If you open the appointment, you will be able to see who the invitation was sent to and whether or not any replies to an invitation have been received (Figure 2-58).

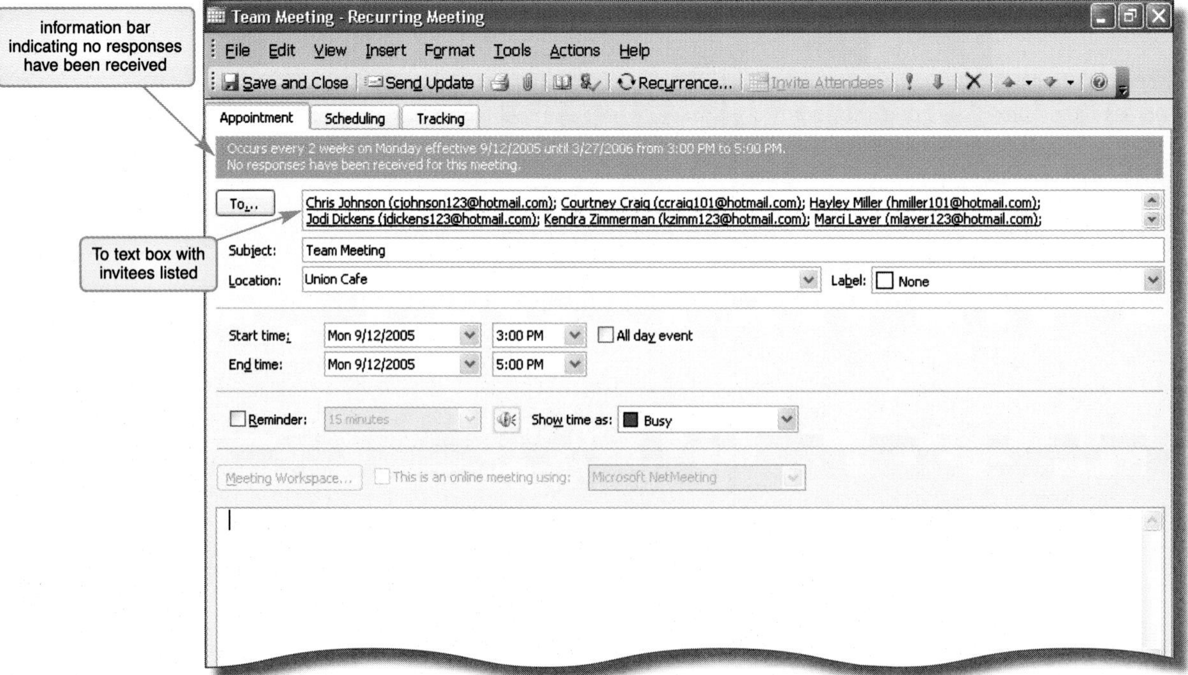

FIGURE 2-58

Scheduling Resources

If you use a Microsoft Exchange server e-mail account, you are able to schedule resources for your meetings in addition to inviting attendees. Resources are items necessary to run your meeting, such as the meeting room where you plan to hold your meeting, or an overhead projector you may want to use for a presentation.

Resources are set up on the server by an individual in the organization. If the resource is available at the time of the meeting, it will accept the invitation automatically, if not, the resource will decline the invitation automatically.

Accepting and Declining Meeting Requests

Once a meeting request has been received, you have to decide to accept it or decline it. A meeting request will appear in your Inbox similar to the one shown in Figure 2-59. Outlook allows you to choose from four responses: Accept, Tentative, Decline, or Propose New Time. The steps on the next page show how to accept a meeting request.

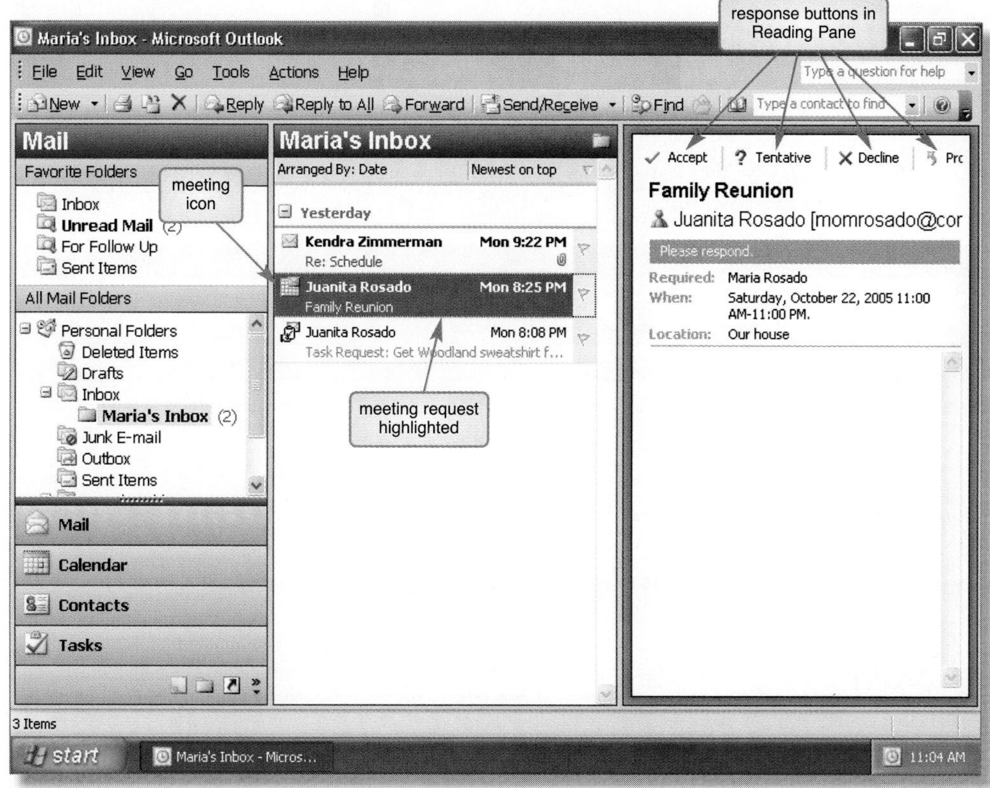

FIGURE 2-59

> *More About*
>
> **Meeting Workspace**
>
> Microsoft Outlook and SharePoint Services offer Meeting Workspace to help you plan your meeting more efficiently. A Meeting Workspace is a Web site for centralizing all the information required for one or more meetings. To learn more about Meeting Workspace, visit the Outlook 2003 More About Web page (scsite.com/out2003/more) and click Meetings.

To Accept a Meeting Request

1

• **If necessary, click the Mail button in the Navigation Pane.**

Outlook displays the Inbox folder with the meeting request selected (Figure 2-60). All the information for the request appears in the Reading Pane along with the Accept, Tentative, Decline, and Propose New Time buttons.

FIGURE 2-60

2

• **Double-click the Family Reunion message heading to open it.**

Outlook opens the Family Reunion - Meeting window (Figure 2-61).

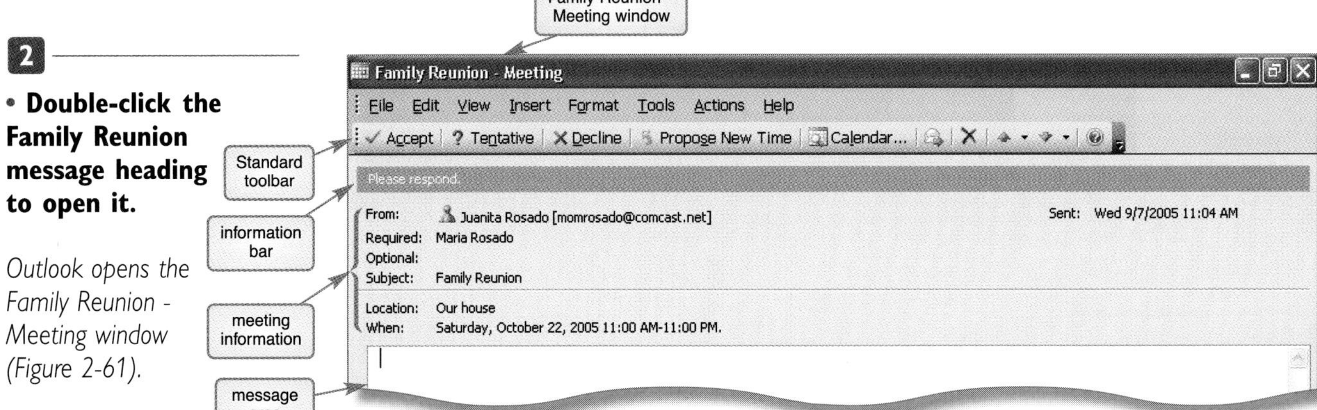

FIGURE 2-61

3

• **Click the Accept button on the Standard toolbar.**

Outlook displays the Microsoft Office Outlook dialog box (Figure 2-62).

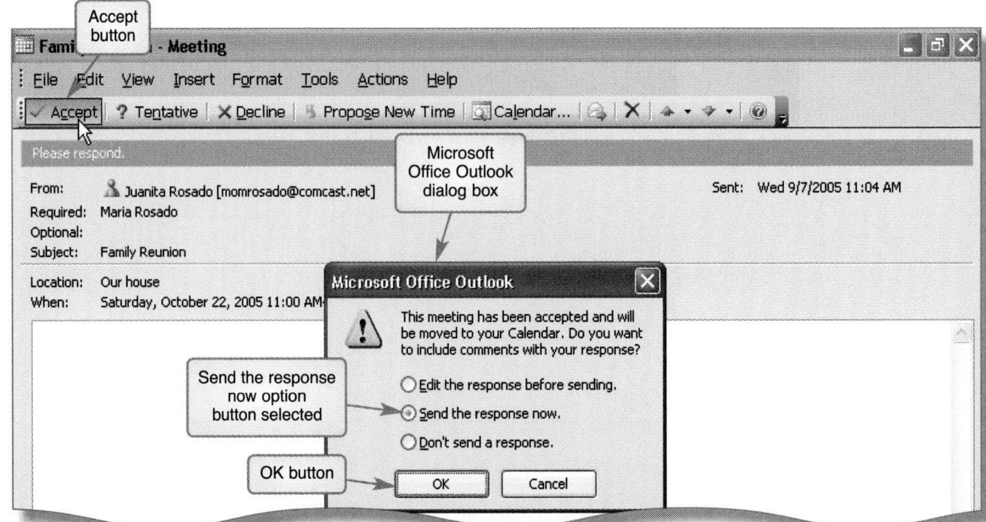

FIGURE 2-62

4

• **Click Send the response now, and then click the OK button.**

Outlook closes the Family Reunion - Meeting window and displays the Inbox - Microsoft Outlook window.

5

• **Click the Calendar button in the Navigation Pane.**

• **Click the right scroll arrow in the Date Navigator so the October 2005 calendar appears.**

• **Click October 22 in the Date Navigator.**

The Calendar - Microsoft Outlook window is displayed (Figure 2-63). The meeting request has been removed from the Inbox folder and placed in the Calendar folder as a new meeting. Outlook may send the meeting request to the default Calendar folder because the invitation was sent to someone other than the current user. To view the new meeting click the Calendar box in the My Calendars pane.

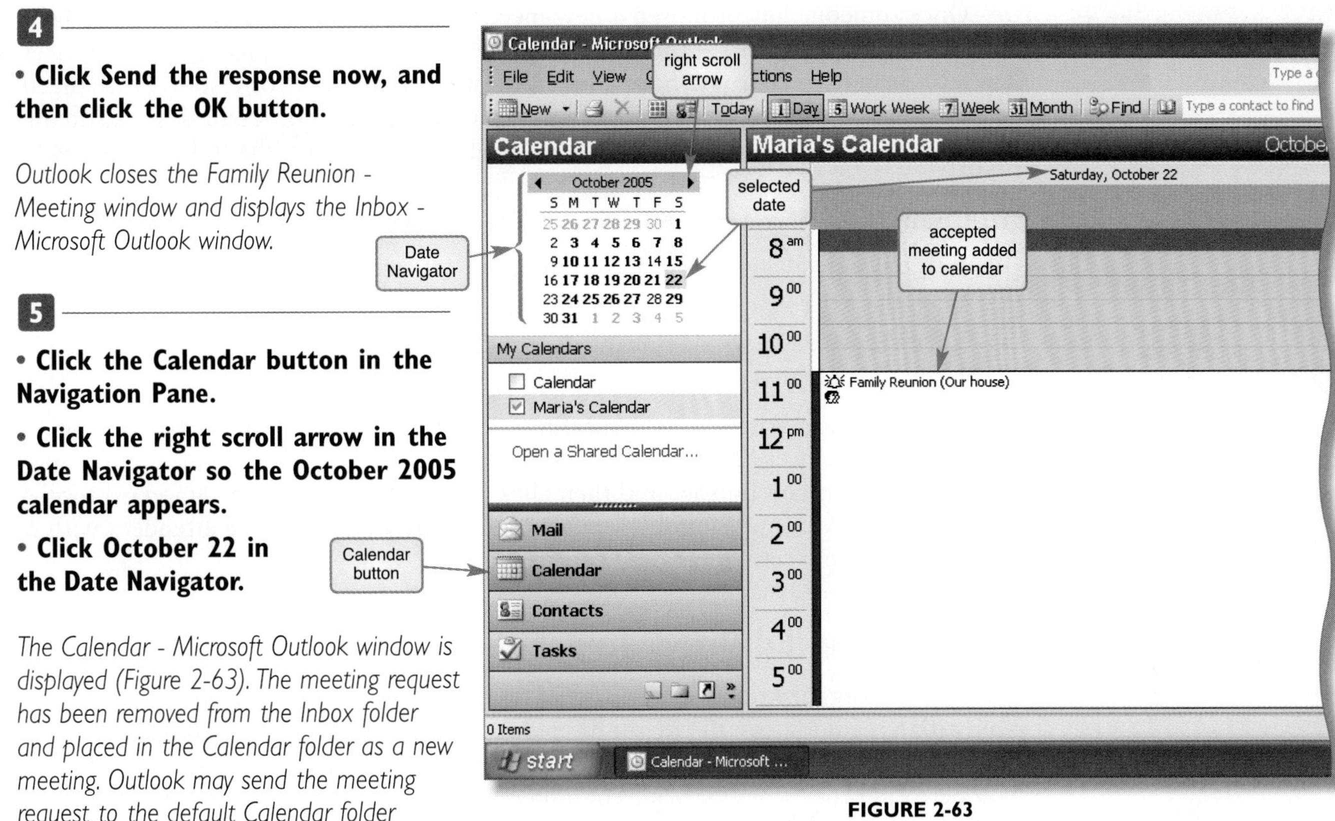

FIGURE 2-63

When a meeting request is accepted, the meeting organizer receives a message indicating that the request has been accepted. If the meeting request is declined, the request is moved to the Deleted Items folder, and the meeting organizer receives a message indicating that the request was declined.

Proposing New Meeting Times

One of the available responses to a meeting request is to propose a new time. When you click the Propose a New Time button, Outlook allows you to send a response to the meeting organizer indicating that you tentatively accept the request, but propose the meeting be held at a different time. To propose a new time for a meeting, you would perform the following steps.

To Propose a New Meeting Time

1. Double-click the appropriate meeting request to open the request.
2. Click the Propose New Time button on the Standard toolbar.
3. When the Propose New Time dialog box is displayed, drag through the time slot that you want to propose, or enter the appropriate information in the Meeting start time and Meeting end time time boxes.
4. Click the Propose Time button.
5. When the New Time Proposed - Meeting Response window is displayed, click the Send button.

Once someone has proposed a new meeting time, it may be necessary to update the meeting request to the other potential attendees. Other reasons to update a meeting request may be that you have added or removed attendees or resources, changed the meeting to a recurring series, or moved the meeting to a different date. To change the time of a meeting and send an update, you would perform the following steps.

More About

Meeting Times

If you use Windows SharePoint Services and have access to other attendees' calendars, use the AutoPick Next button in the Scheduling sheet of the Meeting window to find the next available free time for all attendees.

To Change the Time of a Meeting and Send an Update

1. With the Calendar window active, drag the meeting to its new time.
2. When the Microsoft Office Outlook dialog box is displayed, click the Yes button.
3. When the Meeting window is displayed, click the Send Update button on the Standard toolbar.

If the situation arises that the meeting needs to be canceled, open the meeting window, click Cancel Meeting on the Actions menu, click the Send cancellation and delete meeting option button, and then click the Send button on the Standard toolbar of the meeting window. Outlook sends a high priority e-mail to the attendees with a message that the meeting has been canceled.

Creating and Editing Notes with Outlook

Another organizational tool provided with Outlook is Notes. **Notes** provides you with a medium to write down thoughts, ideas, questions, or anything else that you might write down on a sticky note or note pad. Notes can remain open while you perform other work on your computer. You can add to your notes and your changes are saved automatically. Notes can be color coded per your personal specifications. For example, a blue note may be an issue that you want to bring to the attention of your boss, a green note may be an idea you want to pass along to a coworker, and so on. The following steps show how to create and edit a note.

To Create and Edit a Note

1

- **Click the Notes button in the Navigation Pane.**
- **Click the New Note button on the Standard toolbar.**

Outlook displays the Untitled - Notes window (Figure 2-64).

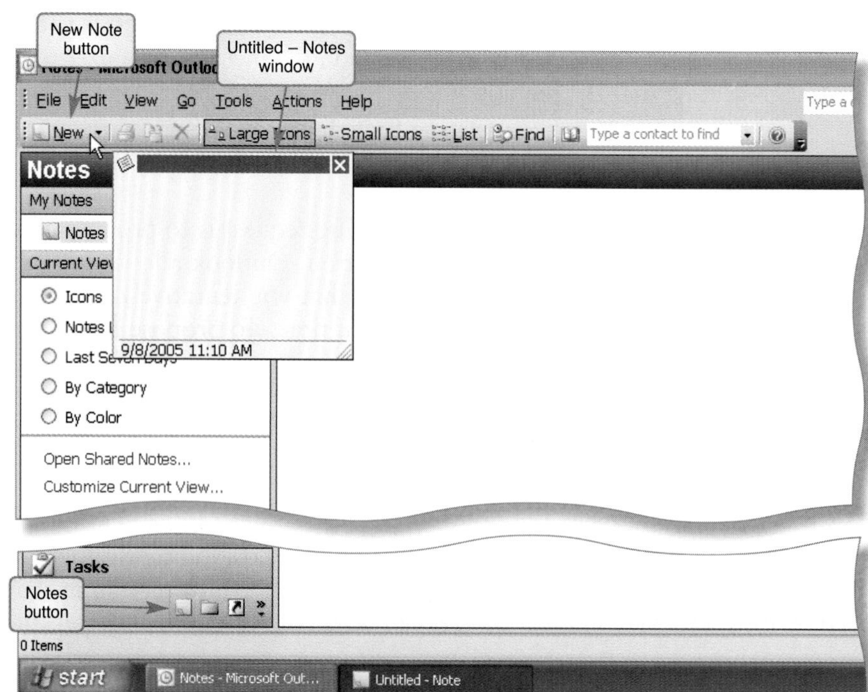

FIGURE 2-64

2

• **Type** `Talk about new warm-up routine with Coach` **as the entry.**

• **Point to the Close button.**

The text appears in the Untitled - Notes window (Figure 2-65).

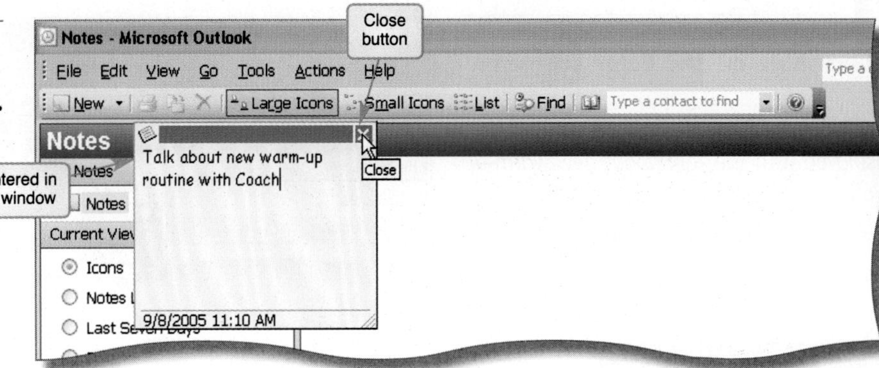

FIGURE 2-65

3

• **Click the Close button.**

Outlook closes the Untitled - Notes window and the note appears in the Notes folder (Figure 2-66).

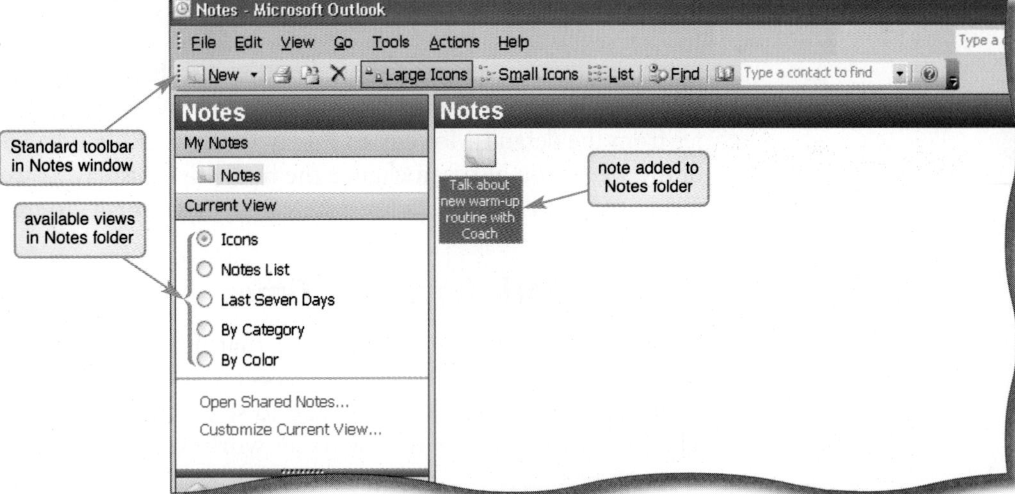

FIGURE 2-66

4

• **Right-click the note and then point to Color on the shortcut menu.**

Outlook displays the Color submenu (Figure 2-67).

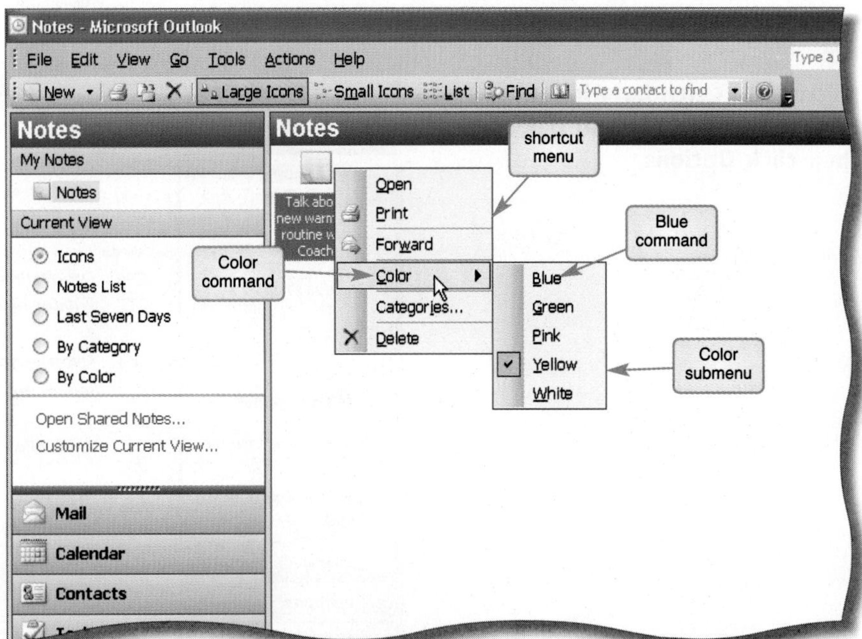

FIGURE 2-67

5

• **Click Blue on the Color submenu.**

The Notes - Microsoft Outlook window is displayed with the Talk about new warm-up routine with Coach note colored blue (Figure 2-68).

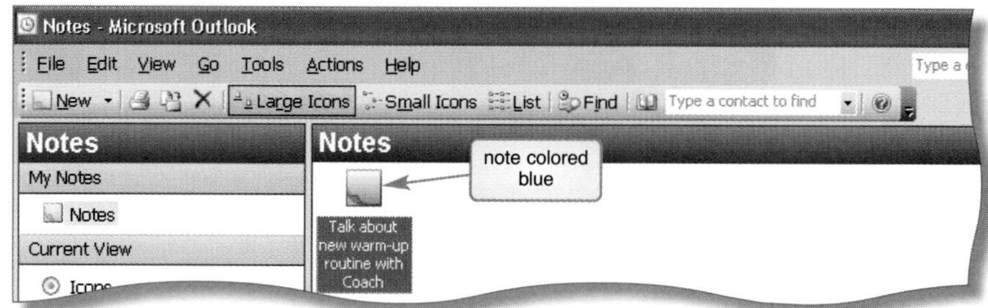

FIGURE 2-68

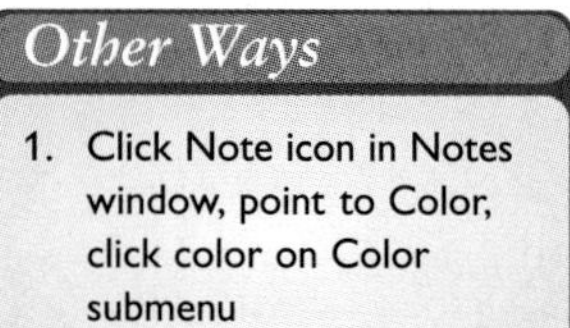

Other Ways
1. Click Note icon in Notes window, point to Color, click color on Color submenu

Customize Calendar Settings

Outlook provides you with several options to change the appearance of the Calendar window. You can customize your work week by selecting the days you work if they differ from the default Monday to Friday work week. In addition to customizing the days of the week, you also can change the hours that display as work hours in the appointment area. You also can color code your appointments to make them easier to view.

Setting Work Days and Times

Some people may have schedules that differ from the standard Monday through Friday work week. Whether it is a six-days-per-week schedule or a four-days-per-week schedule, Outlook allows you to select the days that display in your calendar. The following steps show how to set work week options.

To Set Work Week Options

1

• **With the Calendar window active, click Tools on the menu bar, and then click Options.**

Outlook displays the Options dialog box (Figure 2-69).

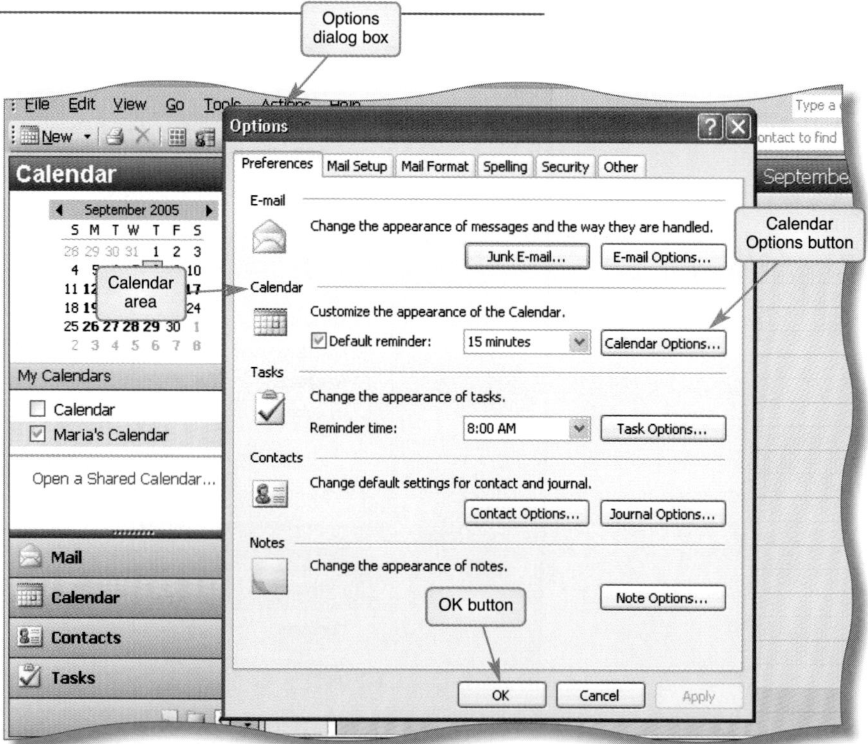

FIGURE 2-69

2

• **Click the Calendar Options button.**

Outlook displays the Calendar Options dialog box (Figure 2-70).

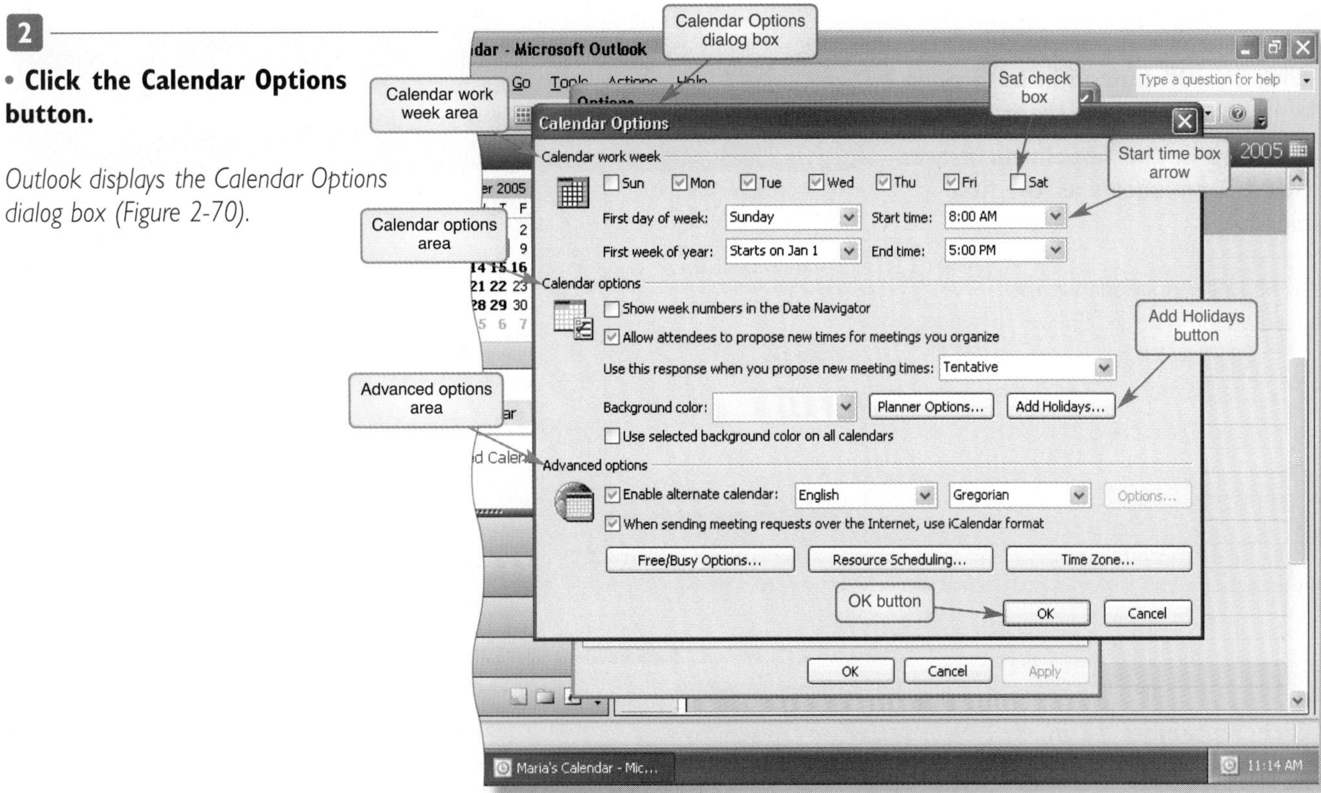

FIGURE 2-70

3

• **In the Calendar work week area, click the Sat check box.**

• **Click the Start time box arrow and then select 7:00 AM as the new start time.**

The work week has been changed to a six-day week with the start time changed to 7:00 AM (Figure 2-71).

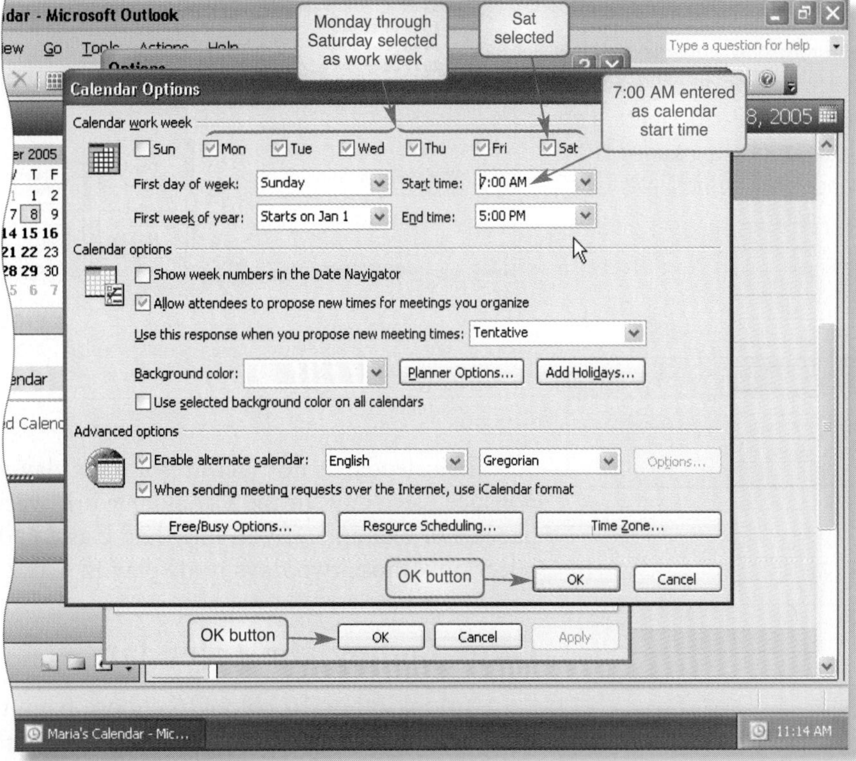

FIGURE 2-71

- **Click the OK button in both open dialog boxes to close them.**
- **Scroll up in the Appointment area so that 6 am shows as the first time slot.**

7:00 no longer is included in the shaded area (Figure 2-72).

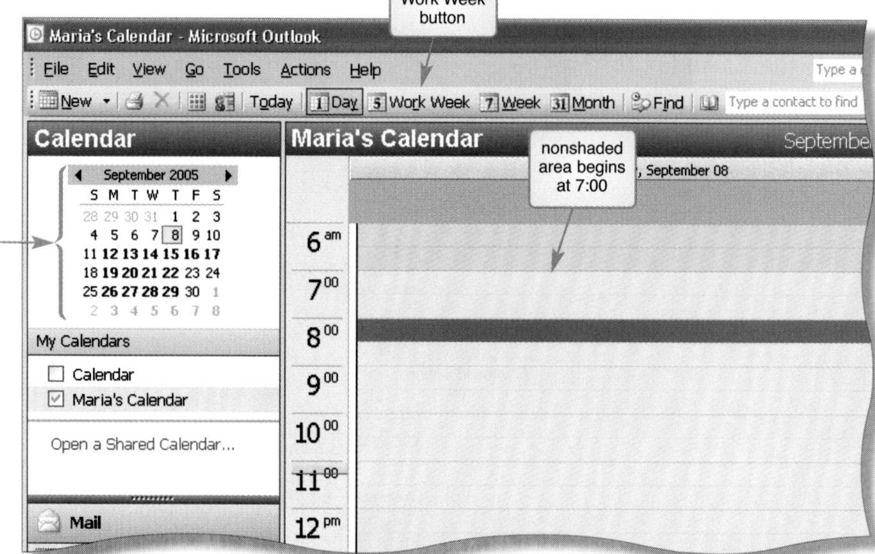

FIGURE 2-72

- **Click September 12 in the Date Navigator.**
- **Click the Work Week button on the Standard toolbar.**

Saturday now appears in Work Week view as an active work day (Figure 2-73). Notice that Saturday also is included in the shaded bar in the Date Navigator.

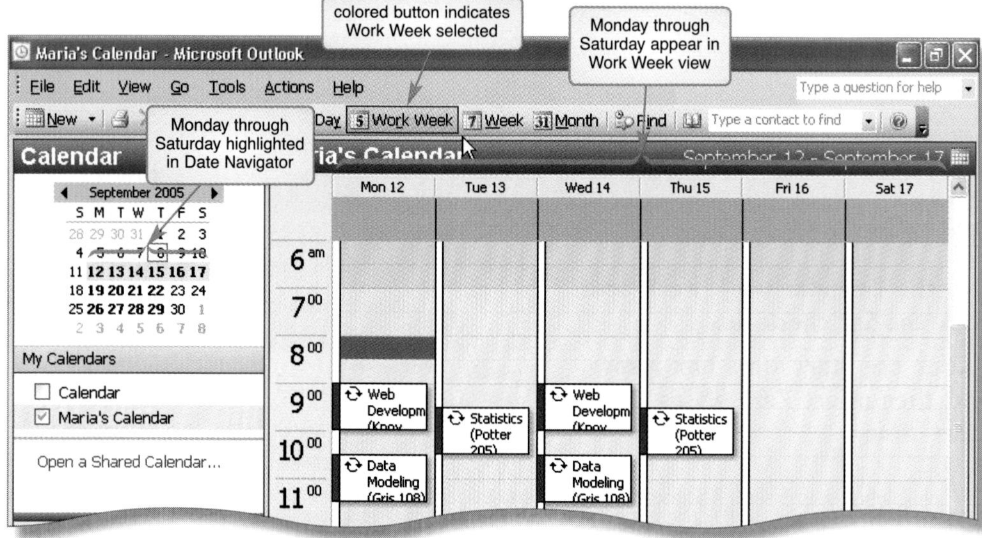

FIGURE 2-73

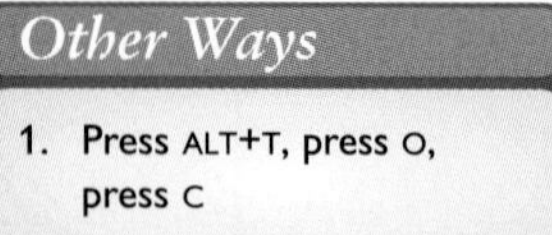

Other Ways

1. Press ALT+T, press O, press C

The calendar is now set up for a six-day work week. You also can select nonsuccessive days in the Calendar work week area (Figure 2-70 on the previous page). For example, if you only had class on Tuesday's and Thursday's, you could select only those two days to display in Work Week view.

Color Coding the Calendar

Outlook offers 10 colors to choose from to color appointments and meetings. For example, you can color your class schedule one color, your work schedule another color, and your extracurricular activities yet another color. Outlook has default labels for the colors that can be changed to fit your needs. The following steps show how to color code the Maria's Calendar calendar and edit the calendar labels.

To Color Code the Calendar and Edit Calendar Labels

1

- **With the Calendar window active, click the Month button on the Standard toolbar to display the calendar in Month view.**
- **Click the Calendar Coloring button on the Standard toolbar.**

Outlook displays the Calendar Coloring menu (Figure 2-74). The color options are not available because an appointment has not been selected.

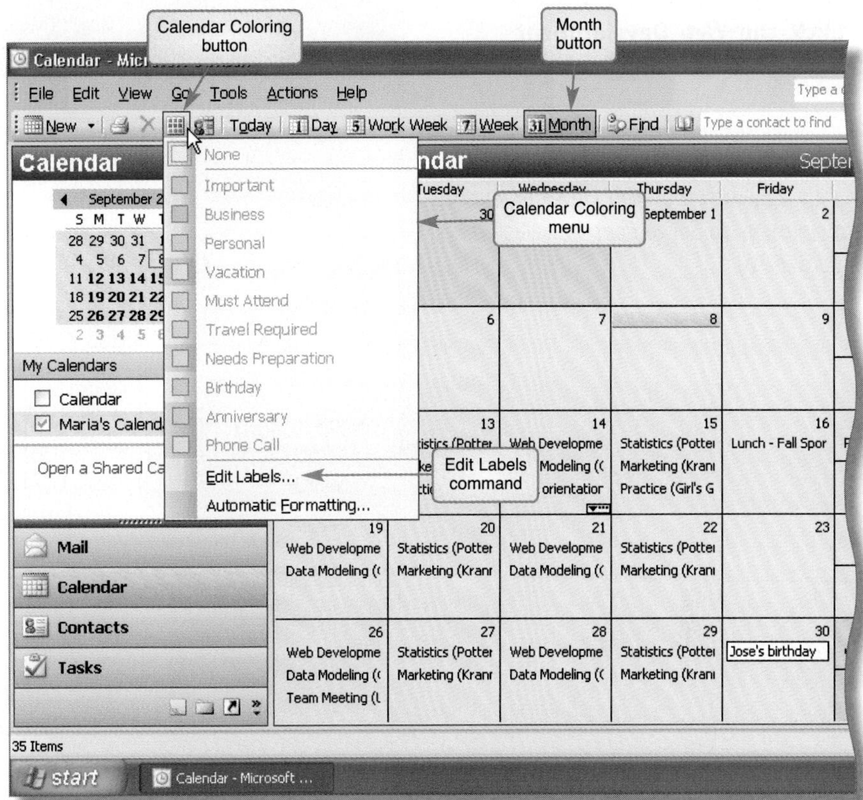

FIGURE 2-74

2

- **Click Edit Labels on the Calendar Coloring menu.**
- **Triple click the Business entry in the second text box in the Edit Calendar Labels dialog box and type** `Work` **as the entry.**
- **Press the TAB key three times, and then type** `Class` **in place of the Must Attend entry.**
- **Press the TAB key once, and then type** `Practice` **in place of the Travel Required entry.**

Outlook displays the Edit Calendar Labels dialog box (Figure 2-75). The three labels have been changed.

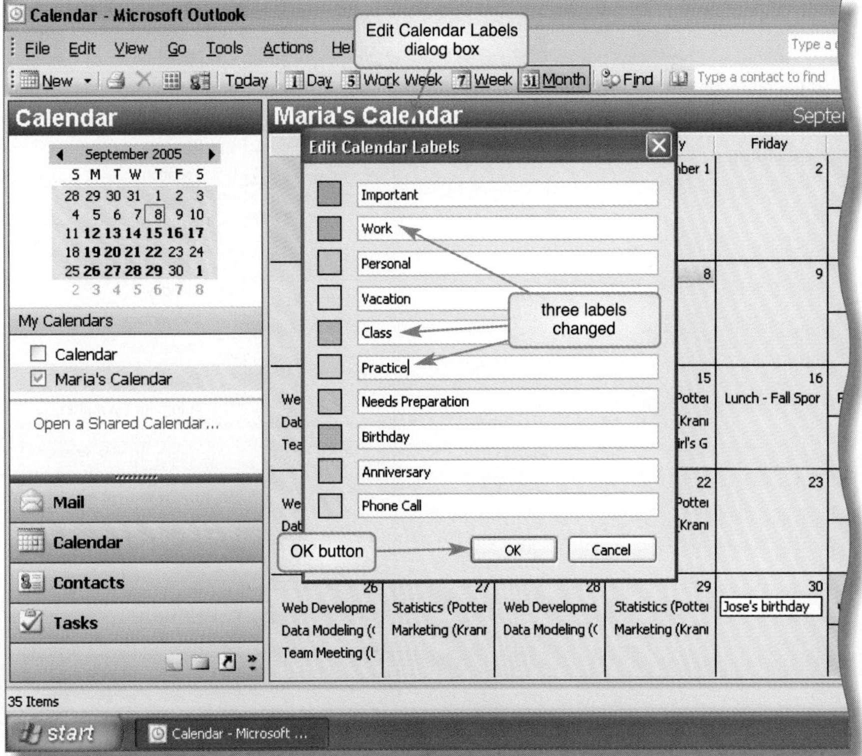

FIGURE 2-75

3

- **Click the OK button.**
- **Click the Web Development appointment on September 12th.**

Outlook closes the Edit Calendar Labels dialog box and displays the calendar in Month view with the Web Development appointment on September 12 selected (Figure 2-76).

FIGURE 2-76

4

- **Click the Calendar Coloring button on the Standard toolbar.**

Outlook displays the Calendar Coloring menu (Figure 2-77). The color options are now available.

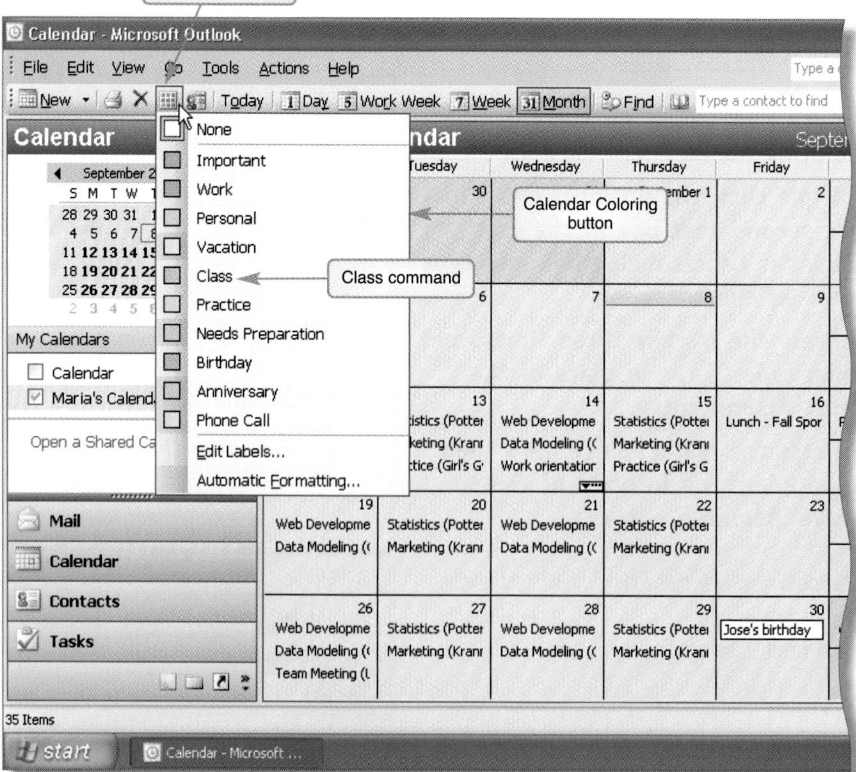

FIGURE 2-77

5

• **Click Class on the Calendar Coloring menu.**

The Maria's Calendar - Microsoft Outlook window is displayed with all occurrences of the Web Development appointment color coded orange (Figure 2-78).

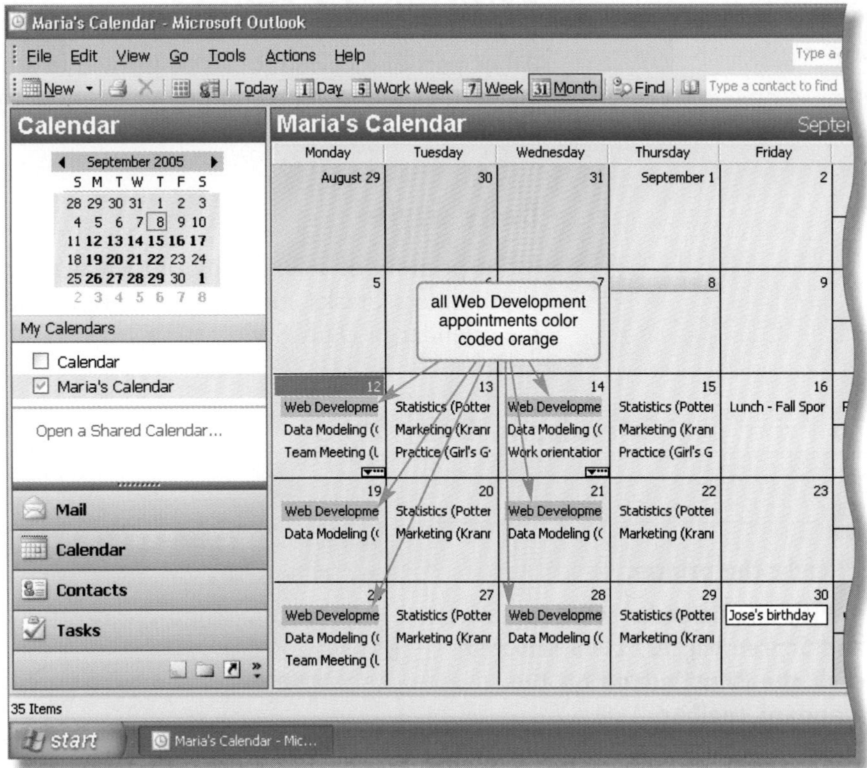

FIGURE 2-78

6

• **Repeat Steps 3 through 5 to color code the remaining recurring appointments in the calendar. Select Important as the label and color for the Team Meeting recurring appointment.**

The Maria's Calendar - Microsoft Outlook window is displayed with the recurring appointments color coded (Figure 2-79).

7

• **Using the methods described in Steps 1 through 5, color code the remaining items in the calendar.**

FIGURE 2-79

The calendar is now color coded. When the calendar is opened, the user will be able to differentiate between the various types of appointments.

Printing a Calendar

All or part of a calendar can be printed in a number of different layouts, or **print styles**. The following section describes how to print the calendar in Daily, Weekly, and Monthly Styles.

Daily Style

A printout of a single day of the calendar, called **Daily Style**, shows the day's appointments, tasks, and a two-month calendar. The steps below show how to print the calendar in Daily Style.

To Print the Calendar in Daily Style

1

- **Ready the printer.**
- **With the Calendar window active and September 12, 2005 selected, click the Print button on the Standard toolbar.**

Outlook displays the Print dialog box (Figure 2-80). Because the Appointment window was in Day view when the Print button was clicked, Daily Style is selected in the Print style list by default.

- **With the Daily Style selected in the Print style list, click OK.**

The daily schedule of appointments for Monday, September 12, 2005 prints on the printer. The printout should display as shown in Figure 2-1d on page OUT 67.

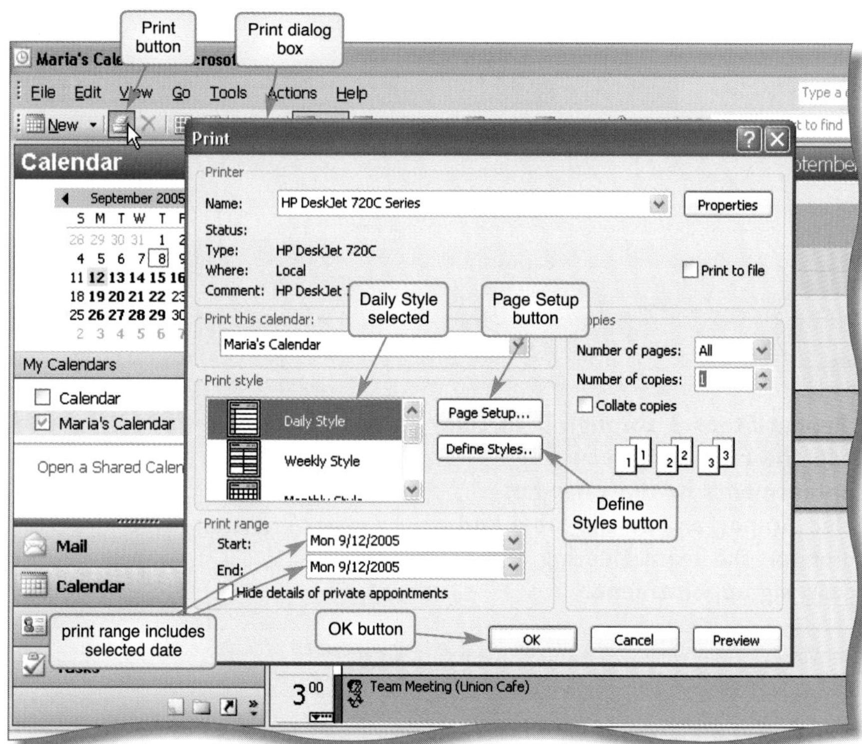

FIGURE 2-80

Other Ways

1. On File menu click Print
2. Press CTRL+P
3. In Voice Command mode, say "File, Print"

The Daily Style printout includes features from the Day view of the Calendar, including appointments, events, tasks, and notes. Dates with appointments print in bold in the two-month calendar. Page numbers and current system dates display at the bottom of the page. The Page Setup button in the Print dialog box allows style modifications to include or omit various features, including the TaskPad and the Notes area. Specific time ranges also can be printed rather than the default 7:00 AM to 6:00 PM.

Weekly Style

Printing a calendar in Weekly Style can be accomplished through the Print button on the Standard toolbar while viewing the calendar in Week view, or by selecting the Weekly Style in the Print dialog box, as explained in the following step.

To Print the Calendar in Weekly Style

1 Ready the printer. Click the Print button on the Standard toolbar. Click Weekly Style in the Print style list and then click the OK button.

The calendar for the week of Monday, September 12, 2005 through Sunday, September 18, 2005 prints on the printer as shown in Figure 2-1e on page OUT 67.

Monthly Style

The following step prints the calendar in Monthly Style.

To Print the Calendar in Monthly Style

1 Ready the printer. Click the Print button on the Standard toolbar. Click Monthly Style in the Print Style list and then click the OK button.

The calendar for the month of September prints on the printer as shown in Figure 2-1f on page OUT 67.

More About

Printing

The margins, page orientation, or paper size can be changed in the Page Setup dialog box. To access the Page Setup dialog box, click the Page Setup button in the Print dialog box (Figure 2-80).

Selecting Monthly Style prints the calendar in landscape orientation. Some appointments are truncated due to the lack of space. The Monthly Style of printout is intended to show the larger picture rather than the detail of a Daily Style printout.

Another useful print style is **Tri-fold Style**, which prints a daily appointment list, a task list, and a calendar for the week. To save styles and setups, use the **Define Styles button** in the Print dialog box.

Printing the Task List

To print only the task list, first open the Task folder. The following steps describe how to print the task list by itself.

To Print the Task List

1 Click the Tasks button in the Navigation Pane to display the task list.

2 Click the Print button on the Standard toolbar. When the Print dialog box is displayed, click the OK button.

The task list prints (Figure 2-81).

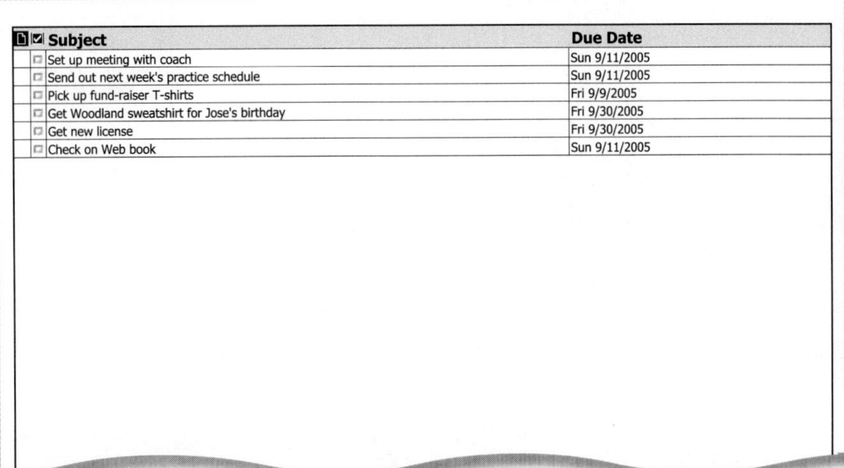

Subject	Due Date
Set up meeting with coach	Sun 9/11/2005
Send out next week's practice schedule	Sun 9/11/2005
Pick up fund-raiser T-shirts	Fri 9/9/2005
Get Woodland sweatshirt for Jose's birthday	Fri 9/30/2005
Get new license	Fri 9/30/2005
Check on Web book	Sun 9/11/2005

FIGURE 2-81

Archiving Items

Outlook has a built-in feature called **AutoArchive** that helps manage Outlook folders. AutoArchive is on by default and can be scheduled to run automatically. AutoArchive searches Outlook folders for items that are used infrequently, and items of which the content is no longer valid (a completed task, and old meeting, etc.). AutoArchive can be set up either to delete expired items permanently, and/or move old items to a special archive file. When AutoArchive is run for the first time, Outlook automatically creates this archive file. Outlook also creates an Archive Folders folder in the Folder List. The Archive Folders maintains the existing folder structure in the Folder List. AutoArchive does not delete any folders from a folder list even if they are empty. If you decide that you want to move archived items back to their original folders, you can use the Import Export wizard to move the items back to the original folder or any folder you specify.

Customizing AutoArchive

Outlook allows you to change how AutoArchive works. The default settings, or global settings, of AutoArchive are set to archive all folders except the Contacts folder. You also can have **per-folder settings** that will override the global settings. With per-folder settings you can have different archive settings for different folders. The following steps show how to change the default settings for AutoArchive.

To Change the Default Settings for AutoArchive

1

- **Click Tools on the menu bar, and then click Options.**
- **When the Options dialog box is displayed, click the Other tab.**

Outlook displays the Options dialog box (Figure 2-82).

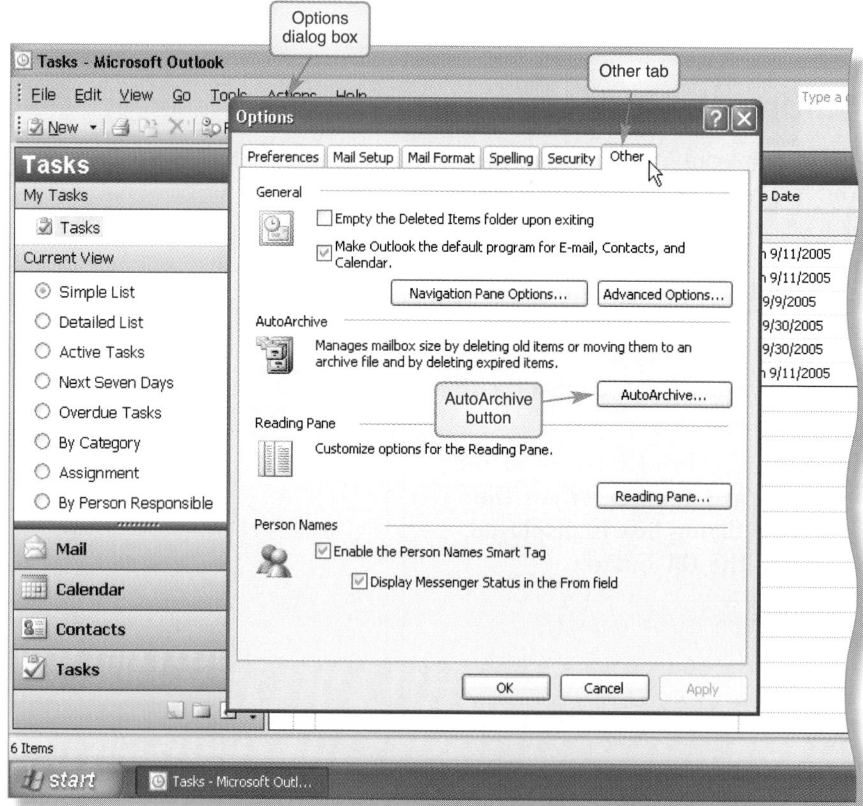

FIGURE 2-82

2

- **Click the AutoArchive button.**

Outlook displays the AutoArchive dialog box (Figure 2-83).

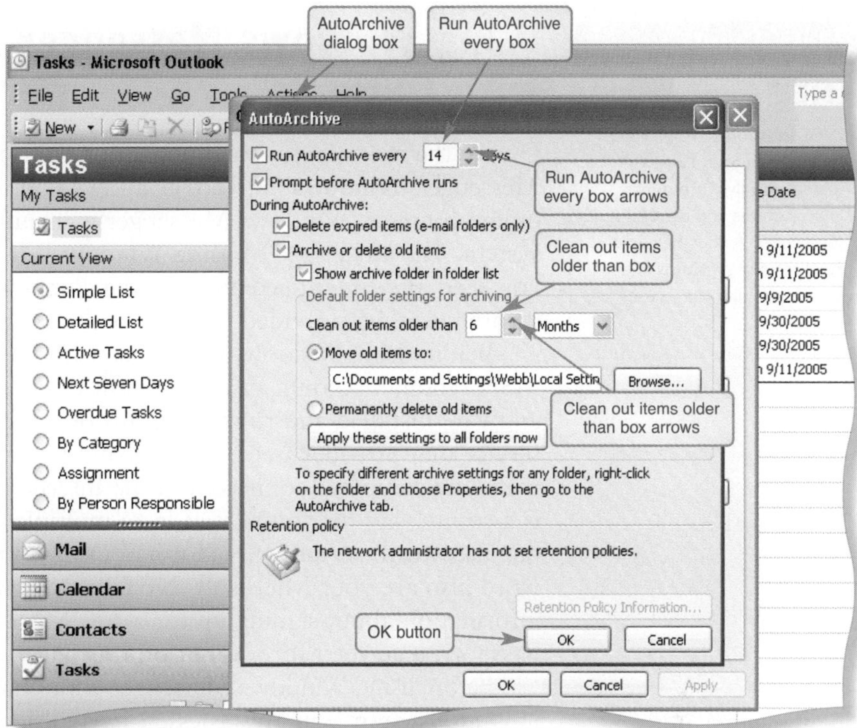

FIGURE 2-83

3

- **If necessary, click the Run AutoArchive every check box.**
- **Change the Run AutoArchive every box to 10 by clicking the down arrow.**
- **Change the Clean out items older than box to 8 by clicking the up arrow.**

The default settings have been changed and are ready to be applied (Figure 2-84).

4

- **Click the OK button in both open dialog boxes.**

Outlook closes the two dialog boxes. AutoArchive is now set to run every 10 days, and any items older than 8 months will be cleaned out.

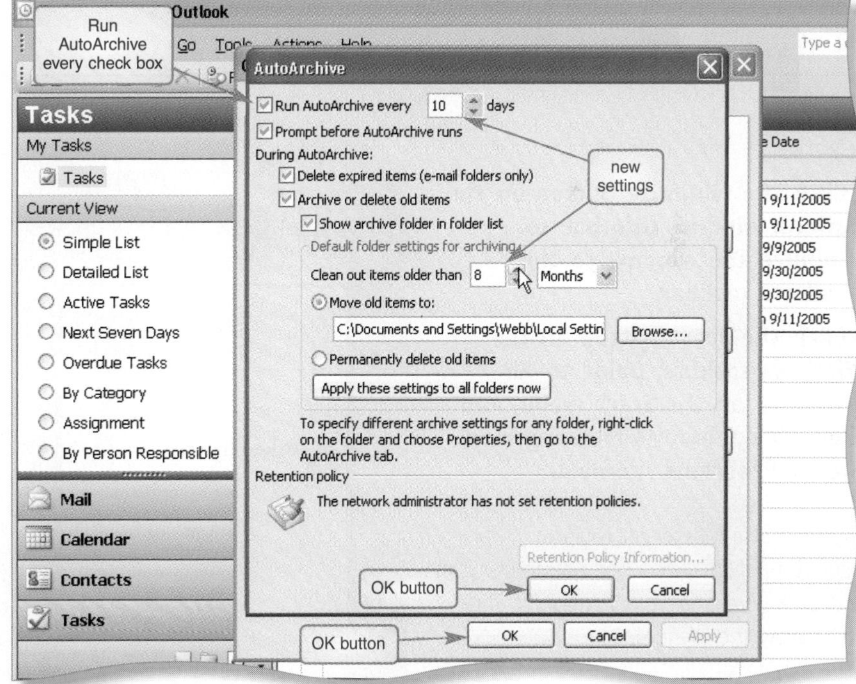

FIGURE 2-84

Other Ways

1. Press ALT+T, press O

The global settings have been changed so AutoArchive runs every 10 days and will clean out items older than 8 months.

To change the archive settings for an individual folder, right-click the folder, click Properties on the shortcut menu, and then click the AutoArchive tab.

More About

.NET Passports

.NET Passports are available for children ages 12 and under who live in the United States and use MSN Messenger. A Kids Passport requires the signature of a parent or guardian to use the service.

Using Windows Messenger and Instant Messaging with Outlook

One of the more useful communication tools available with Outlook is Windows Messenger. **Windows Messenger** allows you to communicate instantly with your online contacts. Windows Messenger is included with the Windows XP operating system. The advantage of using Windows Messenger over e-mail is that the message you send appears immediately on the computer of the person with whom you are communicating, provided that person has signed in to Windows Messenger.

Before using Window Messenger with Outlook, a contact first must have an MSN Hotmail account or a Microsoft .NET Passport and have Windows Messenger software installed and running on his or her computer. **MSN Hotmail** is a Microsoft service that provides free e-mail accounts to allow you to read your e-mail messages from any computer connected to the Internet. The **Microsoft .NET Passport** service is a secure way for you to sign in to multiple Web sites using just one user name and one password. As an MSN Hotmail user, your MSN Hotmail sign-in name and password also are your Microsoft .NET Passport user name and password. For more information about signing up for a free MSN Hotmail account or Microsoft .NET Passport, read the More About on this page.

Before using Windows Messenger with Outlook, you must enable instant messaging in Outlook, start Windows Messenger, and sign in to the .NET Messenger service using your sign-in name and password. The following steps start Windows Messenger and sign in to the .NET Messenger Service using your sign-in name and password.

To Start and Sign In to Windows Messenger

1

- **Click the Minimize button on the Outlook window title bar to minimize the window to the Windows taskbar.**
- **Click the Start button on the Windows taskbar, point to All Programs on the Start menu, and then click Windows Messenger on the All Programs submenu.**

The Windows Messenger window is displayed (Figure 2-85). The Messenger icon and Click here to sign in link display in an area below the menu bar.

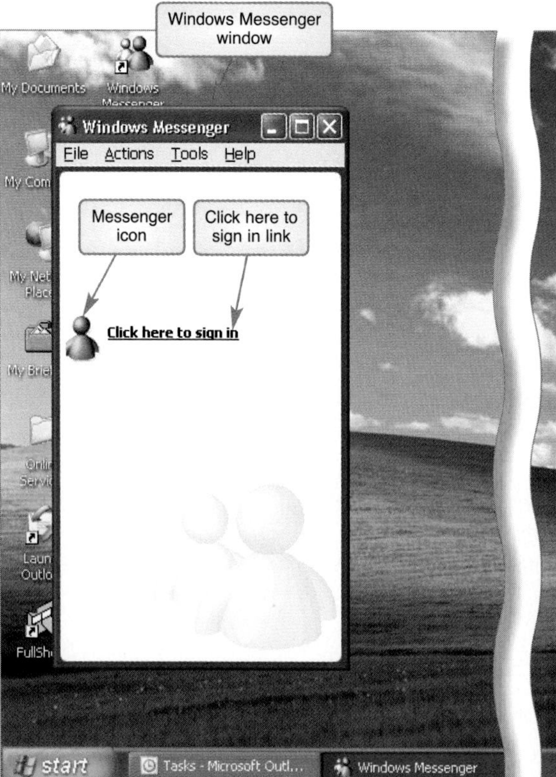

FIGURE 2-85

2

• **Click the Click here to sign in link.**

• **When the Connect to Messaging Services dialog box is displayed, click the .NET Messaging Service box, and then click the OK button.**

• **Type your e-mail address and password in the appropriate text boxes in the .NET Messenger Service dialog box.**

Messenger displays the .NET Messenger Service dialog box (Figure 2-86). The dialog box contains the E-mail address text box containing your e-mail address, Password text box containing your password, Sign me in automatically check box, Get a .NET Passport link, and Help link.

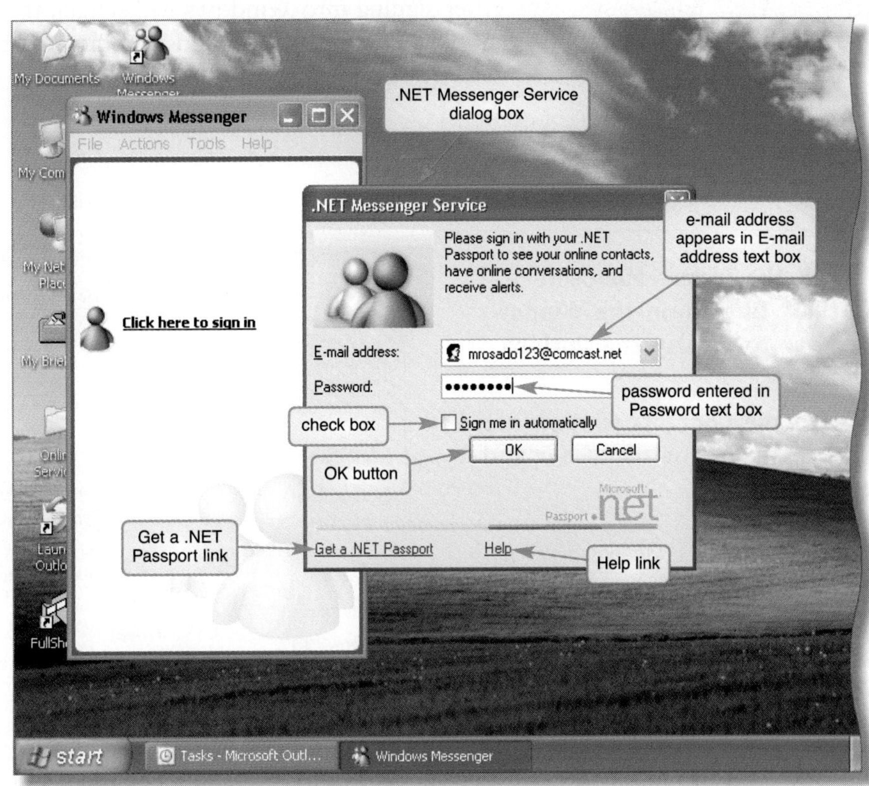

FIGURE 2-86

3

• **Click the OK button.**

The .NET Messenger Service dialog box closes, you are signed in to the .NET Messenger Service, and the contents of the Windows Messenger window change (Figure 2-87). The Windows Messenger window contains a menu bar, three tabs along the left side of the window, and the My Status sheet.

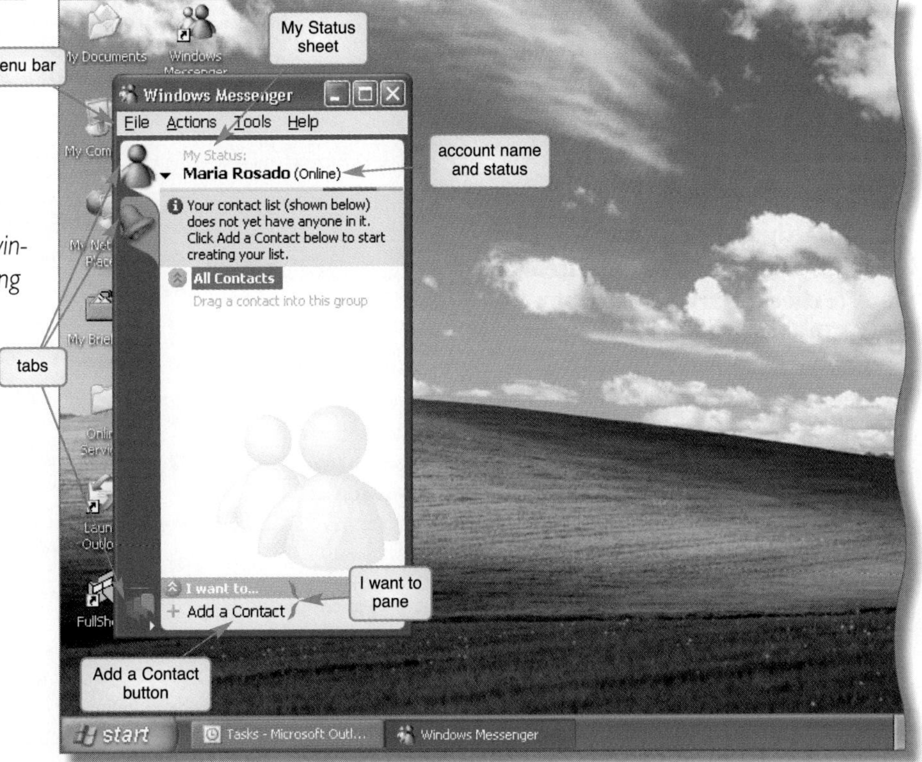

FIGURE 2-87

Other Ways

1. Double-click Messenger icon in status area

After signing into Windows Messenger, the next step is to enable instant messaging in Outlook. The steps below illustrate how to enable instant messaging in Outlook.

To Enable Instant Messaging in Outlook

1

- **Click the Tasks - Microsoft Outlook button on the Windows taskbar to display the Outlook window.**
- **With the Contacts window active, click Tools on the menu bar and click Options.**

Outlook displays the Options dialog box (Figure 2-88).

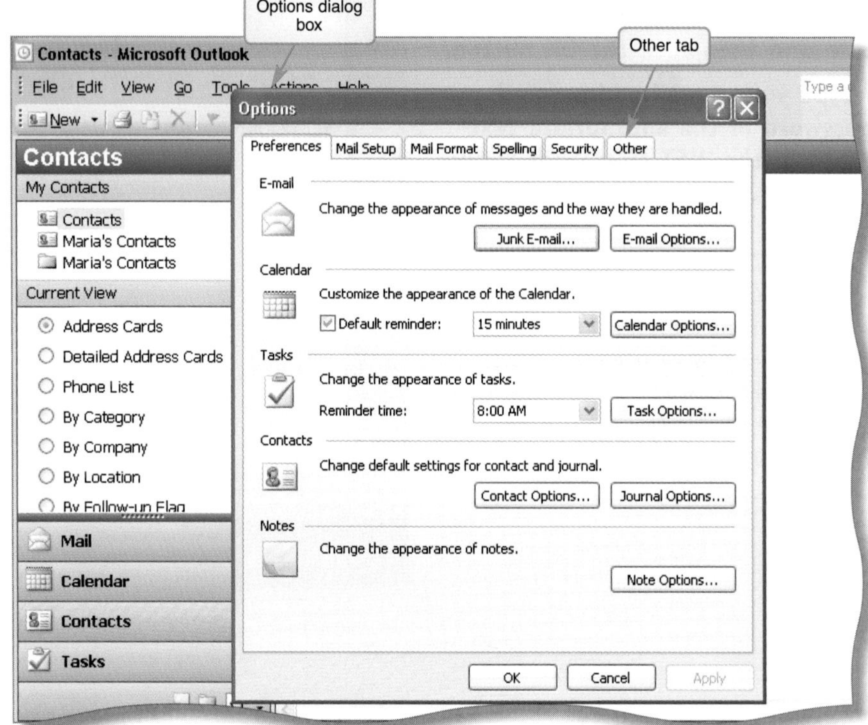

FIGURE 2-88

2

- **Click the Other tab.**
- **In the Other sheet, click the two boxes in the Person Names area to place a check mark in each box as shown in Figure 2-89.**

The Other sheet is activated. A check mark appears in the Enable the Person Names Smart Tag check box and the Display Messenger Status in the From field check box (Figure 2-89).

3

- **Click the OK button.**
- **Minimize the Outlook window.**

Outlook closes the Options dialog box and minimizes the Outlook window to the taskbar.

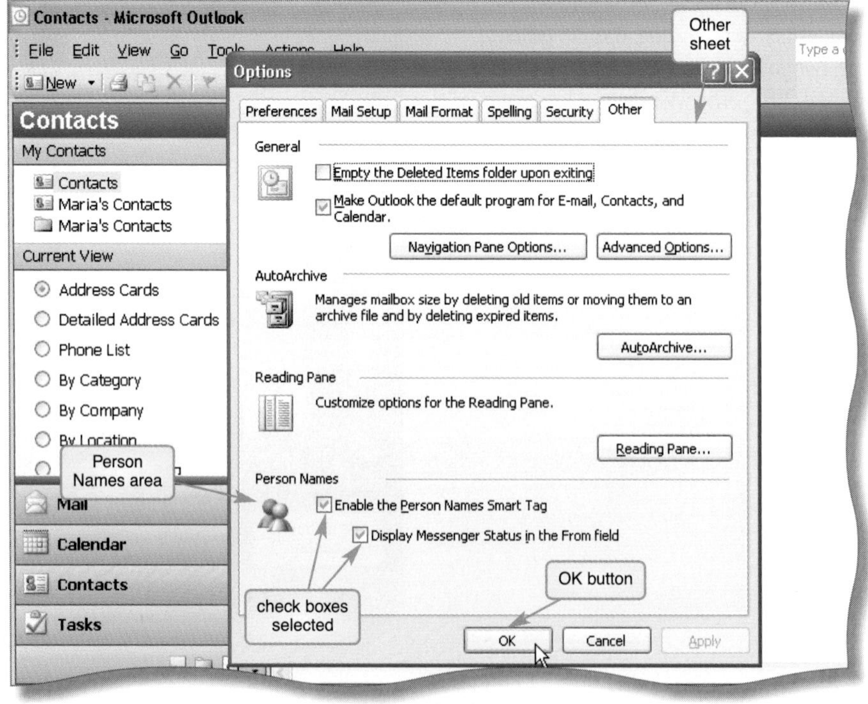

FIGURE 2-89

Clicking the Sign me in automatically check box (Figure 2-86 on page OUT 123) allows you to sign-in automatically each time you start Windows Messenger. Clicking the Get a .NET Passport link allows you to obtain a Microsoft .NET passport.

The My Status sheet in Figure 2-87 on page OUT 123 contains the Windows Messenger account name (Maria Rosado), account status (Online), and a message indicating that the contact list does not have anyone in it.

Adding a Contact to the Messenger Contact List

To use Windows Messenger with Outlook, contacts must be entered in the Messenger contact list, and the contact's Instant Messaging (IM) address must be entered in the Outlook contacts list. Table 2-6 contains the IM addresses for the contacts in the Maria's Contacts contact list.

Table 2-6 IM Addresses

CONTACT NAME	IM ADDRESS
Courtney Craig	ccraig101@hotmail.com
Jodi Dickens	jdickens123@hotmail.com
Susan Hadley	shadley101@hotmail.com
Chris Johnson	cjohnson123@hotmail.com
Marci Laver	mlaver123@hotmail.com
Hayley Miller	hmiller123@hotmail.com
Patti Sabol	psabol123@hotmail.com
Kendra Zimmerman	kzimm123@hotmail.com

After starting Windows Messenger, you can add a contact to the contact list if you know the e-mail address or Windows Messenger sign-in name of the contact. A contact must have an MSN Hotmail account or a Microsoft .NET Passport and have the Windows Messenger or MSN Messenger software installed on their computer. If you try to add a contact that does not meet these requirements, you are given the chance to send the contact an e-mail invitation that explains how to get a passport and download the Windows Messenger or MSN Messenger software.

To simplify the process of adding a contact to the contact list, Windows Messenger allows you to use the Add a Contact wizard. The **Add a Contact wizard** assists you in adding a contact to the contact list. The steps on the next page show how to add a contact to the Messenger contact list using the e-mail addresses listed in Table 2-6.

More About

Instant Messaging

For more information about instant messaging, visit the Outlook 2003 More About Web page (scsite.com/out2003/more) and then click Instant Messaging.

To Add a Contact to the Messenger Contact List

1

- **Click Add a Contact in the Windows Messenger window (Figure 2-87 on page OUT 123).**
- **When the Add a Contact dialog box is displayed, point to the Next button.**

Windows Messenger starts the Add a Contact wizard and displays the Add a Contact dialog box (Figure 2-90). The dialog box contains a question, two option buttons, a message, and the Next button. The By e-mail address or sign-in name option button is selected.

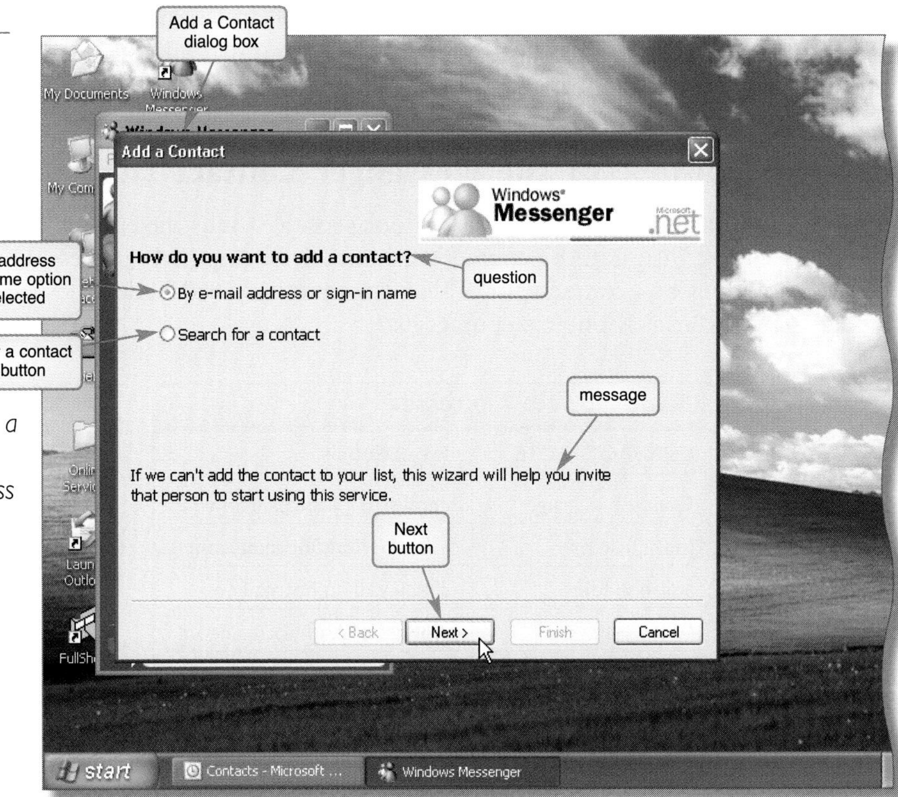

FIGURE 2-90

2

- **Click the Next button.**
- **Type** `ccraig101@hotmail.com` **in the text box.**

The contents of the Add a Contact dialog box change (Figure 2-91). The ccraig101@hotmail.com e-mail address appears in the text box.

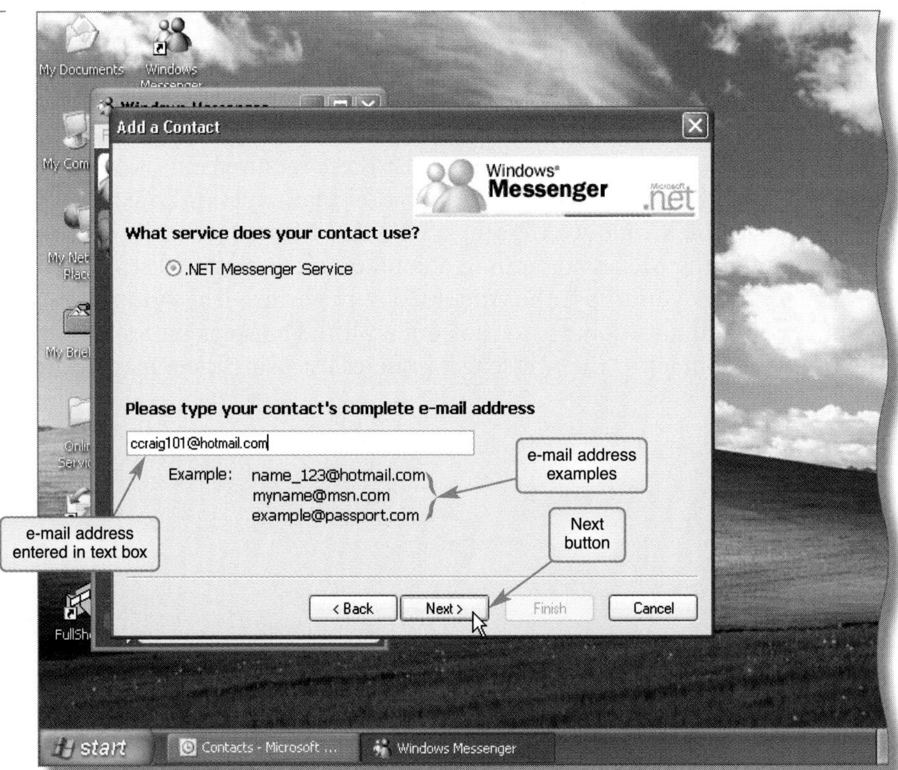

FIGURE 2-91

3

• **Click the Next button.**

The contents of the Add a Contact dialog box change (Figure 2-92). The dialog box contains a message indicating (Courtney Craig) was successfully added to the contact list.

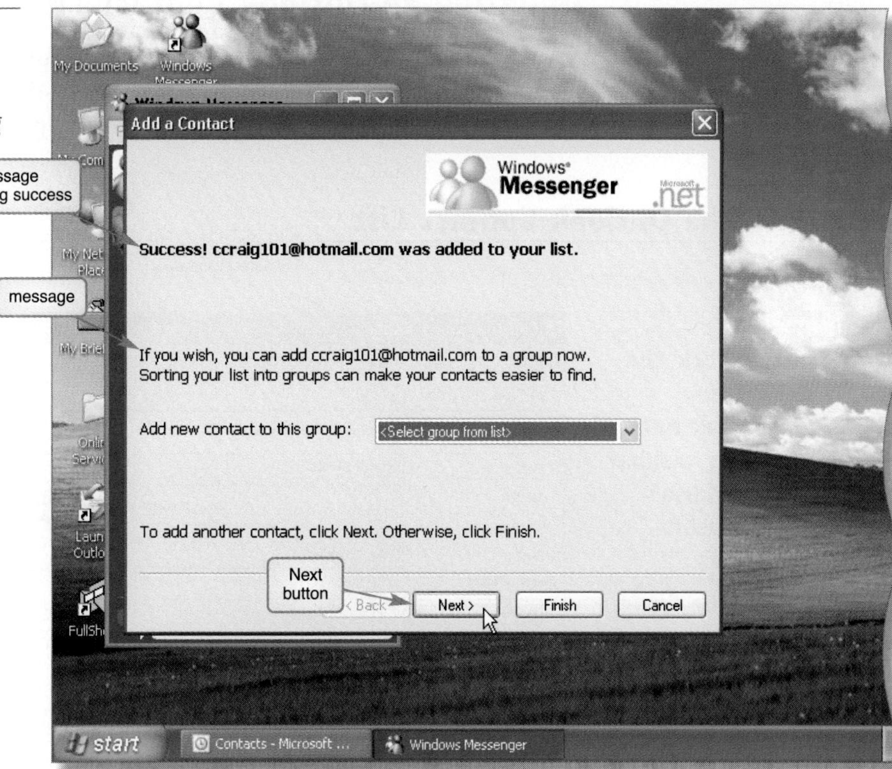

FIGURE 2-92

4

• **Click the Next button two times to advance to the first Add a Contact dialog box (see Figure 2-90).**

5

• **Repeat Steps 2 through 4 to enter the remaining contacts in Table 2-6 on page OUT 125.**

• **After you have added the Kendra Zimmerman entry, click Finish button in the dialog box with the You're done! Message.**

The Add a Contact wizard closes, the contacts from Table 2-6 are added to the contact list (Figure 2-93).

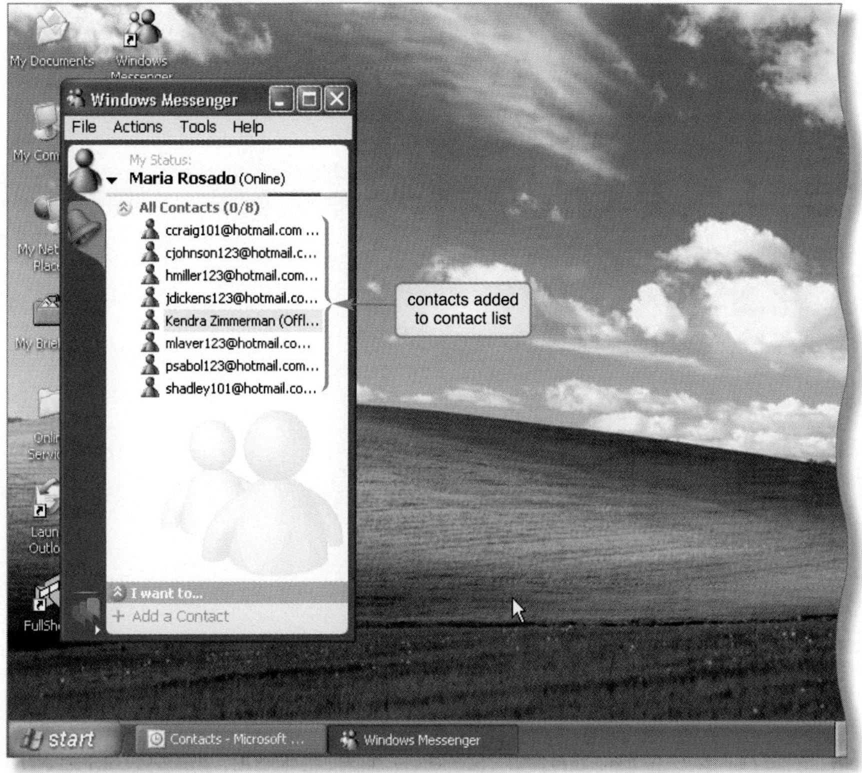

FIGURE 2-93

Updating an Outlook Contact List

To complete the process of setting up instant messaging with Outlook, the contact list must be updated with the IM addresses of the contacts listed in Table 2-6 on page OUT 125. The following steps show how to update the Maria's Contacts contact list.

To Update the Outlook Contact List

1

- **If necessary, click the Maria's Contacts - Microsoft Outlook button on the Windows taskbar to display the Maria's Contacts - Microsoft Outlook window.**
- **Double-click the Craig, Courtney entry to open the Courtney Craig - Contact window.**

Outlook opens the Courtney Craig - Contact window (Figure 2-94).

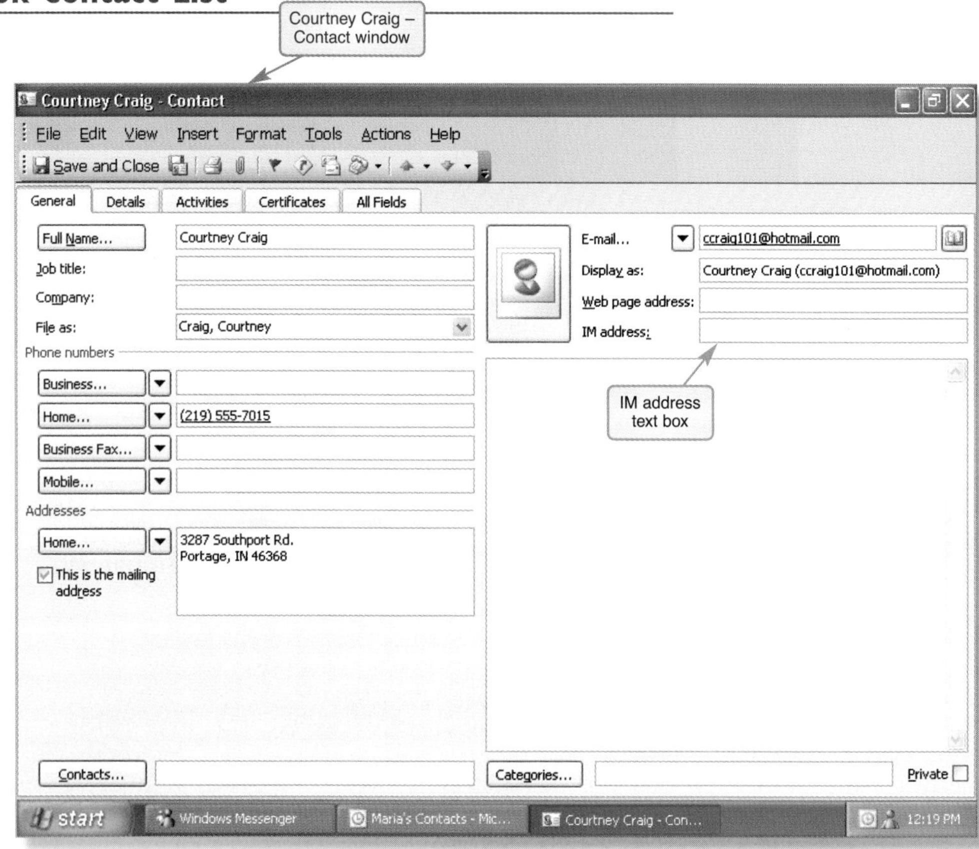

FIGURE 2-94

2

- **Click the IM address text box.**
- **Type** `ccraig101@hotmail.com` **as the IM address.**

The IM address for Courtney Craig is entered in the appropriate text box (Figure 2-95).

3

- **Click the Save and Close button on the Standard toolbar.**

4

- **Repeat Steps 1 through 3 to add the remaining IM addresses from Table 2-6 to the Maria's Contacts contact list.**

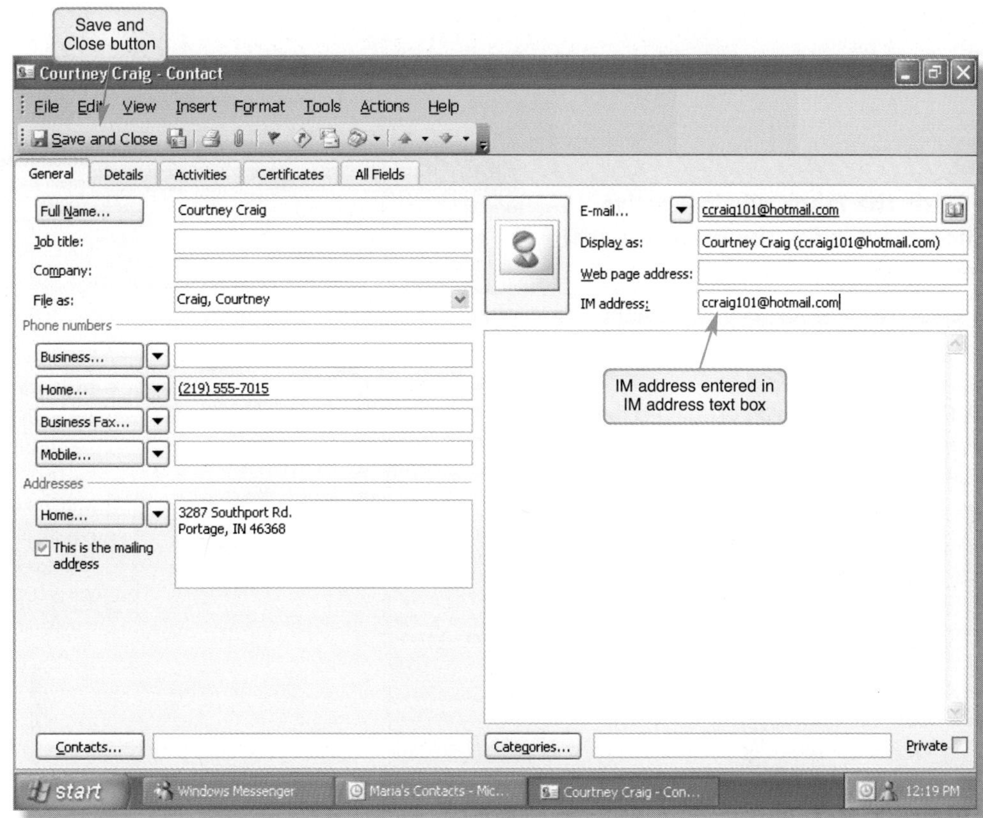

FIGURE 2-95

Communicating Using Outlook and Windows Messenger

To use Windows Messenger with Outlook, the person with whom you want to communicate must be online, and, for this project, must have an e-mail message in an Outlook folder. Using Outlook, when you open an e-mail message from an individual or view the message in the Reading Pane, the Person Names Smart Tag is shown next to the sender's name. Placing the mouse pointer over the Person Names Smart Tag will show a ScreenTip indicating the person's online status. The steps on the next page show how to send an instant message to someone you know is online.

Note: The steps that begin on the next page are for demonstration purposes only. Thus, if you are stepping through this project on a computer, then you must have someone with an Instant Messenger address send you an e-mail so it displays in the Inbox as shown in Figure 2-96 on the next page.

More About

The Person Name Smart Tag

The Person Name Smart Tag can indicate online status for any person whose instant messaging e-mail address you have added to your instant messaging contact list. The Person Name Smart Tag also shows online status for individuals using the Exchange Instant Messaging Service or SIP Communications Service, even if they are not in your contact list.

To Send an Instant Message

1

- **With the Inbox window active, click the Kendra Zimmerman e-mail message.**
- **Click the Person Names Smart Tag in the Reading Pane.**

Outlook displays the Smart Tag menu (Figure 2-96). The message at the top of the menu indicates that Kendra Zimmerman is online.

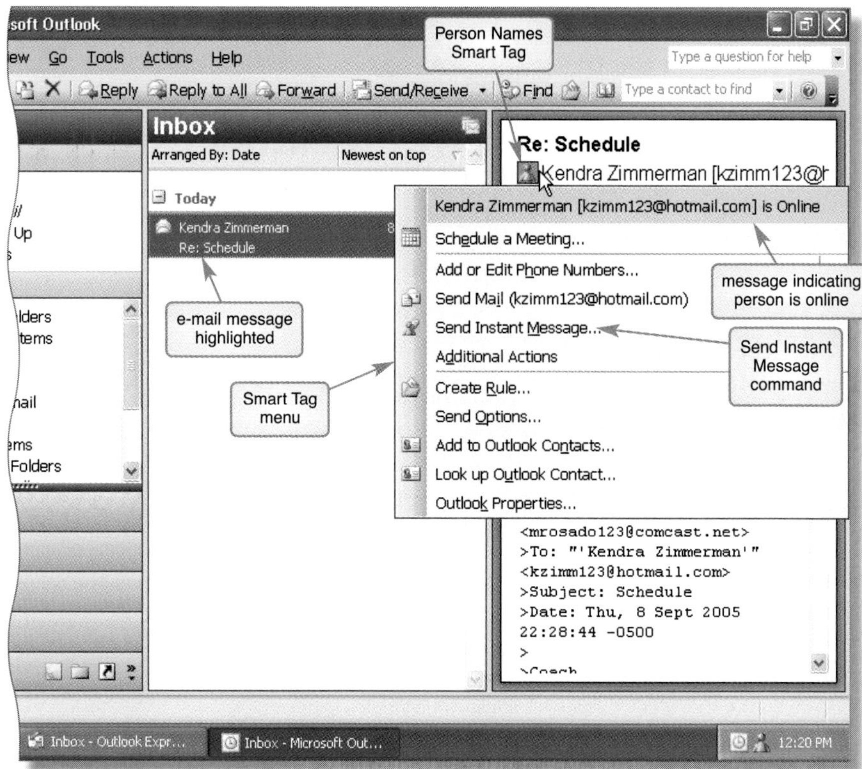

FIGURE 2-96

2

- **Click Send Instant Message on the Smart Tag menu.**

Outlook displays the Kendra Zimmerman - Conversation window (Figure 2-97).

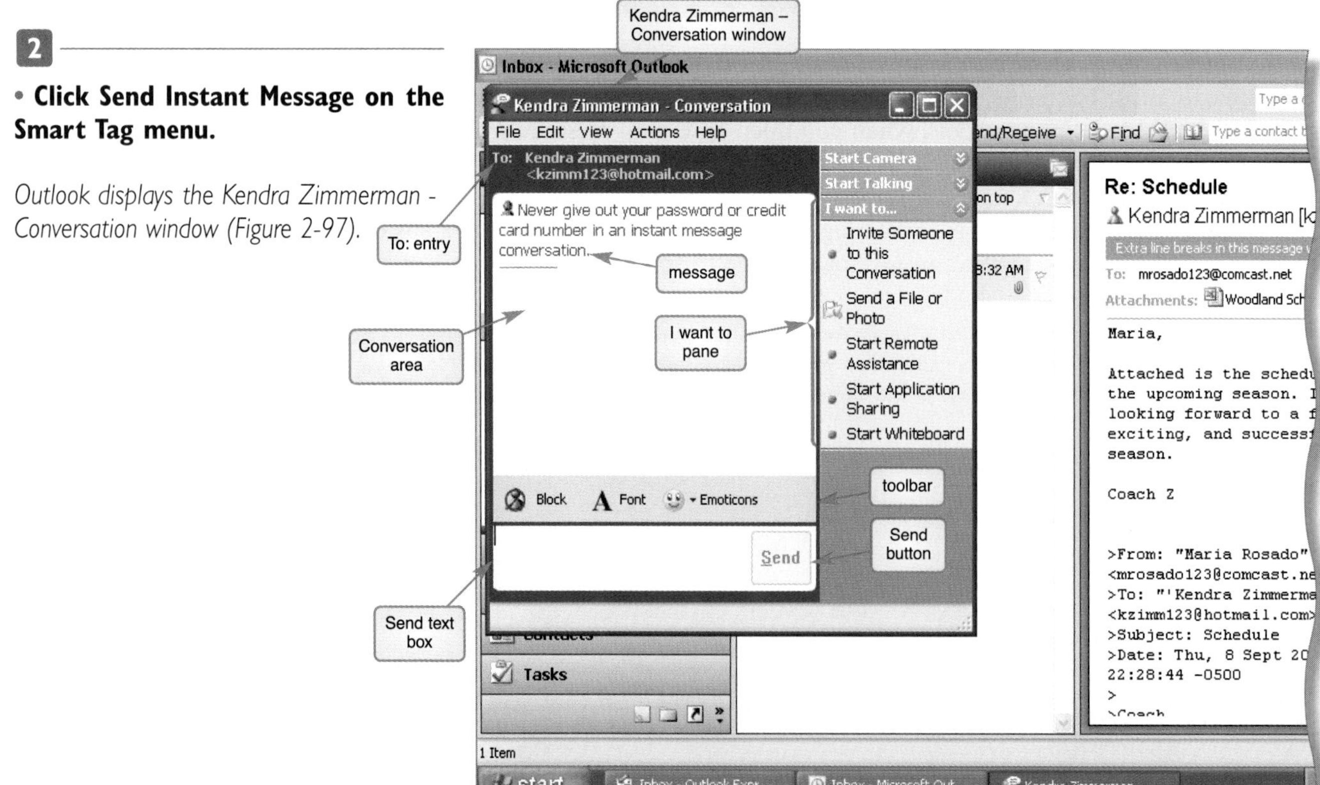

FIGURE 2-97

3

• **Type** `Hey Coach, I'm glad I caught you online. I wanted to get together with you to discuss a new warm-up routine.` **in the Send text box, and then click the Send button.**

Windows Messenger removes the message from the text box, displays the sender's name and message in the Conversation area, and displays the status of the receiver at the bottom of the Conversation window (Figure 2-98). The status indicates that Kendra Zimmerman is typing a message.

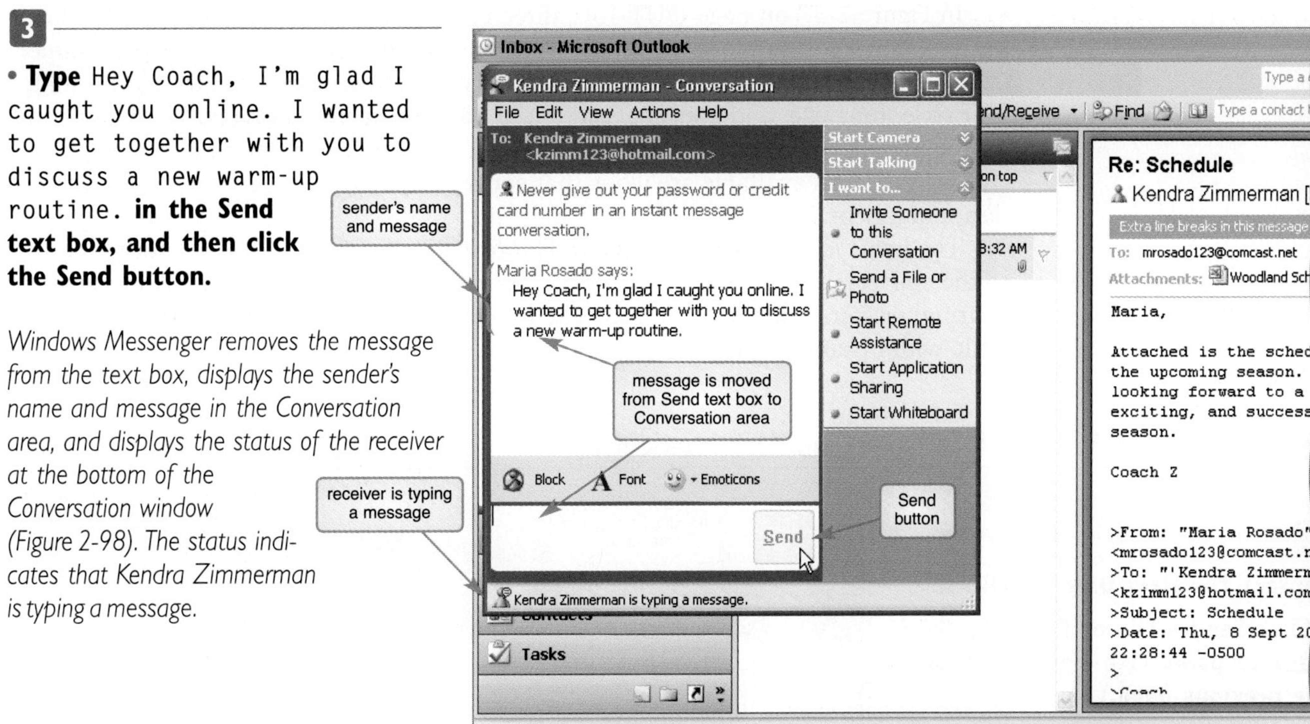

FIGURE 2-98

4

• **The receiver of the message (Kendra Zimmerman) types and sends a response.**

Windows Messenger displays the receiver's name (Kendra Zimmerman) and message in the Conversation area and changes the message at the bottom of the Conversation window to indicate the date and time the message was received (Figure 2-99).

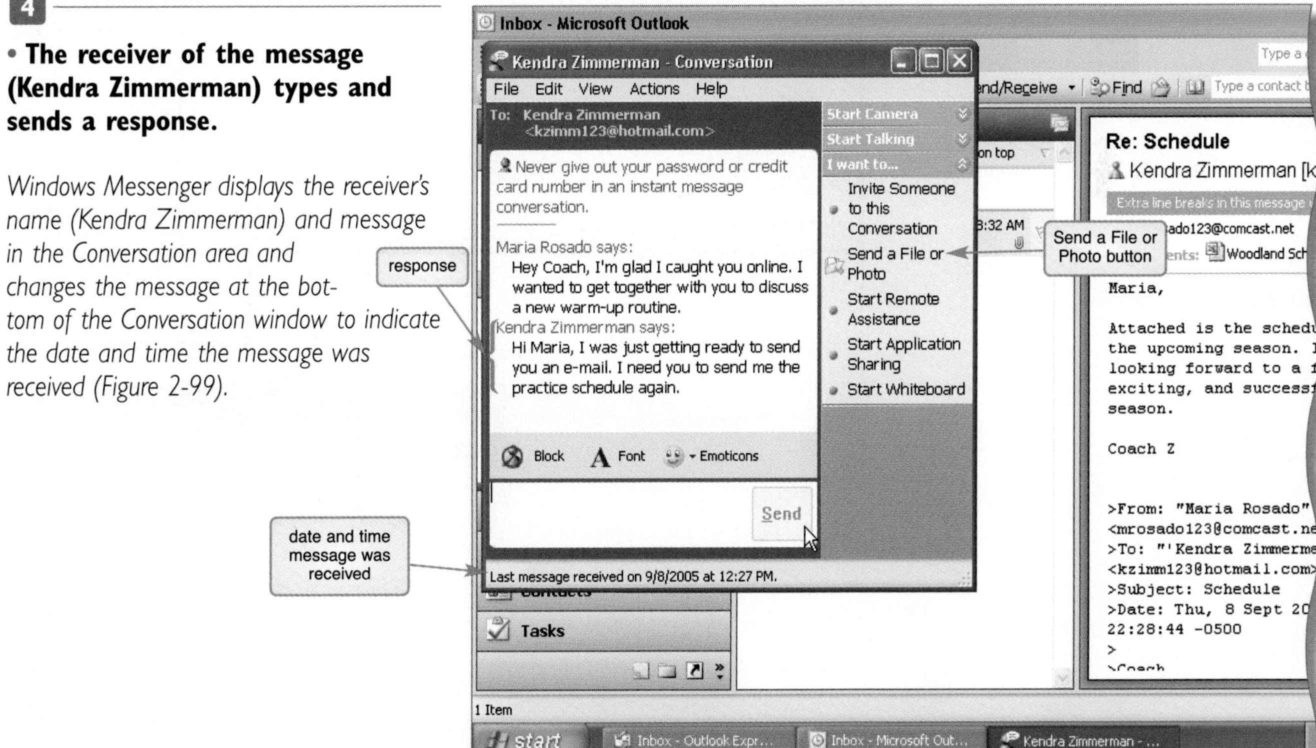

FIGURE 2-99

In Figure 2-97 on page OUT 130, three buttons appear on the toolbar. The Block button allows you to block a contact. The contact will not be able to see your name in his or her contact list or contact you. The Font button allows you to select a font, font style, font size, and apply special effects to the text in a message. The Emoticons button allows you to insert icons in a message that convey an emotion or a feeling. Among the icons available are icons that convey happiness, surprise, confusion, and disappointment.

The items in the I want to pane in Figure 2-97 allow you to invite another person to the conversation, send a file or photo, start Remote Assistance, start Application Sharing, or start using Whiteboard. The following steps show how to attach and send a file with instant messaging.

To Attach and Send a File with Instant Messaging

1

- **Insert the Data Disk in drive A.**
- **Click Send a File or Photo in the I want to pane. (See Figure 2-99 on the previous page.)**

Outlook displays the Send a File to Kendra Zimmerman dialog box (Figure 2-100).

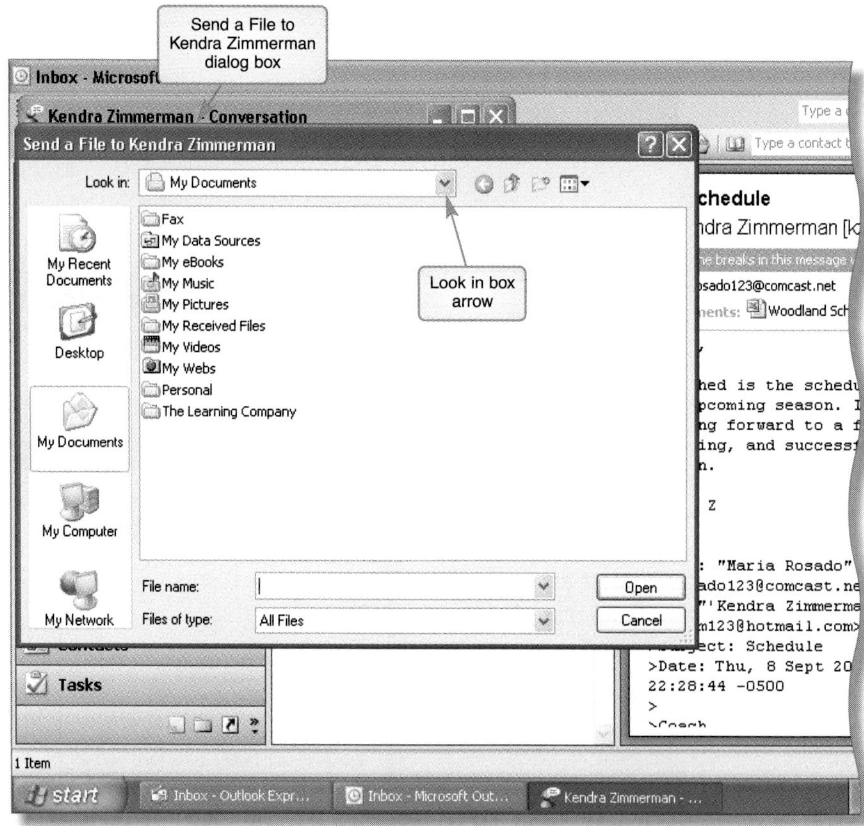

FIGURE 2-100

2

• **Click the Look in box arrow and then click 3½ Floppy (A:).**

• **Click Updated Practice Schedule in the Send a File to Kendra Zimmerman dialog box.**

The Updated Practice Schedule file is highlighted (Figure 2-101).

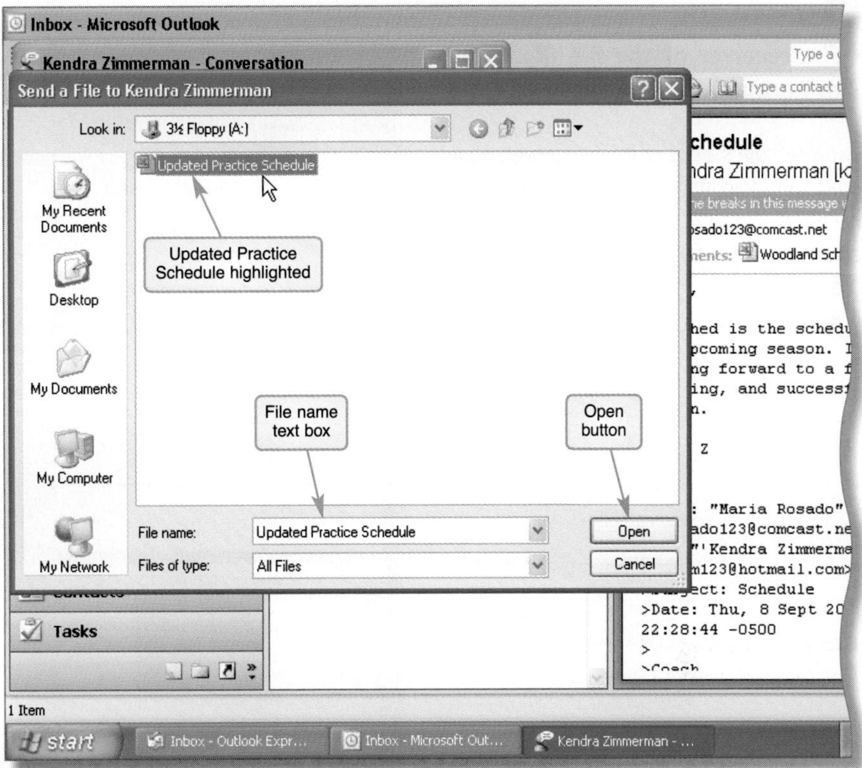

FIGURE 2-101

3

• **Click the Open button in the Send a File to Kendra Zimmerman dialog box.**

The Send a File to Kendra Zimmerman dialog box closes and a message appears in the Conversation area of the Kendra Zimmerman - Conversation window, indicating that you are waiting for the receiver to accept the file (Figure 2-102).

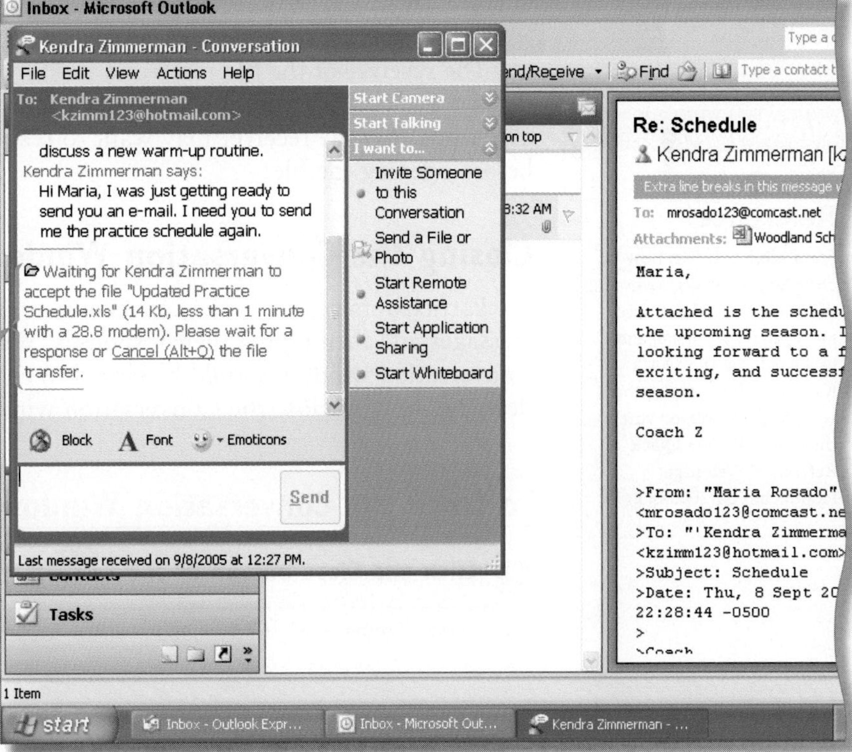

FIGURE 2-102

4

• **The receiver of the file (Kendra Zimmerman) has accepted the file.**

Two messages appear in the Conversation area: (1) indicating the file has been accepted, and (2) indicating the transfer of the file is complete (Figure 2-103).

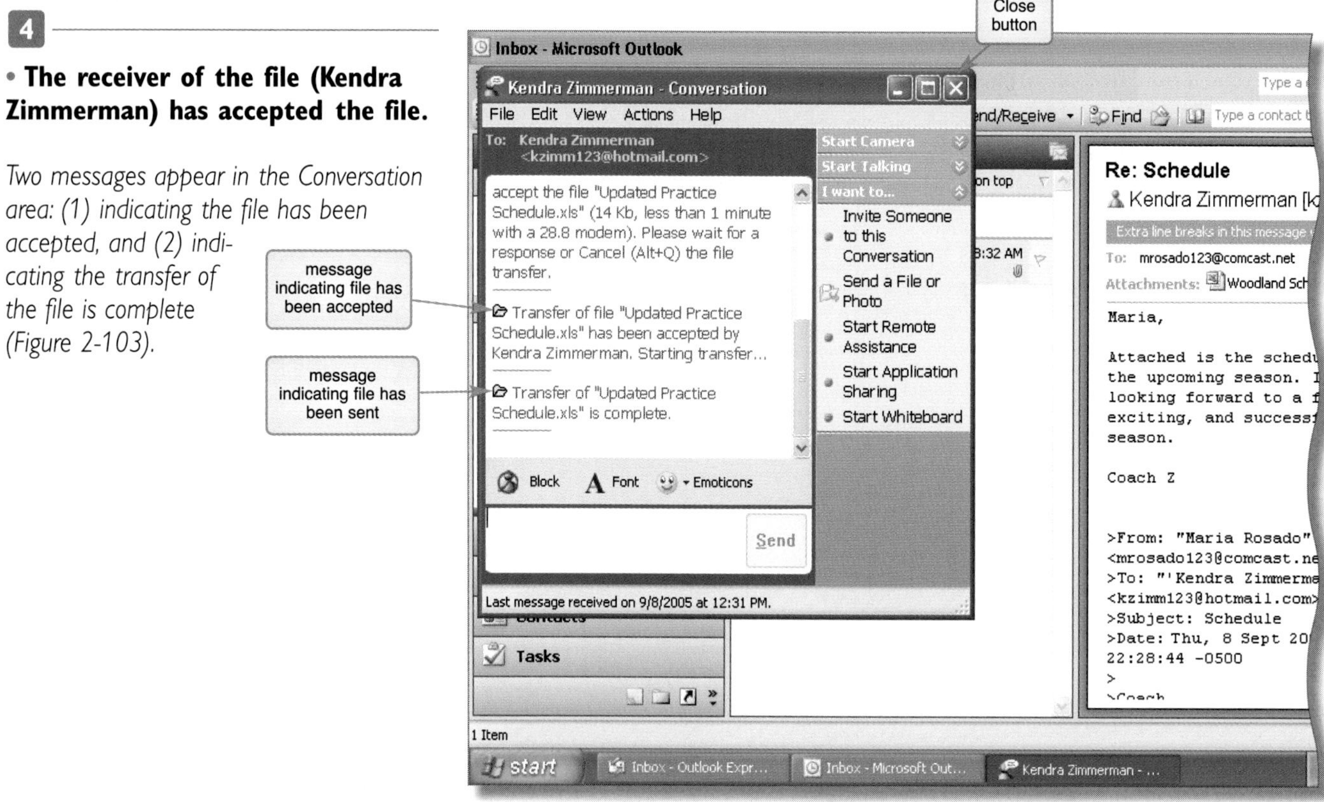

FIGURE 2-103

The receiver of the file receives a message indicating he or she has received the file successfully. The message contains a link with the location of the file along with a warning that the receiver may want to scan the file with a virus-scanning program before opening the file.

> *More About*
>
> **The Quick Reference**
>
> For a table that lists how to complete the tasks covered in this book using the mouse, menu, shortcut menu, and keyboard, see the Quick Reference Summary at the back of this book, or visit the Outlook 2003 Quick Reference Web page (scsite.com/out2003/qr).

Closing the Conversation Window

Participants can continue conversing in this manner, reading each others messages and then typing their responses. When the conversation is complete, the Conversation window should be closed to end the conversation. The following step describes how to close the Conversation window.

To Close the Conversation Window

1 **Click the Close button in the Conversation window.**

The Kendra Zimmerman - Conversation window closes.

Quitting Outlook

With the project complete, the final step is to close the Outlook program and return to the Windows desktop. The following step describes how to quit Outlook.

To Quit Outlook

1 **Click the Close button on the Outlook title bar.**

Outlook closes, and the Windows desktop is displayed.

More About

Microsoft Certification

Microsoft Office Certification provides an opportunity for you to obtain a valuable industry credential — proof that you have the Outlook skills required by employers. For more information, see Appendix E or visit the Outlook 2003 Certification Web page (scsite.com/out2003/cert).

Project Summary

In this project, you learned to use Outlook to create a personal schedule, organize meetings, and create a task list. You learned how to enter appointments, create recurring appointments, move appointments to new dates, schedule events, and view and print your calendar in different views and print styles. You created a task list, assigned tasks, and accepted a task assignment. You learned how to invite attendees and schedule resources for a meeting, accept a meeting request, and propose and change the time of a meeting. You also learned how to color code and label your calendar to make it easier to view. You created and edited notes. You exported your personal subfolder to a floppy disk and later imported subfolders for further updating. You also learned about using AutoArchive and customizing AutoArchive settings. Finally, you learned how to enable and sign into Windows Messenger through Outlook, added contacts to the contact list, and sent an instant message including sending a file through instant messaging.

What You Should Know

Having completed this project, you should be able to perform the tasks below. The tasks are listed in the same order they were presented in this project. For a list of buttons, menus, toolbars, and commands introduced in this project, see the Quick Reference Summary at the back of this book and refer to the Page Number column.

1. Start and Customize Outlook (OUT 68)
2. Create a Personal Folder (OUT 70)
3. Enter Appointments Using the Appointment Area (OUT 72)
4. Enter and Save Appointments Using the Appointment Window (OUT 74)
5. Enter Recurring Appointments (OUT 76)
6. Move to the Next Day in the Appointment Area and Enter the Remaining Recurring Appointments (OUT 78)
7. Enter Appointment Dates and Times Using Natural Language Phrases (OUT 79)
8. Enter the Remaining One-Time Appointments (OUT 81)
9. Delete an Appointment (OUT 82)
10. Move an Appointment to a New Time (OUT 84)
11. Move an Appointment to a New Date (OUT 85)
12. Move an Appointment to a New Month (OUT 86)
13. Create an Event (OUT 88)
14. Change to Work Week View (OUT 89)
15. Change to Week View (OUT 90)
16. Change to Month View (OUT 91)
17. Create a Task List (OUT 92)
18. Export a Subfolder to a Floppy Disk (OUT 93)
19. Delete a Personal Subfolder (OUT 96)
20. Import a Subfolder (OUT 97)
21. Assign a Task to Another Person (OUT 99)
22. Accept a Task Assignment (OUT 101)
23. Add or Delete Fields in a View (OUT 103)
24. Move Tasks to a New Personal Folder (OUT 103)
25. Invite Attendees to a Meeting (OUT 104)
26. Accept a Meeting Request (OUT 108)

Learn It Online

Instructions: To complete the Learn It Online exercises, start your browser, click the Address bar, and then enter the Web address scsite.com/out2003/learn. When the Outlook 2003 Learn It Online page is displayed, follow the instructions in the exercises below. Each exercise has instructions for printing your results, either for your own records or for submission to your instructor.

1 Project Reinforcement TF, MC, and SA

Below Outlook Project 2, click the Project Reinforcement link. Print the quiz by clicking Print on the File menu for each page. Answer each question.

2 Flash Cards

Below Outlook Project 2, click the Flash Cards link and read the instructions. Type 20 (or a number specified by your instructor) in the Number of playing cards text box, type your name in the Enter your Name text box, and then click the Flip Card button. When the flash card is displayed, read the question and then click the ANSWER box arrow to select an answer. Flip through Flash Cards. If your score is 15 (75%) correct or greater, click Print on the File menu to print your results. If your score is less than 15 (75%) correct, then redo this exercise by clicking the Replay button.

3 Practice Test

Below Outlook Project 2, click the Practice Test link. Answer each question, enter your first and last name at the bottom of the page, and then click the Grade Test button. When the graded practice test is displayed on your screen, click Print on the File menu to print a hard copy. Continue to take practice tests until you score 80% or better.

4 Who Wants To Be a Computer Genius?

Below Outlook Project 2, click the Computer Genius link. Read the instructions, enter your first and last name at the bottom of the page, and then click the PLAY button. When your score is displayed, click the PRINT RESULTS link to print a hard copy.

5 Wheel of Terms

Below Outlook Project 2, click the Wheel of Terms link. Read the instructions, and then enter your first and last name and your school name. Click the PLAY button. When your score is displayed, right-click the score and then click Print on the shortcut menu to print a hard copy.

6 Crossword Puzzle Challenge

Below Outlook Project 2, click the Crossword Puzzle Challenge link. Read the instructions, and then enter your first and last name. Click the SUBMIT button. Work the crossword puzzle. When you are finished, click the Submit button. When the crossword puzzle is redisplayed, click the Print Puzzle button to print a hard copy.

7 Tips and Tricks

Below Outlook Project 2, click the Tips and Tricks link. Click a topic that pertains to Project 2. Right-click the information and then click Print on the shortcut menu. Construct a brief example of what the information relates to in Outlook to confirm you understand how to use the tip or trick.

8 Newsgroups

Below Outlook Project 2, click the Newsgroups link. Click a topic that pertains to Project 2. Print three comments.

9 Expanding Your Horizons

Below Outlook Project 2, click the Expanding Your Horizons link. Click a topic that pertains to Project 2. Print the information. Construct a brief example of what the information relates to in Outlook to confirm you understand the contents of the article.

10 Search Sleuth

Below Outlook Project 2, click the Search Sleuth link. To search for a term that pertains to this project, select a term below the Project 2 title and then use the Google search engine at google.com (or any major search engine) to display and print two Web pages that present information on the term.

11 Outlook Online Training

Below Outlook Project 2, click the Outlook Online Training link. When your browser displays the Microsoft Office Online Web page, click the Outlook link. Click one of the Outlook courses that covers one or more of the objectives listed at the beginning of the project on page OUT 66. Print the first page of the course before stepping through it.

12 Office Marketplace

Below Outlook Project 2, click the Office Marketplace link. When your browser displays the Microsoft Office Online Web page, click the Office Marketplace link. Click a topic that relates to Outlook. Print the first page.

Apply Your Knowledge

1 Creating a Schedule

Instructions Part 1: Start Outlook. Create a Calendar folder using your name as the name of the new folder. Create a schedule using the information in Table 2-7. Use the Options command on the Tools menu to set up the calendar for a six-day work week with hours from 7:00 AM to 6:00 PM. Color code the schedule using the following labels: School, Work, and Personal. This calendar is for the fall semester that begins Monday, August 22, 2005, and ends Friday, December 16, 2005. When the calendar is complete, print the calendar in Month view and submit to your instructor.

Table 2-7 Appointment Information

APPOINTMENT	LABEL	DAYS	TIME	OCCURRENCES
Operating Systems	School	M, W	7:30 am - 9:00 am	30
Supervision	School	M, W	11:30 am - 1:00 pm	30
Accounting	School	T, Th	7:00 pm - 8:30 pm	30
Work (Open)	Work	T, Th, Sa	7:00 am - 3:30 pm	August 23 August 25 August 27
Dentist Appointment	Personal	W	4:00 pm - 5:00 pm	August 24
Work (Close)	Work	T, Th, Sa	9:00 am - 6:00 pm	August 30 September 1 September 3
Labor Day 5k Run	Personal	S	8:30 am - 10:00 am	September 4
Accounting Study Lab	School	W	3:00 pm - 4:00 pm	Every other Wednesday for 15 occurrences

Instructions Part 2: Use the Microsoft Office Outlook Help system to learn more about the Calendar Options dialog box shown in Figure 2-70 on page OUT 113. Write a report summarizing all the options available in the Calendar Options dialog box.

1 Planning a Meeting

Problem: You are the project manager for a large government project. The project involves working with individuals from county, state, and federal offices. With the project start date approaching, you need to organize a meeting to get all the required signatures on your contract.

Instructions Part 1: Perform the following tasks.

1. Import the Lab 2-1 Contacts folder into Outlook (Figure 2-104).

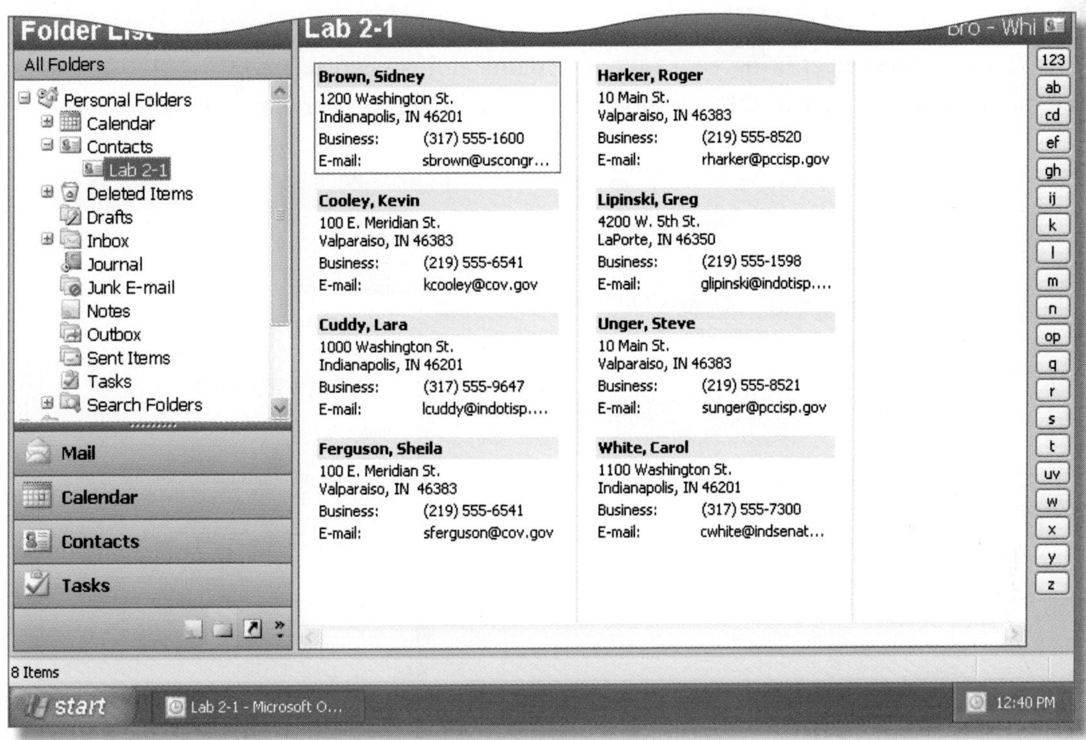

FIGURE 2-104

2. Organize a meeting for Wednesday, November 9, 2005 from 9:00 a.m. until noon inviting only those contacts that hold a county, state, or federal office.
3. Submit a printout of the meeting to your instructor.
4. Change the date and time of the meeting from November 9, 2005 to November 11, 2005 from 1:00 p.m. until 3:00 p.m.
5. Send out an updated meeting invitation.
6. Submit a printout of the updated meeting to your instructor.
7. You have just found out that your presence is required elsewhere on the meeting date. Cancel the meeting using the Cancel Meeting command on the Actions menu.

Instructions Part 2: Use the Outlook Help system to obtain information on scheduling resources. Write a one-page report describing how scheduling resources works. If your instructor has set up resources for you to access, schedule a room and an audio visual device for the meeting described in Part 1.

2 Using Windows Messenger with Outlook

Problem: You are preparing for an important meeting and need a file updated by a coworker in another department. You do not have that individual's information in your contact list, however. You leave a message on her voice mail about the file and she e-mails you requesting that you send the file to her. Because you have only a short time before the meeting begins, you decide to use Windows Messenger with Outlook to communicate and send the file to your coworker. *Note:* To use instant messaging, you should complete this exercise with a classmate.

Instructions: Perform the following tasks.

1. Sign in to Windows Messenger using your own user name and password.
2. Send an e-mail message similar to the one shown in Figure 2-105 to your classmate.

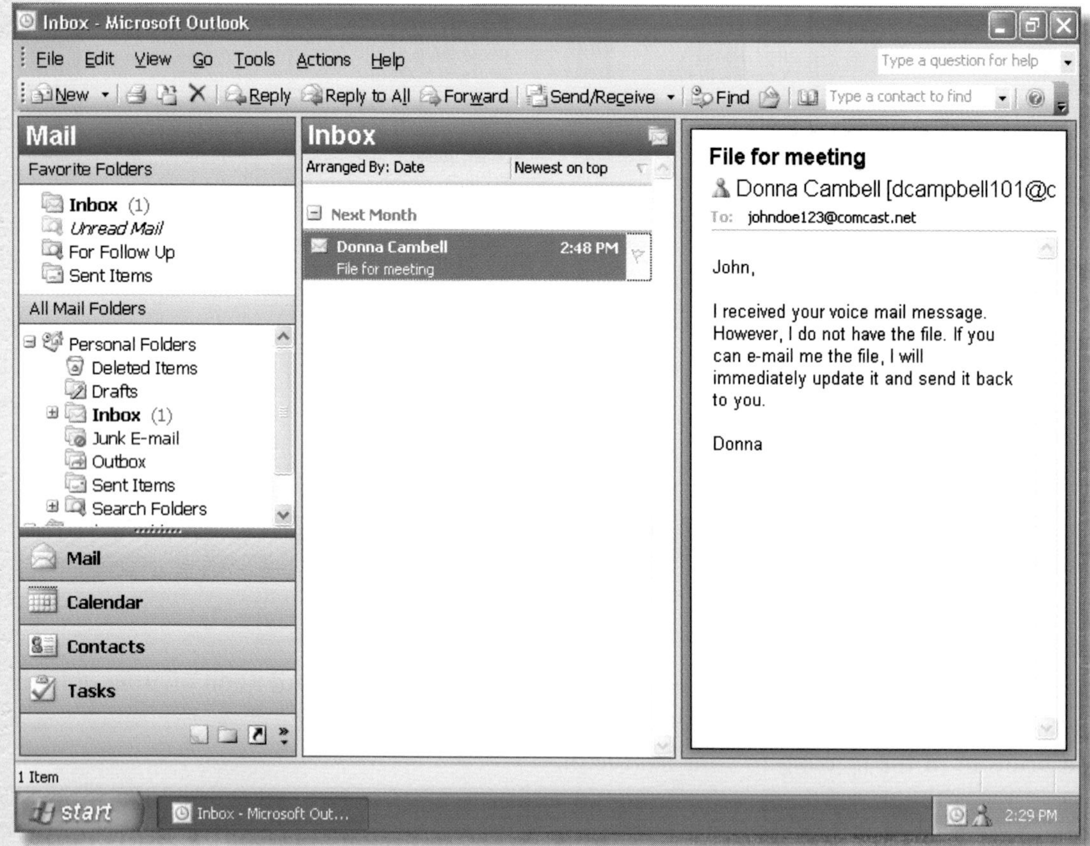

FIGURE 2-105

3. Add the sender to your Windows Messenger and Outlook contact lists. Be sure to include her instant message address in Outlook.
4. Insert the Data Disk into drive A on your computer.
5. Send an instant message indicating that you will send the file using Windows Messenger.
6. Send the Quarterly Report file from the Data Disk to the sender.

In the Lab

7. When you receive the file, open the file and submit a printout with your name and the name of the person you completed the exercise with to your instructor.
8. Sign out of Windows Messenger and close all open windows.

3 Creating a Calendar and a Task List

Problem: You are the owner of a small hardware store. Your company has experienced rapid growth during the last several months, and with spring approaching, you need to change to regular from seasonal stock. As the owner, you also have administrative duties to perform, such as staff meetings, payroll, advertising, and sales campaigns. To make your schedule even more hectic, you coach your child's spring baseball team on Wednesday nights from 5:00 p.m. to 6:30 p.m., and Saturday's from 12:00 p.m. to 2:00 p.m. at Community Little League Fields. You need to create a schedule of appointments as well as a task list to help you keep track of your various jobs and responsibilities each day.

Instructions Part 1: Perform the following tasks.

1. Create a personal Calendar subfolder named A-1 Hardware.
2. Change the start time of the calendar to 7:00 am.
3. Enter the appointments in the calendar, using the information listed in Table 2-8.

Table 2-8 Appointment Information

DESCRIPTION	DATE	TIME
Staff meeting	Every Monday from March 6, 2006 - April 24, 2006	7:00 am - 8:00 am
Meeting to prepare Winter Closeout Sale	March 1, 2006	8:30 am - 10:30 am
Enter payroll	Every Thursday	4:00 pm - 5:00 pm
Ryan's birthday	March 21, 2006	
Conference call with Karen and Bob	March 14, 2006	9:00 am - 10:00 am
Meet with plumbing supplier	March 16, 2006	1:00 pm - 2:00 pm
Lunch with Ruth	March 29, 2006	12:00 pm - 1:00 pm

4. Create a task list containing the following tasks:
   a. Call Kyle to confirm plumbing supplier's visit.
   b. Schedule meeting to discuss spring and summer sales goals.
   c. Call to check lawn fertilizer delivery.
   d. Clear out snow blowers to make room for lawn mowers.
   e. Replace snow shovels with lawn and garden tools.
5. Print the calendar for the month of March and submit to your instructor.

(continued)

Creating a Calendar and a Task List *(continued)*

This part of the exercise requires that you work as a team with two classmates.

Instructions Part 2: With the growth of your hardware store, you have been able to hire a manager and assistant manager. Perform the following tasks.

1. Add the due dates in Table 2-9 to the tasks created in Part 1.
2. Using the tasks created in Part 1, assign the tasks per Table 2-9. Obtain and use the e-mail addresses of two classmates for Manager and Assistant Manager.
3. Have the classmate representing the Manager accept one task and decline one task, and the classmate representing the Assistant Manager accept one task and decline one task.
4. Modify the current view of the task list to include the Owner field using the Customize Current View command accessed by pointing to Arrange By on the View menu, then pointing to Current View on the Arrange By submenu.
5. Print the modified task list and submit to your instructor.
6. Create a personal Tasks subfolder called A-1 Tasks and move the task list you just created to the new subfolder.
7. Export both the personal subfolders created in this exercise to a floppy disk, archive the files, and then delete them from the hard disk.
8. Close all open windows.

Table 2-9 Task Information

TASKS FROM PART 1	ASSIGNMENT	DUE DATE
Call Kyle to confirm plumbing supplier's visit	Manager	March 15, 2006
Call to check lawn fertilizer delivery	Manager	March 10, 2006
Clear out snow blowers to make room for lawn mowers	Assistant Manager	March 30, 2006
Replace snow shovels with lawn and garden tools	Assistant Manager	March 20, 2006

Cases and Places

The difficulty of these case studies varies:
■ are the least difficult and ■■ are more difficult. The last exercise is a group exercise.

1 ■ Create a personal schedule for the next month. Include any work and class time, together with study time. You also can include any extracurricular activities in which you participate. Use recurring appointments when possible. All day activities should be scheduled as events. Color code the calendar as necessary. Print the calendar in Monthly Style and submit to your instructor.

2 ■ At work, you are in charge of scheduling for the month of May. Create a schedule of work times for four employees. Josh works Mondays, Wednesdays, and Fridays from 9:00 a.m. to 5:00 p.m. Julie works Tuesdays, Thursdays, and Saturdays from 9:00 a.m. to 5:00 p.m. Javier works from 12:00 p.m. until 9:00 p.m. on Mondays, Wednesdays, and Fridays. Claire completes the schedule working from 12:00 p.m. until 9:00 p.m. on Tuesdays, Thursdays, and Saturdays. Set the calendar so reflect a six day work week with hours ranging from 9:00 a.m. to 9:00 p.m. Print the calendar in Monthly Style and submit to your instructor.

3 ■ Create journal entries from your personal schedule for the past week. Comment on activities in which you participated and tasks that you accomplished. Write when the activity started and ended. Note the problems (if any) associated with the activity. When commenting on completed tasks, include notes about results of having completed it. Specify what would have happened had the task not been completed when it was. Write a brief summary of your journal and submit to your instructor.

4 ■■ Use the natural language phrase option in the Start time date box to create a list of events for the year. Create a new calendar that contains the following holidays: New Year's Day, Valentine's Day, St. Patrick's Day, Independence Day, Halloween, Veteran's Day, Christmas Eve, Christmas Day, and New Year's Eve. For the last four holidays, indicate that you will be out of the office all day. Also, add events for several family or friend birthdays or anniversaries, using the natural language phrase option. For instance, schedule these events by utilizing the phrase, two weeks from today (or something similar) as a start date. Try different phrase options to schedule these events. Color code the events to separate birthdays from anniversaries, etc. Select two months to print in Monthly Style and submit them to your instructor.

5 ■■ **Working Together** Choose a member of your team to organize a meeting. The organizer will send out meeting invitations to each group member using Outlook. Each member either should accept the meeting time or decline the meeting time and propose a new meeting time based on their individual schedules using Outlook. Use a combination of e-mail and Windows Messenger with Outlook to discuss proposed meeting times with the organizer. Each team member should print out the appointment and hand it in to the instructor.

Appendix A

Microsoft Outlook Help System

Using the Outlook Help System

This appendix shows you how to use the Outlook Help system. At anytime while you are using Outlook, you can interact with its Help system and display information on any Outlook topic. It is a complete reference manual at your fingertips.

As shown in Figure A-1, five methods for accessing the Outlook Help system are available:

1. Microsoft Office Outlook Help button on the Standard toolbar
2. Microsoft Office Outlook Help command on the Help menu
3. Function key F1 on the keyboard
4. Type a question for help box on the menu bar
5. Office Assistant

1 MICROSOFT OFFICE OUTLOOK HELP BUTTON ON STANDARD TOOLBAR

2 MICROSOFT OFFICE OUTLOOK HELP COMMAND ON HELP MENU

3 FUNCTION KEY F1 ON KEYBOARD

4 TYPE A QUESTION FOR HELP BOX ON MENU BAR

5 OFFICE ASSISTANT

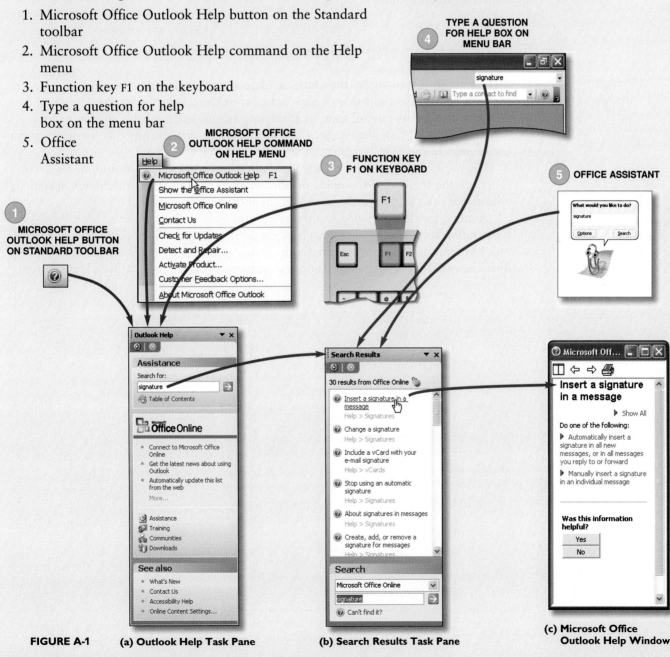

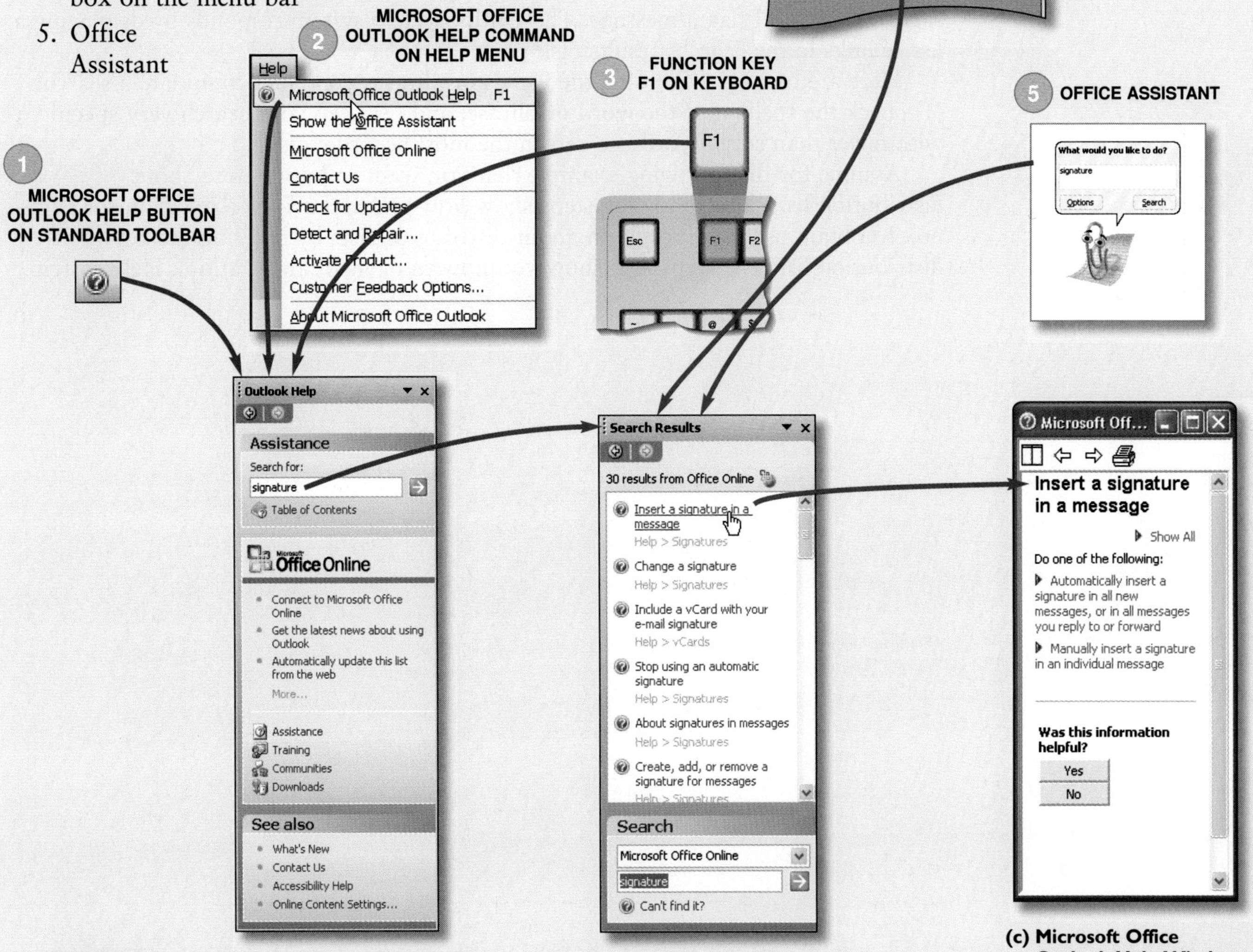

FIGURE A-1 (a) Outlook Help Task Pane (b) Search Results Task Pane (c) Microsoft Office Outlook Help Window

All five methods result in the Outlook Help system displaying a task pane on the right side of the Outlook window. The first three methods cause the **Outlook Help task pane** to display (Figure A-1a on the previous page). This task pane includes a Search text box in which you can enter a word or phrase on which you want help. Once you enter the word or phrase, the Outlook Help system displays the Search Results task pane (Figure A-1b on the previous page). With the Search Results task pane displayed, you can select specific Help topics.

As shown in Figure A-1, methods 4 and 5 bypass the Outlook Help task pane and display the **Search Results task pane** (Figure A-1b) with a list of links that pertain to the selected topic. Thus, any of the five methods for accessing the Outlook Help system results in displaying the Search Results task pane. Once the Outlook Help system displays this task pane, you can choose links that relate to the word or phrase on which you searched. In Figure A-1, for example, signature was the searched topic (Insert a signature in a message), which resulted in the Outlook Help system displaying the Microsoft Office Outlook Help window with information about signatures (Figure A-1c on the previous page).

Navigating the Outlook Help System

The quickest way to access the Outlook Help system is through the Type a question for help box on the right side of the menu bar at the top of the screen. Here you can type words, such as e-mail, font, or filter, or phrases, such as send an instant message, or how do I flag a message. The Outlook Help system responds by displaying a list of links in the Search Results task pane.

Here are two tips regarding the words or phrases you enter to initiate a search: (1) check the spelling of the word or phrase; and (2) keep your search very specific, with fewer than seven words, to return the most accurate results.

Assume for the following example that you want to know more about distribution lists. The following steps show how to use the Type a question for help box to obtain useful information about distribution lists by entering the keywords distribution list. The steps also show you how to navigate the Outlook Help system.

To Obtain Help Using the Type a Question for Help Box

1

- **Click the Type a question for help box on the right side of the menu bar, type** `distribution list`**, and then press the ENTER key (Figure A-2).**

The Outlook Help system displays the Search Results task pane on the right side of the window. The Search Results task pane contains a list of 21 links (Figure A-2). If you do not find what you are looking for, you can modify or refine the search in the Search area at the bottom of the task pane. The topics displayed in your Search Results task pane may be different.

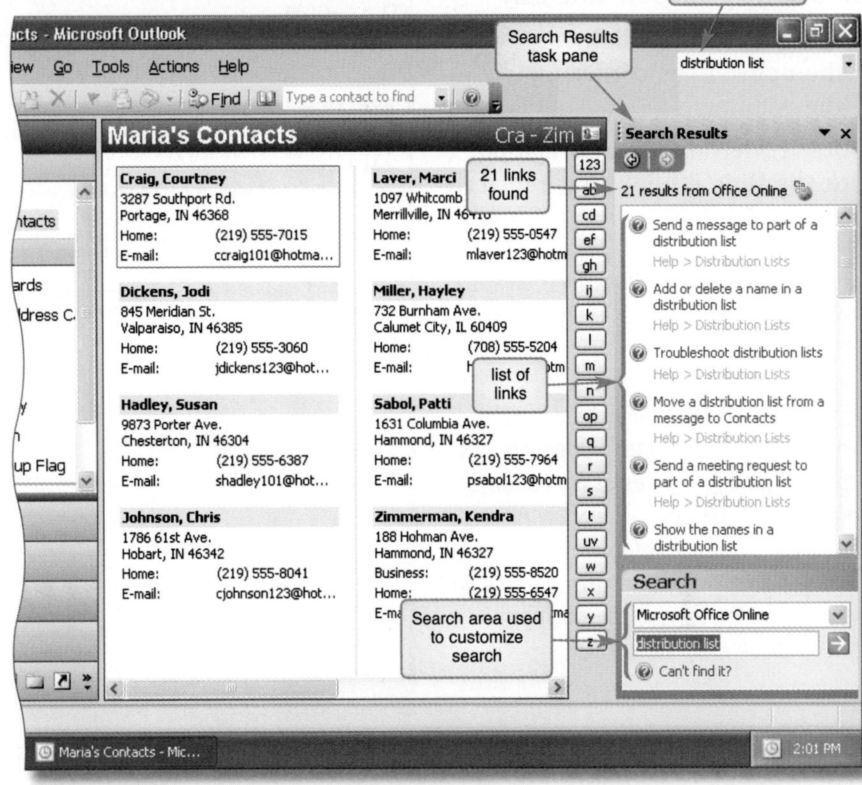

FIGURE A-2

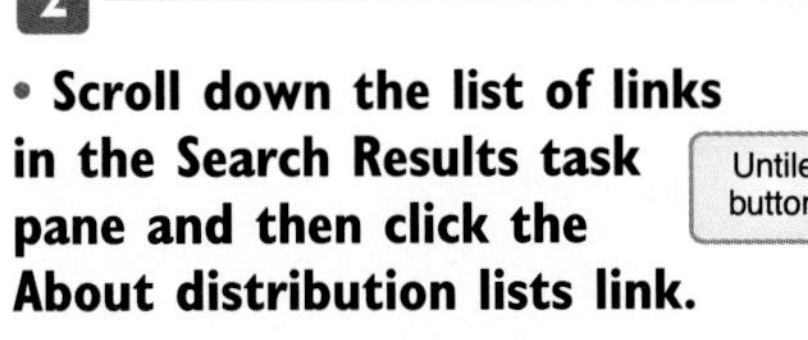

2

- **Scroll down the list of links in the Search Results task pane and then click the About distribution lists link.**
- **If necessary, when Outlook displays the Microsoft Office Outlook Help window, click its Auto Tile button in the upper-left corner of the window (Figure A-4 on the next page) to tile the windows.**

The Outlook Help system displays the Microsoft Office Outlook Help window with the desired information about distribution lists (Figure A-3). With the Microsoft Office Outlook Help window and Microsoft Outlook window tiled, you can read the information in one window and complete the task in the other window.

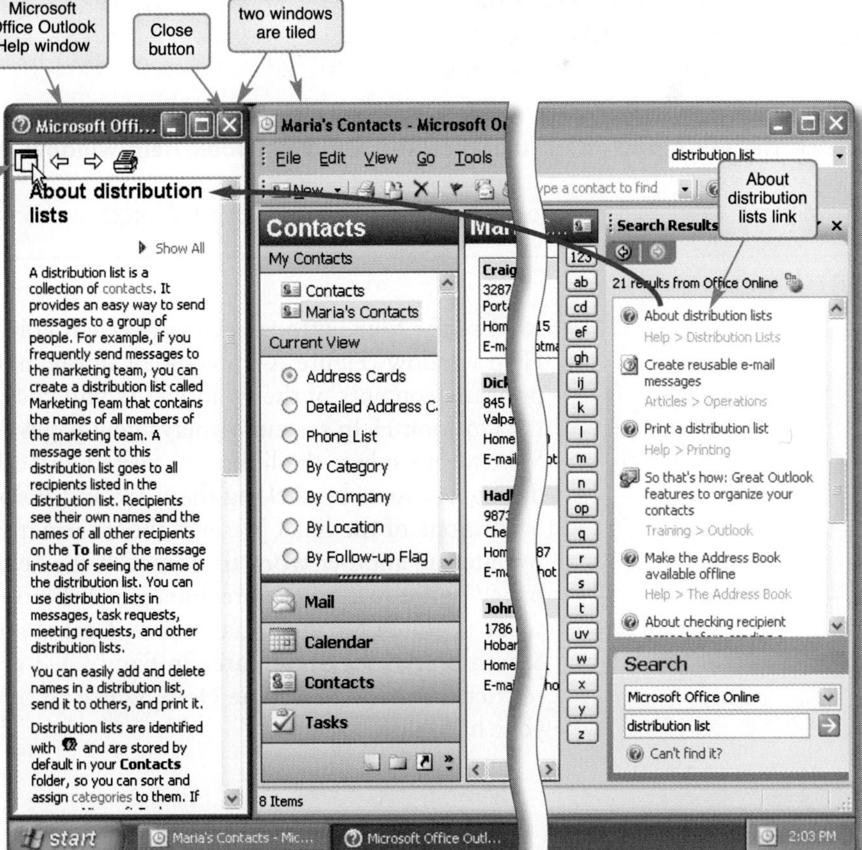

FIGURE A-3

3

- **Double-click the Microsoft Office Outlook Help window title bar.**
- **Click the Show All link in the upper-right corner of the window.**
- **After reviewing the information, click the Hide All link that replaced the Show All link.**

The Microsoft Office Outlook Help window is maximized so it fills the entire screen (Figure A-4). If you are connected to the Internet, you can give Microsoft your opinion as to whether the information was helpful by clicking the Yes or No button at the bottom of the page. The Show All link expands the coverage of information and the Hide All link condenses the information displayed on the topic in the Microsoft Office Outlook Help window.

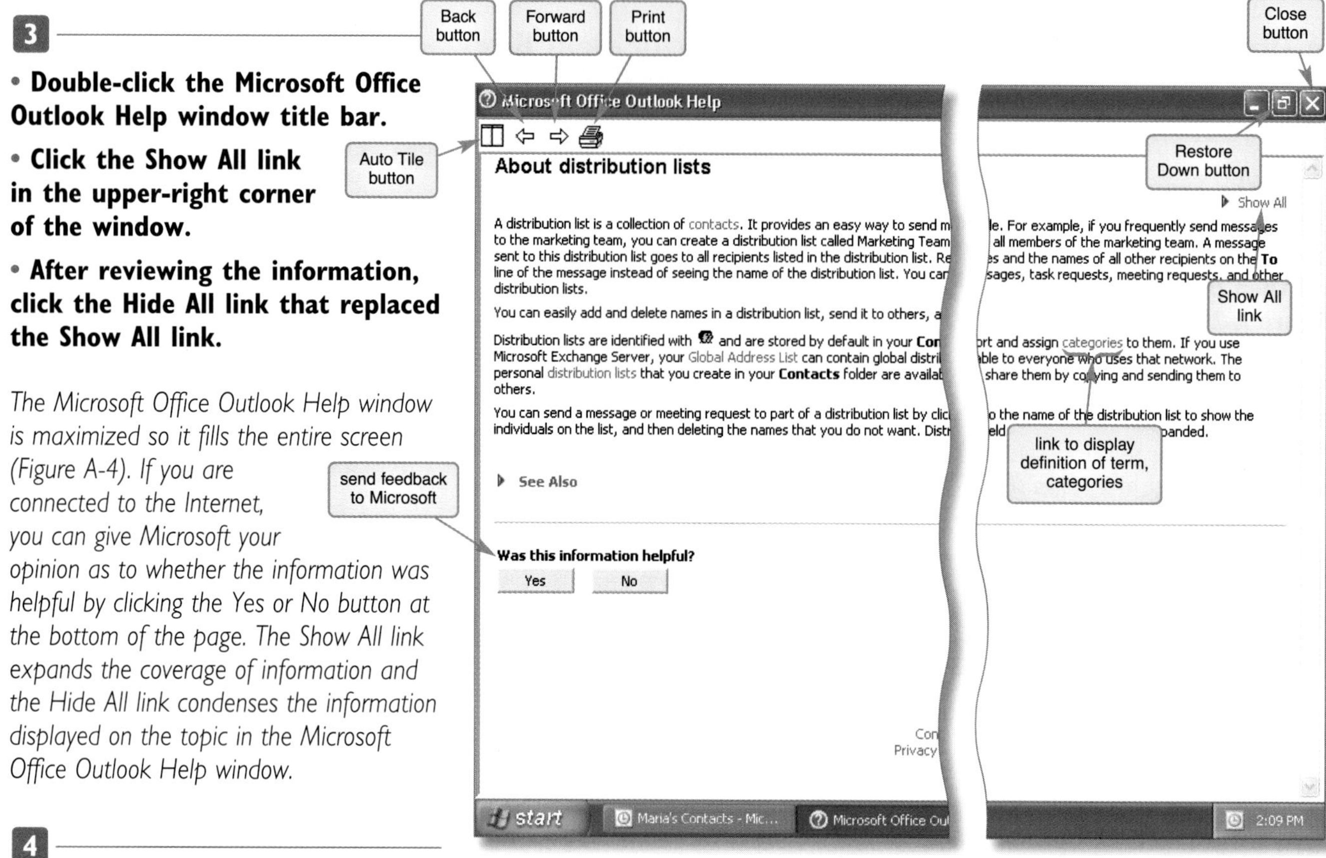

FIGURE A-4

4

- **Click the Restore Down button on the right side of the Microsoft Office Outlook Help window title bar to return to the tiled state shown in Figure A-3 on the previous page.**
- **Click the Close button on the Microsoft Office Outlook Help window title bar.**

The Microsoft Office Outlook Help window is closed and the Outlook Contact window is active.

Use the four buttons in the upper-left corner of the Microsoft Office Outlook Help window (Figure A-4) to tile or untile, navigate through the Help system, or print the contents of the window. As you click links in the Search Results task pane, the Outlook Help system displays new pages of information. The Outlook Help System remembers the links you visited and allows you to redisplay the pages visited during a session by clicking the Back and Forward buttons (Figure A-4).

If none of the links presents the information you want, you can refine the search by entering another word or phrase in the Search text box in the Search Results task pane (Figure A-2 on the previous page). If you have access to the Web, then the scope is global for the initial search. **Global** means all of the categories listed in the Search box of the Search area in Figure A-2 are searched. For example, you can restrict the scope to **Offline Help**, which results in a search of related links only on your hard disk.

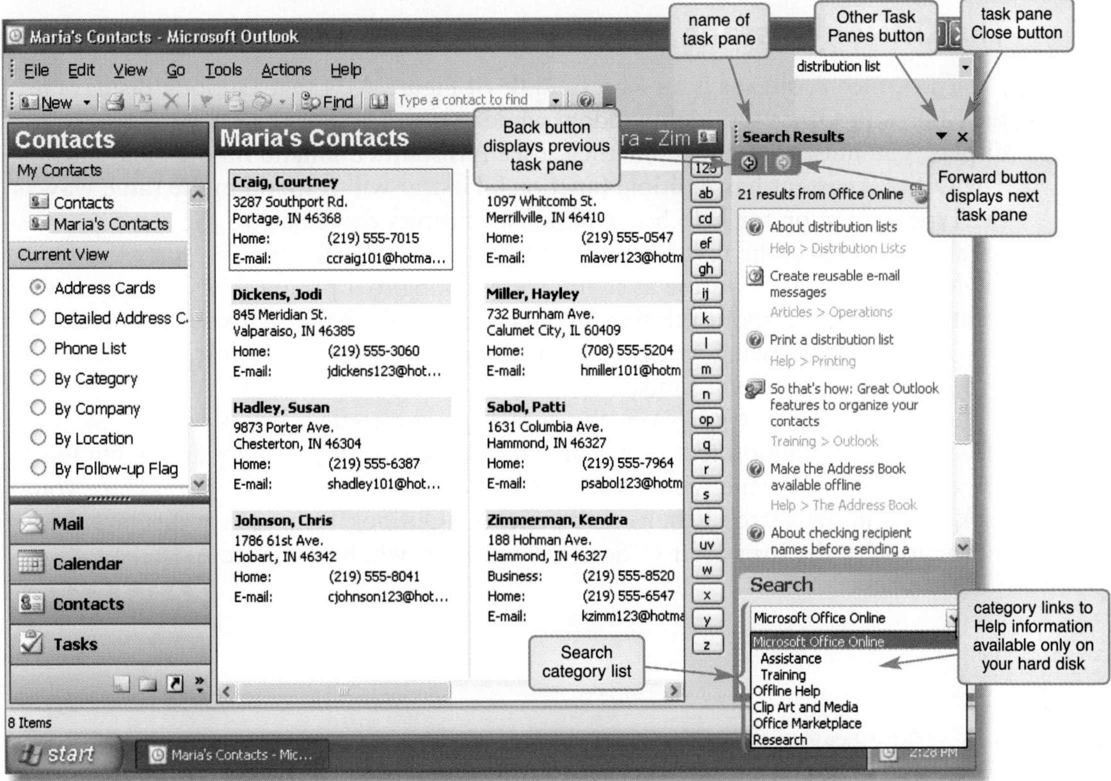

FIGURE A-5

Figure A-5 shows several additional features of the Search Results task pane. The Other Task Panes button and Close button on the Search Results task pane title bar allow you to display other task panes and close the Search Results task pane. The two buttons below the Search Results task pane title bar allow you to navigate between task panes (Back button and Forward button).

As you enter words and phrases in the Type a question for help box, the Outlook Help system adds them to the Type a question for help list. To display the list of previously typed words and phrases, click the Type a question for help box arrow (Figure A-6).

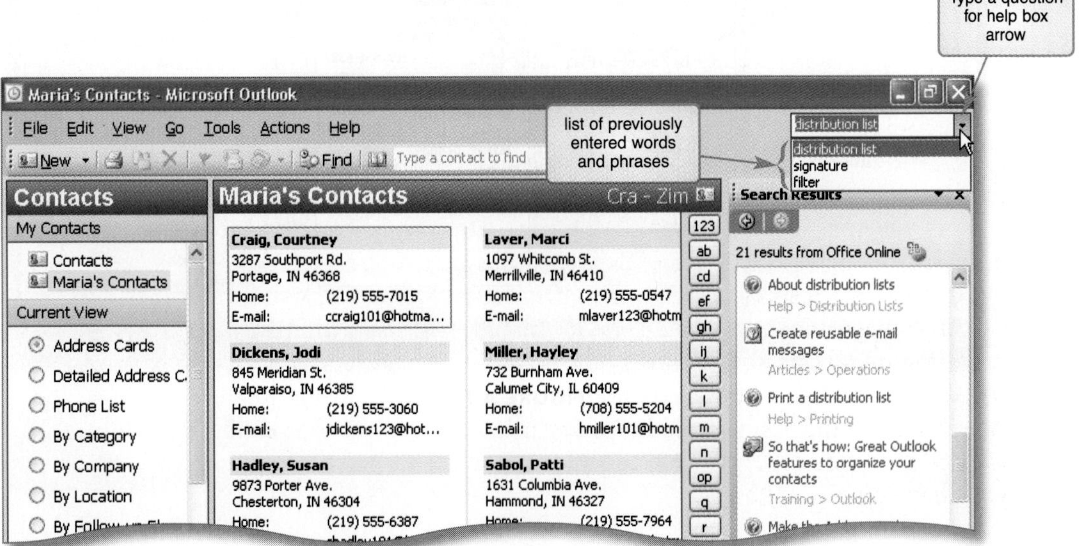

FIGURE A-6

The Office Assistant

The **Office Assistant** is an icon (middle of Figure A-7) that Outlook displays in the Microsoft Office Outlook window while you work. For the Office Assistant to display, you must click the Show the Office Assistant command on the Help menu. The Office Assistant has multiple functions. First, it will respond in the same way as the Type a question for help box with a list of topics that relate to the word or phrase you enter in the text box in the Office Assistant balloon. The entry can be in the form of a word or phrase as if you were talking to a person. For example, if you want to learn more about printing a contact list, in the balloon text box, you can type any of the following words or phrases: print, print a contact list, how do I print a contact list, or anything similar.

In the example in Figure A-7, the phrase, print a contact list, is entered into the Office Assistant balloon text box. The Office Assistant responds by displaying the Search Results task pane with a list of links from which you can choose. Once you click a link in the Search Results task pane, the Outlook Help system displays the information in the Microsoft Office Outlook Help window (Figure A-7).

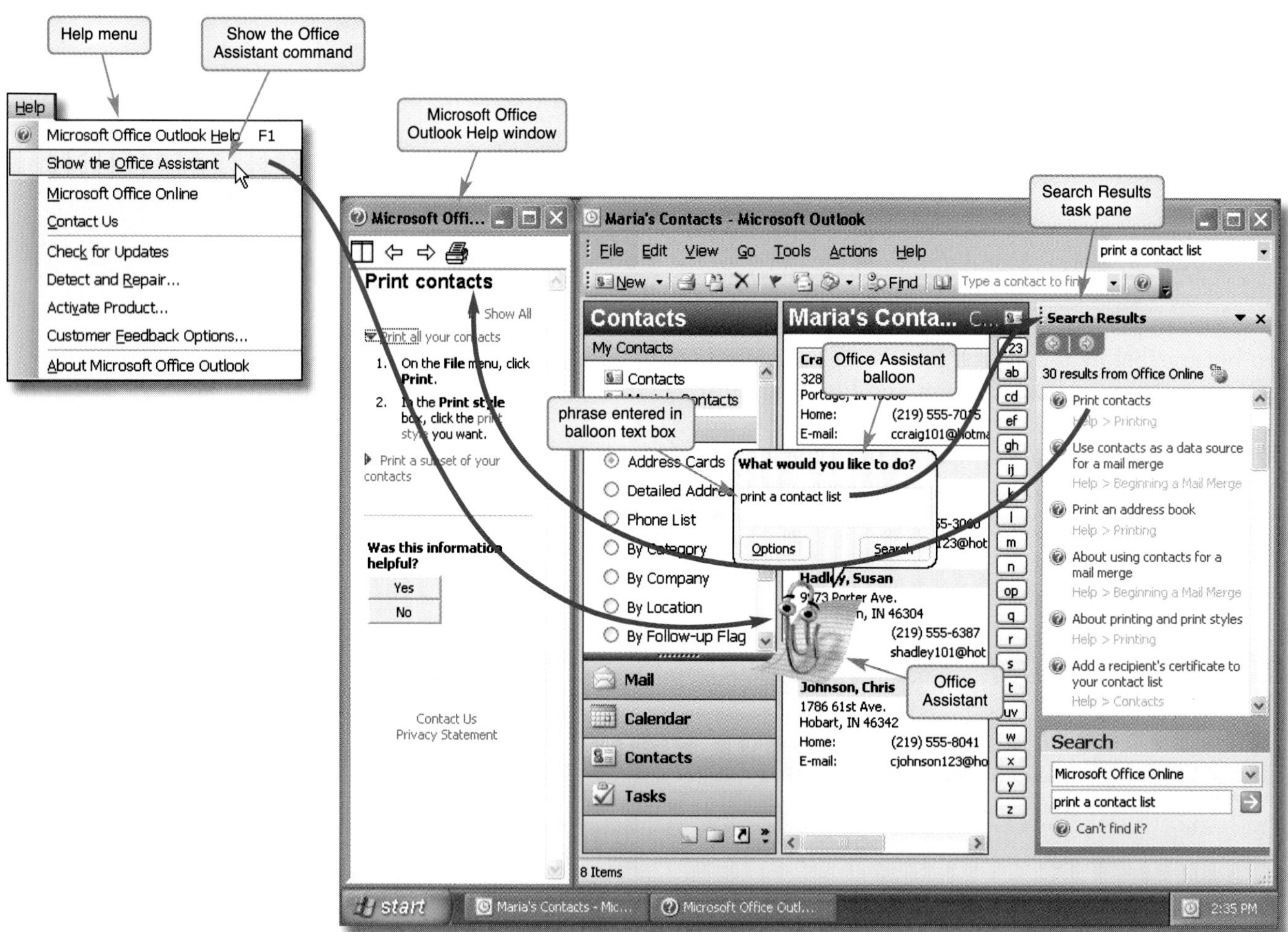

FIGURE A-7

In addition, the Office Assistant monitors your work and accumulates tips during a session on how you might increase your productivity and efficiency. The accumulation of tips must be enabled. You enable the accumulation of tips by right-clicking the Office Assistant, clicking Options on the shortcut menu, and then selecting the types of tips you want accumulated. You can view the tips at anytime. The accumulated tips appear when you activate the Office Assistant balloon. Also, if at anytime you see a light bulb above the Office Assistant, click it to display the most recent tip. If the Office Assistant is hidden, then the light bulb shows on the Microsoft Office Outlook Help button on the Standard toolbar.

You hide the Office Assistant by invoking the Hide the Office Assistant command on the Help menu or by right-clicking the Office Assistant and then clicking Hide on the shortcut menu. The Hide the Office Assistant command shows on the Help menu only when the Office Assistant is active in the Outlook window. If the Office Assistant begins showing up on your screen without you instructing it to show, then right-click the Office Assistant, click Options on the shortcut menu, click the Use the Office Assistant check box to remove the check mark, and then click the OK button.

If the Office Assistant is active in the Outlook window, then Outlook displays all program and system messages in the Office Assistant balloon.

You may or may not want the Office Assistant to display on the screen at all times. As indicated earlier, you can hide it and then show it later through the Help menu. For more information about the Office Assistant, type `office assistant` in the Type a question for help box and then click the links in the Search Results task pane.

Question Mark Button in Dialog Boxes and Help Icon in Task Panes

You use the Question Mark button with dialog boxes. It is located in the upper-right corner on the title bar of the dialog boxes, next to the Close button. For example, in Figure A-8 on the next page, the Print dialog box appears on the screen. If you click the Question Mark button in the upper-right corner of the dialog box, the Microsoft Office Outlook Help window is displayed and provides information about the options in the Print dialog box.

The Search Results task pane includes a Help icon. In Figure A-8, the Help icon appears at the bottom of the task pane and the Can't find it? link appears to the right of the Help icon. When you click the link, and if you are connected to the Internet, the Microsoft Office Assistance window is displayed and provides tips to obtain better search results. If you are not connected to the Internet, the Microsoft Office Outlook Help window will display and provide similar tips for better search results.

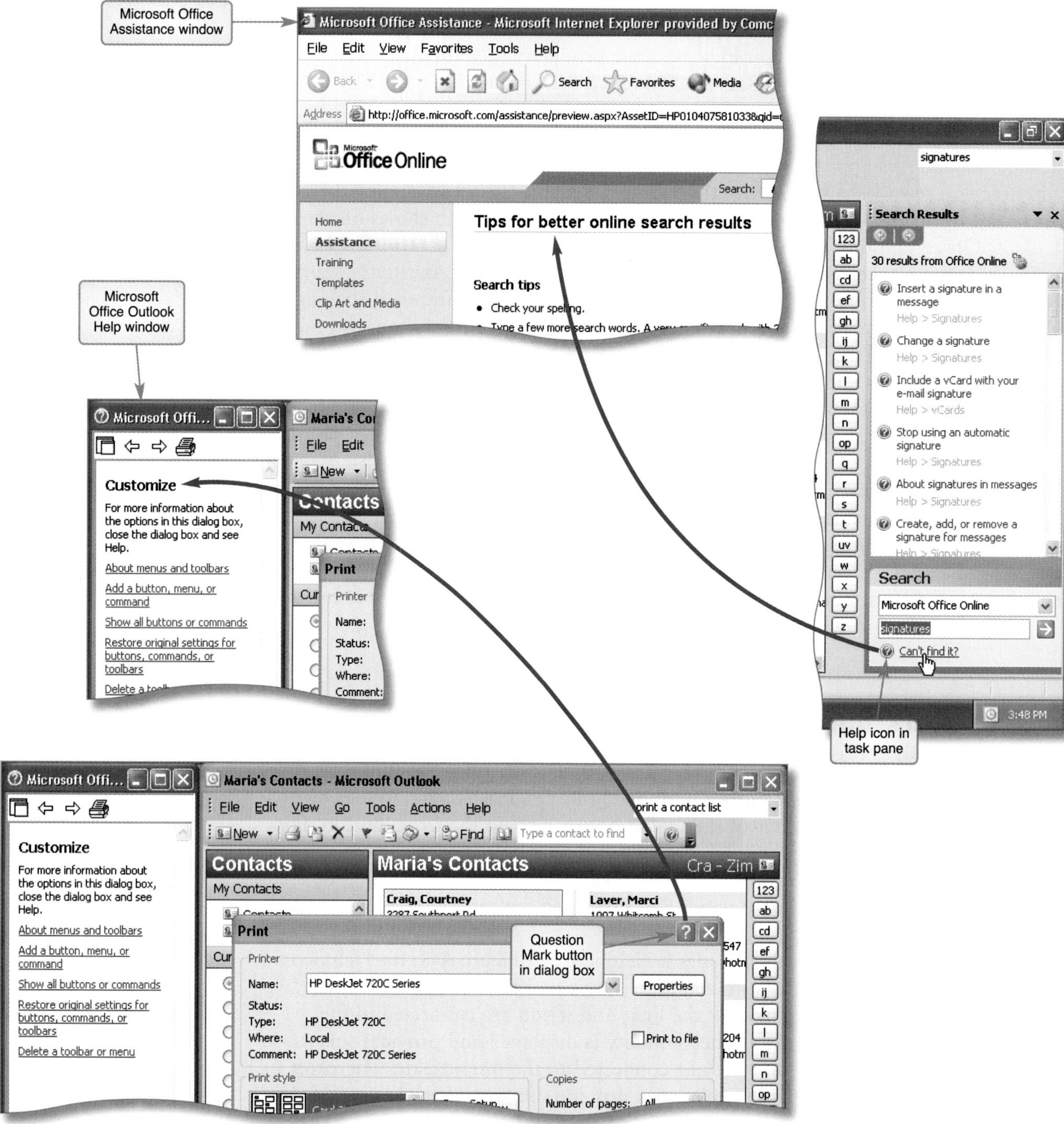

FIGURE A-8

Other Help Commands on the Help Menu

Thus far, this appendix has discussed the first two commands on the Help menu: (1) the Microsoft Office Outlook Help command (Figure A-1 on page APP 1) and (2) the Show the Office Assistant command (Figure A-7 on page APP 6). Several additional commands are available on the Help menu as shown in Figure A-9. Table A-1 summarizes these commands.

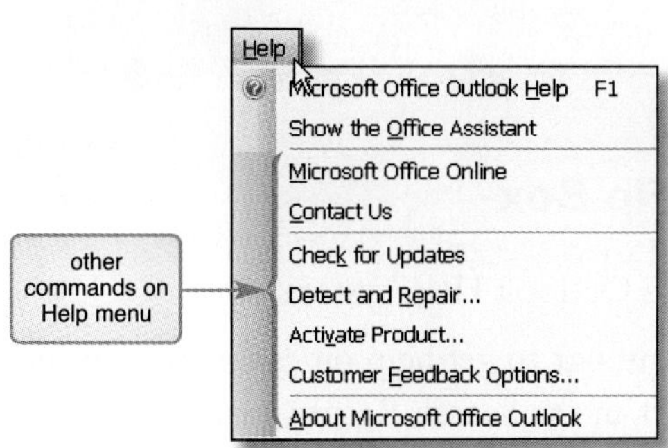

FIGURE A-9

Table A-1 Summary of Other Help Commands on the Help Menu

COMMAND ON HELP MENU	FUNCTION
Microsoft Office Online	Activates the browser, which displays the Microsoft Office Online Home page. The Microsoft Office Online Home page contains links that can improve Office productivity.
Contact Us	Activates the browser, which displays Microsoft contact information and a list of useful links.
Check for Updates	Activates the browser, which displays a list of updates to Office 2003. These updates can be downloaded and installed to improve the efficiency of Office or to fix an error in one or more of the Office applications.
Detect and Repair	Detects and repairs errors in the Outlook program.
Activate Product	Activates Outlook if it has not been activated already.
Customer Feedback Options	Gives or denies Microsoft permission to collect anonymous information about the hardware.
About Microsoft Office Outlook	Displays the About Microsoft Outlook dialog box. The dialog box lists the owner of the software and the product identification. You need to know the product identification if you call Microsoft for assistance. The three buttons below the OK button are the System Info button, Tech Support button, and Disabled Items button. The System Info button displays system information, including hardware resources, components, software environment, and applications. The Tech Support button displays technical assistance information. The Disabled Items button displays a list of disabled items that prevent Outlook from functioning properly.

1 Using the Type a Question for Help Box

Instructions: Perform the following tasks using the Outlook Help system.

1. Use the Type a question for help box on the menu bar to get help on calendar coloring.
2. Click About Calendar coloring in the list of links in the Search Results task pane. If necessary, tile the windows. Double-click the Microsoft Office Outlook Help window title bar to maximize it. Click the Show All link. Read and print the information. At the top of the printout, write down the number of links the Outlook Help system found.
3. Click the Restore Down button on the Microsoft Office Outlook Help title bar to restore the Microsoft Office Outlook Help window.
4. One at a time, click two additional links in the Search Results task pane and print the information. Hand in the printouts to your instructor. Use the Back and Forward buttons to return to the original page.
5. Use the Type a question for help box to search for information on flagging e-mail. Click the About flagging for follow up link in the Search Results task pane. Maximize the Microsoft Office Outlook Help window. Read and print the contents of the window. One at a time, click the links on the page and print the contents of the window. Close the Microsoft Office Outlook Help window.
6. For each of the following words and phrases, click one link in the Search Results task pane, click the Show All link, and then print the page: filtering; date; print preview; office clipboard; junk mail; and themes.

2 Expanding on the Outlook Help System Basics

Instructions: Use the Outlook Help system to understand the topics better and answer the questions listed below. Answer the questions on your own paper, or hand in the printed Help information to your instructor.

1. Show the Office Assistant. Right-click the Office Assistant and then click Animate! on the shortcut menu. Repeat invoking the Animate! command to see various animations.
2. Right-click the Office Assistant, click Options on the shortcut menu, click the Reset my tips button, and then click the OK button. If necessary, repeatedly click the Office Assistant and then click off the Office Assistant until a light bulb appears above the Office Assistant. When you see the light bulb, it indicates that the Office Assistant has a tip to share with you.
3. Use the Office Assistant to find help on sorting. Click the Sort a list of messages, contacts, notes, or files link and then print the contents of the Microsoft Office Outlook Help window. Close the window. Hand in the printouts to your instructor. Hide the Office Assistant.
4. Press the F1 key. Search for information on Help. Click the first two links in the Search Results task pane. Read and print the information for both links.
5. Display the Help menu. One at a time, click the Microsoft Office Online, Contact Us, and Check for Updates commands. Print the contents of each Internet Explorer window that displays and then close the window. Hand in the printouts to your instructor.
6. Click About Microsoft Office Outlook on the Help menu. Click the Tech Support button, print the contents of the Microsoft Office Outlook Help window, and then close the window. Click the System Info button. If necessary, click the plus sign to the left of Components in the System Summary list to display the Components category. Click CD-ROM and then print the information. Click Display and then print the information. Hand in the printouts to your instructor.

Appendix B

Speech and Handwriting Recognition

Introduction

This appendix discusses the Office capability that allows users to create and modify documents using its alternative input technologies available through **text services**. Office provides a variety of text services, which enable you to speak commands and enter text in an application. The most common text service is the keyboard. Other text services include speech recognition and handwriting recognition.

The Language Bar

The **Language bar** allows you to use text services in the Office applications. You can utilize the Language bar in one of three states: (1) in a restored state as a floating toolbar in the Outlook window (Figure B-1a or Figure B-1b if Text Labels are enabled); (2) in a minimized state docked next to the notification area on the Windows taskbar (Figure B-1c); or (3) hidden (temporarily closed and out of the way). If the Language bar is hidden, you can activate it by right-clicking the Windows taskbar, pointing to Toolbars on the shortcut menu (Figure B-1d), and then clicking Language bar on the Toolbars submenu. If you want to close the Language bar, right-click the Language bar and then click Close the Language bar on the shortcut menu (Figure B-1e).

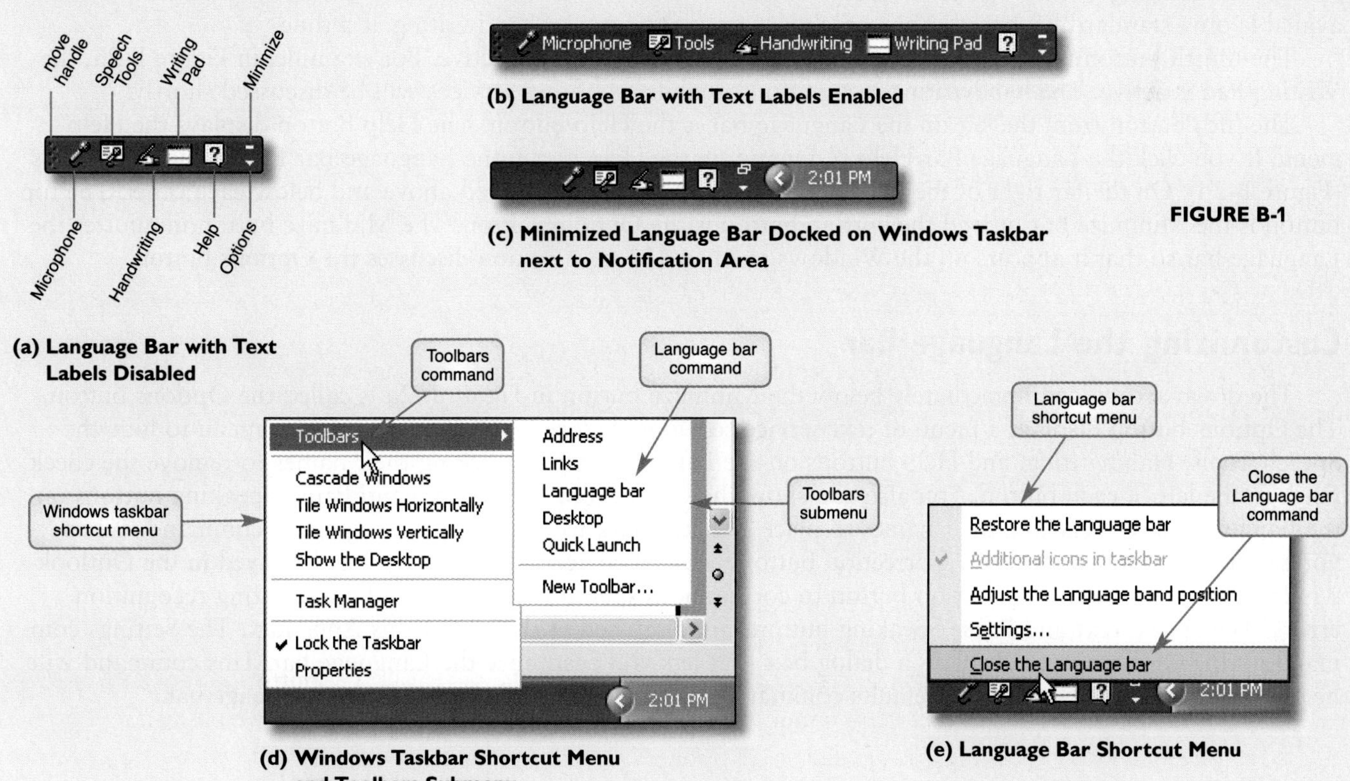

(a) Language Bar with Text Labels Disabled

(b) Language Bar with Text Labels Enabled

(c) Minimized Language Bar Docked on Windows Taskbar next to Notification Area

FIGURE B-1

(d) Windows Taskbar Shortcut Menu and Toolbars Submenu

(e) Language Bar Shortcut Menu

When Windows was installed on your computer, the installer specified a default language. For example, most users in the United States select English (United States) as the default language. You can add more than 90 additional languages and varying dialects such as Basque, English (Zimbabwe), French (France), French (Canada), German (Germany), German (Austria), and Swahili. With multiple languages available, you can switch from one language to another while working in Outlook. If you change the language or dialect, then text services may change the functions of the keys on the keyboard, adjust speech recognition, and alter handwriting recognition. If a second language is activated, then a Language icon appears immediately to the right of the move handle on the Language bar and the language name is displayed on the Outlook status bar. This appendix assumes that English (United States) is the only language installed. Thus, the Language icon does not appear in the examples in Figure B-1 on the previous page.

Buttons on the Language Bar

The Language bar shown in Figure B-2a contains seven buttons. The number of buttons on your Language bar may be different. These buttons are used to select the language, customize the Language bar, control the microphone, control handwriting, and obtain help.

The first button on the left is the Microphone button, which enables and disables the microphone. When the microphone is enabled, text services adds two buttons and a balloon to the Language bar (Figure B-2b). These additional buttons and the balloon will be discussed shortly.

The second button from the left is the Speech Tools button. The Speech Tools button displays a menu of commands (Figure B-2c) that allow you to scan the current document looking for words to add to the speech recognition dictionary; hide or show the balloon on the Language bar; train the Speech Recognition service so that it can interpret your voice better; add and delete specific words to and from its dictionary, such as names and other words not understood easily; and change the user profile so more than one person can use the microphone on the same computer.

The third button from the left on the Language bar is the Handwriting button. The Handwriting button displays the Handwriting menu (Figure B-2d), which lets you choose the Writing Pad (Figure B-2e), Write Anywhere (Figure B-2f), or the on-screen keyboard (Figure B-2g). The On-Screen Symbol Keyboard command on the Handwriting menu displays an on-screen keyboard that allows you to enter special symbols that are not available on a standard keyboard. You can choose only one form of handwriting at a time.

The fourth button indicates which one of the handwriting forms is active. For example, in Figure B-2a, the Writing Pad is active. The handwriting recognition capabilities of text services will be discussed shortly.

The fifth button from the left on the Language bar is the Help button. The Help button displays the Help menu. If you click the Language Bar Help command on the Help menu, the Language Bar Help window appears (Figure B-2h). On the far right of the Language bar are two buttons stacked above and below each other. The top button is the Minimize button and the bottom button is the Options button. The Minimize button minimizes the Language bar so that it appears on the Windows taskbar. The next section discusses the Options button.

Customizing the Language Bar

The down arrow icon immediately below the Minimize button in Figure B-2a is called the Options button. The Options button displays a menu of text services options (Figure B-2i). You can use this menu to hide the Speech Tools, Handwriting, and Help buttons on the Language bar by clicking their names to remove the check mark to the left of each button. You also can show the Correction, Speak Text, and Pause Speaking buttons on the Language bar by clicking their names to place a check mark to the left of the respective command. When you select text and then click the Correction button, a list of correction alternatives is displayed in the Outlook window. You can use the Correction button to correct both speech recognition and handwriting recognition errors. The Speak Text and Pause Speaking buttons are discussed at the end of this Appendix. The Settings command on the Options menu displays a dialog box that lets you customize the Language bar. This command will be discussed shortly. The Restore Defaults command redisplays hidden buttons on the Language bar.

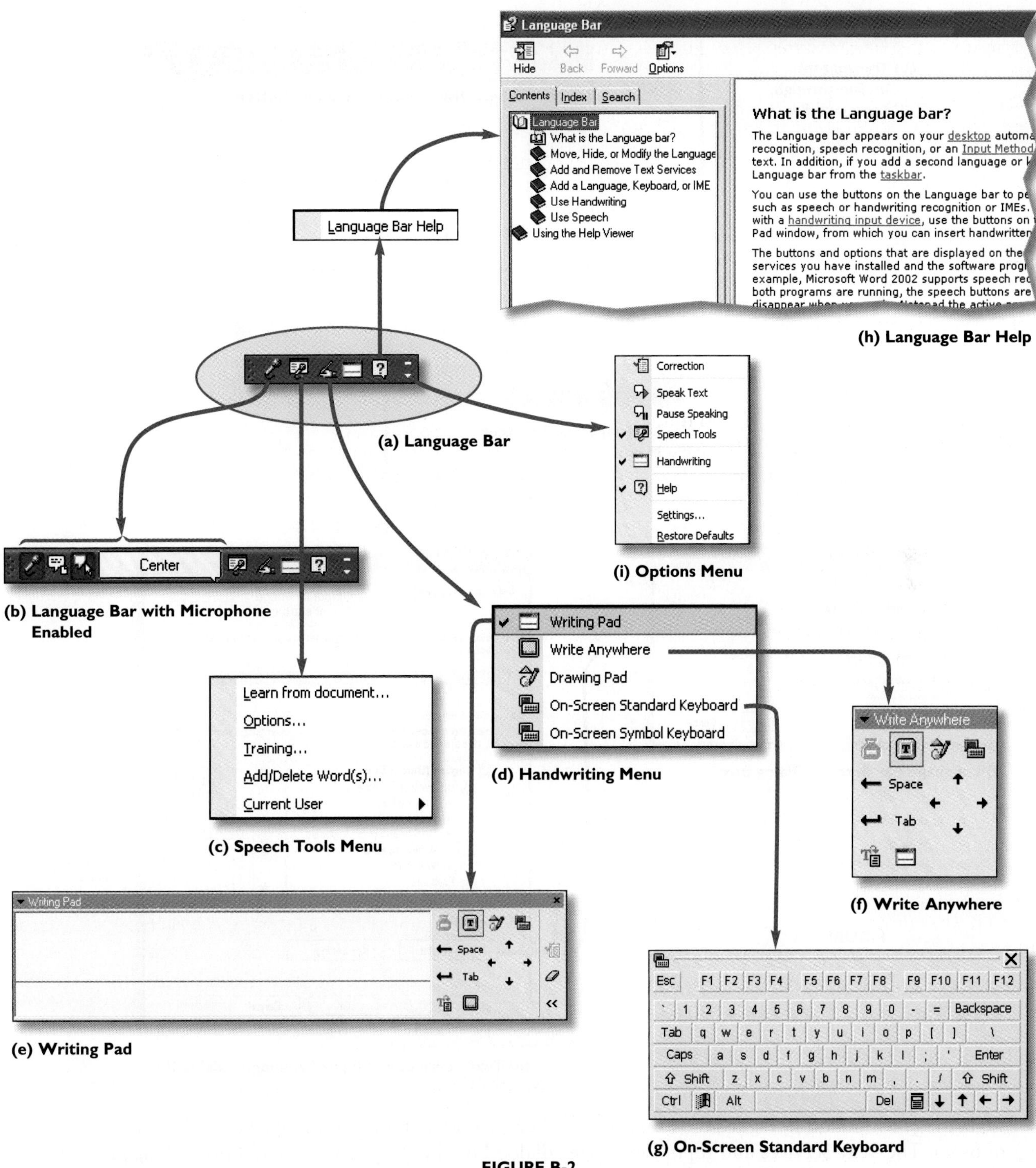

(a) Language Bar

(b) Language Bar with Microphone Enabled

(c) Speech Tools Menu

(d) Handwriting Menu

(e) Writing Pad

(f) Write Anywhere

(g) On-Screen Standard Keyboard

(h) Language Bar Help

(i) Options Menu

FIGURE B-2

If you right-click the Language bar, a shortcut menu appears (Figure B-3a on the next page). This shortcut menu lets you further customize the Language bar. The Minimize command on the shortcut menu docks the Language bar on the Windows taskbar. The Transparency command in Figure B-3a toggles the Language bar between being solid and transparent. You can see through a transparent Language bar (Figure B-3b). The Text Labels command toggles on text labels on the Language bar (Figure B-3c) and off (Figure B-3b). The Vertical command displays the Language bar vertically on the screen (Figure B-3d).

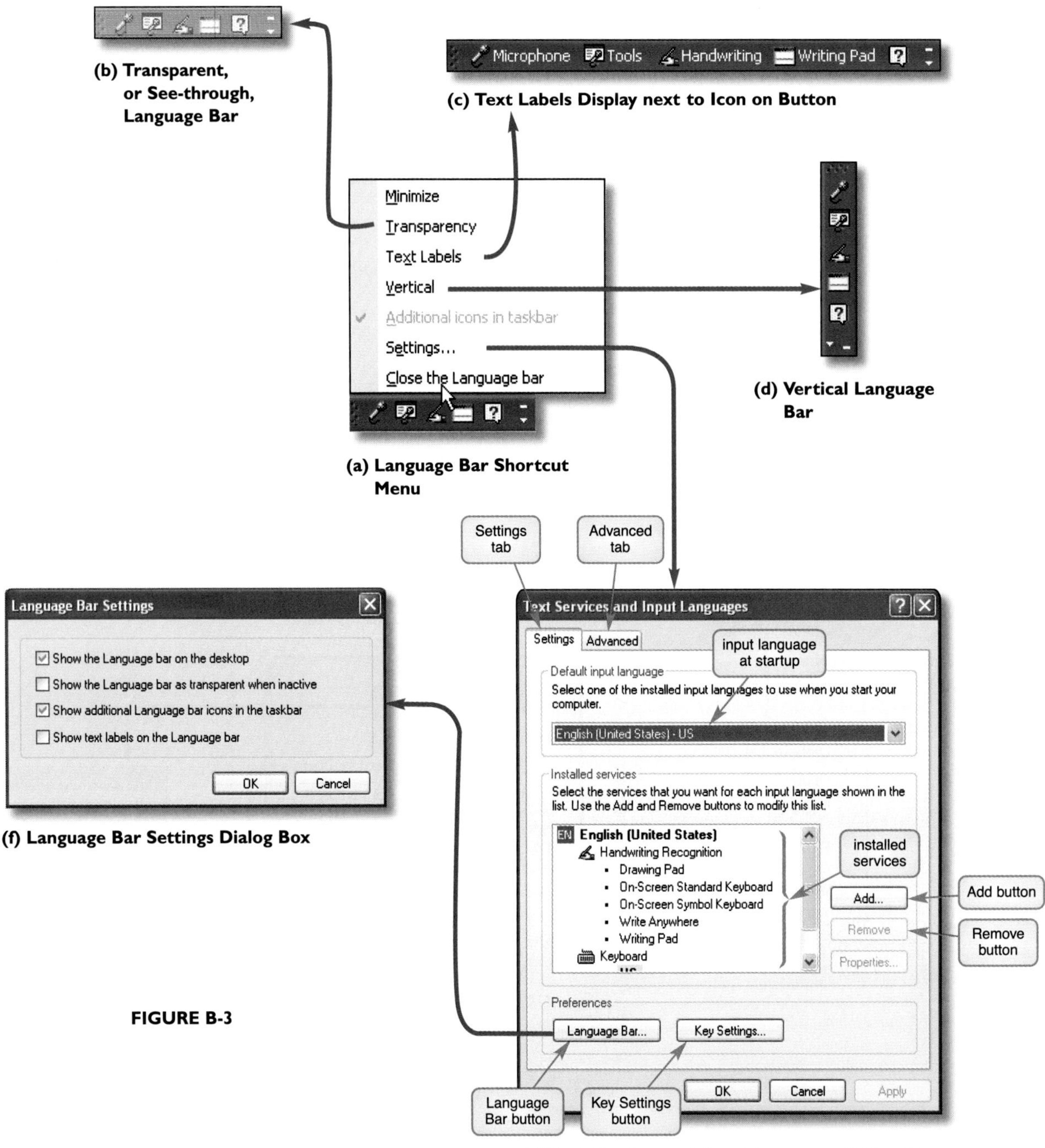

FIGURE B-3

The Settings command in Figure B-3a displays the Text Services and Input Languages dialog box (Figure B-3e). The Text Services and Input Languages dialog box allows you to add additional languages, add and remove text services, modify keys on the keyboard, modify the Language bar, and extend support of advanced text services to all programs, including Notepad and other programs that normally do not support text services (through the Advanced tab). If you want to remove any one of the services in the Installed services list, select the service, and then click the Remove button. If you want to add a service, click the Add button. The Key Settings button allows you to modify the keyboard. If you click the Language Bar button in the Text Services and Input Languages dialog box, the Language Bar Settings dialog box appears (Figure B-3f). This dialog box contains Language bar options, some of which are the same as the commands on the Language bar shortcut menu shown in Figure B-3a.

The Close the Language bar command on the shortcut menu shown in Figure B-3a closes or hides the Language bar. If you close the Language bar and want to redisplay it, see Figure B-1d on page APP 11.

Speech Recognition

The **Speech Recognition service** available with Office enables your computer to recognize human speech through a microphone. The microphone has two modes: dictation and voice command (Figure B-4). You switch between the two modes by clicking the Dictation button and the Voice Command button on the Language bar. These buttons appear only when you turn on Speech Recognition by clicking the Microphone button on the Language bar (Figure B-5a on the next page). If you are using the Microphone button for the very first time in Outlook, it will require that you check your microphone settings and step through voice training before activating the Speech Recognition service.

The Dictation button places the microphone in Dictation mode. In **Dictation mode**, whatever you speak is entered as text at the location of the insertion point. The Voice Command button places the microphone in Voice Command mode. In **Voice Command mode**, whatever you speak is interpreted as a command. If you want to turn off the microphone, click the Microphone button on the Language bar or in Voice Command mode say, "Mic off" (pronounced mike off). It is important to remember that minimizing the Language bar does not turn off the microphone.

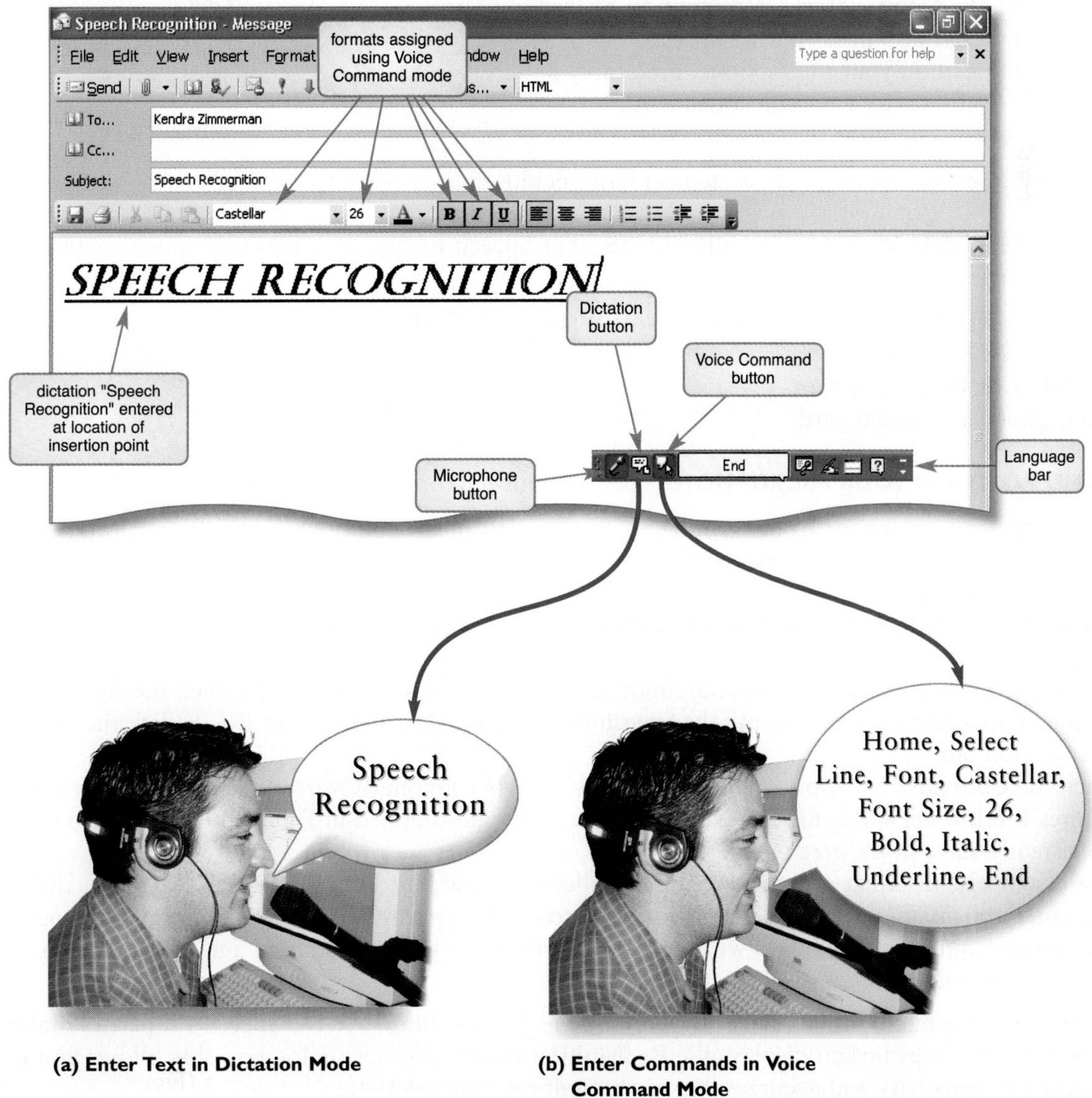

(a) Enter Text in Dictation Mode

(b) Enter Commands in Voice Command Mode

FIGURE B-4

The Language bar speech message balloon shown in Figure B-5b displays messages that may offer help or hints. In Voice Command mode, the name of the last recognized command you said appears. If you use the mouse or keyboard instead of the microphone, a message will appear in the Language bar speech message balloon indicating the word you could say. In Dictation mode, the message, Dictating, usually appears. The Speech Recognition service, however, will display messages to inform you that you are talking too soft, too loud, too fast, or to ask you to repeat what you said by displaying, What was that?

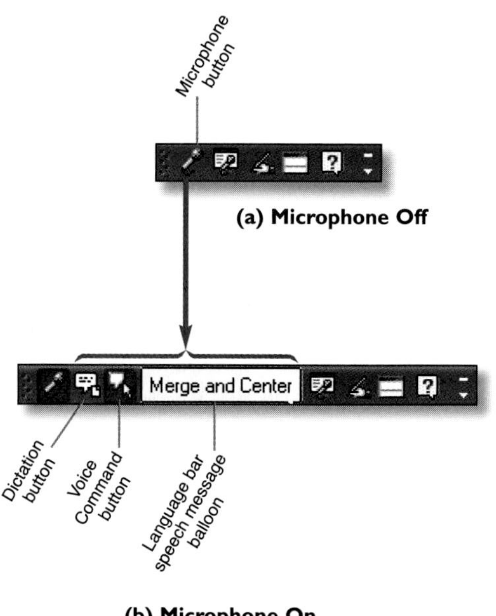

FIGURE B-5

Getting Started with Speech Recognition

For the microphone to function properly, you should follow these steps:

1. Make sure your computer meets the minimum requirements.
2. Start Outlook. Activate Speech Recognition by clicking Tools on the menu bar and then clicking Speech.
3. Set up and position your microphone, preferably a close-talk headset with gain adjustment support.
4. Train Speech Recognition.

The following sections describe these steps in more detail.

SPEECH RECOGNITION SYSTEM REQUIREMENTS For Speech Recognition to work on your computer, it needs the following:

1. Microsoft Windows 98 or later or Microsoft Windows NT 4.0 or later
2. At least 128 MB RAM
3. 400 MHz or faster processor
4. Microphone and sound card

SET UP AND POSITION YOUR MICROPHONE Set up your microphone as follows:

1. Connect your microphone to the sound card in the back of the computer.
2. Position the microphone approximately one inch out from and to the side of your mouth. Position it so you are not breathing into it.
3. On the Language bar, click the Speech Tools button and then click Options on the Speech Tools menu (Figure B-6a).
4. When text services displays the Speech input settings dialog box (Figure B-6b), click the Advanced Speech button. When text services displays the Speech Properties dialog box (Figure B-6c), click the Speech Recognition tab.
5. Click the Configure Microphone button. Follow the Microphone Wizard directions as shown in Figures B-6d, B-6e, and B-6f. The Next button will remain dimmed in Figure B-6e until the volume meter consistently stays in the green area.
6. If someone else installed Speech Recognition, click the New button in the Speech Properties dialog box and enter your name. Click the Train Profile button and step through the Voice Training dialog boxes. The Voice Training dialog boxes will require that you enter your gender and age group. It then will step you through voice training.

You can adjust the microphone further by clicking the Settings button in the Speech Properties dialog box (Figure B-6c). The Settings button displays the Recognition Profile Settings dialog box that allows you to adjust the pronunciation sensitivity and accuracy versus recognition response time.

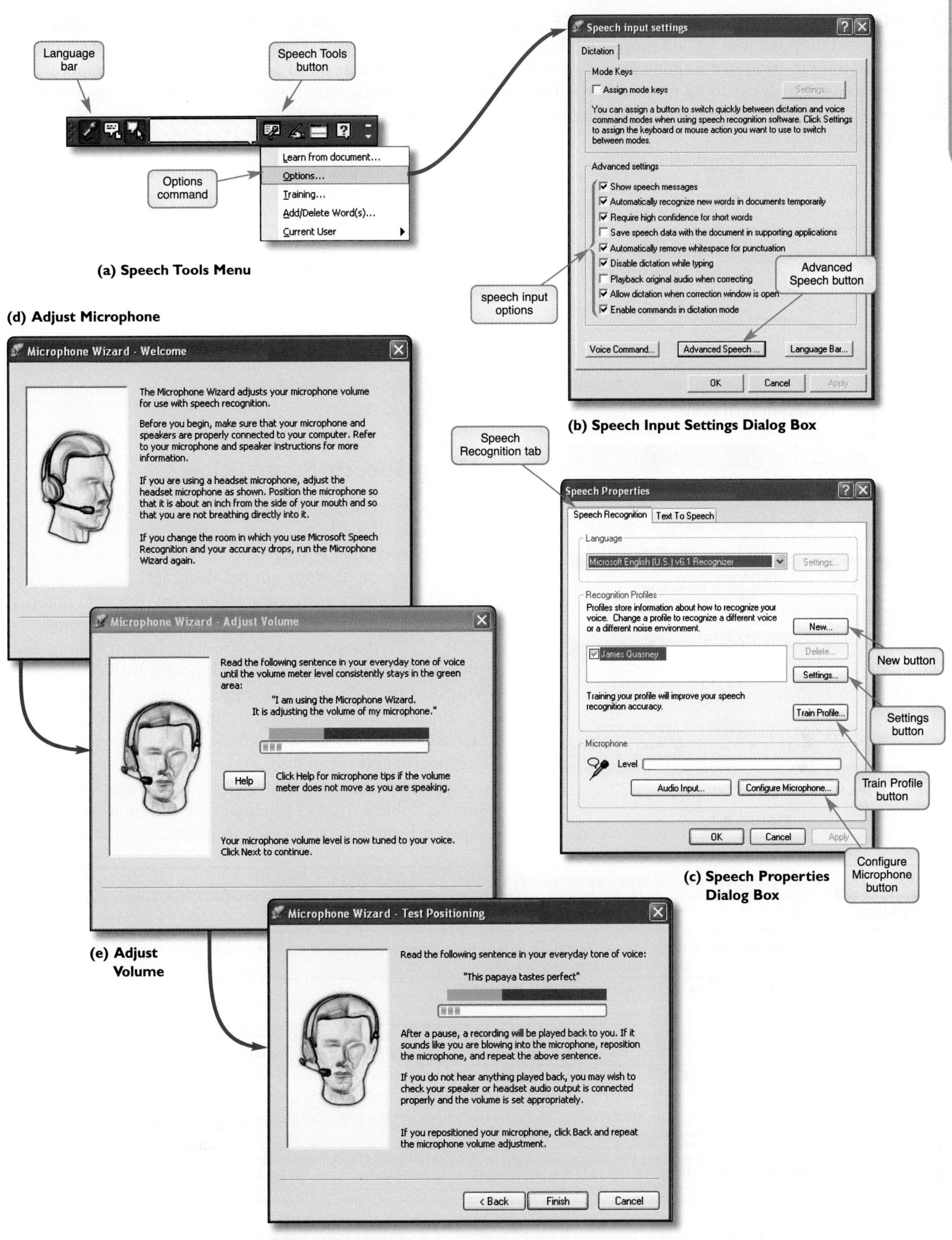

(a) Speech Tools Menu

(b) Speech Input Settings Dialog Box

(c) Speech Properties Dialog Box

(d) Adjust Microphone

(e) Adjust Volume

(f) Test Microphone

FIGURE B-6

TRAIN THE SPEECH RECOGNITION SERVICE The Speech Recognition service will understand most commands and some dictation without any training at all. It will recognize much more of what you speak, however, if you take the time to train it. After one training session, it will recognize 85 to 90 percent of your words. As you do more training, accuracy will rise to 95 percent. If you feel that too many mistakes are being made, then continue to train the service. The more training you do, the more accurately it will work for you. Follow these steps to train the Speech Recognition service:

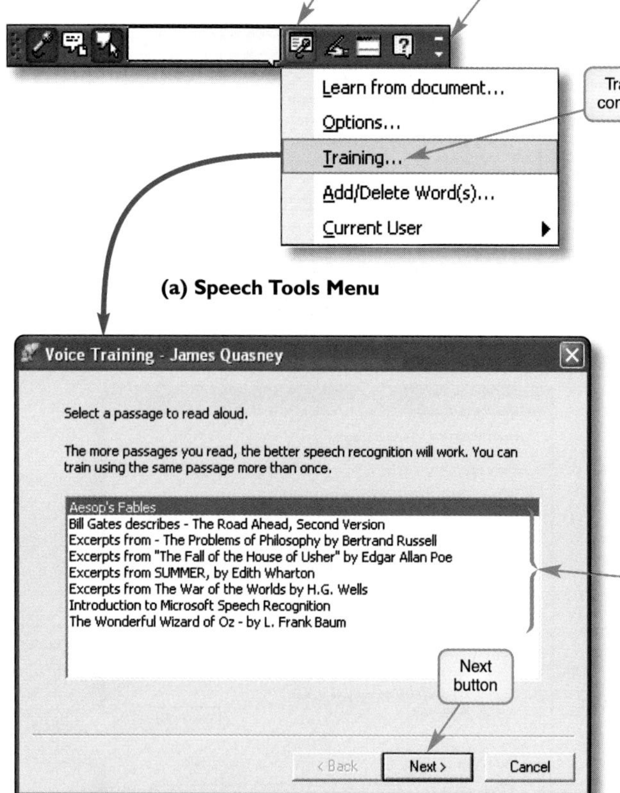

(a) Speech Tools Menu

(b) Voice Training Dialog Box

FIGURE B-7

1. Click the Speech Tools button on the Language bar and then click Training (Figure B-7a).
2. When the Voice Training dialog box appears (Figure B-7b), click one of the sessions and then click the Next button.
3. Complete the training session, which should take less than 15 minutes.

If you are serious about using a microphone to speak to your computer, you need to take the time to go through at least three of the eight training sessions listed in Figure B-7b.

Using Speech Recognition

Speech recognition lets you enter text into a document similarly to speaking into a tape recorder. Instead of typing, you can dictate text that you want to be displayed in the document, and you can issue voice commands. In Voice Command mode, you can speak menu names, commands on menus, toolbar button names, and dialog box option buttons, check boxes, list boxes, and button names. Speech recognition, however, is not a completely hands-free form of input. Speech recognition works best if you use a combination of your voice, the keyboard, and the mouse. You soon will discover that Dictation mode is far less accurate than Voice Command mode. Table B-1 lists some tips that will improve the Speech Recognition service's accuracy considerably.

Table B-1 Tips to Improve Speech Recognition

NUMBER	TIP
1	The microphone hears everything. Though the Speech Recognition service filters out background noise, it is recommended that you work in a quiet environment.
2	Try not to move the microphone around once it is adjusted.
3	Speak in a steady tone and speak clearly.
4	In Dictation mode, do not pause between words. A phrase is easier to interpret than a word. Sounding out syllables in a word will make it more difficult for the Speech Recognition service to interpret what you are saying.
5	If you speak too loudly or too softly, it makes it difficult for the Speech Recognition service to interpret what you said. Check the Language bar speech message balloon for an indication that you may be speaking too loudly or too softly.
6	If you experience problems after training, adjust the recognition options that control accuracy and rejection by clicking the Settings button shown in Figure B-6c on the previous page.
7	When you are finished using the microphone, turn it off by clicking the Microphone button on the Language bar or in Voice Command mode, say "Mic off." Leaving the microphone on is the same as leaning on the keyboard.
8	If the Speech Recognition service is having difficulty with unusual words, then add the words to its dictionary by using the Learn from document and Add/Delete Word(s) commands on the Speech Tools menu (Figure B-8a). The last names of individuals and the names of companies are good examples of the types of words you should add to the dictionary.
9	Training will improve accuracy; practice will improve confidence.

The last command on the Speech Tools menu is the Current User command (Figure B-8a). The Current User command is useful for multiple users who share a computer. It allows them to configure their own individual profiles, and then switch between users as they use the computer.

For additional information about the Speech Recognition service, enter `speech recognition` in the Type a question for help box on the menu bar.

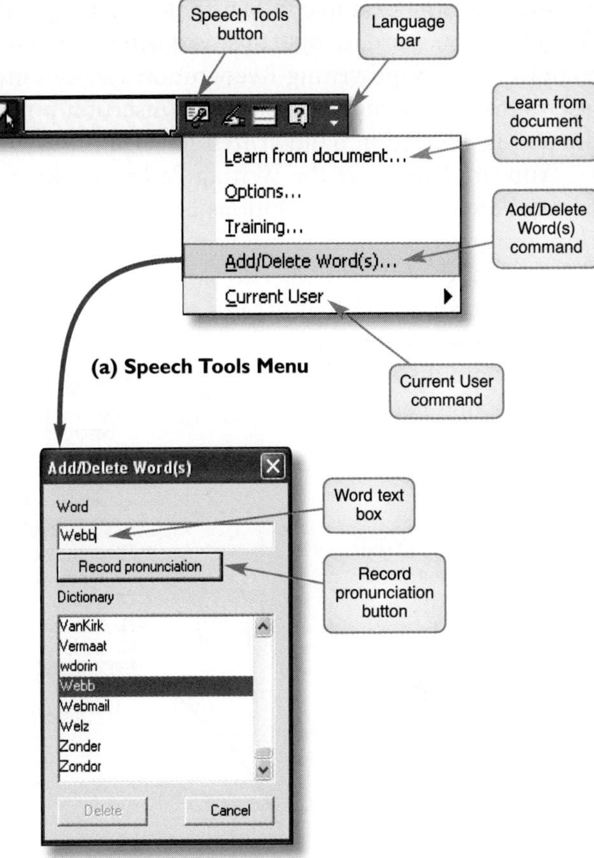

(a) Speech Tools Menu

(b) Add/Delete Word(s) Dialog Box

FIGURE B-8

Handwriting Recognition

Using the Office **Handwriting Recognition service**, you can enter text and numbers into Outlook by writing instead of typing. You can write using a special handwriting device that connects to your computer or you can write on the screen using your mouse. Four basic methods of handwriting are available by clicking the Handwriting button on the Language bar: Writing Pad; Write Anywhere; Drawing Pad; and On-Screen Keyboard. Although the on-screen keyboard does not involve handwriting recognition, it is part of the Handwriting menu and, therefore, will be discussed in this section.

If your Language bar does not include the Handwriting button, then for installation instructions, enter `install handwriting recognition` in the Type a question for help box on the menu bar.

Writing Pad

To display the Writing Pad, click the Handwriting button on the Language bar and then click Writing Pad (Figure B-9). The **Writing Pad** resembles a notepad with one or more lines on which you can use freehand to print or write in cursive. With the Text button enabled, you can form letters on the line by moving the mouse while holding down the mouse button. To the right of the notepad is a rectangular toolbar. Use the buttons on this toolbar to adjust the Writing Pad, select text, and activate other handwriting applications.

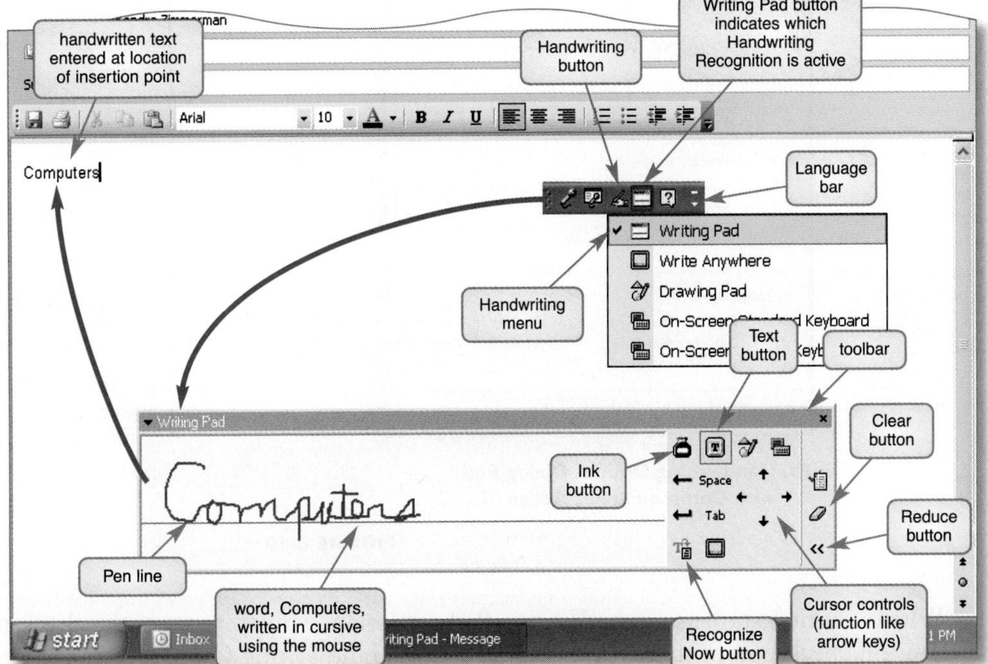

FIGURE B-9

Consider the example in Figure B-9 on the previous page. With the insertion point at the top of the document, the word, Computers, is written in cursive on the **Pen line** in the Writing Pad. As soon as the word is complete, the Handwriting Recognition service automatically converts the handwriting to typed characters and inserts the text at the location of the insertion point. With the Ink button enabled, instead of the Text button, the text is inserted in handwritten form in the document.

You can customize the Writing Pad by clicking the Options button on the left side of the Writing Pad title bar and then clicking the Options command (Figure B-10a). Invoking the Options command causes the Handwriting Options dialog box to be displayed. The Handwriting Options dialog box contains two sheets: Common and Writing Pad. The Common sheet lets you change the pen color and pen width, adjust recognition, and customize the toolbar area of the Writing Pad. The Writing Pad sheet allows you to change the background color and the number of lines that are displayed in the Writing Pad. Both sheets contain a Restore Default button to restore the settings to what they were when the software was installed initially.

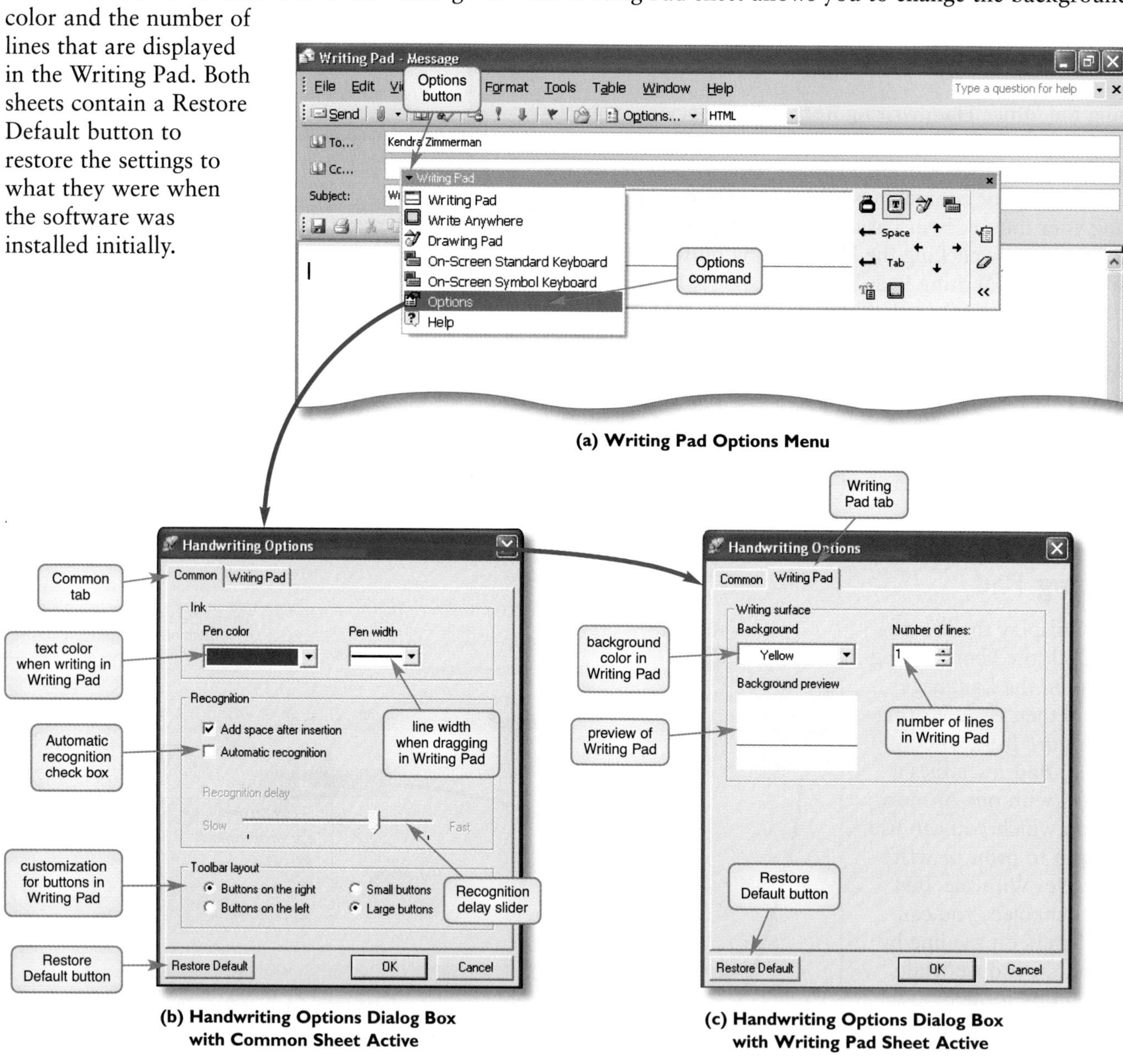

(a) Writing Pad Options Menu

(b) Handwriting Options Dialog Box with Common Sheet Active

(c) Handwriting Options Dialog Box with Writing Pad Sheet Active

FIGURE B-10

When you first start using the Writing Pad, you may want to remove the check mark from the Automatic recognition check box in the Common sheet in the Handwriting Options dialog box (Figure B-10b). With the check mark removed, the Handwriting Recognition service will not interpret what you write in the Writing Pad until you click the Recognize Now button on the toolbar (Figure B-9 on the previous page). This allows you to pause and adjust your writing.

The best way to learn how to use the Writing Pad is to practice with it. Also, for more information, enter `handwriting recognition` in the Type a question for help box on the menu bar.

Write Anywhere

Rather than use Writing Pad, you can write anywhere on the screen by invoking the Write Anywhere command on the Handwriting menu (Figure B-11) that appears when you click the Handwriting button on the Language bar. In this case, the entire window is your writing pad.

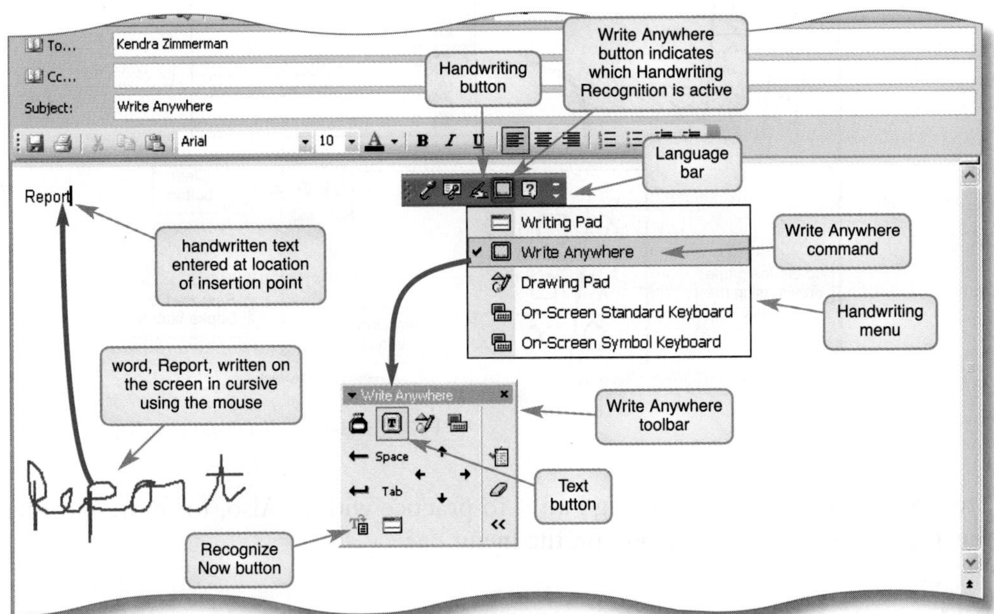

FIGURE B-11

In Figure B-11, the word, `Report`, is written in cursive using the mouse button. Shortly after the word is written, the Handwriting Recognition service interprets it, assigns it to the location of the insertion point, and erases what was written.

It is recommended when you first start using the Write Anywhere service that you remove the check mark from the Automatic recognition check box in the Common sheet in the Handwriting Options dialog box (Figure B-10b). With the check mark removed, the Handwriting Recognition service will not interpret what you write on the screen until you click the Recognize Now button on the toolbar (Figure B-11).

Write Anywhere is more difficult to use than the Writing Pad, because when you click the mouse button, Outlook may interpret the action as moving the insertion point rather than starting to write. For this reason, it is recommended that you use the Writing Pad.

Drawing Pad

With the Drawing Pad, you can insert a freehand drawing or sketch in a Outlook document. To display the Drawing Pad, click the Handwriting button on the Language bar and then click Drawing Pad (Figure B-12 on the next page). Create a drawing by dragging the mouse in the Drawing Pad. In Figure B-12, the mouse was used to draw a tic-tac-toe game. When you click the Insert Drawing button on the Drawing Pad toolbar, Outlook inserts the drawing in the document at the location of the insertion point. Other buttons on the toolbar allow you to erase a drawing, erase your last drawing stroke, copy the drawing to the Office Clipboard, or activate the Writing Pad.

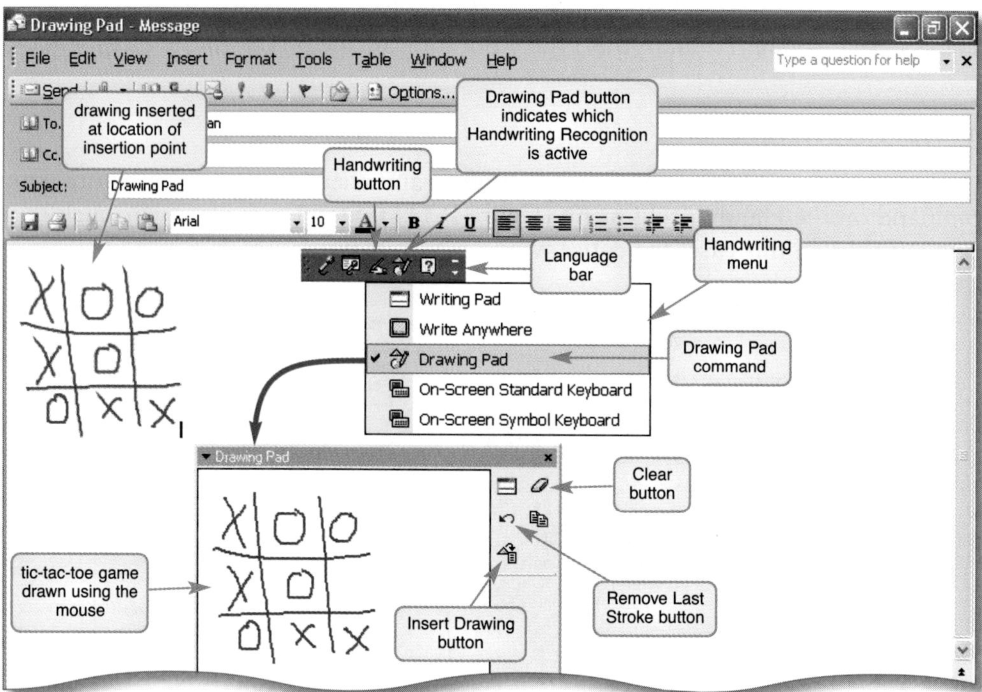

FIGURE B-12

The best way to learn how to use the Drawing Pad is to practice with it. Also, for more information, enter `drawing pad` in the Type a question for help box on the menu bar.

On-Screen Keyboard

The On-Screen Standard Keyboard command on the Handwriting menu (Figure B-13) displays an on-screen keyboard. The **on-screen keyboard** lets you enter data at the location of the insertion point by using your mouse to click the keys. The on-screen keyboard is similar to the type found on handheld computers or PDAs.

The On-Screen Symbol Keyboard command on the Handwriting menu (Figure B-13) displays a special on-screen keyboard that allows you to enter symbols that are not on your keyboard, as well as Unicode characters. **Unicode characters** use a coding scheme capable of representing all the world's current languages.

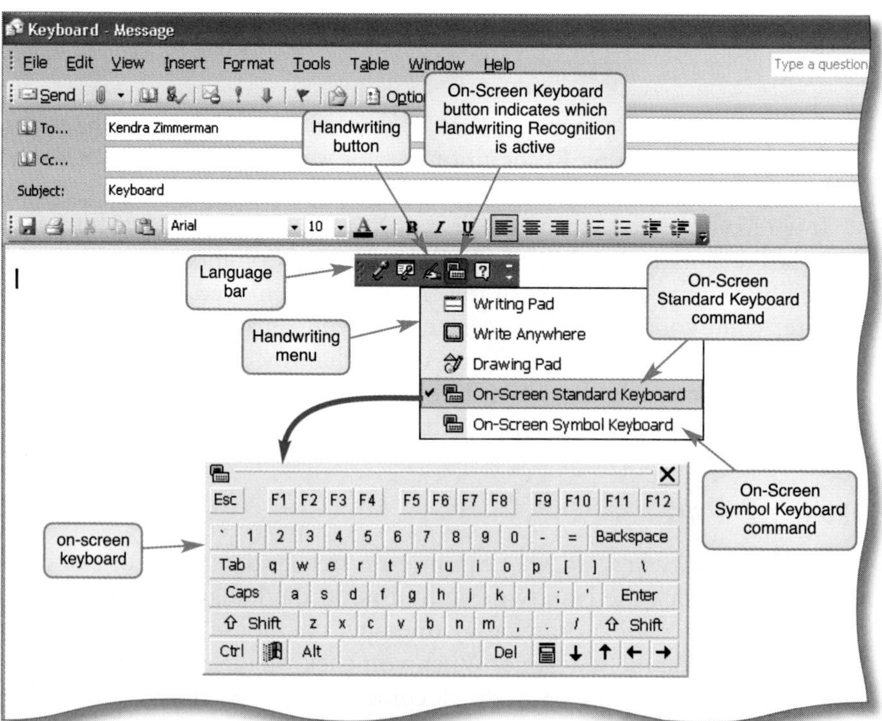

FIGURE B-13

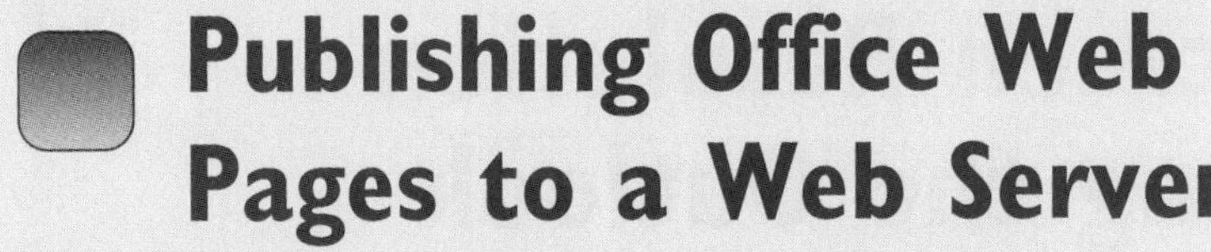

Publishing Office Web Pages to a Web Server

With the Office applications, you use the Save as Web Page command on the File menu to save the Web page to a Web server using one of two techniques: Web folders or File Transfer Protocol. A **Web folder** is an Office shortcut to a Web server. **File Transfer Protocol** (**FTP**) is an Internet standard that allows computers to exchange files with other computers on the Internet.

You should contact your network system administrator or technical support staff at your ISP to determine if their Web server supports Web folders, FTP, or both, and to obtain necessary permissions to access the Web server. If you decide to publish Web pages using a Web folder, you must have the Office Server Extensions (OSE) installed on your computer.

Using Web Folders to Publish Office Web Pages

When publishing to a Web folder, someone first must create the Web folder before you can save to it. If you are granted permission to create a Web folder, you must obtain the URL of the Web server, a user name, and possibly a password that allows you to access the Web server. You also must decide on a name for the Web folder. Table C-1 explains how to create a Web folder.

Office adds the name of the Web folder to the list of current Web folders. You can save to this folder, open files in the folder, rename the folder, or perform any operations you would to a folder on your hard disk. You can use your Office program or Windows Explorer to access this folder. Table C-2 explains how to save to a Web folder.

Using FTP to Publish Office Web Pages

When publishing a Web page using FTP, you first must add the FTP location to your computer before you can save to it. An FTP location, also called an **FTP site**, is a collection of files that reside on an FTP server. In this case, the FTP server is the Web server.

To add an FTP location, you must obtain the name of the FTP site, which usually is the address (URL) of the FTP server, and a user name and a password that allow you to access the FTP server. You save and open the Web pages on the FTP server using the name of the FTP site. Table C-3 explains how to add an FTP site.

Office adds the name of the FTP site to the FTP locations list in the Save As and Open dialog boxes. You can open and save files using this list. Table C-4 explains how to save to an FTP location.

Table C-1 Creating a Web Folder

1. Click File on the menu bar and then click Save As (or Open).
2. When the Save As dialog box (or Open dialog box) appears, click My Network Places on the My Places bar, and then click the Create New Folder button on the toolbar.
3. When the Add Network Place Wizard dialog box appears, click the Next button. If necessary, click Choose another network location. Click the Next button. Click the View some examples link, type the Internet or network address, and then click the Next button. Click Log on anonymously to deselect the check box, type your user name in the User name text box, and then click the Next button. Enter the name you want to call this network place and then click the Next button. Click the Finish button.

Table C-2 Saving to a Web Folder

1. Click File on the menu bar and then click Save As.
2. When the Save As dialog box appears, type the Web page file name in the File name text box. Do not press the ENTER key.
3. Click My Network Places on the My Places bar.
4. Double-click the Web folder name in the Save in list.
5. If the Enter Network Password dialog box appears, type the user name and password in the respective text boxes and then click the OK button.
6. Click the Save button in the Save As dialog box.

Table C-3 Adding an FTP Location

1. Click File on the menu bar and then click Save As (or Open).
2. In the Save As dialog box, click the Save in box arrow and then click Add/Modify FTP Locations in the Save in list; or in the Open dialog box, click the Look in box arrow and then click Add/Modify FTP Locations in the Look in list.
3. When the Add/Modify FTP Locations dialog box appears, type the name of the FTP site in the Name of FTP site text box. If the site allows anonymous logon, click Anonymous in the Log on as area; if you have a user name for the site, click User in the Log on as area and then enter the user name. Enter the password in the Password text box. Click the OK button.
4. Close the Save As or the Open dialog box.

Table C-4 Saving to an FTP Location

1. Click File on the menu bar and then click Save As.
2. When the Save As dialog box appears, type the Web page file name in the File name text box. Do not press the ENTER key.
3. Click the Save in box arrow and then click FTP Locations.
4. Double-click the name of the FTP site to which you wish to save.
5. When the FTP Log On dialog box appears, enter your user name and password and then click the OK button.
6. Click the Save button in the Save As dialog box.

Appendix D

Changing Screen Resolution and Resetting the Outlook Toolbars and Menus

This appendix explains how to change your screen resolution in Windows to the resolution used in this book. It also describes how to reset the Outlook toolbars and menus to their installation settings.

Changing Screen Resolution

The **screen resolution** indicates the number of pixels (dots) that your computer uses to display the letters, numbers, graphics, and background you see on your screen. The screen resolution usually is stated as the product of two numbers, such as 800 × 600 (pronounced 800 by 600). An 800 × 600 screen resolution results in a display of 800 distinct pixels on each of 600 lines, or about 480,000 pixels. The figures in this book were created using a screen resolution of 800 × 600.

The screen resolutions most commonly used today are 800 × 600 and 1024 × 768, although some Office specialists operate their computers at a much higher screen resolution, such as 2048 × 1536. The following steps show how to change the screen resolution from 1024 × 768 to 800 × 600.

To Change the Screen Resolution

1

- **If necessary, minimize all applications so that the Windows desktop appears.**
- **Right-click the Windows desktop.**

Windows displays the Windows desktop shortcut menu (Figure D-1).

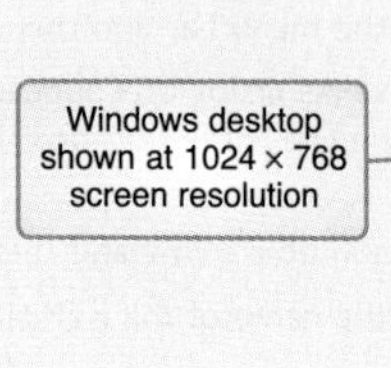

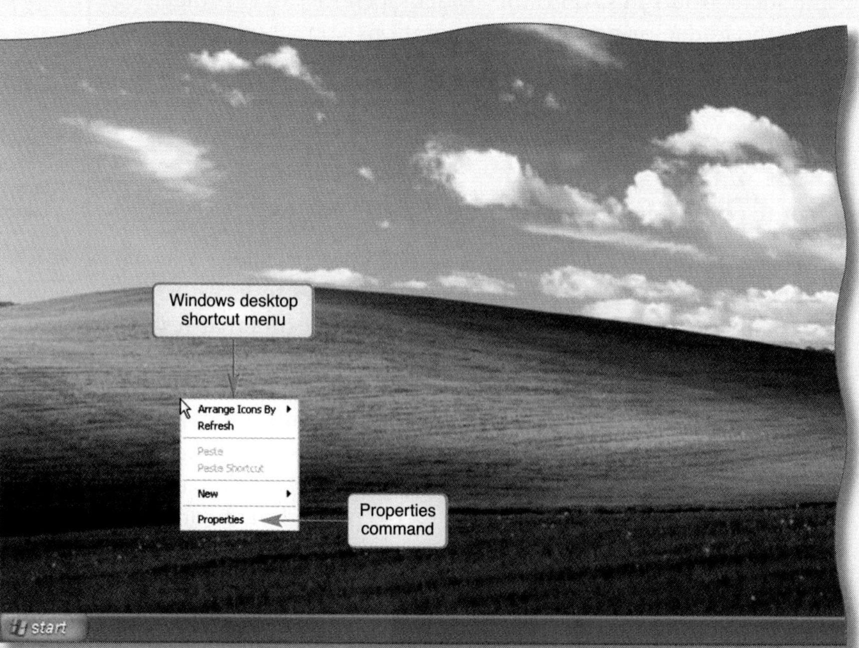

FIGURE D-1

2

• **Click Properties on the shortcut menu.**

• **When Windows displays the Display Properties dialog box, click the Settings tab.**

Windows displays the Settings sheet in the Display Properties dialog box (Figure D-2). The Settings sheet shows a preview of the Windows desktop using the current screen resolution (1024 × 768). The Settings sheet also shows the screen resolution and the color quality settings.

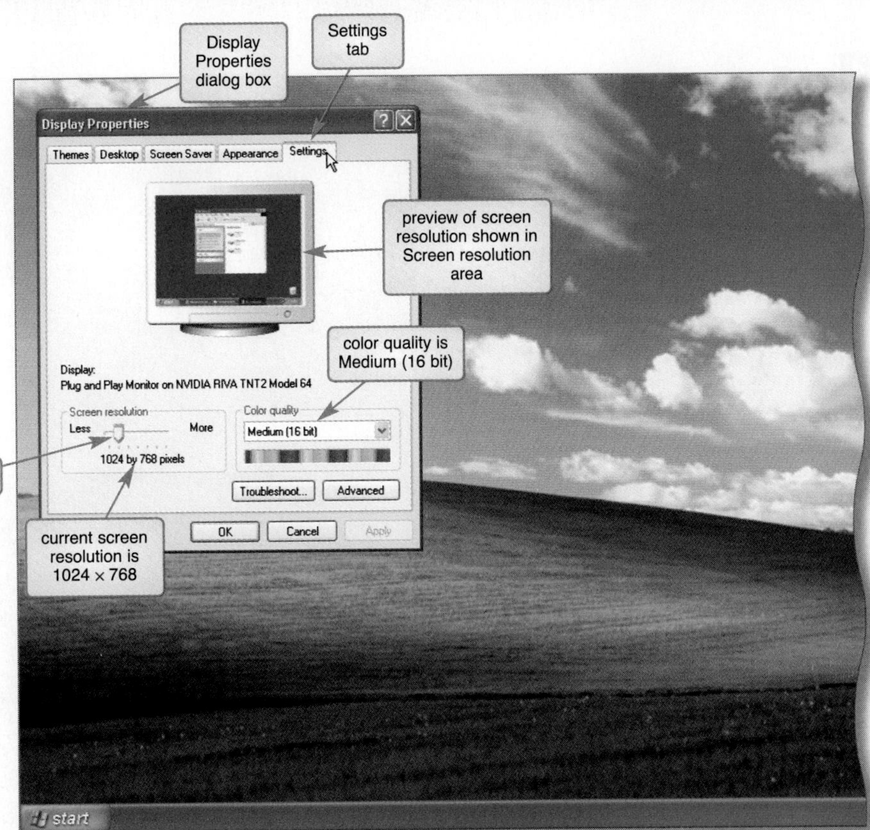

FIGURE D-2

3

• **Drag the slider in the Screen resolution area to the left so that the screen resolution changes to 800 × 600.**

The screen resolution in the Screen resolution area changes to 800 × 600 (Figure D-3). The Settings sheet shows a preview of the Windows desktop using the new screen resolution (800 × 600).

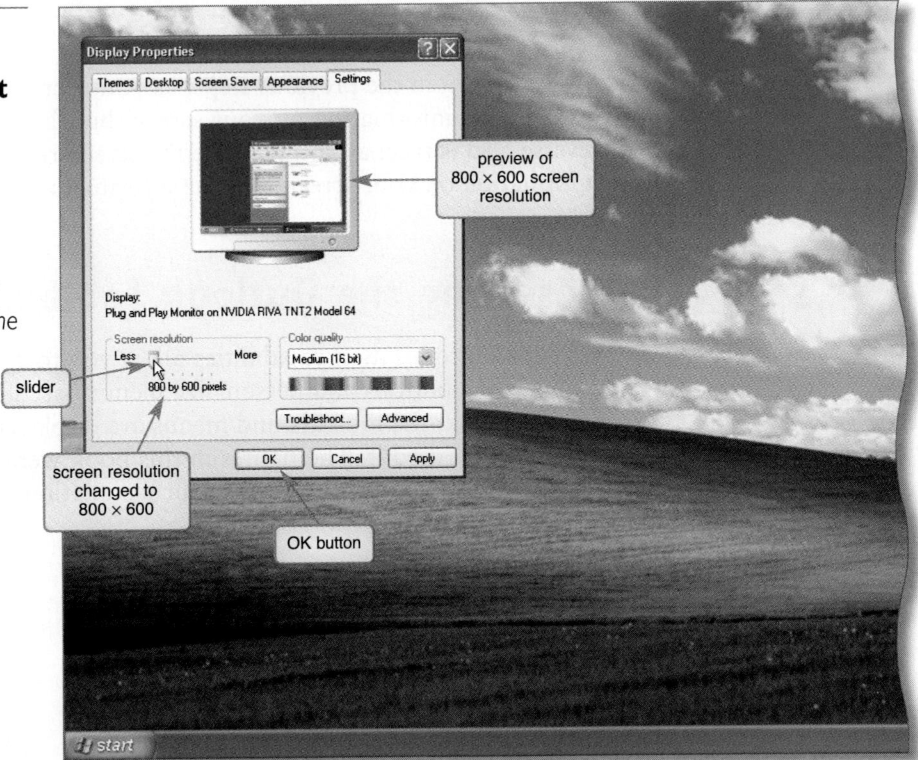

FIGURE D-3

4

- **Click the OK button.**
- **If Windows displays the Monitor Settings dialog box, click the Yes button.**

Windows changes the screen resolution from 1024 × 768 to 800 × 600 (Figure D-4).

FIGURE D-4

As shown in the previous steps, as you decrease the screen resolution, Windows displays less information on your screen, but the information increases in size. The reverse also is true: as you increase the screen resolution, Windows displays more information on your screen, but the information decreases in size.

Resetting the Outlook Toolbars and Menus

Outlook customization capabilities allow you to create custom toolbars by adding and deleting buttons and personalize menus based on their usage. Each time you start Outlook, the toolbars and menus are displayed using the same settings as the last time you used it. The figures in this book were created with the Outlook toolbars and menus set to the original, or installation, settings.

Resetting the Standard Toolbar

The following steps show how to reset the Standard toolbar in the Contact window.

To Reset the Standard Toolbar

1

- **Start Outlook.**
- **Click the Toolbar Options button on the Standard toolbar and then point to Add or Remove Buttons on the Toolbar Options menu.**

Outlook displays the Toolbar Options menu and the Add or Remove Buttons submenu (Figure D-5).

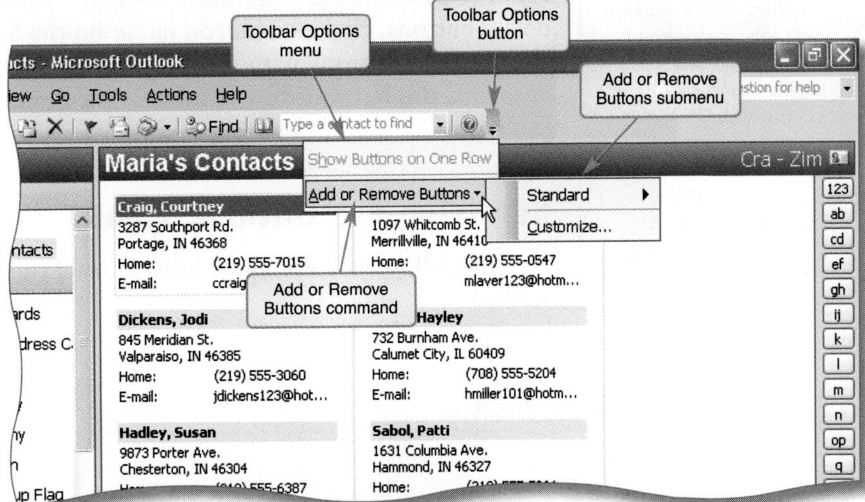

FIGURE D-5

2

- **Point to Standard on the Add or Remove Buttons submenu.**
- **When Outlook displays the Standard submenu, scroll down and then point to Reset Toolbar.**

The Standard submenu indicates the buttons and boxes that are displayed on the Standard toolbar (Figure D-6). To remove a button from the Standard toolbar, click a button name with a check mark to the left of the name to remove the check mark.

3

- **Click Reset Toolbar.**
- **If a Microsoft Office Outlook dialog box is displayed, click the Yes button.**

Outlook resets the Standard toolbar to its original settings.

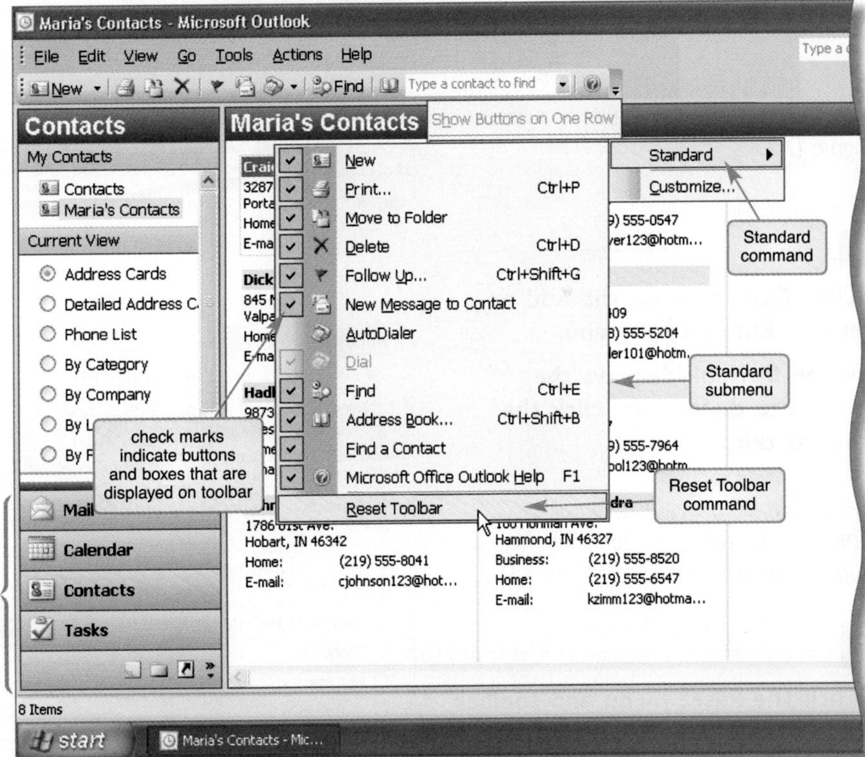

FIGURE D-6

4

- **Reset the Standard toolbars in the remaining Outlook windows by clicking the appropriate component button in the Navigation pane and following Steps 1 through 3.**

Other Ways

1. On View menu point to Toolbars, click Customize on Toolbars submenu, click Toolbars tab, click toolbar name, click Reset button, click OK button, click Close button
2. In Voice Command mode, say "View, Toolbars, Customize, Toolbars, [desired toolbar name], Reset, OK, Close"

Not only can you use the Standard submenu shown in Figure D-6 on the previous page to reset the Standard toolbar to its original settings, but you also can use it to customize the Standard toolbar by adding and deleting buttons. To add or delete buttons, click the button name on the Standard submenu to add or remove the check mark. Buttons with a check mark to the left currently are displayed on the Standard toolbar; buttons without a check mark are not displayed on the Standard toolbar.

Resetting the Outlook Menus

The following steps show how to reset the Outlook menus to their original settings.

To Reset the Outlook Menus

1

- **Click the Toolbar Options button on the Standard toolbar and then point to Add or Remove Buttons on the Toolbar Options menu.**

Outlook displays the Toolbar Options menu and the Add or Remove Buttons submenu (Figure D-7).

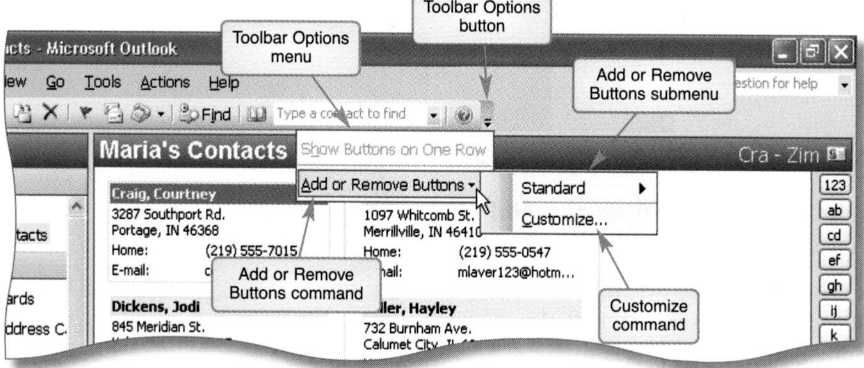

FIGURE D-7

2

- **Click Customize on the Add or Remove Buttons submenu.**
- **When Outlook displays the Customize dialog box, click the Options tab.**

The Customize dialog box contains three sheets used for customizing the Outlook toolbars and menus (Figure D-8).

3

- **Click the Reset menu and toolbar usage data button.**
- **When Outlook displays the Microsoft Office Outlook dialog box, click the Yes button.**
- **Click the Close button in the Customize dialog box.**

Outlook resets the menus to the original settings.

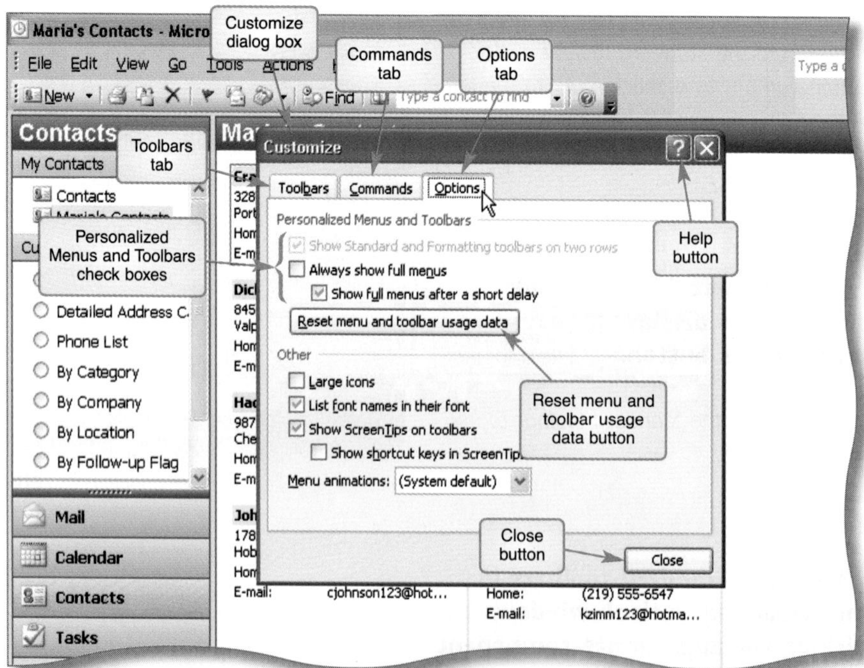

FIGURE D-8

Using the Options sheet in the Customize dialog box, as shown in Figure D-8, you can select options to personalize menus and toolbars. For example, you can select whether Outlook always displays full menus or displays short menus followed by full menus, after a short delay. Other options available on the Options sheet include settings to instruct Outlook to display toolbars with large icons; to use the appropriate font to display font names in the Font list; and to display a ScreenTip when a user points to a toolbar button. Clicking the Help button in the upper-right corner of the Customize dialog box displays Help topics that will assist you in customizing toolbars and menus.

Using the Commands sheet in the Customize dialog box, you can add buttons to toolbars and commands to menus. Recall that the menu bar at the top of the Outlook window is a special toolbar. To add buttons to a toolbar, click a category name in the Categories list and then drag the command name in the Commands list to a toolbar. To add commands to a menu, click a category name in the Categories list, drag the command name in the Commands list to a menu name on the menu bar, and then, when the menu is displayed, drag the command to the desired location in the list of menu commands.

Using the Toolbars sheet in the Customize dialog box, you can add new toolbars and reset existing toolbars and the menus. To add a new toolbar, click the New button, enter a toolbar name in the New Toolbar dialog box, and then click the OK button. Once the new toolbar is created, you can use the Commands sheet to add or remove buttons, as you would with any other toolbar. If you add one or more buttons to an existing toolbar and want to reset the toolbar to its original settings, click the toolbar name in the Toolbars list so a check mark is displayed to the left of the name and then click the Reset button. If you add commands to one or more menus and want to reset the menus to their default settings, click Menu Bar in the Toolbars list on the Toolbars sheet so a check mark is displayed to the left of the name and then click the Reset button. When you have finished, click the Close button to close the Customize dialog box.

Other Ways

1. On View menu point to Toolbars, click Customize on Toolbars submenu, click Options tab, click Reset menu and toolbar usage data button, click Yes button, click Close button
2. Right-click toolbar, click Customize on shortcut menu, click Options tab, click Reset menu and toolbar usage data button, click Yes button, click Close button
3. In Voice Command mode, say "View, Toolbars, Customize, Options, Reset menu and toolbar usage data, Yes, Close"

Appendix E

Microsoft Office Specialist Certification

What Is Microsoft Office Specialist Certification?

Microsoft Office Specialist certification provides a framework for measuring your proficiency with the Microsoft Office 2003 applications, such as Microsoft Office Word 2003, Microsoft Office Excel 2003, Microsoft Office Access 2003, Microsoft Office PowerPoint 2003, and Microsoft Office Outlook 2003. The levels of certification are described in Table E-1.

Table E-1 Levels of Microsoft Office Specialist Certification

LEVEL	DESCRIPTION	REQUIREMENTS	CREDENTIAL AWARDED
Microsoft Office Specialist	Indicates that you have an understanding of the basic features in a specific Microsoft Office 2003 application	Pass any ONE of the following: Microsoft Office Word 2003 Microsoft Office Excel 2003 Microsoft Office Access 2003 Microsoft Office PowerPoint 2003 Microsoft Office Outlook 2003	Candidates will be awarded one certificate for each of the Specialist-level exams they have passed: Microsoft Office Word 2003 Microsoft Office Excel 2003 Microsoft Office Access 2003 Microsoft Office PowerPoint 2003 Microsoft Office Outlook 2003
Microsoft Office Expert	Indicates that you have an understanding of the advanced features in a specific Microsoft Office 2003 application	Pass any ONE of the following: Microsoft Office Word 2003 Expert Microsoft Office Excel 2003 Expert	Candidates will be awarded one certificate for each of the Expert-level exams they have passed: Microsoft Office Word 2003 Expert Microsoft Office Excel 2003 Expert
Microsoft Office Master	Indicates that you have a comprehensive understanding of the features of four of the five primary Microsoft Office 2003 applications	Pass the following: Microsoft Office Word 2003 Expert Microsoft Office Excel 2003 Expert Microsoft Office PowerPoint 2003 And pass ONE of the following: Microsoft Office Access 2003 or Microsoft Office Outlook 2003	Candidates will be awarded the Microsoft Office Master certificate for fulfilling the requirements.

Why Should You Be Certified?

Being Microsoft Office certified provides a valuable industry credential — proof that you have the Office 2003 applications skills required by employers. By passing one or more Microsoft Office Specialist certification exams, you demonstrate your proficiency in a given Office 2003 application to employers. With more than 400 million people in 175 nations and 70 languages using Office applications, Microsoft is targeting Office 2003 certification to a wide variety of companies. These companies include temporary employment agencies that want to prove the expertise of their workers, large corporations looking for a way to measure the skill set of employees, and training companies and educational institutions seeking Microsoft Office 2003 teachers with appropriate credentials.

The Microsoft Office Specialist Certification Exams

You pay $50 to $100 each time you take an exam, whether you pass or fail. The fee varies among testing centers. The **Microsoft Office Expert** exams, which you can take up to 60 minutes to complete, consist of between 40 and 60 tasks that you perform on a personal computer in a simulated environment. The tasks require you to use the application just as you would in doing your job. The **Microsoft Office Specialist** exams contain fewer tasks, and you will have slightly less time to complete them. The tasks you will perform differ on the two types of exams. After passing designated Expert and Specialist exams, candidates are awarded the **Microsoft Office Master** certificate (see the requirements in Table E-1).

How to Prepare for the Microsoft Office Specialist Certification Exams

The Shelly Cashman Series offers several Microsoft-approved textbooks that cover the required objectives of the Microsoft Office Specialist certification exams. For a listing of the textbooks, visit the Shelly Cashman Series Microsoft Office Specialist Center at scsite.com/winoff2003/cert. Click the link Shelly Cashman Series Microsoft Office 2003-Approved Microsoft Office Textbooks (Figure E-1). After using any of the books listed in an instructor-led course, you should be prepared to take the indicated Microsoft Office Specialist certification exam.

How to Find an Authorized Testing Center

To locate a testing center, call 1-800-933-4493 in North America, or visit the Shelly Cashman Series Microsoft Office Specialist Center at scsite.com/winoff2003/cert. Click the link Locate an Authorized Testing Center Near You (Figure E-1). At this Web site, you can look for testing centers around the world.

Shelly Cashman Series Microsoft Office Specialist Center

The Shelly Cashman Series Microsoft Office Specialist Center (Figure E-1) lists more than 15 Web sites you can visit to obtain additional information about certification. The Web page (scsite.com/winoff2003/cert) includes links to general information about certification, choosing an application for certification, preparing for the certification exam, and taking and passing the certification exam.

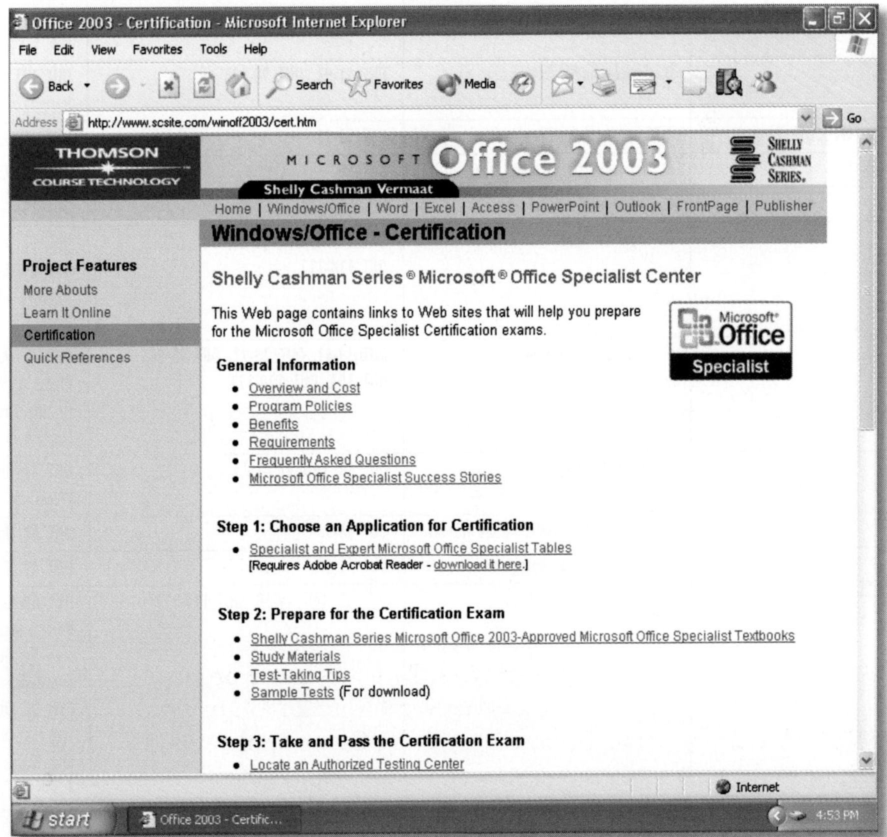

FIGURE E-1

Microsoft Office Specialist Certification Map for Microsoft Outlook 2003

This book has been approved by Microsoft as courseware for Microsoft Office Specialist certification. Table E-2 lists the skill sets and activities you should be familiar with if you plan to take the Specialist-level examination for Microsoft Office Outlook 2003.

Table E-2 Specialist-Level Skill Sets, Activities, and Locations in Book for Microsoft Office Outlook 2003

SKILL SET	SKILL BEING MEASURED	SKILL DEMONSTRATED IN BOOK	SKILL EXERCISE IN BOOK
I. Messaging	A. Originate and respond to e-mail and instant messages	OUT 13-16, OUT 23-25, OUT 51-53, OUT 129-131	OUT 62 (In the Lab 1 Part 2 Step 1), OUT 63 (In the Lab 3 Part 2), OUT 64 (Cases and Places 3), OUT 140 (In the Lab 2 Steps 3, 6), OUT 141 (In the Lab 2 Step 7), OUT 143 (Cases and Places 5)
	B. Attach files to items	OUT 27-29, OUT 132-134	OUT 62 (In the Lab 1 Part 2 Step 3), OUT 141 (In the Lab 2 Steps 7-8)
	C. Create and modify a personal signature for messages	OUT 19-23	OUT 63 (In the Lab 3 Part 1, Part 3 Step 4)
	D. Modify e-mail message settings and delivery options	OUT 15, OUT 29-31, OUT 34-38	OUT 62 (In the Lab 1 Part 2 Steps 2, 4-5, In the Lab 2), OUT 63 (In the Lab 3 Part 2)
	E. Create and edit contacts	OUT 41-44, OUT 125-127, OUT 128-129	OUT 61 (Apply Your Knowledge 1), OUT 64 (Cases and Places 1-5), OUT 140 (In the Lab 2 Step 4)
	F. Accept, decline, and delegate tasks	OUT 98-102	OUT 142 (In the Lab 3 Part 2)
II. Scheduling	A. Create and modify appointments, meetings, and events	OUT 72-77, OUT 79-81, OUT 88-89, OUT 103-107	OUT 138 (Apply Your Knowledge 1 Part 1), OUT 139 (In the Lab 1 Part 1 Step 2, Part 2), OUT 141 (In the Lab 3 Part 1 Step 3), OUT 143 (Cases and Places 1, 4-5)
	B. Update, cancel, and respond to meeting requests	OUT 107-110	OUT 139 (In the Lab 1 Part 1 Steps 4-5, 7), OUT 143 (Cases and Places 5)
	C. Customize Calendar settings	OUT 112-117	OUT 138 (Apply Your Knowledge 1 Parts 1-2), OUT 141 (In the Lab 3 Part 1 Step 2), OUT 143 (Cases and Places 1-2)
	D. Create, modify, and assign tasks	OUT 91-93, OUT 98-100	OUT 141 (In the Lab 3 Part 1 Step 4), OUT 142 (In the Lab 3 Part 2)
III. Organizing	A. Create and modify distribution lists	OUT 53-56	OUT 61 (Apply Your Knowledge 1 and In the Lab 1 Part 1)
	B. Link contacts to other items	OUT 58	OUT 64 (Cases and Places 3)
	C. Create and modify notes	OUT 110-112	OUT 143 (Cases and Places 3)
	D. Organize items	OUT 31-34, OUT 44-48, OUT 103, OUT 114-117	OUT 61 (Apply Your Knowledge 1), OUT 62 (In the Lab 2), OUT 64 (Cases and Places 3, 5), OUT 138 (Apply Your Knowledge 1), OUT 142 (In the Lab 3 Part 2 Step 4), OUT 143 (Cases and Places 1)
	E. Organize items using folders	OUT 39-41, OUT 70-71, OUT 95-96, OUT 103, OUT 120-121	OUT 61 (Apply Your Knowledge 1 Part 1), OUT 64 (Cases and Places 4), OUT 138 (Apply Your Knowledge Part 1), OUT 141 (In the Lab 3 Part 1 Step 1), OUT 142 (In the Lab 3 Part 2 Steps 6-7)
	F. Search for items	OUT 38, OUT 46-47	OUT 63 (In the Lab 3 Part 3 Step 2), OUT 64 (Cases and Places 2)
	G. Save items in different file formats	OUT 56-58	OUT 62 (In the Lab 1 Part 3)
	H. Assign items to categories	OUT 47-49	OUT 64 (Cases and Places 4)
	I. Preview and print items	OUT 12, OUT 49-50, OUT 118-119	OUT 61-62 (Apply Your Knowledge 1 and In the Lab 1 Part 1, Part 2 Step 6), OUT 63 (In the Lab 3 Part 1, Part 2, Part 3 Step 5), OUT 64 (Cases and Places 1-5), OUT 138 (Apply Your Knowledge 1 Part 1), OUT 139 (In the Lab 1 Part 1 Step 6, Part 2), OUT 141 (In the Lab 2 Step 8, In the Lab 3 Part 1 Step 5), OUT 142 (In the Lab 3 Part 2 Step 5), OUT 143 (Cases and Places 1-5)

Index

MICROSOFT Office Outlook 2003

Quick Reference Summary

In the Microsoft Office Outlook 2003 application, you can accomplish a task in a number of ways. The following table provides a quick reference to each task presented in this textbook. The first column identifies the task. The second column indicates the page number on which the task is discussed in the book. The subsequent four columns list the different ways the task in column one can be carried out. You can invoke the commands listed in the MOUSE, MENU BAR, and SHORTCUT MENU columns using Voice commands.

Table 1 Microsoft Office Outlook 2003 Quick Reference Summary

TASK	PAGE NUMBER	MOUSE	MENU BAR	SHORTCUT MENU	KEYBOARD SHORTCUT
Accept Meeting Request	OUT 108	Accept button on Standard toolbar in Meeting window	Actions | Accept	Accept	ALT+C
Accept Task Assignment	OUT 101	Accept button on Standard toolbar in Task window	Actions | Accept	Accept	ALT+C
Address E-Mail Message	OUT 51	To button in Mail window			CTRL+SHIFT+B
Assign Task	OUT 99	Assign Task button on Standard toolbar in Task window	Actions | Assign Task	Assign Task	ALT+N
Attach File to E-Mail Message	OUT 28	Insert File button on Standard toolbar in Message window	Insert | File		ALT+I, L
Change to Day View	OUT 91	Day button on Standard toolbar	View | Day		ALT+V, Y
Change to Month View	OUT 91	Month button on Standard toolbar	View | Month		ALT+V, M
Change to Week View	OUT 90	Week button on Standard toolbar	View | Week		ALT+V, K
Change to Work Week View	OUT 89	Work Week button on Standard toolbar	View | Work Week		ALT+V, R
Color Code Calendar	OUT 115	Calendar Coloring button on Standard toolbar	Edit | Label	Label	ALT+E, L
Compose E-Mail Message	OUT 24	New button on Standard toolbar	File | New | Mail Message		CTRL+N
Create a Note	OUT 110	New button on Standard toolbar	Actions | New Note	New Note	CTRL+SHIFT+N
Create a Task	OUT 92	New button on Standard toolbar			CTRL+SHIFT+K
Create an Event	OUT 88	New button on Standard toolbar	Actions | New All Day Event	New All Day Event	CTRL+N | ALT+A, N
Create Contact List	OUT 42	New button on Standard toolbar	Actions | New Contact	New Contact	CTRL+N | ALT+A, N
Create Distribution List	OUT 54	New button on Standard toolbar	File | New | Distribution List		CTRL+SHIFT+L
Create E-Mail Signature	OUT 20		Tools | Options		ALT+T, O
Create Personal Folder	OUT 40		File | New | Folder	New Folder	CTRL+SHIFT+E
Create Subfolder	OUT 70		File | New | Folder	New Folder	CTRL+SHIFT+E
Create View Filter	OUT 32		View | Arrange By	Custom	ALT+V, A, M
Delete an Appointment	OUT 82	Delete button on Standard toolbar	Edit | Delete	Delete	CTRL+D
Delete E-Mail Message	OUT 17	Delete button on Standard toolbar	Edit | Delete	Delete	CTRL+D
Delete Folder	OUT 96	Delete button on Standard toolbar	File | Folder | Delete	Delete	ALT+F, F, D

Table 1 Microsoft Office Outlook 2003 Quick Reference Summary *(continued)*

TASK	PAGE NUMBER	MOUSE	MENU BAR	SHORTCUT MENU	KEYBOARD SHORTCUT
Display Contacts in a Category	OUT 49	Find button on Standard toolbar	Tools | Find		CTRL+E
Enter Appointments	OUT 74	New button on Standard toolbar	Actions | New Appointment	New Appointment	CTRL+SHIFT+A | ALT+A, O
Find a Contact	OUT 46	Find button on Standard toolbar	Tools | Find		CTRL+E
Flag E-Mail Messages	OUT 30		Actions | Follow Up	Follow Up	ALT+A, U
Forward E-Mail Message	OUT 16	Forward button on Standard toolbar	Actions | Forward	Forward	ALT+W
Import/Export Folders	OUT 93		File | Import and Export		ALT+F, T
Invite Attendees to Meeting	OUT 104	Add Others button in Appointment window	Actions | Invite Attendees		ALT+N
Move an Appointment	OUT 86		Edit | Cut | Edit | Paste		CTRL+X | CTRL+V
Move to Next Day	OUT 78		Go | Go to Date	Go to Date	CTRL+G
Open Calendar	OUT 68		Go | Calendar		
Open E-Mail Message	OUT 11		File | Open	Open	ALT+F, O
Organize Contacts	OUT 48		Tools | Organize		ALT+T, Z
Print Calendar	OUT 118	Print button on Standard toolbar	File | Print		CTRL+P
Print Contact List	OUT 50	Print button on Standard toolbar	File | Print		CTRL+P
Print E-Mail Message	OUT 12	Print button on Standard toolbar	File | Print		CTRL+P
Print Task List	OUT 119	Print button on Standard toolbar	File | Print		CTRL+P
Propose New Meeting Time	OUT 109	Propose New Time button on Standard toolbar in Meeting window	Actions | Propose New Time	Propose New Time	ALT+A, S
Recurring Appointments	OUT 76	Recurrence button on Standard toolbar in Appointment window	Actions | New Recurring Appointment	New Recurring Appointment	ALT+A, A
Reply to E-Mail Message	OUT 13	Reply button on Standard toolbar	Actions | Reply	Reply	ALT+R
Save Contact List as Text File	OUT 56		File | Save As		ALT+F, A
Send E-Mail Message	OUT 29	Send button on Standard toolbar	File | Send To		ALT+S
Send Instant Message	OUT 130		Actions | New Instant Message		ALT+A, S
Send Meeting Update	OUT 110	Send Update button on Standard toolbar in Meeting window			ALT+D
Set Message Delivery Options	OUT 34	Options button on Mail toolbar in Message window			ALT+P
Set Message Importance and Sensitivity	OUT 34	Options button on Mail toolbar in Message window			ALT+P
Sort E-Mail Messages	OUT 31		View | Arrange By		ALT+V, A